For Lewis Wirshba—
May this book remind you
of your time on the hill
With best wishes,
Carol Kammen
August 2007

Christopher J. Torre, class of 2008

# First Person Cornell

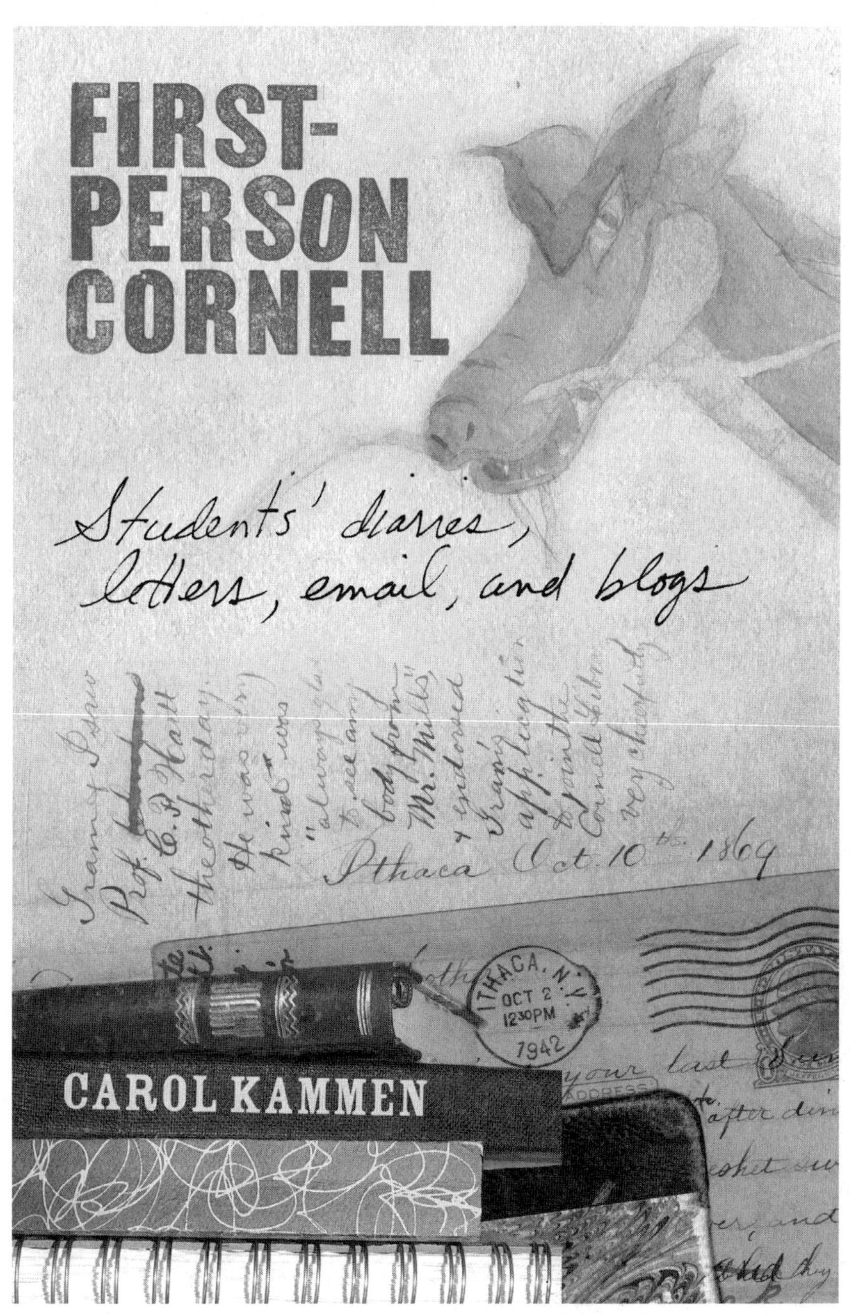


CORNELL UNIVERSITY LIBRARY

*To the students of History 126*
*from whom I have learned so much*



Printed in U.S.A.

Cloth 978-0-935995-07-7
Paper 978-0-935995-05-3

Library of Congress Control Number 2006923062

# CONTENTS

# FOREWORD

In her new book, Cornell historian Carol Kammen captures the essence of the undergraduate experience at Cornell through first-person student accounts that span nearly 140 years of university history. Mining archival materials in the Cornell University Library as well as the writings of contemporary students in her own classes, Kammen presents a view of Cornell that comprises the individual perspectives of one of the university's most important constituencies.

Kammen deftly sets out the scope of her endeavor and briefly describes commonalities and trends she has discovered—from the role that music has played in student life across generations to the changing climate for women students—but mainly she allows the students their own voices. They discourse passionately, if not always grammatically, about their professors and the amount of work they are required to complete. They worry about being on probation and about whether or not to join a sorority. They report to their parents on their expenditures, and they ask for advice on everything from whether to buy a class blazer to how best to rework a poor essay in order to raise their grade.

Amid the mundane details of daily life, there are moments of introspection and kernels of wisdom. Jessie Mary Boulton, class of 1883, for example, wonders why she is getting an education: "I have no particular objective but the mere getting of the education. I don't seem to know whether I will make any use of it or not ..."; and Maeva Curtin, class of 2000, describes her life as an architecture student: "I spent my morning in the library, and then all day reading books, except for that short span of time I spent in studio ...," and then she adds, "If I avoid wasting time, if I work consistently, I cannot feel guilty and will be a much happier person."

Having made the journey from 1868 to the twenty-first century in the company of such a diverse group of Cornell students, who speak candidly and spontaneously about the many strands of their undergraduate lives, one develops an overall impression of Cornell as an infinitely varied place and of its students as individuals one would enjoy knowing better. Kammen's latest work offers a stimulating reading experience that can be enjoyed by Cornellians and non-Cornellians alike.

Hunter R. Rawlings III
President, Cornell University

# INTRODUCTION

College students spend a great deal of time writing. They write laboratory reports, compile notes, and document their research; they draft and, if we are lucky, revise term papers, book reports, critical essays, and senior theses. They also write personal letters, and many have kept diaries. Rarely do deans, administrators, professors, or even other students get to read these private commentaries, in which the first-person pronoun is predominant. That material, however, is profoundly interesting because it reveals a great deal about the individual, friends, classes and professors, housing, food, money, the times in general, and sometimes the important questions of life itself.

When I began teaching the history of Cornell, it seemed obvious that in addition to reading the previous histories—and good ones at that—and working in the archives and library collections, students should also read what other students have had to say about their experience at Cornell. Students are often the overlooked segment of institutional histories, yet they are the reason the university exists in the first place; they are the hyphen that connects the past to the present, and they see and experience a university in distinct and particular ways.

I began to tease out of the archives past Cornell students' experience. These became reading assignments for my students, who looked for trends, themes, and singularities. My idea was to engage modern students with their counterparts so that they could read how John Henry Comstock, class of 1874, helped build McGraw Hall, in which our class meets; they could meet M. Carey Thomas (1877), who looked out from Sage College to describe the view across Library Slope, which my students walk each day. I wanted them to see that originally students arrived by train and that later they were "left off by passing Buicks," as E. B. White '21 observed, whereas modern students most often come via airplane or in the family's sport utility vehicle. I wanted my students to get a sense of a time when people communicated by means of the post office, and I wanted them to see what happened when telephones became prevalent and as email flourished. I wanted them to meet students who knew precisely where their studies were leading and to encounter others who hadn't a clue why they were in college. I wanted them to hear through the words of earlier students the topics of "bull sessions," the angst of new love, the excitement of being away from home, and to understand that others, too, longed for the comforts of home and found the workload impossible yet managed nonetheless to "gafoodle"—to waste time. I wanted them to experience the joy some students found in their courses, and the disdain with which others wrote of their professors, for such conflicting emotions and the reverse are alive on campus today. Mostly, I wanted to show my students that it is not only the famous alumni but also students like themselves who contribute to our shared history.



What follows are the words and voices of Cornell students from the first day in 1868 to the present, along with images from three students who have recorded their Cornell experience on camera. Pulled from letters and emails, from diaries and commentaries made in notebooks, here is a look at the culture students create at college, and what they have observed and thought and written.

An eager crowd gathered at Library Hall in Ithaca on the morning of Wednesday, October 7, 1868, to be present at the ceremonies inaugurating Cornell University. Faculty and trustees mingled with residents of the village. Visitors from out of town were drawn to the celebratory event, but the governor, fearful of retaliation at the polls by Methodists and Baptists, sent the lieutenant governor in his place. Also present were many students, accepted by letter or examination, who were amazed and delighted at the promises made and the predictions that this university would usher in a new educational era, that this day represented not a culmination of efforts but a new beginning, that nothing was completed, that everything at Cornell University would always be in a state of becoming.

In the afternoon, the ceremonies moved up the hill, where a set of chimes given to Cornell by Miss Jennie McGraw was dedicated. The nine bells hung from a wooden support adjacent to South University (now Morrill) Hall, with the exterior stone walls of uncompleted North University (now White) nearby. Among those standing on the brow of the hill that day was John Davis of Auburn, New York. Two days later, he sat down in his room in Cascadilla Hall to write home about the inauguration and the start of classes. Other students surely wrote about these early days at the university and recorded this inaugural day in diaries or notebooks or jotted notes on the official program (as the young president, Andrew Dickson White, was moved to do), but if they did, their words have not survived. We have printed texts of the speeches given by White, Ezra Cornell, and Harvard Professor Louis Agassiz, among others, and there are newspaper articles about the ceremony, but only John Davis has left us a student's account of what the day was like. Davis described the reception at Library Hall, where he was introduced to a Presbyterian minister and his wife "and a great many ladies and gentlemen besides." He learned that the students were to be taught to dance—this, at a time when some narrow religious denominations considered dancing immoral—and have entertainments to which they could invite young women.

Davis tells us in interesting detail about the dimensions of his room in Cascadilla Hall and the plentiful food served in the dining hall—although his opinion would swiftly change, and by the end of the semester, Davis and other students were looking for better and cheaper places to board. He gives us a sense of the excitement of being at Cornell at the very start. "As yet," he wrote, "everything is in an uproar and confusion." Still, he predicted that when things got straightened out, he thought he would like Cornell "very much."[1]



John Davis wrote the sort of letter that travelers in exotic destinations write to those who are unlikely to see such places for themselves. He came to Cornell when going to college was not a common experience. Cornell, called a "Godless" school where Satan would easily find "raw recruits," was considered not only strange but a danger to the soul. Davis's letter, with its clear picture of the university and the important, upstanding people in the village he was meeting, was intended to reassure his family.

In 1870, there were approximately 50,000 students—1.7 percent of young people aged eighteen to twenty-one—in 311 colleges in the United States. In the 1960s, there were 2,026 institutions of higher education in the United States educating approximately 3,500,000 students. By 1970, the number of students had doubled. In 2003, 64 percent of all high school graduates went on to college, with some 16.7 million students enrolled in colleges and universities throughout the United States.[2] Today, college experience is common, pictured in films, written about in novels, depicted in advertising. Universities are known and ranked, and gaining admission is something to crow about rather than justify. The four years after high school have become, for a great many Americans, a stage of life all its own. Walter Todd '09 wrote that college years were "the finest phase of life ever invented."[3]

The lives of men, and sometimes of women, have been parsed in many ways. In *As You Like It*, William Shakespeare wrote of seven stages; Thomas Cole painted the *Voyage of Life* (1839–40) in four scenes; Currier and Ives showed life in four panels: childhood, youth, manhood, and old age. Some folk paintings depict ten stages; the psychiatrist Eric Erickson schematized eight.[4] When I ask my students what they are, however, they are at a loss to label themselves. They are no longer of high school age; they do not consider themselves adolescents or teens, even though most of them are seventeen and eighteen years old when they begin college. One student wrote that college students were "between stages." They are certainly not adults, they readily admit, if being an adult means that they are responsible for themselves. Even students who are working their way through college are generally not financially independent, and their emotional attachments to the homes they have just left are complex. Some say they are "getting away," but others feel they have been wrenched out of their families. What are they? I ask. What is their stage of life? The answer is always, "Well, we are college students." With so many young people heading into college after high school and with widespread recognition today that higher education is not only desirable but necessary, perhaps it is time for us to recognize the college years as a separate and distinct phase of life.

There are several notable books about college life. Historian Helen Lefkowitz Horowitz in *Campus Life* has looked at student life over time; Michael Moffatt studied students as anthropological subjects in his book *Coming of Age in New Jersey*, where he portrays college years as a rite of passage. Most recently, Rebekah Nathan, a professor of anthropology, writing under a pseudonym, moved into a student dormitory and enrolled as a freshman. In her book *My Freshman Year* she writes of college years as a state "where normal rules of society are lifted." At college and university, students "leave the strictures and comforts of their parents' home; they enter a geographically removed youth-based college culture with its own rules and values." It is a time, she notes, when "students bond with one another, sometimes for life, and, amid rules of suspended normality and often hardship, explore their identities, wrestle with their parents' world, and wonder about the future."





Given the number of college students—both those currently in college and those who have passed through and graduated—it is surprising that few histories of educational institutions recognize or use the materials generated by students about their college experience. College histories are generally about the origins and growth and governance of an institution. Most histories detail the overbearingness or benignity of deans, the initiatives or neglect of presidents, the inertness or interference of the trustees; they describe departmental growth, significant alumni, generous donors. Athletic programs and particular schools within a university are a common subject for historians. About Cornell alone, we have a history of hockey, a three-volume history of the New York State College of Veterinary Medicine, and a history of the chimes.[5]

Two exceptions to historians' general lack of attention to college students come from opposite ends of the country. Washington State University (Wazzu, say its students) opened at Pullman in 1892 as the Agricultural College and School of Science. William L. Stimson, in his *Going to Washington State: A Century of Student Life*, writes, "few universities (I'm not sure that there are any others) feel compelled to devote a book to the history of their students. I suppose that taken collectively students seem like hurricane forces without discernable structure. They blow in and they blow out." Yet, as he points out, college is a four-year period of life when students select careers and often spouses, establish friendships and form "lasting attitudes about the world." His book looks at what students wrote in the newspaper and, in particular, at students' reaction to university regulations and administrative restrictions.[6]

*Carolina Voices: Two Hundred Years of Student Experiences*, about the University of South Carolina, uses students' writings to tell the story of the university. The quotations come from letters, diary entries, editorials in the student newspaper *(The Gamecock)*, and emails. Founded in 1801, the University of South Carolina has a rich history that is amplified by this surprising array of documents. The editors write, "nothing more clearly reveals the personal nature of Carolina than the voices of thousands of students, past and present," and in *Carolina Voices* students get to tell their own versions of Carolina's story. From the start of the nineteenth century, when a freshman wrote about his entrance exam and his initiation into college life, to a very recent memoir of a 2003 alumna reflecting on her college years, the excerpts are vivid. They describe the joys, problems, activities, homesickness, appreciation for good teachers, and even the dangers in the 1880s of tainted water, but all relate in some way to university policies and institutional history.[7]

This book about Cornell is nothing like those other two. Students have much to tell us, and their story is both of the particular individual from a particular time, and of students over time. The extracts here are drawn primarily from the riches of the Rare and Manuscript Collections in Kroch Library, from some published sources, and from letters and diaries sent to me by alumni who responded to a notice about my search in the *Cornell Alumni News* in the fall of 2004.[8]



Through these documents we meet individual students reacting to the experience of arriving at Cornell, taking courses, interacting with classmates and professors, engaging in extracurricular activities, and in some cases, experiencing the thrill or the nostalgic tug of graduation. Read the 1946 diary of David Kogan '50, in which he wrote about his classes and his search for a career in which he might live a useful life. Because his diary has survived, he is plucked from the past for us to encounter. We might assume that he was typical of that postwar era, but then Elizabeth Severinghaus Warner '47, Anita Ades Goldin '50, and Janet Hamber '51 expand our understanding in their accounts of the same period.

As we read these letters and diaries, we can wonder whether there is a "Cornell culture." Is there a similar experience that all Cornell students share? What are the important features of the university? Is the environment always inspiring, the weather always awful, the workload always intense? What connects alumni across time? What are the things they talk about? The selections in this book allow us to see both particular students and the common experience.

Although there are continuities, change over time is especially apparent in the writings of Cornell women. Through their letters and diary entries, we can envision them at specific times and track changes in how they are regarded by male students and how they approach their education. We experience them first through the letters of M. Carey Thomas (1877) and Jessie Mary Boulton (1883)—among the few who enrolled when coeducation was unusual. Then, after the turn of the century, we meet Adelheid Zeller '16, Katherine Lyon '16, and Helen Bullard '18, when young women in college had to create their own social life in the face of male disdain. We can read about the wartime experience of Katie Pierce Putnam '44, who marries, sets up an apartment, and then moves back to the dorm when her husband is sent to a military base. And finally, we meet very different women of the recent past—Molly Darneider '98, Karen Klingele '01, and Meava Curtin '04—who nonetheless face the same challenge of adjusting to college life.

The documents presented here are not the only written commentaries about the university created by Cornell students. There are chapters of biographies and autobiographies devoted to time at Cornell, and there are many alumni memoirs. Anna Botsford Comstock (1885) wrote *The Comstocks of Cornell* (Ithaca, 1953) to tell her own and her husband's story; Stanton Griffis (1910) wrote of his college years, but especially of his time as an editor of *The Daily Sun*, in *Lying in State* (New York, 1952);

Sara Lawrence Lightfoot wrote *Balm in Gilead: Journey of a Healer* (Reading, Mass., 1988) about her mother, Margaret Morgan Lawrence '36, and the racial prejudice she encountered at Cornell; Gene Case '25 turned his father's memoirs into *The Shoe Box Notebooks* (Chapel Hill, 1992). These are all books crafted to tell about the past; they are sometimes witty, often well written. There are also countless oral histories that probe the student experience. These works, however, are programmed by an interviewer who has a purpose in mind and poses particular questions, or they are offered by those who have long considered their college experience and want to convey something about it. All such reminiscences represent a backward view—one that is consciously shaped and crafted.



The first-person accounts in this book, by contrast, have a spontaneity about them that is tremendously appealing. They lack the polish of the memoir, but they are "in the moment"; they resound with the language of the day; they reveal the unreflected sentiment, and they ring very true to the ear and eye. They are not better than their more polished relatives, but they resonate with a special liveliness and the times. These documents tell us a lot if we but listen to what they have to say. What they relate is not a history of student life, or a history of Cornell University. They represent instead moments in an individual's life, a voice out of time that we can connect to other voices and other times.

If there is one theme that resounds throughout all these selections it is music. Cornell students sing: they belong to choirs, they sing in class meetings; they sing under the arches and they sing on stage; they sing as they pass the dorms at night and they listen as others sing and make music. Though I know of many groups—Cayuga's Waiters, the Symphony Orchestra, the Brass Ensemble, the Gamelon players, Nothing but Treble, as a small sample—that make music on campus today, and I have for forty years listened to concerts of all sorts, I had no idea how deeply ingrained music was in student life until I began reading these accounts. Royal Taft (1871) marveled that the concerts he attended were a "rich musical feast. The best I ever heard." He attended Ole Bull's violin concert, too: "Music was grand. I could listen to him much longer and not get bored." But Taft had a good ear, and after listening to a concert given by the Cornell Glee Club, he wrote that he thought the musicians "did not distinguish themselves." Several female students report that men serenaded the coeds outside Sage College. "Sounded very pretty," noted Adelaide Taber Young (1899). In later years, the music heard on campus was of many types. Attending Harold Thompson's lectures about folk music in the 1940s, David Kogan found Thompson's pronunciation of Yiddish lyrics amusing but loved the professor's enthusiasm and wide-ranging knowledge. Ann Meigs '61 wrote about listening to folk music in the 1960s at Willard Straight. And of course, there were Jennie McGraw's chimes, which every student heard. Webb Hayes (1875) described the five buildings on campus in 1872 and exclaimed in particular about the chimes. Cornellians of every era have found the music of the bells pealing over the hillside a unique feature of life on campus.

Cornell students have always had a distinct sense of being at a special place. John Rae, one of the "Immortal Eight"—his term, not mine—who graduated in 1869, wrote that he was "most enthusiastic over the hill and the environment," which he saw first from a lake steamer. When a group of his friends founded a literary society, "we did not want a Latin or Greek name, for this was a new institution, one that had never existed before, and we must have something better." They consulted Andrew White and decided upon Washington Irving to honor one of America's best-known writers—and a New Yorker to boot. In 1929, Harold Gulvin '30 wrote to his future wife about his Cornell experience; there were "some things you can't get anywhere but in college," he said. Modern students are more likely to speak about their pleasure being at an Ivy League school.

Students of every age remark about the beautiful campus. W. Forrest Lee (1906) summed it up in 1902: "this is a mightily pretty place." Many students report walking in the gorges. John Moffatt thought he was climbing in a place where "ladies would find it difficult" but quickly pulled up his socks when he discovered that "ladies do go there." Almost every writer, and just about every student I have taught, has mentioned at one time or another the ever-changing weather. In May of 1870, Royal Taft reported that he awoke one morning to find a foot of snow outside. Typical, most students would say today: "Ithacation."[9]

Today one topic likely to be asked about is Cornell during the war protests and social upheavals of the 1960s, and in particular the spring of 1969, when a group of African American students occupied Willard Straight Hall. Two previously unpublished letters appear here, from Stephen Appell '65 and Knight Kiplinger '69. These thoughtful young men's letters were written in response to those confused days.[10]

Students who were at Cornell while Ezra Cornell was alive—and that was until 1874—wrote about encounters with him. John Rae "never saw Mr. Cornell in a classroom but [Cornell] had great hopes for the University. He told a friend that within five years there would be 5000 students on the hill." And later he noted, "The boys all liked him—those who came in contact with him." Rae liked him as the "new and great figure in the educational world. We thought his gift"—the university—"unprecedented in college history." The university celebrated Cornell's gift each January 11, his birthday. By 1893, according to Gertrude Nelson, no students were invited to the Founder's Day celebration, only faculty and guests, and the event has fallen off the calendar altogether in modern times. Although Rea quoted the Cornell motto about any person and any study, few other students of his era mentioned it, and I suspect we hear it cited more today than one did in earlier times.

What we do hear in these documents is student slang. In 1871 the word for leaving class if the professor had not arrived after twenty minutes was "bolt." In 1894 Gertrude Nelson thought a student who became friendly with a professor had "leg pull." We recognize this as "apple polishing," or as "brown nosing" and "ass kissing" in somewhat cruder parlance. Arthur Wessels '41 frequently wrote "swell" in his 1930s letters home. Today, students are more likely to say "wicked," or "phat," or "mad."

In 1945, Elizabeth Severinghaus referred to the "Big Red Tape" emanating from Day Hall. The first instance I have seen of that term dates from 1926, in the Cornell humor magazine *The Widow*.[11]



One of the complaints about Cornell, by those eager to find fault, was that the university had no denominational affiliation, and President White, like all those who followed him, was a scholar but not a clergyman. "Godless Cornell" was the epithet. One student wrote that Cornell was not popular with the downtown Ithaca churches because of the "infidelity in many pupils." According to a student who attended a local Methodist service, the preacher prayed, "O Lord, deliver us from this flood of infidelity that is flowing upon us." He also observed that the Presbyterian minister rapped the university for serving a wine punch at an 1869 entertainment given by Ezra Cornell. When the preacher wrote a letter to the local press complaining about students' drinking, Mrs. Whittlesly, wife of the commander of the Cornell militia, replied that he should "mind his own business." Despite the university's strident nonsectarianism, however, students' letters and diaries testify to the fact that Cornellians were not without religious inclinations, and any number of Cornellians have become religious leaders. Even unlikely candidates report going to church, though few as attentively as Royal Taft, who sometimes went three times on a Sunday and commented on the quality of the sermon, the singing, or the attentiveness of the congregation. Students also attended religious services at Sage Chapel. Today, students come with a variety of beliefs, from nonobservant to fundamentalist Christian, Jewish, and Muslim; some are pagans.

Not only did the students evaluate the preachers, they judged members of the faculty. John Moffatt wrote of James Hart, "I hate him. He is the laziest professor." Anna Botsford Comstock recalled Bela MacKoon as a man who "struck terror in students," though she insisted that he was an excellent teacher. Jessie Boulton thought Professor Wait "ignored the girls," but Gertrude Nelson went off to a theatrical performance escorted by Professor Adams. Adelaide Taber Young thought, "Mr. Segall is, if possible, a little more disagreeable than Mr. Otto"; both men were instructors of French. Students had opinions about President White, whom they called "prex" and "prexy." (Is it possible that those terms were used to his face?) Royal Taft commented that White had not given a good lecture and liked it better when he spoke "off hand" rather than when he read from a prepared text. What the students did approve of were the new teaching methods. President White told his class that he would talk for half an hour and that the students would talk for the remaining time. And one of the best compliments a professor could make was to say, as Professor Evans did of his 1869 analytical geometry students, that the Cornell class "did better than his class at Yale."

Each time an additional language or other new course was offered, students would remark on it and crow that other schools did not provide similar opportunities. When another college boasted of offering a subject that was standard fare at Cornell, the students hastened to let others know they already had that opportunity—and more. In 1894 when music was first introduced as a university subject, Gertrude Nelson squealed with joy. She also described Cornell's newly established honor system.

There would be no proctors, and students were expected to neither give nor receive aid. If caught, the accused would face judgment by a committee of students. Cheating in college—by looking at another's paper, getting an advance copy of an exam, plagiarizing, or handing in an essay written by someone else—has always been considered inevitable. Some thought of cheating as the "game" that students play, with the professors constituting the opposing team. When President White handed out an exam consisting of fifty-two questions, however, he announced, "Gentlemen, I have a faculty meeting. I put you on your honor," and left the room. That was to set the standard. Yet less than a year later, there was a report that the "wholesale Ponying" had "disgraced our university last year." In 1870, a student who copied most of a German essay was judged by his fraternity, which voted to "sever" him; in 1871, cheating was considered a thing of the past because of "strict surveillance" by the professors. When asked by his parents about cheating, one student wrote, "I think the rule still puts us on our honor, as gentlemen." The Cornell experience regarding cheating would seesaw back and forth between an honor system and proctoring; cheating was one of the subjects investigated in a survey of Cornell students in the 1950s. It continues today in various forms, many of them electronic, as students do what they need to do to stay afloat, to avoid being "busted."[12]



Another Cornell tradition involved the beanie. That little freshman cap with its tiny brim and black button took on, over the years, a kind of sanction beyond belief. Its original purpose was to mark the new men on campus that they might be legitimately hazed by upperclassmen, and also to create solidarity among the members of the freshman class. In 1870, a student reported that he wore his cap but saw several first-year "boys who did not comply with the order." In February 1871, he wrote that the university had issued a demand that all freshmen wear their caps. At the end of the year, students met to bury their caps, but in some years, caps were burned. In 1893, Ruth Nelson reported that the women had adopted a cap they would wear—headgear, she wrote, made "like a mortar board." Into the 1930s, there are reports of women adopting hats, though theirs were nothing like those worn by the men. Recent traditions include chalking and quarter-carding, both used to advertise student events and opinions.

One tradition at the university that prided itself on having no traditions was that students were to be treated as adults: the faculty would not oversee students' behavior. Students were to board themselves, and there are a number of accounts of students, like Jared van Wagenen (1891), who stepped from the train at the Ithaca station and walked through town looking for a place to live. Students report looking for rooms, changing rooms, worrying about roommates, disliking the food, and finding new places to eat. John Davis complained about the food, and so did Jessie Boulton—but though she approved of coeducation, she was bothered by "coeating" when men were allowed to board at Sage College. Adelaide Taber Young in 1896 thought the food had improved and was pleased to be offered fruit every day. Later female students recalled that ice cream was served because an alumna had left money in trust that the women have dessert. Modern students comment rather favorably about the food at Cornell and worry more about gaining the "freshman fifteen" than about the quantity or quality of food in the dining halls.

Being away from home for the first time, students encounter a number of problems. Having things to wear and having clean clothing are a recurring theme. Women in the nineteenth century at Sage College frequently reported that they sewed new flourishes on old dresses to make them appear different. They took dresses apart, added collars, shifted necklines, and altered sleeves. In some cases, clothing was sent home to be washed and then returned in a box, usually with homemade treats tucked inside. These deliveries were much anticipated and constituted the basis of a "spread"—a party in a dorm room for a special few. Other students hired washerwomen to clean their clothing; Jessie Boulton had trouble finding someone who would live up to her standards of cleanliness without wearing out her clothes by harsh treatment.

Students always need new things, and the traffic up and down East Hill, from campus to the merchants in Ithaca, is steady and unrelenting. They went to shops in the 1870s, and to Rothschild's Department Store all through the first two-thirds of the twentieth century. They frequent Pyramid Mall today. For some, however, new clothing posed a challenge. When John Moffatt needed new hose, he wrote to his mother, "I do not know how to buy socks: what shall I ask for, how shall I know if I get what I want, and how much ought I give?"

Students asked other questions of their parents. Shall I join a club? Might I go boating on the lake? Shall I buy the expensive edition of the book I need, or should I make do with the cheaper volume? We can hear the desired answer, even if their parents did not. As they reported home on money spent—in a great number of cases, on every penny—students received advice. "Supply yourself, not extravagantly," wrote Moffatt's father, "but so that you will regret nothing." Moffatt's parents also told him where they thought he ought to place his furniture, and even without having seen his room, they sent along a diagram in case he didn't understand their directions. His mother worried about his health and sent a warning not to change from his winter underwear until the leaves reached full size. "Elect one of the later trees for guidance," she wrote, and he dutifully replied that he had decided to follow the lead of a locust.

The Moffatts were members of the Swedenborgian Church, or the New Church, so John came to Cornell with his box of homeopathic medicines. He doctored himself, with the advice of his father, and he provided medicines for his friends, dosing one classmate with arsenic. Moffatt himself became sick from the carbon monoxide produced by the coal fire in his Cascadilla room. The Nelson sisters, not wanting to be quarantined, hid the fact that they had the measles. Midway through his junior year, in 1948, doctors diagnosed David Kogan with lymphoma.

When John Comstock became terribly ill with typhoid fever, he was nursed back to health by Professor Burt Green Wilder. In 1902, Forrest Lee reported he felt sick: "I guess this water has put me on the bum," he wrote, and indeed, in 1903, the community suffered a major typhoid epidemic. The water provided by the university proved to be safe, but the public drinking water drawn from Six Mile Creek was contaminated. Thus, the women at Sage College, whose drinking water came from Beebe Lake, were untouched, but many male students living in fraternities and in boarding houses scattered over East Hill fell ill.

Suicide among students has not been uncommon, and students here have reported on those for whom the pressures were just too great. John Detmold '43 wrote about a young woman who jumped from the bridge into Fall Creek Gorge. Modern students tell of visits to Gannett Clinic and even to the Cayuga Medical Center. There was always danger of fire, there were accidents, and there was the constant worry about fraternity hazing, especially after 1872, when a young man fell to his death in Six Mile Gorge.



At Cornell the word hazing has two meanings. As we understand the word today, it refers to rituals of humiliation and sometimes corporal discomfort leading to admission into the Greek system of fraternities. In Cornell's early days, hazing was the ongoing battle between the freshman and the sophomore classes, the one intent upon standing up to the older guys, the other determined to do unto the freshmen what had been done to them the previous year. These were the class rushes, which could involve wrestling in the mud on Library Slope, rioting through the commercial area of Ithaca, and forcing the other class into the creek that lay behind the Fairgrounds, where Wegman's is today. Students also write about other kinds of hijinks. "Blanket tossing was in vogue," wrote Royal Taft. On "gate night," no homeowner with a gate or unsecured trashcan was safe. One student in Cascadilla Hall prepared an electric battery to shock anyone entering his room.

Through the years, student letters and diaries often reveal ongoing prejudice—against Cornell women, against Jews, against African Americans, against those perceived as "other." In this, students mirror common attitudes in the country, and their language reflects that of their parents and of society beyond Cornell. It is unattractive to read this prejudice today, but it is here—unvarnished. Narrow ideas, of course, were not restricted to the students: read what Vice-President Russel said when Anna Botsford received an invitation to attend a dance with a Brazilian student; read M. Carey Thomas's description of a "colored youth" in her class, and Adelaide Taber Young's description of a "Jewess" in the dorm; see what David Kogan wrote about anti-Semitism. At Cornell, many students had their first encounters with people unlike those they had known at home. They often did not think about what they were writing or lacked the language to say things differently. Times change—sometimes, and about some things, for the better.

---

This book necessarily presents only a selection of what students thought about their Cornell experience. Not all students wrote letters or diaries, not everything that was written survived, and not all surviving letters or diaries have made their way to an archive. I have not reprinted whole letters or entire diary entries—that would have made this volume unwieldy and enshrined a great deal of uninteresting material, since many letter writers went on at length about inconsequential matters and about friends and family members unrelated to Cornell. The selections here are extracts: sentences and paragraphs that offered interesting, important, or funny perspectives of student life. Some of the diary entries were short to begin with—see the entries of

Adelheid Zeller and Donna Fulkerson LaVallee '76, who made daily entries of one sentence or less—and even these are excerpted.

Over time, the kind of materials created by students has changed. In the earliest days, students wrote letters and kept diaries. The telephone later siphoned off some communication between parents and students, but before 1970, few students called home with any frequency. In those days, the phone was reserved for dire news. Since the mid-1990s, however, students appear to be talking on cell phones all the time and just about everywhere—even in class. But phone conversations, important or otherwise, do not supply historical documentation. Letter writing has fallen off, and of those letters that are written, many fewer are kept than in the past. In addition, it will be decades before most letters and diaries written today are donated to a repository. As traditional correspondence and diaries have waned, however, email has filled the void and become the vehicle for thousands of letters of varying length, spelling, and taste. A bit of email correspondence is represented below, along with a blog, or on-line diary.



The ease with which photographs can be taken today and transmitted in digitized form to friends and family via email enables students to communicate their experience in images. Offered here are three views of the university, taken from the scrapbooks and photo portfolios created by current Cornell students. Leah Barad, class of 2007, is in the Arts College, where she is studying psychology; she comes from Bennington, Vermont. Devon Goodrich '08 is an English literature major from Pennsylvania. Christopher J. Torre '08, who comes from Medford, New Jersey, is a prevet animal sciences major in the College of Agriculture and Life Sciences. Eric Tobis '08 comes from North Palm Beach, Florida, and is studying electrical and chemical engineering.

The bulk of the most recent material has been generated by students in History 126: The History of Cornell University, for which students have been required to keep a scrapbook. Students have always kept scrapbooks of wondrous artifacts: dance cards, concert tickets, postcards and birthday cards, ribbons, and other items of personal interest. Rarely, however, are these older scrapbooks explained—the items are left to explain themselves, and often they do not. My students' scrapbooks must be annotated, a requirement that students understand variously. Some write a great deal, and others think three sentences suffice. Currently, more than three hundred of these annotated scrapbooks, each tremendously interesting, each full of information about the individual and his or her relationship to the university, now exist, and selecting from these books has been difficult. Space permits only a few entries that give a flavor of the lives of recent students.

In selecting the extracts—whether from traditional correspondence or today's material—I sought to let each individual speak in his or her own voice, explain him or herself, be natural and spontaneous. Thus, this book offers selections that reveal the individual as well as those that speak of the more general university experience. I was looking for expressions of their concern about making friends, about their courses and professors, about doing well or doing well enough. I wondered what they worried about, what pleased them, and what they thought of the faculty, their classes, and classes, and the purpose of their education. I have been alert to what the men have said about the women and vice versa. These were not limiting subjects, but these were my interests when reading the material. I have not hidden the warts, which would have been easy to do, but instead hope that these students will help us understand their own times as well as their links to students of other eras, and that their comments will challenge us to think about student life as well as student achievement. 

All this material has passed through filters: what was created, what has survived, what was available, and what I found of interest. The variety of materials is impressive. All but one author are identified, and the selections appear with permission. In introducing the selections, I have not made any attempt to write biographies of the students. For those no longer living, I have used Deceased Alumni Files in Kroch Library; for living alumni, I used *The Cornellian*, alumni class listings, and information obtained from the donors. Most of the younger writers from my classes are now making their way in the world: their lives are still taking shape, and so they appear here identified only by name and year of graduation.

I have quietly corrected misspelled words when it appeared that haste was most likely the reason for them, and I have smoothed a few grammatical glitches for readability. Underscored words have been italicized. The essence of these selections, however, remains true to the originals. The blog and email in particular I kept as close to the originals as possible, with their deliberate misspellings, lowercase letters, and incomplete thoughts.

The appendix indicates the locations of the original sources; most come from the Rare and Manuscript Collections in Kroch Library.

A great many people have been exceedingly kind and helpful as this project developed. My touchstone is always Elaine Engst, Cornell University Archivist and Director of the Rare and Manuscript Collections in Kroch Library. Her knowledge of the university is impressive and always generously shared. Her staff has been exceedingly cooperative and has made me feel most comfortable as I settled in among them. My appreciation goes especially to Cheryl Rowland, Susette Newberry, Margaret Nichols, Nancy Dean, Eileen Keating, C. J. Lance, Laura Linke, Brenda J. Marston, Peter Martinez, Katherine Reagan, Patrick J. Stevens, and Brian Vliet. You are wonderful colleagues.

Along the way, I have met numerous Cornellians who have happily dug for material and found gems, while exhibiting a wonderful enthusiasm for their Alma Mater. They, and my students in History 126, have taught me a great deal, and I appreciate my contact with all of them. I have talked or corresponded with a number of people. My thanks to Seth Lloyd '69, Shannon Murray '94, Prof. Daniel Krall, C. J. Read-Jones, Peter Hirtle, Anita Ades Goldin '50, Ezra Cornell IV '70, Mary Berens '74, James H. Roberts '71, Margaret M. Gallo '81, Donna LaVallee '77, Michael Patrick Hearn, Thomas Nytch '58, Janet Hamber '51, Diane Christopulos '70, Bruce and Christine Kowalski and their son Geoffrey '07; Steven Appell '65, Robin E. Wechkin, Knight Kiplinger '69, George Ubogy '58, Deb Barth, Kathleen Pierce Putnam '44, and Philip Gruen. I also appreciate the comments and friendship of students in my Cornell Alumni University course taught during the summer of 2004: Lois Dow '64, Mary Esther Haggerty '65, Diane Lucek, Marilyn Merryweather '57, Charles Shelley '53, Beatrice Szeckley, Marjorie L. Thayer '51, and Maureen Whitefield '73. Ralph Janis invited me to lead that discussion of family history, which often turned to the history of Cornell.



It is a pleasure, as always, to work with my friends Sally Atwater, who edited this book, and Lou Robinson, who designed it. Tom Hickerson backed the project from the start and has provided crucial support. My husband, Michael, has lived through this project with enthusiasm, suggestions, and good-natured humor.

## NOTES

1. The best starting point for anyone investigating Cornell's history is Carl L. Becker's Cornell University: Founders and the Founding (Ithaca, 1943), essays that were first delivered as the Messinger Lectures. See also Morris Bishop, A History of Cornell (Ithaca, 1962), and Carol Kammen, Cornell: Glorious to View (Ithaca, 2003).

2. www.census.gov.

3. See Frederick Rudolph, *The American College and University: A History* (New York, 1962), especially page 486. See also Helen Lefkowitz Horowitz, *Campus Life: Undergraduate Cultures from the End of the Eighteenth Century to the Present* (New York, 1987), Michael Moffatt, *Coming of Age in New Jersey: College and American Culture* (New Brunswick & London, 1989), Anne Matthews, *Bright College Years: Inside the American Campus Today* (Chicago, 1997), and Rebekah Nathan, *My Freshman Year: What a Professor Learned by Becoming a Freshman* (Ithaca, 2005). Although most university histories were not told from the students' point of view, students have always been subject to surveys of their opinion. The most famous Cornell study is *What College Students Think*, by Rose K. Goldsen, Morris Rosenberg, Robin M. Williams, Jr., and Edward A. Suchman (Princeton, 1960).

4. See "Changing Perceptions of the Life Cycle in American Thought and Culture," by Michael Kammen, in *Selvages & Biases: The Fabric of History in American Culture* (Ithaca, 1987), 180–221.

5. See Ellis Person Leonard, *A Cornell Heritage: Veterinary Medicine* (Ithaca, 1979); Ed McKeown, *The Cornell Chimes* (Ithaca, 1991), with an introduction by Kermit C. Parsons; and Adam Woden, *Cornell University Hockey* (Charleston, S.C., 2004).

6. William L. Stimson, *Going to Washington State: A Century of Student Life* (Pullman, 1989), especially page xi for quotes.

7. *Carolina Voices: Two Hundred Years of Student Experiences*, Carolyn B. Matalene and Katherine C. Reynolds, editors (Columbia, S.C., 2001).

8. My appreciation to Mary Berens, Ezra Cornell, and James H. Roberts, editor of the *Cornell Alumni News*.

9. John Rae's memoir, called "The Immortal Eight," appeared in *Half-Century at Cornell: A Retrospect* (Ithaca, 1930), 51, 91–92.

10. See Donald A. Downs, *Cornell '69* (Ithaca, 1999).

11. Slang can be defined as any unusual or nonstandard use of one word as a substitute for another. Student slang can be witty, and it can be vulgar. It is usually grammatically correct. See B[enjamin] H. Hall, *A Collection of College Words and Customs* (Cambridge, 1851). Hall defines bolt as "an omission of a recitation or lecture." The modern expert on college slang is Connie Eble, whose book *Slang and Sociability* (Chapel Hill, 1996) discusses in-group language among college students. She does not include "bolt" as a slang word used by students she studied; they were more likely to use say "cut" or "blow off." "A Dictionary of Slang for the Uninitiated" appeared in *The Cornellian* in 1892. "Bolt" was here defined as a "general cutting of recitations; to cut with most of the class." An updated version of Cornell slang was written by John Detmold (1943), some of whose letters appear in this book; he was influenced by Morris Bishop. Since the 1980s, students in History 126: A History of Cornell have collected student slang, which includes such words as *sexile,* to be "kicked out of your room when your roommate has a visitor of the opposite sex," and *sketchy,* "suspicious, unknown in a bad way," and *word,* "I agree," or "OK, I hear you." The Internet has also changed slang, which now moves about the country at lightning speed. Emailese includes such shortenings of words as brb, "be right back," and lol, "laugh out loud." There are also typed symbols that convey meaning, just as shaped fingers can denote a number of emotions and ideas.



12. See Rose K. Goldsen et al., *What College Students Think* (Princeton, 1960). For the current honor code, see http://cuinfo.cornell.edu/Academic/AIC.html.

# JOHN Y. DAVIS

## CLASS OF 1872

John Yawger Davis was one of 412 students who registered when Cornell opened. Of these, 9 were seniors who had transferred from other colleges. There were 23 juniors, 32 sophomores, and 143 freshmen, plus some students outside the degree programs. The faculty consisted of 26 professors, and there were three buildings: Cascadilla, where John roomed; South University, now known as Morrill Hall; and North University, dedicated in 1869 and renamed White Hall in 1883. Everything else was future. Davis left the university after two years, before completing the requirements for a degree, to become a dairy farmer in Cayuga County, dealing in thoroughbred Jerseys. He died in Auburn in 1923.

Oct. 9, 1868. I have just got into my room. It is in the water cure building called Cascadilla building or Cascadilla place. In this building the students take their meals.

My room is No. 158 first floor south wing south side of the hall and second west of the main entrance. My room is nine feet one way and twelve feet the other and twelve feet high. I have one large window on the south side three feet wide and eight feet high.... My door opens opposite the dumb waiter room by which the coal is hoisted from the basement and where we will get our coal every morning and evening.

Nearly opposite is the dining room door. There is a large and elegant dining room sufficient to accommodate all the students. The tables are large enough to accommodate twenty each. The room is about thirty feet high ... there is a splendid table set for every meal. For dinner we have three courses, first soup then three or four kinds of meat including fish, and one kind of pie for dessert. Thus far we have had plenty of every thing and the best of it.

As yet every thing is in an uproar and confusion but when we get a full start I think we will like it very much. I wish you were here I would like it so much.

Yesterday morning at nine o'clock according to notice given we all met at this building and formed in line in the hall, first the Seniors or those that come from other colleges as seniors, and next juniors sophomores and ... those commence[ing] their first term in this college, the seniors going in first and the other classes next. They first drew rooms set apart for captains.... We then went and found our rooms.

We are now under the command of Major Whitelsey who will require us to be in readiness for his orders and I believe he will require us to form in line immediately after breakfast and march over to the university chapel and at one o'clock to march back again to dinner and at some time in the forenoon to drill a little. There has been a requisition made on the governor for five hundred stands of arms.

Major Whitelsey will be our governing officer. All that he will require is that we are here at meal times and at chapel and that we put out our lights by a certain hour and that we keep ourselves and rooms clean and in order, and all that the other officers will require is that we are at recitations and that we have our lessons well. The rest of the time we will have to ourselves to go where we please. There will be no smoking in recitations but it is required that we have our lessons. On [October 7] we all attended the inauguration exercises in the morning at which president White and the faculty were sworn into office and the president gave his inaugural address. Lieutenant Governor Woodford administered the oath of office and delivered the address. Mr. Cornell also spoke some. In the afternoon we went upon the hill and listened to speeches by Professor Agassiz and George Wm. Curtiss and Mr. Weaver the superintendent of public instruction of this state and also to a speech made by a person in behalf of Miss Jenny McGraw who gave the chime of bells to the University. They are splendid bells, the largest one being like the one on the big factory, and eight smaller ones.

After the speaking the chimes were rung to play Old Hundred, Hail Columbia, and other tunes. It sounded nice. In the evening the citizens had a reception and jubilee. The reception for the students and the jubilee for the boys. In the town the reception was in the library hall and the jubilee was in the streets. The hall was cleared of seats and the ladies appeared in full dress costume with the Grecian band. In many cases it was like the bazaar, excepting the booths, and the citizens vied with [each] other in making it pleasant for the students. I got introductions to the Presbyterian minister and his wife and a great many ladies and gentlemen besides. We expect to have a sociable once every week in the reception room which is larger and [or] as big as the dining room hall.

Oh I forgot to say that among the other requirements we will have to learn dancing under the instruction of the cadets so that we may invite ladies to our sociables and dance with them. I expect we will have great times those times. When things are more settled we will have a bathing room in each hall where we can take a shower bath either hot or cold or get water to wash ourselves whenever we wish.

I can't think of anything more I am sitting on the corner of my bed and writing on my wash stand because we have no chairs yet.

3

JOHN Y. DAVIS

1872

# ROYAL TAFT

## CLASS OF 1871

Royal Taft came to Cornell in 1868 and began his diary in January 1869. His entries provide a full view of student life: he studies, he attends concerts, he joins student clubs, and he goes to church, sometimes two or three times a day. The university's critics thought it a "Godless university," but Royal tells us that many Cornell students chose to attend church services. He also participates in class rushes, those extended battles between the sophomores and the freshmen, and takes a keen interest in the ladies. When he graduated in 1871, he earned one of forty-one undergraduate degrees, the faculty numbered thirty-two, and there were two new buildings, McGraw Hall and West Sibley. After graduation, Royal returned to Pennsylvania to manage the family's general store and eventually settled into a job with the Post Office. He returned to Ithaca in 1940 to attend reunion, seventy-two years after entering the university.

January 8, 1869. I started back to college.

January 10, 1869. In the morning attended M[ethodist] E[piscopal] Church. A stranger preached. His text was from 1 John 2nd chap. A part of the first verse. Stayed to Sunday School. Dr. Wilson preached at 4 o'clock in the faculty room. Went to hear him. Attended evening services in the M. E. church. Mr. Crippen preached ... stayed to evening prayer meeting and had a good time.

January 11, 1869. The crowing event of the day was a reception given at Cascadilla

Place by Mr. and Mrs. Ezra Cornell. All the students were invited. It was a grand success. The music was excellent, the dancing graceful, the ladies handsome, and the refreshments delicious. Being unacquainted with the fair sex and but slightly knowing how to "trip the light fantastic toe" I did not venture to dance.



January 12, 1869. In consequence of keeping late hours last night did not wake up until 8 1/2 o'clock. The snow was piled up against our windows and is 8 or 12 inches deep on the ground. Did not go to any recitations ... studied very little.

January 14, 1869. This morning recited German to Professor Fiske, the first time. He is an excellent teacher and I am sure we shall like him. In the afternoon practiced in the laboratory. Chum and I commenced with the 5th group. From our room I have seen people skating and have had a desire to try ice instead of poring over books.

January 21, 1869. During the afternoon practiced in the Laboratory and finished group V. In the evening attended anniversary exercises of Cornell Library, which were held in Library Hall. Col. Sprague our Prof. of Rhetoric delivered an address, which was very good. Music by Whitlock's band and the University glee club. I think the glee club did not distinguish themselves.

January 24, 1869. Attended Dutch Reformed services in the morning. Dr. Strong preached a good sermon. The church was trimmed for Christmas and the trimmings have not yet been taken down they look beautiful. Went to M.E. church in the evening. Stayed to prayer meeting. Pleasant day. Had chicken for dinner.

January 25, 1869. Had but one recitation to day, which was in Physics. In the evening went down town to hear Prof. Goldwin Smith lecture. His subject was Oxford. It is a beautiful moonlight night. Weather is cold and thus endeth the chapter.

January 26, 1869.Was called upon to day to demonstrate a proposition in analytical Geom. and could not do it.

February 7, 1869. A pleasant beautiful day. Attended M.E. Church and Sunday school in the morning. In the afternoon attended the young men's prayer meeting in our building. Went to Episcopal church in the even. After services we went to the Methodist prayer meeting.

February 9, 1869. Practiced in laboratory in the afternoon. In the evening attended a party at Prof. Crafts. It was a stylish affair. Most of the gents were members of Prof's Chemistry class. He lives in fine style and has a very nice wife. The fair maids of Ithaca were of course present. Pleasant day. Thaw.

February 11, 1869. Weather is still warm. Practiced in laboratory. Capt. Nichols left on the evening train. He was one of the parties engaged in hazing Hale. The affair has created considerable excitement.

February 12, 1869. The Hale excitement still rages. Prof. Russel talked about it to a large number of students. Attended society meeting in the evening. Elected officers and had considerable sport. Weather is yet warm.

February 22, 1869. Blanket tossing was in vogue this morning. No recitations on account of its being the anniversary of Washington's birthday. This forenoon Ryman, Kasson and I had our heads examined by a Phrenologist. There is a little truth and considerable humbug about the science. Morley, a Freshman, fell through a hatchway the height of two stories and broke his leg.

February 27, 1869. In the evening went downtown again and was initiated into the Phi Kappa Psi society. The ceremony was at the room of Foraker and Buchwalter. Weather very cold. Wind blows hard.

March 1, 1869. Attended a concert given by the Hall Bros. of Boston. Camilla Urso performed on the violin. Miss Ridgway sang several times. It was a rich musical feast. The best I ever heard.

March 3, 1869. Went down town and visited the velocipede school. Chum and I each tried one. He succeeded in riding very well but I did not quite get the "knack" of the thing.

March 4, 1869. Today Gen. U. S. Grant assumed the duties of President of the United S's.

March 23, 1869. Had no Chemistry to day. Boss, the darky that helps around the laboratory was nearly killed last night by Carbolic acid. Practiced in Laboratory in the afternoon in the evening studied Analytical Geometry. Weather is very cold considering the time of year.

March 27, 1869. Studied Chemistry a little to day preparatory to examination. Went down town twice.... Phi Kappa Psi fraternity met to night and elected officers. I was chosen Recording Sect'y.

April 6, 1869. Was examined in chemistry and passed all right. Did not attend recitation in An Geom but the boys said Prof. Evans gave our class a high compliment. Said it had done better than his class at Yale. In the evening attended Episcopal Mite Society and escorted Miss Howard home.

April 9, 1869. After dinner called on Misses Tucker and Betts. Went to Ole Bull's concert in company with Miss Flora Platts and had a very pleasant time ... Ole Bull's music was grand. I could listen to him much longer and not get bored.

April 19, 1869. Mr. L. H. Pratt a member of our class died this morning. He had been sick about two weeks and very few of us knew anything about it. I was not much acquainted with him but he was a very good student.

April 23, 1869. The Freshman class made a rush or "raid" upon a few members of our class as they were going from University to laboratory. The Fresh think it is a "big thing." Went down in town after dinner to see a balloon ascension. It proved to be a sell. The balloon was paper and would not ascend.

April 27, 1869. Felt very sleepy in consequence of being up so late for the past few nights. Practiced in laboratory in the afternoon. The boys are quite enthusiastic over baseball and played a game this afternoon. I do not expect to take any part in the game unless I have more time to spare than at present.

April 30, 1869. Drilled from 5 to 6 P.M. after supper and went down town to the Irving Literary Association. Question: Resolved that the best interests of the United States demand a compulsory system of Education. Ryman was leader on the Negative and I on the aff.

May 24, 1869. The day passed about the same as usual. Studied chemistry from 3 to 5 P.M. then went over to University and drilled an hour. In the evening attended Mr. Curtis' lecture: Subject Chas. Dickens. His introduction was principally about Sir Walter Scott. Weather quite warm.

May 26, 1869. Commenced to rain as we were coming from recitations to dinner. Took a bath in afternoon. Prof. James Russell Lowell delivered his first lecture this evening to the students. His delivery is not as good as Curtis's but his ideas are good and his criticisms to the point. After lecture closed went to M.E. Mite Society.

May 27, 1869. Van Ambaugh's menagerie entered town to day by the road leading past Cascadilla. The procession made a very fine appearance. In the afternoon went down town to see the animals. The collection is a choice one and worthy of commendations. Ithaca was thronged with people who had come to see the menagerie. Some of the sightseers were about as much of a curiosity as the animals themselves. Rained in the evening. Felt tired and did not attend Prof. Lowell's lecture.

June 8, 1869. Last night just after I had retired and before I had gone to sleep I was awakened by unusual noise in the halls. Soon the gong sounded and...fire was heard. The old building directly back of us was in flames. For a time considerable excitement prevailed. Cascadilla was scorched but not seriously damaged. The building burned to the ground. Several hundred dollars worth of beds and blankets were stored in it and were also consumed. The fire companies were on hand and one engine played upon the fire. Curtis delivered his last lecture this evening.

June 21, 1869. Last night the boys pulled down the No. 10 Privy at the University.

June 22, 1869. Was examined in Calculus, Chemistry and analyzed a solid at the Laboratory. Considerable excitement now prevails concerning the tearing down of the privy. Expulsion is threatened but I guess the affair will be settled. Everybody is very busy preparing for examinations.

June 23, 1869. Was examined in English Literature two hours and Calculus one hour. Made a "flunk" in Calculus. Spent the afternoon at the library studying German authors. Went down town after supper.

June 24, 1869. The students who for the past few nights have been summoned to the "Cornell University Privy Council" were each fined ten dollars. Rather a dear trick. Was examined in Calculus. Went down town after dinner.

June 30, 1869. At 3 P.M. the corner stone of the McGraw building was set amid the ceremonies by the Masonic order. Speeches were delivered by several prominent public men of the state. A large bell, the gift of Mrs. A. D. White was presented to the university.

July 1, 1869. This morning at 9 o'clock began the first Commencement exercises of Cornell University. The graduating class, eight in number, delivered orations, which were very good. Pres. White then made a neat speech and presented the diplomas. Reception in Cascadilla parlor in the evening. The ladies' dresses were rich and costly. Refreshments consisted of strawberries, ice cream, cake and lemonade. There was no dancing as Mrs. White did not approve of it. Thus closes the first year at Cornell. It was full of joy and scarcely darkened by sorrow. May each succeeding prove as happy and may our university grow and prosper from year to year.

September 13, 1869. Left home this morning on my return trip to Cornell.

September 14, 1869. Took my first meal at our new boarding place and am well pleased with the fare ... A great many new students are here and examinations are now going on. The Profs are severe and the poor Fresh. who are applying for admission go about with anxious faces.

September 15, 1869. Examinations were continued to day. About three hundred have been admitted.

September 22, 1869. For the first time attended Dr. Wilder's lecture. His subject was the heart. I shall be in his class all of this term. Just before I came down from the university to dinner I went out in the field to see Dr. Law.

Sept. 24, 1869. Prof. Sprague lectured to the Juniors and Seniors this morning on the Origin and Growth of Language. Drilled an hour before supper in Military Hall. In the evening The Irving Literary Society held a meeting. H. L. Jones, the president made a good inaugural speech. Weather warm.

Oct. 6, 1869. Played my first game of billiards at Clinton Hall with Case. There is no bar attached to the room.

Oct. 29, 1869. Dr. Wilder gave a lecture in which I think he rather upheld the use of liquor at least that of wine. I think it will produce some discussion.

Jan. 11, 1870. Arose at 8 1/4. No reason to get up early as we had no recitations on account of its being Founders Day. Employed my leisure moments in reading *Domby & Son*. It is good but some parts are rather tedious.... went to Cascadilla to a reception given by Mr. Cornell in honor of his birthday. The refreshments were simple consisting of biscuits, coffee, cake and ice cream. After supper dancing was in order. The music was good and all present seemed to enjoy themselves.

Mar. 4, 1870. Read my essay on Divorce before the class this morning. Goldwin Smith gave his first lecture of the present term. The subject was the reign of Chas.

II. He talks slowly and it is quite easy to take notes from him. Spent the afternoon in reading and playing chess.

Mar. 7, 1870. Our minister called on us and we had quite a long conversation discussing the university &c.



Mar. 13, 1870. Went to hear Dr. Stebbins the Unitarian minister. Text from Prov. I: 24 Because I have called and ye refused. The sermon was on the freedom of the will and against the Calvanistic doctrine of preordination. He is a very able man and the sermon was excellent. I do not understand the Unitarian doctrine. I supposed that they received the Savior only as a good man. Dr. Stebbins however, made both of his prayers and pronounced the benediction through Christ.

Mar. 16, 1870. When we arose this morning the ground was covered with a foot of snow. The flakes continued to fall thick and fast and now the snow is between two and three feet in depth. It is the greatest snowstorm I have ever seen. The roofs of a few buildings have fallen in, business is dull, the mails are stopped and everybody stays at home as much as possible. We did not go up to the university at all.

Mar. 31, 1870. Was examined this morning in Law and Polity. Dr. Wilson is an easy old soul and I think that few or none of the class will be conditioned. During the remainder of the forenoon studied Zoology.

April 1, 1869. Was sold this morning at the breakfast table by means of a pancake, which had a piece of paper in it. I did not however put any of the cake into my mouth. At 9 1/4 was examined in Eng. Lit. The examination was easy and I think none of the class will be conditioned. At 3 P.M. was examined in Zoology.

April 17, 1870. Took my first breakfast at my new boarding place, viz at Mr. Rood's the Sheriff. Eight students are now boarding there.

April 18, 1870. This morning at the first hour Dr. Wilson commenced his lecture to the Juniors on Logic. At the fourth hour we had a lecture from Prof. Blake on optics.

April 25, 1870. Bayard Taylor lectured this evening on Frederick Schiller. He repeated from William Tell the song of the boy on the lake. The lecture was excellent. Chum took Miss Rose and Peters, Miss Atwater. Think I will try to get some company for next Wednesday evening.

April 26, 1870. Went to the university as usual. Dr. Wilson informed us that he would be absent during the remainder of the week. I did not notice anyone shed tears at the announcement.

September 19, 1870. ... paid my tuition went to Cascadilla and was registered after which I proceeded to the University. Heard Goldwin Smith lecture at the last hour. He began with a description of England & its early inhabitants. Had a fine dinner of chicken, sweet potatoes &c. Read some of *Robertson's History of the State of Europe* &

found it quite difficult. We have several new Profs and I presume all of them are fine scholars.



September 22, 1870. This evening the Freshmen had a meeting in military hall for the purpose of class organization or something of the kind. The Sophs gathered about the building and when the Fresh came out there was a grand "rush." Clothes were torn, canes broken, plug hats smashed &c. The police were on the spot & put a few of the students in the police station but let them out in a few minutes.

September 23, 1870. At the 5th hour the Sophs & Fresh had a "big rush" & the latter being in the majority came out ahead. Fresh exhibited considerably generalship in marshalling their forces & commencing the attack. Prex drove up just about the close of the performance, made a speech & advised them to desist from such conduct in the future. The Sophs triumphantly exhibit pieces of canes, pieces of plug hats & bits of clothes taken in the rush last night.

September 28, 1870. Hunted up our old washer woman Mrs. Ford & engaged her to wash for me again.

September 30, 1870. Has rained all day making the walk to and from the university rather disagreeable. Prof. Roehrig started a class in Chinese today. A large number of the boys attended and are quite enthusiastic upon the subject. Wilson gave the final lecture of a course on Physical Geography and Climatology. Spent the afternoon in Cornell Library reading literary reviews on Lothair. *The Era* came out to day. In the evening read some in Hist. of Philosophy and Robertson's Chas V. Sophomore class elections take place to night.

October 4, 1870. Prex White did not give any lecture. Dr. Wilson gave us a miserable lecture supposed to be on the Hist. of Philosophy but really a rehash of what he has told us several times before. Read Hist. in the afternoon.

October 7, 1870. It is just two years ago that the inaugural exercises of the university took place. Today we have at least 700 students and I presume much more. The weather has been beautiful. At the first hour Prof. Corson read a lecture to the Senior & Junior classes and hereafter on Friday this system will be continued. Our Spanish class is now quite large. After dinner copied up some Spanish exercises. Juniors & Sophs had a game of ball, which the latter won by a score of 38 to 17.

October 11, 1870. I went up to the cider mill at Free Hollow and had all the cider we could drink. Prex White did not read his lecture today as is his usual custom but delivered it off hand. I like this way much better as it is easier to take notes. Read History during the afternoon and evening.

October 17, 1870. Attended lecture in Hist. & then came to my room cutting Spanish.... Then we went down to the ball ground where the boys were playing a match game of ball for the benefit of Mr. [Thomas] Hughes. He seemed to be very much pleased. After the game was finished the boys got up a game of football. Mr. Hughes

& Prof. Russel mingled in with the crowd & kicked the ball. Mr. H., I think could beat Prof. He drove away amid the cheers of the crowd. A beautiful day.



October 26, 1870. It was announced yesterday that Prex. wished to/would meet the whole body of students in the chapel this morning. There was a general turn out & the room was "jammed full." He made a nice speech and a short one too. The objects: He began with minor matters such as "manliness," from that to secret societies, then rushes, next the great question of obliging students to wear the military cap, and as a clincher (especially for the Fresh) he agreed to furnish planks for a walk between Cascadilla & University.

November 1, 1870. This morning we were very much amused by seeing people hunting for gates and carrying them home. Last night being Holly Eve a general raid was made upon the gates. A lot were placed in the park, others were loaded on wagons & drawn into Cascadilla Creek. The greatest event of the day or rather night was the burial of "chapeau." The four classes united and made quite a demonstration. They met at Clinton Hall & disguised themselves in all sorts of ways but mainly every one wore a long nightshirt & some sort of a mask. A band was hired for the occasion and many had tinhorns, which made the noise of a Rabble and drowned the music of the Band. The procession then marched through the streets of Ithaca & then up on the hill where they burned & buried a large coffin filled with old hats. Dismal howls rent the air & the whole spectacle was ludicrous & grotesque. Ceremonies being over at the graves the procession marched back to Cascadilla & called at Prex who made a speech. Next they visited Prof Russel who was in fine spirits. They also called at Mr. Cornell's but he was either away from home or would not come out. The procession then disbanded. I should also have mentioned that many were provided with torches.

November 4, 1870. The day has been beautiful and if it only continues a little longer we shall see the wings of the McGraw building roofed over. They are also putting a roof on Mr. Cornell's house.

November 7, 1870. After supper Peters, Kasson and I went down to Inghman's & McNair's room & put it in general disorder. We took the bedstead apart, placed the spring bed upside down on the floor & filled it full of books. We also hid the bed slats, bookcase, top of the stove &c.

November 8, 1870. After dinner went to the polls (Tompkins house) and deposited my maiden vote without being challenged. I took the Republican ticket (straight).

November 16, 1870. Wore my cap up to the university for the first time. Several of the boys however did not comply with the order but wore their hats. Dr. Wilson took up the subject of climatology in his lectures to day. In Spanish we commenced Gil Blas. After dinner went up town & exchanged my cap for which I was obliged to pay twenty five cents extra. The other one hurt my head it being too narrow in front but the one that I now have is very comfortable.

December 1, 1870. The Catholic Priest was present at Prex. White's lecture. Also quite a number of ladies.

December 13, 1870. As I was going up the hill this morning I met Chum, Chuck & Bright who told me that Nobby had got into an unfortunate position. He was one of the competitors for the prize essay on German literature & copied largely from a work on Lessing translated from the German by Prof. Evans. Prof. Fiske was very much provoked and posted up his name on the bulletin board. To preserve the honor of our fraternity we drew up a paper severing him from the fraternity but did not use the word expel. He felt very badly & it was with reluctance that we took such a measure. Individually we like him as well as ever and will befriend him.

December 15, 1870. Prex White's examination in History took place this P.M.. The boys say there was no chance at all for ponying.

January 7, 1871. Had breakfast my first meal at Mrs. Boy's our new boarding place. It is a decided improvement upon last terms board. Spent the forenoon in the room. About 3 o'clk went skating. I expected to see quite a number of ladies out but there were only a few.

January 9, 1871. Went up to the university at the first hour to attend the lecture on Roman History but as Prof. Russel had a cold and another lecture to deliver he did not give any on Roman Hist. At the third hour attended the lecture on Geology given by Prof. Hartt, who has just returned from his Brazilian expedition. At the fourth hour attended a lecture on Ancient Hist delivered by Prof. Russel. Having nothing the fifth hour I came down town. During the afternoon wrote up four pages of the history lecture. In the evening went to see the pantomime of Three Blind Mice, played by Fox & Dernier troupes. It was the first pantomime that I ever saw. The audience were well pleased.

January 11, 1871. This being Founders Day, there were no university exercises. Did not study much. Mr. Cornell gave a reception this evening in Cascadilla parlor....I did not go up to the reception until 10 o'clk. All of the students were invited as well as a great many of the people of Ithaca. The ladies toilettes were very fine. A good band was in attendance, which furnished excellent music for dancing. In all there were nine dances. I missed none but the first. Refreshments were furnished to the guests but I did not take any as the lady that I was with did not wish any. The entertainment broke up about 1 o'clk or a little after.

January 12, 1871. Pres. White today announced that he had been unexpectedly called away and would perhaps be absent from the country several weeks if not months. I have since learned that he is going to San Domingo to settle some question for the government. In the mean time we shall have lectures from Prof. Corson in Eng. Lit instead of the President's lectures on Hist.

January 23, 1871. Colder than blitzen! Had the pleasure of sitting in the North University Chapel for two hours and it was cold enough to freeze.

January 28, 1871. Had a frat meeting in the evening and initiated Goldsmith, Frankenheimer & Rosenblatt all splendid boys. Each made a few remarks very appropriate for the occasion. Had apples &c and a good time generally. F & R were rushed by the Alpha Delta Pi.

February 6, 1871. Prof. Russel excused all of the History class who felt too cold to remain in the lecture room & the consequence was that nearly the whole class went out.

February 10, 1871. Went up to the university at the usual hour ... the order has been repeated that we must wear the university cap and I suppose for the present at least we shall be obliged to obey it.

March 4, 1871. Had Phi Kappa meeting and received the resignation of Goldsmith. His uncle is opposed to secret societies and so he was obliged to withdraw.

April 11, 1871. In the evening attended Anna Dickinson's lecture, in company with Miss Sarah Atwater. Her subject was Jeanne D'arc or Joan of Arc, and she treated it in a masterly way. Anna is eloquent & possesses a great deal of that individual magnetism which she attributes to the Maid of Orleans. The audience showed by their actions that they were pleased with the lecture. Miss A. looked nice. We have had several showers today.

May 6, 1871. ... spent the forenoon in the Cornell Library reading up for my commencement oration.

May 18, 1871. Rulloff [a murderer] was hung to day in Binghamton. The papers of that city contain a full account of the affair.

June 7, 1871. Had strawberries for Tea, which tasted very good although they were brought from a distance.

June 9, 1871. Prof Dwight delivered his last lecture of the course on Constitutional law. That was the last lecture of my collegiate course.

June 20, 1871. Class Day: went up to the university via Cascadilla & saw the sights & came back through the cemetery. Also visited Cornell's new house. Our Class Day exercises took place this afternoon in Library Hall.

June 22, 1871. Commencement: The last day of my college life. Commencement exercises took place this morning and were quite good. The university band furnished music & every thing passed off pleasantly. Prex. White looked care worn ... but he made the graduates a very good speech. The speakers came on in alphabetical order & that brought me last on the list. It was therefore a disadvantage as the exercises were long. All of us were favored with an abundant supply of bouquets, I receiving fourteen.

# JOHN LITTLE MOFFATT

## CLASS OF 1873

The letters between John Moffatt and his parents in Brooklyn constitute an extraordinary family dialogue, each writer expressing great affection and interest in the physical and spiritual condition of the other. The Moffatts were adherents of Swedish scientist and theologian Emanuel Swedenborg (1688–1772), who believed in the spiritual nature of the universe. A small New Church congregation had formed in Ithaca, and John describes the professors and townspeople involved. He writes of his health and the health of his friends, requesting advice about using homeopathic medicines to alleviate ailments. Father and son discuss the challenge of new scientific theories, especially Darwinism. John Moffatt graduated from Cornell in 1873 in a class of ninety-five and went on to medical school in New York City. His three children also graduated from Cornell. He practiced homeopathic medicine in Brooklyn until 1917, when he became ill and moved his family to Ithaca.

October 10, 1869. My Dear Father and Mother. I understand your explanation of the Origin of Evil. Dr. Wilder does not explain much, he says he is a pupil with us, in Swedenborg's writings.... I have formed an acquaintance with a very nice fellow from New York, E. Williams. His family are New Church.... I think the rule still puts us on our honor as gentlemen; I have not heard of any change. Are there many velocipedes in the streets?

Oct. 17, 1869. We are awakened by the gong or bugle. The bugle summons us to meals, and we form in the halls by companies, and each company marches into meals. We do not drill in stormy weather.... [we] march up to the University Buildings where the co. is generally broken up into squads of four or eight men each and drilled. We then march back to supper. I believe the captain recommends cadets for promotion and by the approval of the faculty, the major promotes them. I think the best way to rise would be, first merit, & then (very important) join the secret society in which the officers are; but I will do no such thing as the latter.... I dress in my common clothes for class but have to appear in uniform for drill.

Oct. 17, 1869. The servant girls come around every day, a little after 12, I believe, and empty the slops. There is a fellow down stairs who has made an electric battery; he is going to connect it to the door, so that when anybody opens the door, the outside and inside of a leyden jar are connected, and the person coming in will receive a shock.

Oct. 24, 1869. My board will be due on Sat. It will be $24.18, I believe. I have now on hand $6.67. Aubert, a friend, and I are going to have a couple of geological hammers made if they do not cost over .50 each, for Prof Hartt set us to collecting fossils. At the end of each month, I shall endeavor to send home an account of my finances & a trial balance.

Aubert & I walked up Fall Creek this afternoon. We went to the lower falls and found out that it cost 15 cents each to walk up the gorge. I did not believe in that and turned back; but we climbed up the hill some distance from the gate, and after hard climbing reached what afterwards proved to be the path. I found that they have made a very good path the whole length of the gorge, and the walk, now is worth 15 cts. We came to a rather dangerous place in the path where there were two boards put up, viz, "Johnson's Tumble." John Johnson fell from here Aug. 24, '69 & went 200 feet, was not much hurt. These are not the exact words on the 2nd board, but they are the idea.

The different falls are magnificent, and I want you to see them. There are some places where ladies would find pretty difficult climbing, but ladies go there, as we saw several.

Nov. 14, 1869. One of our discomforts is, on Sunday, we cannot get any water without going way down in the cellar to the kitchen or wash room. I do not think Dr. Wilder any more distant or less kind than he used to be. There are some fellows that dislike him but they are mostly those one would not be anxious to have as friends.

Nov. 19, 1869. We are going to read Shakespeare's plays (our class) and Prof. Sprague recommended each to get a copy of the plays with notes. Tues. I went down town & priced some copies. There was a copy of the Globe Edition, quite small & fine print, for $2.00.... Then there is an edition of $3 that I like best. I can get a second hand copy for $2.50. It has I suppose, between 600 & 700 pages, clear type, notes at bottom of the page, bound in calf, about the size of Boyer's Dictionary, though thicker.

Which should I get? I must wait for money before I get one, I suppose I will need one about the 25th.

Nov. 28, 1869. I am behind in my Physiology lectures, and in Eng. Literature. I hope to make up soon.

Jan. 12th, 1870. In the evening the reception came off. I did not go in until 9 o'clock. It began at half past eight. There was a great crowd, and dancing did not begin until about 11 o'clock. During the first dance the supper room opened and kept open for an hour or two. They had a counter, and the gentlemen would go and get refreshments for their ladies. There was a great crowd. I believe refreshments were Ice Cream, Cake, Coffee & Sandwiches. The dancing continued until about 2 o'clock. There were about 11 or 12 square dances; Mrs. Cornell would not allow any round dances. Most people, I suppose, paid their respects to Mr. & Mrs. Cornell on entering; I did not. I shook hands with them at the close, however. I danced twice with Miss Nichols & once with Mrs. Wilder.

Jan. 19, 1870. We have a new professor here, Prof. Russel told us his name was Roehrig & that he was the greatest linguist in America, probably in the world. On three months notice he will go as interpreter to any location in the world. If he doesn't know the language, he will learn it in that time. He knows about 23 or 25 different languages.

Feb. 27, 1870. I have a great many of those little black specks on my face but they are not what troubles me chiefly. I have larger red pimples that generally come to a white head, but not always, and my face is getting very rough to the hand. A day or two ago I found I had what look'd like a boil in the left corner of my mouth on the lower lip. It did not hurt but was merely a hard collection of white matter growing larger & larger ... I opened it with my knife and squeezed out all the matter I could. In so doing I broke off the top. I put a plaster on and after about a day the plaster came off ... [it] begins to hurt when I open my mouth very wide and draw my lips apart. There are others of these on my face but they are much smaller & do not trouble me though they look bad.

Friday evening I felt a little chilly as I sat in my room and put on the fire coal to get up heat. After it was hot I put on more coal & left the stove door open, thereby permitting, aiding, and abetting Carbinie Monoxide (C.O. a poisonous gas) to come in the room. After a time I felt dizzy and a nausea, I opened the window to blow out & then went into the W.C. I took some N. Vom. & felt a little relieved ... I laid on my back in bed trying to get better but that made me worse so I turned on my side & went to sleep, waking up in the morning all well.

March 13, 1870. Prof. Roehrig is our French teacher this week, and we all look forward to a pleasant time. We change profs every [week] and always look forward to Prof. Roehrig's week as the pleasantest & most instructive; he tries to make us speak French only, on Fridays.

[From Mother] 19 Apr 70. Do not change your underwear till the leaves have their full size. Select one of the later trees for guidance. You may lighten your outer garments safely, but not the underwear at all.



19 May, 70. I have chosen the locust tree for my standard when to change my winter clothing. Barrett says it is about the latest tree in these parts to have its leaves attain their full size.

Thursday evening. I ... with some others, were elected members of the Cornell Natural History Society and I signed the constitution.... Friday I attended the second meeting of the "Independent Cadets" as our company is called. We signed articles of agreement and had a drill. In the evening I attended the meeting of the Independents for the purpose of inaugurating the officers.

May 22, 70. ... there were some young ladies coming [along Buttermilk Falls] and we scampered back to put on our shoes and stockings and make ourselves as presentable as might be.... As it turned out, the place was too steep and difficult (I think) for ladies to ascend and when we looked, we saw they were sitting down looking at the falls.

June 12, 70. I understood from Dr. Wilder that Swedenborg does not explain the origin of species. If I understand the question right, it is embodied in three principal theories. Agassiz, Darwin's (so called), and Mr. Ferris's. There are others, but these seem to be the most prominent & likely.

Agassiz' theory is that when man was made, he was made by a miracle from the dust, as the Bible says. I think Darwin says that there were a great many species of animals on the earth each differing in an imperceptible degree from those on each side of it, until the series led up to man. He says that then a great many of the intermediate species died out so as to leave gaps between those remaining. This might be illustrated by a number of marbles each successive one a little larger than its predecessor, but so little difference between them that we can not conceive it. Then if we take away nos. 2.3.4.5.6.7.8&9 and compare nos. 1 and 10 we will see a decided difference in size. I think that is Darwin's theory, but this does not account for the *origin* of species, even if it be true.

There is some theory (I do not know what) that says that all animal life originally was derived from one cell of the lowest order of life. From this cell sprang others of higher orders and differing in the course of time until all the present diversity of the animal kingdom.

Mr. Ferris's theory is (I think, but I am not very clear on his theory) that some family of animals were especially made by degrees higher than the rest of their species by miracles and finally they brought forth man in his lowest state. But I should hardly credit this theory as all animals have from birth the instinct, which they possess through life, and man has not, and I do not see that he ever could have had this instinct.

But the lower human beings now living were found in the center of Africa by Du-Chailler (I think) or Livingstone; they are dwarfs, and live but little better than the monkeys, and seem not to know much more. For my part I am not going to accept any of the theories now current until I have studied the subject thoroughly....





Prof. Wing said that he believes animals have what, for want of a better name, you might call souls. That you cannot kill an animal forever if you kill him on this earth. His reasons for this, if I recollect right, are that animals possess life or power, which is indestructible.... Prof. Wing says that the soul or life of animal is not to be compared with man's soul any more than an animal is to be compared to man on this earth. They are parallel and do not meet at infinity.

And where God gave life ... we cannot destroy it: I can't explain this well, but I think I understand it.... Will you please explain this to me?

June 16, 70. Today I heard Greene Smith lecture on "Birds" showing how they are the friends of man. It was very interesting.

June 19, 1870. Father, I think I can see what you mean in your letter but I can hardly accept the train of reasoning yet, though I cannot refute it. The Ferris I mentioned is our Mr. Ferris of Ithaca I am sure. It seems to me that you hold Agassiz's theory, of spontaneous generation, or man's being made by a miracle from the earth ...

PS: I did not show your letter to Dr. Wilder as Gram [John's cousin] thought the Dr. might not like to be corrected.

Nov. 20, 1870. Church has had a bad cold for two or three days. At first it was a running cold and I gave him arsenic; the next day it was no better, but his head was stopped up. I gave him Asa Foetida. He says when his cold breaks up he generally has a cough in the evenings as if his throat was swelling & choking him. A loose prolonged cough that does not raise matter. What is the right medicine for him? I want to cure him by Hom[eopathic] Practice, for his father is an allopath. doctor.

Feb. 26, 1971. Friday, Prof. Russel told the students that the trustees have decided not to have anything to do with boarding us next term. They will rent us rooms in the building. They may possibly supply us with coal and gas. And will rent the kitchens to any one who wishes to set up a restaurant....If they don't give us gas, we will burn kerosene, and if they won't supply us with coal we will club together and get it ourselves. I don't know how they will manage about taking care of our rooms, etc. Some say that the trustees have lost about $11,000 on Cascadilla in the two years. This was mainly by board, and *I think* Bailey [the building manager] could account for a considerable portion of it.

I have given up Latin. I don't know what to do about it. I try to read a little French every day. Our German teacher is a humbug. We passed the last examination with honor and hence are in the advanced class. But, it happens that our old teacher, McKoon was taken from us, and now Prof. Hart teaches us. He is about the laziest professor I have ever seen. I almost go to sleep in the class every day. We have read the Geigirlex once and now we are going over it yet again translating from Eng. to German. The other classes are far ahead of us in the reader and have been taking the Grammar also, so instead of our being the Advanced class, they are really. I feel mad at Prof. Fiske and despise Prof. Hart while I hate him.



Mar 12, 1871. Prof. Fiske is an Ultra Prussian. Yesterday he got all the German sections up in the chapel and gave us a very interesting abstract of the condition of Germany since the thirty years war (which ended, I believe, in the 17th century) and said something about the last war. We ought to hear someone now, who sympathizes strongly with the French so that we can draw our own conclusions. He then read us some beautiful German pieces from our reader.

April 28, 1871. Please send me $30 if convenient because my wash bill has just drained my pocket.

Sept. 27th, 1871. Please send me twenty dollars ($20). I will pay for three weeks board and the five dollars will keep me in funds to the next installment. I hope.

Nov 1st, 1871. I do not know how to buy socks; what shall I ask for, how shall I know whether I get what I want, & how much ought I give.... This morning I heard Prof. Goldwin Smith read half of his lecture "The Thirty Years War," it was very interesting indeed.

Nov. 9, 1871. Last night quite a number of students met in Military Hall to bury the caps, many in masks & night shirts or sheets. We formed a procession, first came the hearse and priests, next a wagon, with the University Band, then the Independent Cadets with three drums; then a society called "the Owls" with fish horns, and finally other students. Being so near the head of the procession I could not see how many there were in it, but Church thinks there were not more than 150; there were about a hundred students armed with clubs in the crowd which accompanied the procession, so no outbreak occurred.

Nov. 12, 1871. Comstock of '74, Dr. Wilder's assistant, is down with the Typhoid fever, but is improving. Dr. W. has him in his rooms and has been very kind to him indeed. I have not heard of small pox around here. Is there much of it in Brooklyn or New York? My face has broken out with pimples badly; I have been putting glycerin on them, & taking Hyd. apparently without effect.

Nov. 22, 1871. Last Friday the class in Hist. waited twenty minutes for Prof. Russel, and during that time some of the students shouted "Bolt!" very often but apparently could not screw their courage up to the sticking point. Prof. Russel heard them as he came upstairs and as he came up the aisle there was a dead silence all over the room. When he had reached his desk he turned around and quietly said, "You are dismissed," and immediately went out again.

Nov. 22nd 71. I had to write four essays for Prof. Schackford on: 1st Sir W. Scott as a Man; 2. The direction, "Do your work having regard to its Excellence, & not to its Acceptability"; 3rd. The Natural Scenery of Ithaca; & 4th. The Rise of the German Empire. I have written the first two.... I have the Psychology syllabus of 120 questions of long answers to get out. And I must study up Rhetoric, History & German. I take lectures on Hist. of civilization by Prof. Russel; Lectures on Psychology by Dr. Wilson; German (Wallenstein) under Prof. Fiske; Rhetoric under Schackford; & French under Crane. These I will be examined in. Then I have Lab. Pract. & recitations (with Prof. Wing).

Dec. 3rd, 1871. In my freshman year, when the professor did not come to the class for half-an-hour, and it was probable that he would not come, we would "Bolt!" that is, *cut* or go away. The Faculty are keeping very good order among the students by keeping their sentence of suspending those arrested for gate-lifting yet in abeyance; they say that they shall hold them for the present as hostages for the good behavior of the others. So the poor fellows loaf around town, studying, but not attending the University Exercises.

Comstock made me a visit to day and spoke to me about how kind every one had been to him, a stranger. As soon as he got sick, Dr. Wilder brought him over to Cascadilla and gave up two of his rooms, and paid a great deal of attention to him. Dr. Morgan's bill was $30, Mr. Finch the bookseller down town paid $10 of it, tho' he had never seen Comstock. Comstock is a Freemason. I don't know whether Finch is one. Leavitt nursed C. and would take no pay. C. has a mother in California, but no other relations in the world. I guess he don't know much about her as he told me he was alone in the world, and had lived with an old couple since he was a little boy. From what he says, he seems almost ready to accept Swedenborg's doctrines.

January 10th, 1872. Tomorrow being Founder's Day is a holiday, and Mr. Cornell holds a reception in the evening. I will tell you about it in my next.

The board here is wretched!!!! The food is of poor quality & not enough of it. This morning I had one roll, two pieces of *tough* beefsteak for breakfast. For dinner there was a mouthful of chicken, *two* pieces of beef, poor bread, & could help myself only once to mashed potatoes! We are going to speak to Mr. Taylor about it, and if that don't improve the fare, we will have to make some other arrangement; probably go downtown. So I shall not be in a hurry to pay my board or room rent.

April 7th, 1872. I shall not be able to take Prof. Wilder's course in Embryology on account of the President's History. The ice still extends about seven miles down the lake but I suppose it is very rotten. There was a snowstorm here on Thurs., and I see snow around the fences, & on distant hill tops.

April 11th, 1872. I am charmed with Pres. White & his lectures, but the latter are so comprehensive and hurried that I find I must read up with them.

May 12, 72. Prof. C. F. Hartt was advertised to deliver his first lecture of a course of four on "Brazil" on Tuesday night. He was going to have a sort of stereopticon so

Prof. Caldwell was making Oxygen for him in the laboratory. He left the room to hear a class recite and the oxygen burst the bag, setting it & the window frame on fire. Some one coming along (this was about 12 o'clock I think) saw the flames coming out of the window & gave the alarm, and the fire was soon put out. I hope this will be a warning to the authorities to get a fire extinguisher & keep it there. In fact, there ought to be half a dozen, for it is a wooden building & would soon go, if once fairly burning. The fire was in the Assaying room, first floor southwest corner. In the picture in the Register the N.W. cor is towards you.

Friday was the day of the Regatta, the first race was at first appointed for half-past two, and then for three o'clock. There had been a north wind all day which blew until sunset, if not later, and there was consequently a heavy swell. There were a great many people who had driven to the lake in carriages which were drawn up along the roadside for quite a distance. Many more came on foot, and a large barge full was towed down from the steamboat landing & anchored off the starting point.

Profs Fiske & Wait were the judges. A four oared crew brought their shell up from Union Springs, and their Captain, Courtney, a blacksmith with a splendid physique, brought his boat to row a race with Elseffer in his paper shell. The waves were so high that the race was delayed in hopes of their abating until about four o'clock; then the "Tom Hughes" six oared crew (belonging to the navy), the seventy three crew in our six oared lapstreak, and the "Townies" as they are called (a four oared crew of people of the town) entered for the first race. I had a boat and rowed down about a quarter of a mile to see the crews pass me. They say that '73 made a splendid start. But I know that one of the boats made a tremendous splashing. The Tom Hughes men pulled beautifully. When the "Townies" had gotten about halfway to the point where I was they broke one of their oars; they steered for the shore and the man jumped overboard in about five & a half feet of water & swam ashore while the other three continued the race. But after going maybe half a mile further they broke another oar & had to give up.

The '73 crew had hardly pulled a dozen strokes before they began to go under. The water came in over the bow continually and filled the boat; the crew stood upon the thwarts and the boat rolled over and spilled them into the drink. Immediately a number of boats crowded around, picked them up, and towed the boat ashore. Jayne, the bow oar, was the only one who couldn't swim; I believe he went under twice, but he kept up finally with the aid of the other fellows, and of the boat. The waves had gone down slightly but the '75 crew in the 8 oared barge got frightened & declared that they wouldn't row. So the races were postponed until 9 a.m. Sat.

Yesterday at about quarter past one o'clock I was reading in the library when I heard an alarm of fire and saw a large volume of smoke ascending from near Cascadilla; I ran here and found that it was Morse's carpenter shop just below us, which was burning fearfully. I ran up to exchange my straw hat for my cap and met Pres. White hurrying to the scene.... We set to work to save this & got it all out. It seemed a very long time before the engines came, but they had to climb that hill, which was plenty of excuse. Finally they arrived, two old hand machines & two steamers, the

# WEBB HAYES

## CLASS OF 1876

Webb Hayes was one of four sons of Rutherford B. and Lucy Hayes who attended Cornell. Birchfield Austin Hayes ("Birch" in his brother's diary) was a member of the class of 1874; Rutherford Platt Hayes graduated with the class of 1880, and Stanley Wolcott Hayes graduated in 1891 with a degree in mechanical engineering. Webb Cook Hayes entered Cornell in 1872 but withdrew when the elder Hayes won the White House in the contested election of 1876; he became his father's secretary and went with him to Washington in March of 1877. Webb describes the fraternity hazing of 1873 that led to the death of a pledge. He uses the slang of the day: "peelers" are the police; "plugs" are hats; "A. B. C." is Alonzo Cornell, Ezra's eldest son, then living in Ithaca. The catcall "Custom house, custom house" refers to Alonzo Cornell's appointment by President Grant as port naval officer in the New York customhouse, a post from which he was removed in 1878.

When President Hayes left the White House, Webb entered the Army. He won a Congressional Medal of Honor during the Spanish-American War for a daring feat in the Philippines, was wounded in Cuba, served on the Mexican border, and went with the China Relief Expedition in 1900. In his early sixties, he served on the Italian front and in France during World War I. Between wars, Hayes was vice-president of the National Carbon Company in Cleveland; he identified himself as a manufacturer. He died in 1934.

September 9, 1872. I started for Cornell University at Ithaca, N.Y. at 7 P.M. Birch stayed to take part in a Base Ball match. I changed cars at Cleveland, arriving at Rochester at 7 A.M. where I again changed cars arriving at Cayuga where I took a Steamboat for Ithaca passing down Lake Cayuga and landing at Ithaca about 6 P.M. I went up to Cascadilla Place and went to bed in Birch's old room.

September 11, 1872. I met some of the boys that I was introduced to last June. At 3 P.M. I went to an examination in Grammar. It was pretty hard but I guessed I passed.

September 12, 1872. I visited the University buildings this morning. There are five buildings completed and another has its foundation laid. Three of these buildings were built by the University: The North and South University buildings and the Laboratory. The former are large buildings built of stone. They contain the recitation rooms and some of the lecture rooms. The Laboratory is a wooden building and contains the rooms for Laboratory practice and so forth. The McGraw building is situated between the University buildings. It is larger than either of these buildings and contains the Library, Museum and lecture rooms. In the Library are 35,000 volumes. In the tower of the McGraw building are the University chimes consisting of nine bells and the large University bell. The Sibley building is situated at the head of the quadrangle and contains the Machine shops, the University press and lecture rooms. The Sage building has its foundation laid.

September 14, 1872. I get a little homesick once in a while because I have nothing to do.

September 16, 1872. I went to a recitation in German in the North University building at 8:15 A.M. In Algebra at 9:15 A.M. in the same building and to a lecture in Physiology at 11:15 A.M. in the McGraw building. At 4:30 P.M. we drilled on Campus.

September 17, 1872. I went to Algebra and German and to Rhetoric at 10:15 A.M. in the Laboratory. I like it here very much. I have to study pretty hard.

September 20, 1872. The Freshmen had some bills printed with Songs on them to sing. It was announced that Pres. White intended to speak to the students this morning but he did not come on time. After Physiology the Class of '76 held a meeting in the lecture room.... The Soph's were in the hall below yelling and singing and making all the noise they could. Two or three times the Soph's made a rush to get up to the lecture room but were driven back. They threw up a cane and a plug hat with '76 printed on it. We chalked ourselves and then started down in a solid body, one fellow wearing the hat and two or three carrying canes. The soph's were put out of the hall a great deal quicker than they came in. The rush began. There were four knots of fellows, which showed where the canes and the hat was. A conceited little '75 man who thought he was some in a Rush got hold of me but I dropped him pretty lively and the second time so hard that it settled his sport with me. During the Rush I mixed in the different knots but the fellows were too large for me though I did some good. While I was working away at some fellows a large '75 man picked me up as it seemed to me and deposited me none too gently on a pile of stones. The Rush went on being in favor of '76 who had the remains of two canes and the hat. The Rush had been going on nearly two hours and some of the men began to leave when the Soph's left tussling and went for the cane and succeeded in getting it away from the Freshmen and then they ran into one of the buildings with it and so got away. A great disadvantage to the '76's was that they did not know each other. Once during the Rush I was having it with a fellow of my size nip and tuck when I noticed that the students near by were laughing so we stopped and found we were both of '76. This was the 5th Rush at Cornell. Great pluck was shown on both sides. The upper classmen say that it was the best Rush that they had ever seen. A great many clothes were torn, coats being with out tails and so forth.... Folks may talk about rushes as they will but I see nothing wrong in them for there is no ill feeling between the classes other than a little rivalry. It is simply a trial of strength.

September 21, 1872. This afternoon I played ball. There is very little to write about college Life, it being the same over and over but intermixed with a great deal of fun and enjoyment.

October 31, 1872. Tonight is "Hallow e'en'" or Gate night. Last year about 6 students were suspended for partaking of this innocent amusement but that kept none back this evening. About 10 o'clock I went down to Ingersoll's ('73) room where there were a lot of fellows and pretty soon we all went down town singing and yelling. We met a lot of fellows and then started for the University buildings where there were altogether about 100 students discussing what to do. After a while they started for the cellar of the McGraw building where there was a bear belonging to Prof. Wilder. Some of the fellows went into his cage and got two ropes fastened to his collar when they led him up and out of his cellar. There were so many fellows that they skared poor Bruin out of his wits. Then they took him to the South University building where they took him down into the cellar and then up, up to the Chapel in the 3rd story and led him up near the pulpit where they tied him and then lit out.... they took the three large excavators and went for the nearest fence and loaded the excavators with rails and all the gates on the way to the bridge. At the bridge they piled the excavators, rails, logs, gates, etc. etc. so as to make it impassable even to a person on foot without great climbing and squirming. They then blockaded the other bridge. While the fellows were blockading the bridge there were two or three alarms that some Prof's. were coming but they proved only alarms although the fellows ran away quite lively. I got in bed about 1 A.M. after getting very nearly caught two or three times. After I left they put a calf in the bear's den. And then went down town and lifted a great many gates. Thus ended Gate Night A.D. 1872.

September 11, 1873. Sheldon got in without an examination, entering the Freshman Class. My recitations this term are Trigonometry, on Mon. Tues. Thurs. & Frid. at 9.15 under Prof. Arnold; French daily at 10.15 under Prof. Roehrig; Chemistry,

Tues. & Thurs. at 12.15 under Prof. Schaeffer; Physics, Mon., Wed., & Fri., at 12:15 under Prof. Anthony; and Elocution under Prof. Corson.



September 16, 1873. Went to recitations in Trig. and French and attended a lecture in Chem. This afternoon after putting on all my old clothes I started down town with Lamb '76 as part of the class of '76 to see that no Freshy wore a plug or carried a cane but for a limited space of time. Near the P.O. we met about a dozen of our fellows and lounged around till we saw a party of big Freshmen one of whom wore a plug. We immediately started to gain possession of said plug and before some of the fellows could get out of the P.O. the hat was gone and ye Freshies running like sheep ... the Freshmen under charge of Will Cook had formed in fours, locked arms in front of the Clinton House and with Will Cook in the center carrying a cane, forward marched for Journal Hall. There were seventy-two Freshmen in the procession while only about twenty-five of our fellows, had as yet come to time. We decided to attack them just as they would enter the stairway, when Lo! The Honorable Alonzo B. Cornell, Speaker of the Assembly of the State of New York, placed himself at their head and with peelers on the flanks and in the rear, they marched in midst groans & shrieks and yells. Then a scene ensued. As soon as the Honorable A. B. C. had them safely seated he returned to the door to watch over the entrance of the retreat of his lambs.

Soph's, Juniors and even Seniors hailed him with cries of "Custom House, Custom House," Candidate for President of (Freshman Class), and the like. Two peelers with clubs stood by him and "Hell was to pay" generally. He ordered one of the Cops to arrest a Soph. But said Cop "darsent tich 'em."

...In the mean time a large crowd had gathered in the streets. The Cops who were guarding the door not relishing the idea of being mixed up in a Rush and wanting to appease the students said that as soon as the first freshman made his appearance they were going to leave. The Sophs now numbered from 40 to 50 while the freshmen both in the hall and out numbered from 80 to 100.... One freshman, after the Rush had everything torn off of him but one boot and sock. All of our fellows but the Anti-Rushers went in [as] well. Senator was badly used being so conspicuous. I came out all right with the exception of having my right elbow cleared of its skin when I came down in the street on the cobblestones.

October 10, 1873. This evening while Birch and I were coming up from Town, it being late, we met prof. Fiske who said that several students had been hurt by tumbling into Six Mile Creek gorge.

October 11, 1873. The report that we heard last night has proved to have been most horribly true. It seems that a Freshman named M. M. Leggett was about to join the Kappa Alpha and as they say they were taking a "preliminary" walk as they called it, which most probably meant being initiated.... Leggett was blindfolded and was being led about by Wason and Lee both of '76 when they all three suddenly disappeared and the other members running up found that they had tumbled over into the Gorge. They found a path leading down into the Gorge and found them. Leggett was moaning indistinctly "Oh don't," "Oh don't" and "Take it off." He died soon afterward. His skull was broken and he was otherwise injured. Wason had his collarbone broken and Lee was badly injured internally.... In the coroners inquest the members of K.A. testified that they were not aware how near they were to the Gorge; never any hazing done in the society and nothing done to intimidate the candidate. He was with them of his own free will....



October 14, 1873. A challenge has been received from Michigan University to play a game of Football at Cleveland, Ohio. 30 men on a side. Much interest is taken in football and will probably accept if we find that we can get the money and also leave of absence which I think we can.

October 15, 1873. 45 men have been chosen from whom to pick the 30 players to go to Cleveland. Birch and I are of the number.

February 7, 1874. Fred Baker was invited to go to South America with Prof. Woeikof, a Russian savant, who goes out under charge of the U. S. government. Fred has written home to his father; he says he don't have a shadow of a chance to going and I hope he don't. It is a little selfish in me but then Baker is a fine fellow and liked by us all.

June 29, 1874. Most of the boys have left but the poor subfresh and Alumni make up for them. A son of President Grant is here being examined. He is quite small and boyish looking. The "Kaps" are rushing him.

June 30, 1874. This afternoon I rode around the city of Ithaca ... and had a pleasant time. There have been about 60 applicants for admission to the University. 5 females.

July 1, 1874. After these [Class Day] exercises the Band got in a Bandwagon and followed by the procession of Seniors marched up to the Campus. An Ivy was planted on the south side of the chapel each senior casting some earth upon it. After the Ivy was planted G. R. Van De Water delivered the Ivy Oration, which was very good. The Pipe of Peace was then smoked and the Class sang college songs and the Band tried to play the tunes in which they balled. S. D. Halliday, '70 was elected Trustee of the Cornell University by the Alumni. He is the first Trustee elected by the alumni. In the evening the Seniors had their Concert. Gilmore's Band was the great feature. I did not go, not being able to get a reserved seat. I staid in Tompkins' room, nearly opposite to the Hall and heard all the pieces which were very fine indeed, the "Pot Pourri" especially took my ear.

July 2, 1874. This morning I got up early i.e. earlier than usual for me and went to Library Hall. The commencement Exercises were to commence at 9 A.M. but at 8.15 A.M. when I got there the hall was pretty full. I got near one of the East windows and hence had a very pleasant, cool seat.

At 25 min. to 10 A.M. the Trustees, Faculty, Seniors and Alumni entered the Hall. The exercises consisted of 22 Orations, Essays and theses, 11 of which were to be delivered ... the Agricultural, Architectural and Engineering theses and Essays were rather dry but the others were good.

After this the degrees were conferred as follows B.A. to four (one to Miss Fleming), B.L. to four (one to B.A. Hayes Esq.).... Thus '74 graduated 73 men and 3 certificated; 11 have been thrown out this term, not being up to the standard 3 1/2% or else conditioned.

In the evening the President held his reception in Cascadilla and the Seniors had their Class Ball in Wilgus Hall. Thus endeth the 2nd lesson and the Class of '74 is no longer an undergraduate class. Birch will enter Harvard Law School next Fall or else study Law in an office.

July 4, 1874. "The Day we celebrate." Only a few Seniors are left in Ithaca. Birch and I leave for New England on Monday. There are several picnics near here today.

$160 & the tuition $60 making a total of $420 a year. In fact all the desirable rooms looking down the lake & on the front are 5.00. The others ... looking out back with a partition are 2.00 & 3.00 a week, making the whole amount $300 or $340 a year. I think I could get one of those lovely blue rooms with a parlor looking way down the lake.... If you think this too expensive I am perfectly willing to take two back rooms ... I also like the prestige of having a nice room at first but [will] do just as you think best. We must decide Wednesday & there is the worst of it. The prices are unequal I think. If I can not get this parlor I shall take one of the rooms at $2.00 no other rooms are worth the sacrifice of $120 a year more but these are, if you think you can afford it.... Telegraph.

September 14 [1875]: I have just come out of Latin examination—from half past two till seven o'clock. I think that any more such examinations will be too much for even my nerves. About fourteen young men came in from other colleges—one from Amherst the freshman year, to be examined for the Sophomore, and *all* of them failed and had to go into the freshman [year]. You can tell from this what an ordeal it was. He examined me on every book I had read except Livy and in Allen's *Prose Composition* because I had studied Arnold, he said. He asked questions about formation of verbals, etc., things I had never had, but at any rate I am not as hopeless as the fourteen boys. My geometry comes Thursday and Greek. Professor Flagg has been sick and says I may enter Junior and be examined afterwards. Now to leave studies & come to news.

The reason Sage College is not open is that the bedding & crockery come on a "religious railroad" as Prof. Russel says & were delayed over Sunday but they arrived today & we can sleep there tomorrow night. Nothing in the world could be kinder than Prof. Russel. He has taken the greatest interest about my rooms & I have concluded to take his advice about the rooms to take that blue parlor & two bedrooms opposite for $5 for this term—it is 13 dollars a term more than the only other desirable rooms, which would have to do for bedroom & study in one & infinitely nicer. Then next term if I find no roommate I can give them up. As it is they are the nicest rooms in the building I think & for no more than others, which are not worth the price. The Steward is very polite & every thing is complete about the rooms—beautiful blankets & beds as soft as any thing ... Miss Mills of Syracuse stands in the middle of [her] room before her trunk & refuses to take out a thing till she hears from her examinations. It is too funny! There is a *rara avis* staying with Professor Russel till the Sage is open—Miss Ruth Putnam, daughter of the great publisher & sister of Dr. Putnam Jacobi, the great New York lady Dr. who has just had a baby & it is five weeks old but she receives patients & gives courses of lectures as usual. She & her husband, also a Dr., Miss Ruth says, are wild over it & when she sees patients he kneels down by its crib & looks at it & vice versa. She, Ruth, is a sophomore & has a room right by me, is short & stout & jolly looking, short curly red hair, bright brown eyes, worships her sister & came here because she wished her to. She asked me about my family tree before we had been together two hours, expressed great amazement because I was a Friend on account of my voice, which she says sounds like a lady who had been out a great deal in society. She evidently thinks Friends are cooks or something.

The students call Pres. White "Prexy" & one of the young ladies suggested that Vice President Russel should be called "Proxy" so he goes by that.



[September] First Day 10th [1875]. I shall have to break a piece of news to you gently—I mean to Father. They allow anyone to take their meals at the Sage and a good many gentlemen have come. Among others the Sioux Society, fifteen men who have turned a large house halfway up the hill into a club and room there and take their meals here. Also they scatter gentlemen among the ladies, without saying by your leave. I have taken a seat at the end of one of the tables and barricaded myself with Miss Putnam on my left and Miss Hicks on my right hand ...

[Sept.] 19, 1875. On Sixth day I went into Analytical Geometry & found a class of about 20 men, the engineers of the University, & no lady ... two came in however. Prof. Byerly teaches it entirely by lectures & a most interesting one he did give. It was introductory on the relations of algebra & geometry & at the close of each lecture he gives problems to be worked over illustrating the principles. They say he is the finest teacher of Math. in the University. Then Prof. Hewitt, a young Prof. whom we had met up at Pres. White's the other evening gave the beginning class in German, a first rate lesson. There are about 60 men in the class & two girls besides myself.... In Prof. Shackford's Junior Literary, I saw the Junior Class together & among them a sprightly colored youth as black as jet, not a particle of Cuban or Brazilian about him!

October 3 [1875]. I was in the slough of despair last week. I made a bad recitation in Tacitus, and by the way his *Annals* are the hardest Latin I have ever met with. Then I got so confused reciting before so many men in the German class ... Professor Flagg ... admitted me into the Junior Class. He said he had to look over my paper to see if he should have me make up in Greek Composition. But now I am happy for I have entered full junior, which seems to be rather an unusual thing for anyone to do.

[no date, 1875] There go the students two and two, tramp, tramp, down the hill, with here and there a girl or two scattered in between. Professor Russel has just passed; soon will come "Beauty and the Beast," university parlance for Professor Wilder and his big black dog ...

I have no recitation this last hour so I always study my Greek at the window and watch the moving panorama. The autumn foliage is glorious. The trees scattered over the hills opposite and along the shores of the lake look like so many little bonfires. So much for the world outside. Within, my room is so comfortable and warm and furnished, in contra-distinction to most of the other rooms here, that it is a pleasure to be in it.... Yesterday I forgot about the men and went into the parlor to waltz with Miss Hicks.... Nothing could be more deferential and polite than the way the gentlemen behave and that funny Mr. Harris, who used to wear a flannel shirt and a gray coat when he first came to our table, now appears resplendent in a white shirt and black coat. "Refining influence of women!"

[no date, 1875]... here ... you are absolutely on your own responsibility. I like it and yet it is lonely. Our position here is *perfectly* nice—the faculty one and all, behave to the ladies as if they were out at a party together and think of not the least impoliteness or familiarity. Their wives meet those they know more than halfway in advance. The students, who before would not even be introduced to the university girls, are now quite the other way. And as far as I can see it is not considered in the *least* derogatory to ladyhood to attend the university. Even Doctor Wilder, Mrs. Wilder said, encourages his young sister-in-law to come next year and one of the strongest "anti cos" as the term is here, sent over an invitation to the young ladies of the Sage to come and take as many pears as they wanted from his orchard. I wanted to make this statement for Father's benefit.

[To Anna, November 21, 1875] The gentlemen students treat the ladies with the greatest deference and respect. They will even wait in the halls to open a door for you. And in Analytical Geometry, I happened to get there the other morning before the recitation and there were about fifteen men talking and laughing rather loudly, and immediately every hat was taken off and their whole manner changed. This is a sample. I am a complete convert to "Coed," as the term is here. And even when last week I stood up on the platform, gazed at by eighty masculine junior eyes, and read my essay (though it was a severe proof) my belief did not waver.

How do I occupy my leisure time when I have any? Take a look at my center table! Two volumes of Roman History I am reading in connection with Tacitus, English Literature and Canterbury Tales for Corson's lectures on literature which are grand, Sainte-Beuve's "Causeries du Lundi" Professor Russel lent me, and on top of all Music and Morals, which Mr. Gardiner, the champion skater of Cornell brought me the other day ....

Well, I have been and gone and done it—I may as well confess. Ever since the first I have struggled against it. I made up my mind that up here, at least, I would not have a friendship that was in the least absorbing. It takes time and I don't approve of them.... I knew from the first that I should like Miss Hicks very much but not one advance did I make. Indeed the first week we were here, it came up in the course of conversation and I said that I had made up my mind not to have any more intimate friendships and she took that as a hint and carefully avoided showing that she liked me. So matters remained in this interesting state and if the fates had not made her fall in love with me, I should have kept my resolution. It was dancing and Swinburne that did it...

January 23, 1876. My lessons are really such a pleasure that the time goes faster when I study them ... Romney's and Aurora's characters in Professor Corson's readings afford a grand field for discussion. Miss Putnam, Miss Hicks and I had a fierce discussion on that point. I held that Aurora's mission, that of a poet to raise the few and inspire them with heaven-sent visions, was higher than Romney's to be a raging philanthropist and give soup to the masses ....

[no date, 1876] It is a most glorious spring day.... There is a *rara avis* here, she came this last week—a tall, sad, poetical-looking woman who drops her head and looks up at you with her dark languishing eyes. She came here to take the course in Journalism and we knew there was some mystery. On the flyleaf of her notebook was Sarah S. and the last name scratched out and Sternes written over it. We knew her as "Miss Sternes," but finally she told Miss Johnston and she told me, as she tells me everything, that she was a divorced woman, though her husband adores her and is physically and intellectually her ideal man. She had come here because [she is] not strong enough to practice medicine, though she graduated from Edinburgh Medical College. She writes really very pretty poetry and is a sort of wonder to me.... I shall be very careful about not getting intimate with her but she is a study. I'm afraid she may be a believer in free love but at any rate her views are decidedly revolutionary ...



October 15 [1876]. I am just enamoured of my life here. After the do-nothing summer, it is glorious to be at work again. Latin and Greek, Sanscrit, Philosophy and Literature and Essays are my studies and they are all congenial.

[1877] ... This is the program for commencement week. On First Day the seventeenth of June, James F. Clark delivers the sermon to the graduating class. On the Second and Third Day evenings there is speaking. Thomas W. Higginson being the principal speaker. On Fourth morning, the twentieth, is class day and on that evening a grand concert provided by the senior class, and on Fifth Day commencement.

[From M. C. Thomas's journal]

June 12, 1877. Sage College, Cornell University. It is almost two years since I have made an entry. I have now finished all my senior examinations and have nothing to do for the next nine days except wait for my degree.... At last the object of my ambition—the one purpose that runs through my journals has been attained. I have graduated at a university. I have a degree that represents more than a Vassar one.

I wish I had kept a slight, at least, record of my experience here and now it is too late to recall it. The first two years I had a difficult time to get into the new methods of study and especially in Latin I entered behind.

Altogether I have learned a great deal and it has been thoroughly profitable to be here—it has given me a new outlook. Though I feel very far from a good Latin and Greek scholar, yet I do see light somewhat. My life here has been very hermit like, except seven girls. I have seen very few people, half the men here are uncultivated and Cornell misses all that glorious culture that one reads of in college books. The girls are for the most part of a different social station and I have seen very little of them as they had nothing to counterbalance that fact.

I want to write about my fifth friendship, for in spite of myself I have one. When I came here I made up my mind that at Howland [boarding school] I had wasted a great deal of time with friends and that it amounted to very little except pleasure.... The first girl I saw was a young lady in Algebra examination—lace-dressed, in gray with a brown hat with a wing in it. She was up at Pres. White's to tea and we had a little talk. I thought she was smart and well prepared in the examinations next day. I "rather hoped" I should see her again next fall. Next fall came—she was the first person I saw as I drove up to the Sage College. Her mother was with her and together we chose our rooms on the same corridor third hall.... Miss Hicks, Miss Putnam, Miss Mills, Miss Head and Miss Mitchell—they seemed more interested in fun than anything else. And not one of them was smart except Miss Hicks; the other girls in the Sage were good enough students but not ladies, and the gentlemen, except Prof. Boyesen, were second rate, "half cut" Bessie would say.

Well, I began to see more and more of Miss Hicks. She got in the habit of coming and reading me her mother's letters and of bidding me good night. We used to go and study some time in Cascadilla woods and when it would get dark we would sit under her blue shawl and talk. Then we came across Swinburne's "Atalanta in Calydon" and Miss Hicks would come in her wrapper after I was in bed and we would read it out loud and we learned several of the choruses. One night we had stopped reading later than usual and obeying a sudden impulse I turned to her and asked "Do you love me?" She threw her arms around me and whispered, "I love you passionately." She did not go home that night and we talked and talked. She told me she had been praying that I might care for her.

That was the beginning and from that time, it was the fall of '75, till June '77 we have been inseparable. I put this all down because I cannot understand it. I am sure it is not best for people to care about each other so much. In the first place it wasted my time—it was a pleasure to be with Miss Hicks and as I cared to be with no one else. I would have spent all that time in reading.... All our ideas were opposite.... She likes everyone. She cares for everyone's opinion ...

September 23, 1877. Yesterday I made application to the Johns Hopkins University to study for a second degree. Mr. Gilman was very polite and it will come before the Trustees in a month and I (Oh I hope there is some chance for ladies!) am in great anxiety.... I am glad I went [to Cornell], I learned far more than was possible at home. I broke away from old rules and mingled with different classes of people; but there was no real earnest intellectual companionship, not much earnest heartfelt study.

# JESSIE MARY BOULTON

## CLASS OF 1883

Jessie Mary Boulton came to Cornell in September 1879 and lived in Sage College, where she encountered "co-eating" along with coeducation. Jessie was one of the founders of Kappa Alpha Theta, the first woman's sorority at Cornell, and she was elected a member of the Cornell *Daily Sun* board and to Phi Beta Kappa. Her letters are witty, intelligent, and playful. She conveys strict standards of etiquette and a sense of independence. Her comments about politics and other students are particularly interesting; when she writes "freshmen" or "students," she is referring to male students. Jessie's mother copied her letters into a ledger that was deposited in the University Archives. These extracts are from her mother's copies. After graduation, Jessie married a Cornellian. At least seventeen members of their family have graduated from Cornell.

September 20, 1879. Papa told me not to write till I got my entrance exam returns and as I just received the last this morning I thought I would write now. I just passed in Latin and Arithmetic, have a creditable in Geography, I think an honorable in Spelling, Grammar, Algebra and Geometry. I am going down town this afternoon for my books so I have not much time to write. I am going to change my room and take a roommate. I concluded seven dollars a week was too much for board so I thought I would come down a little. Anyhow the girls all fix up their rooms here so much and I concluded that I would rather take a cheap room and fix it up a little than have a dear one not fixed up. I am feeling kind of queer now—it seems to me that everybody is ahead of me; but I guess I passed....

Miss Briscoe and I together with Miss Yost whom we met on the way went down town to get books. I bought a Physiology in cloth binding for $5.40, the leather would have been $6.30 or $6.50. I don't know which so I thought I would be economical and buy the cheaper one. I also paid $1.50 for a Latin book and .50 for a German together with an Algebra which I bought second hand from one of the girls (because she wanted to sell it and it looked like new and was seventy five cents cheaper) and one or two more books, which I shall need, make up quite a nice little sum. It is ever so nice here, the girls are so sociable....



Mr. Wilson took Miss Yost and myself through the museum and library in McGraw on Thursday morning; I think that was a place which you missed, and you missed a treat too. They have almost everything you would want to see in the museum. He took us also to Fall River [Creek], up one hill and down another till our strength was almost given out; but we have survived. I have been down to town three times and you know what that hill is, so I think I deserve some credit.

There are about 140 odd in the freshman class this year 17 of whom are girls I have heard. Boys or young men (as I guess they call themselves) abound everywhere; we have been surrounded everywhere we went. It gets rather monotonous but I suppose we will get used to it after awhile. They stare at the girls too. There is a Brazillian in our class, Miss Yost says "He is a daisy." I don't know whether you can understand that expression or not, I can't. He is a little bit of a fellow, I don't think he is as tall as I am....

September 24, 1879. I have been to three days recitations and think they are splendid; but the question comes up again, when am I going to learn all this? It is almost discouraging to note how much the Professors know. In Latin particularly I am mixed up but I guess I will get straightened out in a few days. The girls here are very pleasant but I can hardly distinguish one from the other, some of them I know by name but the others I have to call she or her, almost all of them have called on me but I have returned very few calls as yet. I think Mr. McCrea was mistaken when he said the girls at Cornell were all old and ugly excepting a few who lately came in. I think he is either a very poor judge or else he has not seen very many of the girls here....

P.S. I did not miss a word in the examination in spelling. We had fifty of them.

September 26, 1879. In Algebra we had an oral examination today and Professor Wait entirely ignored the girls till I put up my hand once and he gave the question to me. Physiology under Professor or rather Dr. Wilder is just splendid. The only thing I object to in this is the drawings and I would not object to them only that I can't draw decently. He dissected a cat for us on last Monday and explained it all to us. In anticipation I took a front seat and had a full view, I enjoyed it ever so much. The number of girls at Sage, I cannot tell exactly, I think there are about 30.

October 2, 1879. My time is scarce although I do spend two or three hours a day idling. I have to study on an average of about four hours a day. Then on most days recitations of 4 hours; on some days five hours but after next week I will not have any more than four hours on any day and only three on Thursday. Mamma wants to know about how I spend my Sabbaths. On the first one there was no church in the Chapel so I did not go down town. In the afternoon I went to Y. M. C. A. prayer meeting in the North Building. Last Sunday Rev. G. G. Munger (Congregationalist) preached in the chapel twice and I attended both services. In the afternoon I again attended the Y. M. C. A. ... As to exercise in the Gymnasium I am hardly able to report as I do not observe much progress. But I have not exercised every day in that direction. However I make it up in walking as I walked one day about three miles.... There are only two grievances for me here. One is that I have to make my own bed and the other is that it is so warm I hardly know what to do with myself sometimes. One of them is not very grievous, but it is lasting and the other is grievous but I don't think it will be lasting.



October 4, 1879. I attended the Irving Literary Society last night with Miss Buck, one of the seniors. By the way, I think she is the nicest girl at Sage. The Society has about seventeen or eighteen members. The exercises were very good but I think I expected more. Almost all of those who took part were seniors. They sang some college songs at recess, some of which were very amusing, especially one about little Injuns which is a kind of round ... Rules have been posted up now ... we are not to be out after ten unless we get permission from Mrs. Kinney. These do not affect me much only when I want to go to Literary ... I am getting along nicely with my studies and like all my Professors but one and he is Assistant Professor of Rhetoric. I am going to bring pictures of all of them at the Holidays as we can purchase two for a quarter....The study of Physiology is just splendid here: I have a book for a student of medicine so you see as far as appearance goes I am progressing rapidly ... We have a room with a partition making a parlor and bedroom. The only objections I have to the place are that the bedroom is not carpeted and there is no door to the closet.

We have one senior here so I heard yesterday, who is only nineteen years of age. She is the daughter of Professor Roberts. I suppose Papa remembers him and she applied for admission when she was fifteen but they would not allow her to come in. So she attended the lectures (you can do this even if you don't register) took the notes and passed the examinations. She says the Professors examined her papers out of kindness. Then when she came to be seventeen she entered two years ahead and so will graduate at nineteen.

I did not suppose I would feel so at home here. I can be introduced to people and talk to them as if I had known them for years. I really almost feel as if I had been a student here for a long time. I see so many things new that nothing seems especially surprising. There is a free singing class to be organized on Monday.

October 8, 1879. I want to tell you some of the exercise I have been taking since I came here. Don't be frightened there is no danger. I have been out rowing. The lake is just delightful, the only objection is that it is about a mile and a half there and the same back which would make three miles on level ground but makes four nearly as there is a steep hill on the way.

The boys are quite rude here and they seem to be very fond of applauding.... when the girls came in ... immediately we received a perfect round of applause. Yesterday I was about ten minutes late at a lecture in Rhetoric and when I came in I went up front and took a seat. Immediately they interrupted the speaker by applauding me. Those are two specimens of their behavior.

October 15, 1879. Dr. Wilder called on *Mr.* Boulton to recite this morning and as I arose, I received a rather smothered applause. There are about 100 students in the class so of course he is not expected to distinguish sex by just the names. I am getting used to these boys so I don't mind them much.

October 17, 1879. The more I get acquainted with the girls the more I like them. I think on the whole I never saw a collection of girls where there were so many nice ones.

November 1, 1879. I get a little discouraged sometimes when I think how I prepare my lessons. But I guess I study them as thoroughly as any of the girls, or boys either. It is impossible when a person has so much to do to get everything thoroughly. The examinations are passed here mostly by cramming just before. A syllabus of the studies, or at least of the lectures is given and the thing is "crammed" till it is "dead." These are two Cornell slang words. The first is as far as I have gotten yet. I haven't used the second.

November 8, 1879. I must tell you about Professor McKoon. Miss Yost is in his class. He has not been calling on her to recite for quite a while so she went up to him the other day and said, "Prof. McKoon will you be so kind as to tell me why you do not call on me to recite? I am anxious to improve and would like to recite." He says: "Well, Miss Yost I will tell you but it is rather a delicate matter; it is because you wear a veil and I never speak to a lady that wears a veil." They had some more conversation but that is enough to show you how queer he is. He is about as eccentric a man as there is in the University.

I paid my board bill for this last month today and when that is drawn out of the bank there will be a remainder of sixteen dollars besides seven, which I have on hand. Don't be astonished at the amount; I have been as careful as I could. I have paid about twenty-two dollars out for books. I have not bought my hat yet.

November 12, 1879. I was not getting along satisfactorily in Latin for I do not know enough about the Grammar and when I would recite in the class I always showed my ignorance to such an extent that it became monotonous. I disliked to leave the class for one reason: because I hate to have those boys think that I was unable to keep up. But I thought it was better to have a few studies well done than more only partly done. Meanwhile, I will study Latin grammar and enter the class next year and see if I can get along then. It was not doing me any good to study it and I might as well drop it.

November 22, 1879. I am the only girl in any of the classes that I am in that will ask a question. The others are too backward. They don't see how I can do it.

January 8, 1880. I am rejoicing over not having to get up for an 8 o'clock recitation. My hours all arrange nicely without it.... You know it makes no difference what you register. My Zoology and Anglo Saxon conflicted so I took Zoology in preference. My studies as near as I make out will be Algebra, German, Rhetoric, Chemistry & Zoology. That is all.



January 10, 1880. I invested in a Zoology today. I suppose perhaps the next thing I will be buying will be the book on Evolution (Darwin). I don't know that I care very much about having descended from an "amphioxus" but I guess the truth of the matter is that it does not make much difference what I descended from. I don't like the Professor of Chemistry very much so far. He lectured a whole hour the other day without saying much of anything. I think it will be about as easy to take notes in his lectures as it is in Professor Shackford's. I think Zoology for the first part of the term, at least, will be very interesting.

January 17, 1880. In the first place I am in trouble about our table again. It is a source of misery to all of us girls, but I don't know how we can get out of it. Mr. Welby has left and Mr. Kent and Mr. Jonas who are so disagreeable to me are still here; besides we have four new gentlemen!! So that makes four ladies and six gentlemen. I ate scarcely anything at dinner yesterday....There are several very nice gentlemen at the table but still I do not like it. I go down and get through with my meals as soon as possible. I am just tired of eating with gentlemen every meal; I think they might all go. I believe in co-education but I get tired of co-eating. I can endure a surplus of gentlemen in the classes but when it comes to the table it makes one drop too many in my cup of sorrow....Our lectures on Zoology are grand but he gives us evolution hot and heavy.

January 20, 1880. I found out yesterday why Mr. Hayes comes to Sage to board. I don't know whether I told you or not but he is very bitter against coeducation. Miss Boyer, who is not a student but is taking drawing lessons here, asked him. He told her that he had not changed his views but was willing to be convinced; and had come here to see for himself if coeducation was a failure. I hope he will be convinced but I don't think that I want to meet him.

January 30, 1880. I bought myself five quires of note paper today for forty cents like this on which I am writing (but this does not belong to the lot), just eight cents a quire, is that not cheap? I used nearly five quires last term. You speak of my learning something at table as well as elsewhere.... I get along all right in my classes and if I do say it myself I think I can surpass Mr. Kent in German, but then everybody knows things about History, Science, Philosophy, Poetry, Literature, Civil Service. I have not the least idea about more than the name. Here is one: "The survival of the fittest." I have heard that mentioned but am ignorant of its application. I hear so many things mentioned and I don't know what half of them mean. It's awful to be in such a state but I guess the case is hopeless.... Dr. Wilder showed us today one bone of a fossil animal (the arm bone), which was found twenty miles from here; it was about a yard long and about a foot and a half in circumference. He could hardly lift it.

February 17, 1880. The Class of '83 will give a class supper next Saturday evening and rumor says that they will have wine. Of course the girls are not expected to attend. I heard today that there were only seven gentlemen in the whole freshman class that got honorable in everything at the last examination. Just think of that out of about 110 members.

February 21, 1880. I have been thinking lately and wondering a little what I am getting my education for. I have no particular objective but the mere getting of the education. I don't seem to know whether I will make any use of it or not. And whether it would not be a less waste of money if I turned my attention to something else.

March 9, 1880. ... there are several ballot boxes up in different parts of the building for the students to deposit ballots for 1st or second choice of Presidential candidate. This morning we found one up at the ladies' room requesting the ladies' votes. I deposited mine immediately. I did not care much whom I voted for but I gave Blaine 1st and Sherman 2nd. It may be the only time that I will have an opportunity to vote for the nomination of President and I thought I might as well embrace it.

September 19, 1880. There are eleven freshmen girls at Sage. More, by five than there were of us last year. There are some rather fine looking girls in the number also.

September 22, 1880. Cornell has a daily paper now.

September 29, 1880. I have joined a Shakespeare class, which meets in the evening at Professor Shackford's. It is composed entirely of girls.

October 6, 1880. I told you about a lively girl in the freshman class ... Her mother is Mrs. Joselyn Gage. I think I told you about her. I came to the conclusion long ago that Cornell was no place for girls (myself excepted i.e. no place for lively girls) and Charley has gone farther he thinks it is no place for girls at all. He has heard so much talk since he came; you know they always stuff the freshmen. He says the boys talk terribly about the girls here; but that he has never heard anyone speak anything but good of me. There I am praising myself again, shall I never get over that? I am alarmed for the future Freshmen girls ... A girl who is the least lively and can scarcely repress her life has no peace at all.

October 13, 1800. Today the Senior, Junior and last but greatest, the Sophomore [class]-elections. The Seniors and Juniors ran one ticket but '83 would always be ahead. Last year we had six or seven tickets in the field. This year up till this morning there was but one; when lo upon the dawn of this important day, another ticket came to light. It was headed Co-Ed and Psi U.-President Miss Yost, Vice Miss Wetherell, Treasurer Miss Baum, and the other offices filled by members of the Psi Upsilon fraternity. Suffice it to say the first ticket was elected. Miss Wetherell took it very hard; she almost felt like going home....Now you need not ask me more why I did not wish Sadie to come to Cornell. I have luckily escaped all this and Sadie would also perhaps but—there is Miss Wetherell the Quakeress—after that who could expect to be safe? Miss Van Pelt came to me today, and asked me if I would volunteer my services as alto in a choir for chapel.



October 20, 1880. I have not quite made up my mind if I shall return to Cornell in the Winter Term or not. There is a bare possibility that I may be conditioned in Latin and English Literature; and French one can never be certain of, so you observe that my time at Cornell may be limited.

November 17, 1880. This afternoon one of the girls a senior, Miss Neyman, came to me and asked me if I would be in favor of a secret society among the girls, and if I would join. They have received a letter from one of the Western Colleges stating that they would like to establish a chapter of the Kappa Alpha Theta society here. The object of the society or fraternity is to further Literary culture as well as social and draw girls into a closer bond of union in order that they may think more of each other's welfare or something to that effect. I have long wished that we could have such societies for I thought that they would be a very good thing. I at once told her that I would like to it very much and would join ... There are only three of us at present; Miss Neyman, Miss Baum and myself but we expect one or two more ... I can see no objections to it save that it will cause a little talk at first, and there may be some fun made of it but that will soon blow over and I think that we would really be doing some good, as fraternities certainly do make a bond of union between persons which would not otherwise exist.

November 21, 1880. There was quite a startling wedding here on last Wednesday. Two of the Juniors took that awful step and have filled the mouths of the Cornell world with something to talk about. The lady is resident of town so it is not so bad as it would be were she from a distance.

January 27, 1881. Prof. Corson's work is very easy, and some try to make it easier by not studying it at all. I think I should go wild if I were he, by the way they recite; he does get a little disgusted. He gave us a lecture yesterday about being able to impart our knowledge and made this funny expression. "Some students consider themselves walking buckets going around the different Professors to be pumped into." He gets off some of the queerest expressions. He says that if you go to a door and somebody asks "who is there?" it is perfectly proper to say "It is me." He does not think that language is governed by rule but by feelings.

February 13, 1881. The speakers for the Woodford stage are decided upon and I am sorry to say that Mr. Wilson is not one of the six. He is feeling very badly over it, so I have heard. There is one girl selected—the second that has ever been on—Miss Van Pelt. You have heard me speak of her. The first one was a Miss Bradford of '75.... Some of the boys are agitating the matter of allowing us to be represented on the Board of Editors of the *Cornellian*. That would give us a good deal of honor and very little work as there is only one publication a year. But it is rather doubtful whether all the boys will agree or not.

February 27, 1881. Mrs. Gage, Maud's mother lectured here on Woman's rights last night, you remember that I told you she was a member of the Woman Suffrage Association.



April 13, 1881. Vice President Russel has been requested by the trustees to resign his office and Professorship and he has done so—you remember perhaps that he is Prof. of History and that History does not come until the Junior year which throws me in a rather bad state as regards that branch. He is one of the lights of the University and the Trustees give no reason for their action. It is supposed that they disagree with his liberal views on religion. It has created quite a sensation here; the seniors held an indignation meeting and sent in a petition to the Trustees; I do not know whether it has been successful or not but I suppose scarcely as I hear that the request was made to Prof. Russel early last term. If Cornell loses one of her best Profs. every year as she has the last three or four it is not hard to prophesy her future. I feel like saying what next?

April 24, 1881. Prof. Russel's difficulty is not yet settled ... I think I told you that the ladies sent in a protest to the Trustees. Mr. Sage remarked to one of the girls, that if they had come to him before they sent in that protest they would not have sent it in, for he would have told them the reasons of the action. It is also said that the Trustees gave Prof. Russel their reasons, and asked him if he would rather they would make them known, and he said no he did not wish them made public. And so the matter stands.

May 22, 1881. The man who is expected to take Prof. Russel's place is here. His name is Tyler; I believe he is from Ann Arbor.

May 26, 1881. Only one more week of my Sophomore year and then comes the transition between Sophomore boastfulness and Junior dignity. Next year I shall enter very sober and very quiet, different from my usual state.

November 4, 1881. Mr. Kinney put up a notice the other day saying that the indulgence in regard to the price of the rooms is to be withdrawn at the end of this term. That will increase our joint expense $1.50 a week. Do you think you can afford it?

November 19, 1881. There is a lecture on women's rights in town tomorrow night but it is too near examinations to attend and aside from that I should be most afraid to go for fear the students will make some fuss.

December 14, 1881. The law has been passed that all the University girls will *have to board* at Sage and the result is general dissatisfaction.

January 27, 1882. Sadie and I went to the concert last night with three other girls—Mrs K[inney] looked very sober when we told her we were going but that did not influence us. I do not see why five girls cannot go down to the Opera House in a bus and back without people holding up their hands in holy horror and saying that "it is not proper." I have been reading on Woman's rights today; perhaps that is what makes me so strong in my protestations.



March 5, 1882. The Woodfords took place on Friday night and were pretty good ... I told you I think that Miss Lizzie Van Pelt was to be one of the Woodford speakers. She had an elegant oration as well written as almost any of the boys and delivered it with force and almost as well as any girl could do with the voice that every girl has.... I was to hear the Fisk Jubilees last night; they almost all had colds and consequently did not sing so well as usual but I enjoyed it very much.

April 23, 1882. The freshmen cremated Algebra on last Friday night. They put on nightshirts instead of overcoats and wore masks. They carried torches and marched past Sage up to the lawn in front of South building. The girls did not know whether it would be the proper thing to go over or not; but at last we concluded that we could go. I went with a crowd of girls with Mr. Gilbert as escort....They had a prayer and speech and consigned the Algebra to the flames. The exercises were very good but the boys were rather outwitted. They did not expect the girls to be present and they had a good many jokes in about them—such as this: One gentleman remarked that he was bald for all his hair had been taken out by Algebra and the co-eds. The boys had a good time and I suppose it payed.

April 30, 1882. I have some news for you which I think will rejoice your heart—it is not the goal of your ambition for me but it may be a means to that goal. I have been appointed one of the editors on the *Sun* board for next year. Mr. Kent has been one of the editors this year and very kindly proposed my name. I do not know whether I shall like it or not. I hesitated for a long while about accepting it. I did not let you know for I wanted to make up my own mind about it.

May 8, 1882. I sometimes wonder if my College education is paying but when I think that it is but a matter of five hundred dollars or less besides my board (which would have to be paid anywhere) I think that it is certainly worth it. It is not so much what we actually learn as it is what we get started in. I often wonder if I shall continue in the same studies I have now after I leave College. I think a good many of them I shall never look at again.

May 14, 1882. A chapter of the Phi Beta Kappa is being established here. You may remember that that is the fraternity which held its 100th anniversary I think last spring at which [Wendell] Philips made the address. Of course, they will only admit seniors who have a good standing in the University. I am anxious to learn whether it will be restricted to gentlemen or not. I am very much afraid it will be ... I would very much like to belong and if girls are admitted at all, I think I might stand a very good chance.

October 1, 1882. Last night, Mr. Gilbert told us that President White had forbidden us to dance on Saturday night except for a very few minutes just after supper. Verily things are becoming narrow. I expect very soon to hear that only occasional callers are allowed and those not without the President's permission. No that is unjust—I do not believe that it will ever be that bad.

October 19, 1882. Senior class committees were posted today and I was very much provoked that I am the only girl whose name appears at all. In former years there has always been more than one girl on. Not more than one on a single committee for 3 or 4 on altogether. It is an insult to the girls, and I cannot imagine why my name is on unless the boys have some secret game to play that I know not of.

November 2, 1882. The President called a meeting of the ladies last night in the parlor. We had no idea what it was for, but we were not long in finding out. He talked on all sorts of subjects among which were coeducation, health, attitude toward the young gentlemen, etc. Some things he said about our treatment of the young gentlemen amused me very much and some of it exasperated me. He said that if he met a young lady and gentleman walking on the campus after night he would inform the lady the next morning that her presence was no longer desired in the University. He may not have meant exactly that but he certainly said it. I felt like telling him that I had frequently walked on the campus and in the gorge also and he might expel me if he wished.

January 18, 1883. I am the only girl in the Shakespeare class and I don't think I shall stay: I am not anxious for the honors. There is a class of girls in Shakespeare but I do not want to go into that for there will be no fun in it at all, and Shakespeare is such a sleepy work if there are no jokes.

January 25, 1883. Vaccination is the all-absorbing topic at present. Each one greets the other with the interesting question "How is your arm?" Several of us have begun to take in earnest but most of them have not noticed it yet. Mine is working beautifully and I did not expect it would take at all. Sadie was only vaccinated yesterday so of course hers has not begun yet. The Professors also are undergoing the initiation, so we are all rejoicing together.

January 31, 1883. We are having lectures now from Prof. Charles Kendall Adams of Ann Arbor, on the "History of Institutions" and they are exceedingly interesting.

March 8, 1883. Last night we had a concert given by a colored glee club in town. They came up to the parlor and gave us the concert gratis. The leader is one of the waiters here so that accounts for the extraordinary generosity. It was quite good and very amusing.

March 14, 1883. Tonight some of us are invited out to Mrs. Comstock's for tea; I am afraid I shall disgrace myself by eating too much for I have been pretty nearly starved lately. It seems to me that things are getting worse and worse here as regards eating. Some who are a little pessimistic would say that everything was degenerating but I shall not go quite so far as that.

March 28, 1883. I don't know how I am going to get along with my thesis; the library is going to send either to New York or Boston to get me some books so I hope to commence pretty soon.



April 8, 1883. I asked Dr. Wilson if there would be any objections to my taking only eleven hours when there were thirteen required. He said he would compromise on twelve—that the reason they were so strict about the third term of the Senior year was, that in the early days of the University it had been the habit of students to do extra work in the earlier part of their course, and have nothing to do the last term of their senior year; this spare time they spent in lounging around town, drinking beer, playing billiards, etc.; so the faculty concluded to be strict; he immediately added, as he saw a smile gathering on my face, that of course they could not fear such trouble in my case.

Mr. Mathews came to see me yesterday and asked me if the ladies of '83 would smoke the class pipe on class day. (It has always been the custom to smoke the "pipe of peace" before separating). I disappointed him very much by telling him that I did not know what the other girls would do, but I should certainly *not* do anything of the kind. He said that he had hoped none of the ladies would make any objection to it. In former years some of the girls have done it and some have not—I prefer to be among those who refuse.

May 27, 1883. I have an appointment to Phi Beta Kappa and I am so happy. Phi Beta Kappa is an honorary society—the oldest society in the U. S.

June 3, 1883. Pres. White told me last night that we nine who were appointed [to Phi Beta Kappa] stood out prominently from the rest of the students in the Latin Course (for only those are admitted) and that there were only a few in the other course who could come up to us. He also said that we stood very much alike especially the first six who were chosen and that I was one of them, he thought. I was very much rejoiced to hear that for I was positive that I had just squeezed in. This is the first class also which has had the honor of membership in this chapter. They are going to make appointments from the back classes next year, but we have our names first.

# GEORGE A. KRAUS

## CLASS OF 1893

Little is known about George Kraus. He was born in 1871 and came to Cornell in 1892 from his hometown of Clarence, New York, to study electrical engineering. His class selected old gold and white as its colors, and the class cheer was "Rah Rah Ree; Rah Rah Ree; Cornell, Ninety-Three." His letters to his mother echo those of many students who were concerned about getting money from home. George also writes about Cornell athletics.

September 26, 1892. Everything is going along smoothly. I work ten hours a week in the Electrical Laboratory and nine hours at designing electrical machinery, and have also three hours a week in mechanical Laboratory at experimental work. The remainder of the work is lectures and shop work. The freshman class this year is a large one. There is football practice every day, and one game has been played and won by a score of 16 to 0.

Oct. 1, 1892: We have had good weather during the past week. There have [been] two football games. Cornell beat Syracuse 58 to 0 and beat Bucknell 54 to 0. Books cost forty dollars this term, so that I will need fifty dollars ($50) next week.... After this term will need only a few dollars worth more of books. Shop and laboratory dues cost $9. I would like to have Pa or some[one] see that my name is registered, so that I can vote.

Dec. 4, 1892. Dear Mother: I said that I would need $40 and you have sent $25. Please send $20 as soon as you can and it will be sufficient for this term. Send it the first part of next week if possible.

Jan. 4 [1893] I arrived in Ithaca at 1:20 yesterday and registered. Have the work nearly the same as last term. We will not have much work until next Monday and then the lectures in the Steam Engine and Electrical Machinery begin. Books and dues this term amount to about $20 and I also need shoes. I wish to have about $40 (forty dollars). Please send it as soon as you can.

Jan. 24, 1893. I have already performed three experiments in the Mechanical Laboratory, two Engine tests and one test of an air pump used for operating airbrakes. Will have to perform about four more. The candidates for the baseball team have begun training in the Gymnasium. I will need money the last of this month. Please send $40 (forty dollars) the 31st of this month or not later than the 2nd of February if possible. This will last nearly to the end of the term.

Mar. 17, 1893. I have finished all my work except the two examinations. We had expected to take three examinations but Prof. Thurston concluded not to have an examination and to mark on the term's work. I have gotten some of my photographs and will send one soon. Will begin thesis work as soon as we can. We will make over an alternate current motor that was built in 1891.

Apr. 16, 1893. Am working on thesis every day and have taken the motor apart. We will probably not finish it until some time in May. The winding of the wire takes a good deal of time, as we have to wind about one thousand turns. The baseball team practices every day and the crew rows every day. During this week there will be three ball games.... There was an entertainment at the Wilgus Opera House for the benefit of the baseball team last Friday night. There was reading by two of the Professors and an address by the President, J. G. Schurman. The Glee, Banjo and Mandolin clubs also gave some selections. I will need some money before the end of the month.

May 14, 1893. We have finished our motor but have not yet tried to run it. The motor is quite small but weighs about two hundred pounds on account of the iron with which it is built.... Commencement Exercises are held this year on Thursday June 15. Expenses around commencement time and from now on are pretty high, such as class tax $15, and also the fee for graduation. Will need money.

# GERTRUDE NELSON

**CLASS OF 1896**

&

# RUTH NELSON

**CLASS OF 1897**

In 1891 Gertrude "Trudy" Nelson entered Cornell. She majored in philosophy and was a member of Delta Gamma, Asteroids, and Der Hexenkreis, a women's honor society. In 1893 her sister Ruth entered the university. Gertrude graduated in 1895 and married a Cornellian. Ruth was inducted into Phi Beta Kappa and took a music degree at Columbia University. She became a music teacher with private pupils and later married. Both young women write home frequently. They request that their mother visit them at Cornell, and they seek their parents' permission for everything from contemplated purchases to attendance at dances. They provide information about clothing and shopping in Ithaca, and they challenge accepted practices, such as going into town without a chaperone and entertaining gentlemen callers in the parlor of Sage College. They also write about their finances. A "spread" is a feast held in a student's room, usually with food sent from home. These letters were written sometimes by one sister, sometimes the other, and often both. The writer is identified at the end of each entry.

Oct. 1, 1892. Wednesday night Elizabeth had a little spread in her room. I ate a pear, one ginger snap, a chocolate-cream and a half and drank some lemon soda and ginger ale, about half a cup of each. We sang college songs and one of the girls told a terrible story about a crazy man while Emily related her ghost story.

We won't be fully at work until next week. We have been running around from one class to another, receiving lessons for next week. Emily and I went down town

Wednesday afternoon and purchased a waste basket, ink, knobs for curtain poles, a hammer and package of tacks and brought some matches at the C.G.[Cornell General Store].

...Yesterday [several girls] took a long walk down to the tunnel. The other girls all wanted to go through the tunnel and so, although I was afraid, I went through it too. There was very little water going over Ithaca Falls, so we stood on the dam just above them and had a most beautiful view. Oh the country here is simply grand, and beautiful. The hills are partly hidden by an autumn haze and the lake looks very inviting. Alas! Poor Gertrude has no young man to take her rowing.



We have had to pay $3.00 for physiology stuff already and will have to pay more later on. Our histories cost $1.75 and I ... will have to buy other books. Consequently I am afraid I must ask for more money ... the entering class of girls isn't as nice as our class was.

President Schurman gave an opening address yesterday noon to all the students and his talk was very fine, though he said rather more to the men students than to the women students [Gertrude].

Jan. 24 '93. Last Friday I was called on in American History for the first time since I began that subject and though quite frightened I managed to recite creditably. Consequently I didn't study my lecture for Monday as I knew I wouldn't be called on that day. Monday afternoon I worked for two hours after history in the library. After supper Emily, Dot, Blanche and I went over to the large gymnasium and watched the sophomore and freshman girls practice. They are getting ready to give an exhibition in eight weeks and some of the things which they are going to do are very pretty. They have fancy marching, dumb bell drills, and figures with hoops. When the drill was over we danced a while and then returned to Sage. Then I read Latin.

Mrs. Hooker [warden of Sage College] has made a rule that all skaters must be in Sage by nine o'clock, reporting to her when they go and return. She also advises freshmen to get their parents' consent before going. Have you any objections to Ruth's skating? I suppose Ruth's case would be different anyhow since I am here to look after her.

Prof. Crane lectured us this morning because of the dreadful way which most of us pronounce French. I shall have to read my lessons aloud in the future for I know that I am one who reads very badly. [Gertrude]

Apr. 30, 93. The boys who live in the Alpha Tau Omega house were poisoned this week with rat poison. Their cook made some pancakes out of meal into which some rat poison had gotten and some of the boys were awfully sick. They said there were three doctor's carriages at the house the morning after the poisoning. Fortunately they all recovered. [Gertrude]

May 10, 93. I went to a lecture on sculpture this afternoon with Grace and then watched the boys drill from my window. There has been a new order of things established here in regard to examinations. In the future we are to have no proctors in examinations, but each student is to make this declaration at the end of his paper and sign it "I have neither given nor received aid in this examination." There is also to be a student court to judge persons who are reported for cheating with Pres. Schurman at the head of the court whose decisions are to be referred to the faculty for approval. They hope the duties of the court will be exceedingly light and think much cheating will be prevented by the new system.



The election for the editors for '95 *Cornellian* Board next year took place to day. We girls nominated a girl as one of the editors and are very much disappointed because she didn't get elected. Some of the men here are just as *mean* as they can be and wouldn't vote for a girl for anything. It is the first time that a girl has been a candidate for a place on the *Cornellian* board and it is *too* bad she was defeated. [Gertrude]

May 22, 1893. There were twelve speakers and Jennie Jenness was the only girl. All of them did well. Jennie did very well and the judges were Profs. Burr, and Tyler, and a minister from Buffalo. They awarded the prize to Mr. Chapman who did very well but I should have given the prize to Mr. Hegersmann. The one who gets the prize always gives a banquet to the other speakers. Of course Jennie didn't go to the banquet being the only girl but her roommate gave her a banquet here in Sage.... Prof. Smith the elocution prof. advised her what to wear, told her to have her dress made long to cover her feet and to have large puffs on her sleeves to her elbow and then tight cuffs. She wore a black dress and followed his advice. [Gertrude]

June 4, 1893. I had examinations in Psychology and Logic until six o'clock this afternoon and I was just frightfully tired.... Imagine my surprise to find that my German instructor Mr. Adams had written asking me to go to the concert with him. I wrote and told him that I took part in the concert so we couldn't sit together, but that I should be pleased to have him escort me over and back. He came last night all dressed in a dress suit with a fancy white vest and was very pleasant. We had quite a large audience to hear us sing and on the whole did very well.

There is a caterer down town named Andrews. Yesterday was St. Andrew's day and he treated all Sage to ice cream and cake. Wasn't that nice of him? [Gertrude]

June 8, 1893. I was rather frightened at the prospect of going out with one of my instructors fearing I shouldn't know what to say to the gentleman. However, we got along beautifully, as he is quite a talker and didn't act at all like a dignified teacher. [Gertrude]

Sept. 29, 1893. My work is about evenly arranged. I have Latin, German, and French Mondays, Wednesdays and Fridays, Geometry at noon, Tuesday, Thursdays and Saturdays, and Rhetoric and History Tuesdays & Thursdays and a lecture on Hygiene Saturday morning.

Yesterday noon Pres. Schurman gave his address. It was very fine indeed. He spoke about smoking on the campus and requested the men not to do so. He said whenever he saw a man smoking on the campus he thought it must be a workman, or some green young freshman who didn't know the rules.

My legs ached dreadfully yesterday. I think it is going up and down so many stairs and up and down hill, so much. Mrs. Hooker in announcements last night said that if the girls wished she would help them organize a Threadbare Club to meet once a week and mend while she read aloud to them. Pretty good idea isn't it. [Ruth]



Oct. 8, 1893. As you probably know this is the time of the 25th celebration of Cornell's founding. We had a holiday yesterday. Friday night there was a reception of the alumni, faculty and invited guests. No students invited. Yesterday morning there were exercises in the Library lecture room and many distinguished people sat upon the platform. [Ruth]

[1893] My dearest momsie & popsie, Yesterday afternoon the athletic contest between '96 & '97 was held down on Percy Field. Several of us girls went down with Mrs. Hooker. We freshmen wore our caps, for we have adopted a cap, it is very much like a mortar board, but not exactly like one, and is very becoming to everybody. Lavender and purple are the class colors, and we made little flags of them and pinned them on our umbrellas and waved them vigorously whenever the freshmen won. We also wore knots of ribbon of the class colors. The games were wildly exciting, and the freshmen did nobly although they did not win, the sophomores got 66 points and the freshmen 50.... Our yell is Zip a la, Zip a la, Boom, la la Cornell, '97, Rah Rah Rah. [Ruth]

Oct 11, 1893. I have voted for once in my life if never again. It was a vote in regard to the *Sun* question. There are at present two papers by the name of *Sun* each claiming to be *The Sun*; and it is to be decided by the votes of the students to day which one shall continue. It was very exciting I assure you. At one o'clock I vote again for class officers and I have my ballot all ready. It is a pity that all our class meetings have to come at one o'clock for we are ravenously hungry before the meetings are over. [Ruth]

October 15, 1893. The storm here Friday night was awful, the building shook, the windows rattled, and the wind howled so, that we did not get very much sleep.

Nov. 12, 93 ... it is very hard on nice cloaks to wear them every day and try and jam them into narrow recitation seats.

Nov. 19, 1893. I hardly have the heart to write home to night for we at Sage are mourning over one of the saddest accidents that I ever heard of. Miss Yeargin and Dr. Merriam went down the lake early yesterday afternoon and nothing has been heard of them since. Today their boat was found full of water. Dr. Merriam was the instructor whom papa took for a freshman, he was a very bright fellow, an instructor in Political Economy. Miss Yeargin was in the law school and was one of the finest women in the University and liked by everybody. It was quite cold yesterday and the lake was very rough. They were expected back to dinner but when they did not come and it grew later and later and they did not come Miss Yeargin's friends got worried and at half past ten they went down and told Mrs. Hooker. She did not sleep a bit all night long she worried so. She told James about it and he went down the lake early this morning. It was so cold that he had to go back and he then telephoned to the President. President Schurman told him to come up and talk with him … a committee of the faculty was formed and went down on the lake in a steam launch but could not find the slightest trace of them. After the boat was found full of water and with the oars outside they gave up all hope. The man who rented them the boat rowed along the shore of the lake for about twenty miles but could find no trace of them.… There is a sort of gloom all over the building.

Nov. 26, 1893. Yesterday afternoon I was to have gone through the shops with Mr. Clark but Mrs. Hooker said that I must take some third person with me, my sister, or Miss Stoneman or some one of the older girls, as it would be criticized if we went alone. Well as Gertrude did not know the gentleman I could not very well drag her or anybody else along, so when he came I had to go down and tell him I couldn't go. I was awfully mad and I guess he was too. But it was not my fault and I hope I made him see it that way. [Ruth]

I put my wintery union suits on to day and how they scratch. [Gertrude]

Dec. 13, 1893. Such a change as is going to take place here probably next term! We are to have *no more final* examinations, but prelims all the time during the term and I suppose class work will count for something. Then in the future, college will open earlier in the fall; there will be no vacation at Thanksgiving but Thanksgiving day, the winter vacation will begin Dec. 23 and only four days vacation in the spring … how are we to get any sewing done in the spring? Blanche declares the faculty are in league with the Ithaca dressmakers. [Gertrude]

Jan. 21, 1894. Went to the Ethical Society and heard Sabbath Breaking discussed. They did not arrive at many conclusions however.…The buses are on runners now and when we got almost there the runners slid, something broke, and one side went down. Nobody was hurt however. [Ruth]

Jan. 27, 1894. The University had decided that this Junior Ball should not last so long as those before, and would only furnish electric lights until three o'clock. At that hour while everyone was dancing out went the lights, but everybody kept right on, the light from the piano [and] lamps in the boxes furnishing the illumination, and it was twice as beautiful as it had been before: the dim light softened everything, and there was one waltz, which I am sure only violins and harps played and which was the loveliest thing that I have ever heard. They kept right on dancing until about four o'clock, and that was the loveliest part of the evening. There were a great many University girls at the Junior this year. In fact there were not so many girls imported this year as usual, and the University girls looked just as well as those from out of town. One man said to me on seeing my fraternity pin "I see you are a fraternity girl, Miss Nelson, from what college?" I could not think what he meant at first, as I had no idea that any one would take me for a girl from out of town.

Jan 28, 1894. Everybody who goes skating in the evening has to get back at nine o'clock … I had an invitation to go to a meeting of the Mathematical Club on Saturday night, on the card it stated that from the quality of my work I was supposed to be interested in Mathematical discussions. Everybody above a certain standard received one. Several of us girls went over, but they did not do anything but discuss Projective Geometry and although it was rather interesting, it was too deep for me, and I decided not to join the club. Friday evening: played cards, made beef tea and ate crackers and jelly: had a nice little spread.



February 4, 1894. Only five Sage girls went to the Cotillion and nine or ten to the Junior. Fewer and fewer Sage girls are each year invited to these big affairs and I think it is a shame. These balls are college affairs and I think college girls ought to have a chance to participate in them. One girl in the sophomore class went to her class Cotillion. Some of the girls had an indignation meeting tonight over the way we girls are treated here. Many of the men look down on us and snub us, some of the faculty also, and the president of the university thinks that co-education is no good. What are we to do? [Gertrude]

February 11, 1894. If Mrs. Hooker had her way she would soon abolish co-education here by sending girls home whom she thinks aren't strong enough to stay here. Now she is after *me*.... Last week one of the professors made a bust of Henry Sage out of snow. It was an excellent likeness and several people took pictures of it. [Gertrude]

Feb 25, 1894. Saturday night a colonial party; Mr. and Mrs. George Washington, etc. had tableaux. The girls were going down to have our pictures taken en costume tomorrow, but Mrs. Hooker thought it would be dreadful for the girls to appear before the photographer when dressed up as men, so we cannot have the pictures taken, unless we get one of the girls to do it and amateur photographs are not very good as a rule.

Feb 28, 1894. The professors in this university treat us like a lot of machines especially Prof. Tyler who exacts entirely too much time for his work. It's all very well to say "don't work" but it isn't so easy not to do so when work piles up fast. [Ruth]

Mrs. Hooker doesn't approve of girls dressing up as men *at all.* [Gertrude]

April 8 1894. A colored man, a Mr. Washington from Georgia, spoke and was very good [at Bible class] Jessie Capron and I are almost persuaded that our calling is to go South and teach the Negroes. [Ruth]

April 8, 1894. We had terrible food to eat most of last week, the bread was dreadful, and of course my stomach began to ache again, but we bought some oranges, and we had a very good dinner and supper to day. [Gertrude]

April 22, 1894. Mrs. Myers is the mother of one of our DG girls and has come to Ithaca to live here until her daughter finishes college.... I don't think it is safe for Ruth to go out in a canoe on the lake. Last year two men upset in the very canoe that she has been invited to go in. I don't care how many times she goes in a row-boat but canoes are so small and they upset in the slightest provocation. Don't you think I'm right? [Gertrude]

April 29, 1894. Margaret, Genevieve, Mae, Emily and I decided to go and pay our own way [to *The Gondoliers* at the Opera House] since no gallant youths had volunteered to take us. We got seats in the third row in the balcony for fifty cents and we could see and hear splendidly. [Gertrude]





May 6, 1894. You know college men steal all the signs that they can find & decorate their rooms with them and as Grace and I had been longing for some signs we eagerly seized one. We had some trouble in getting it concealed sufficiently so as to carry it across the campus but we finally succeeded. [Ruth]

Miss Crandall thinks "Marcella" is flat & she & another woman in the Cornell Library have started a petition *against* woman suffrage and have left it in the library for girls to sign!! What do you think of that? Nellie Reed signed it & Blanche said she was going to do so. [Gertrude]

May 8, 1894. It rains here nearly every day either a steady downpour all day or a storm in the afternoon. [A visit to Professor Wilder's zoo in McGraw Hall] took us down stairs to see the alligators, the raccoon, armadillo and the cats. We also saw some white mice and a cage of snakes besides seeing a poisonous lizard. Then we wandered about the museum and the museum of casts.

Agnes was my partner for that dance and as we didn't wish to dance the reel we danced the two step by ourselves all the time in the hall and had an *elegant* dance. We had lemonade and salted wafers for refreshments and danced until twelve o'clock.... It was quite an innovation here to have a large dance in the drawing room to which no men were invited and I think it was quite nice. [Gertrude]

May 9, 1894. Monday night there was organized here a "L.I. Club" to which people who lived in Long Island or who had been prepared in any school on that island were eligible for membership. There was a great time over the adoption of the constitution and election of officers. Then those who wished to join were requested to write their names on a piece of paper on the desk. Emily, Ruth and I after some deliberation decided to join and subscribed our names. About twenty-seven names were signed in all a pretty good beginning. The dues are .25 a year and the object of the club is for the students who lived on Long Island to become better acquainted with each other. [Gertrude]

May 13, 1894. You know here if a student is particularly friendly with a professor, he is said to have a leg pull.

Dr. Buckley preached in chapel this morning & in one part of his sermon told that wives should yield to the dominating influence of their husbands. Such a remark provoked much discussion among the girls most of whom thought the sermon showed narrow mindedness and conceit. Leona has heard him preach several times and she says that he always introduces that idea into his sermons. [Gertrude]

May 16, 1894. Monday evening Prof. Pratt lectured on "Music as a University study" in Barnes Hall. The Cornell Musical Union sang two songs before the lecture. The

Union is the mixed chorus of men and women's voices of which I have the honor to be a member. I thought the Union sang very well that evening, as well as it had ever done. The lecture was very interesting and scholarly. Prof. Pratt sketched out a plan for forming a department of music in a university, which if followed out should be as difficult as any course now in this university and lead to a degree of doctor of music. I do hope at some future date such a department will be established here.



Monday afternoon instead of our regular American History lecture, Dr. Wells who is a candidate for Prof. Tuttle's position lectured to us about Napoleon. The lecture was well written but was delivered in a monotonous tone, which made me very drowsy. Mr. Sage, Pres. Schurman, Dr. Willcox, Prof. Crane and Prof. Burr were there to listen and judge of the merits of the lecturer. I suppose Prof. Tuttle has been taken back to the asylum. [Gertrude]

Oct. 8, 1894. We had our first practicum in Physiology yesterday. When I first went into the room it smelt so horribly that it almost made me sick and it did not seem at first as if I could ever touch the cat, which was placed on a platter before me but as soon as I got started I got very much interested and I just enjoyed it. It was such a satisfaction to find all the things. [Ruth]

Oct. 17, 1894. I have had two prelims this week, one in Physiology and one in Rhetoric. The former was not hard, but the latter was sort of mean. I am very glad that they are over with, for I detest prelims. [Ruth]

Feb. 6, 1895. Poor Peggy has got the genuine old-fashioned measles. She has been feeling rather poorly lately, and Monday night she broke out in a rash. We all laughed at her and told her that she was getting the measles, but she did not have all the symptoms. However, Tuesday morning she was redder and more broken out so we sent for Dr. Baker and he pronounced it measles. We have not dared to tell a soul about it, or the house would be quarantined.

February 24, 1895. You should have seen the sewing which we girls did to get ready for the military [dance]. Blanche put new sleeves in her pink crepe and put stiffening in the back of her skirt, Eleanor made new sleeves for her pink crepe, Emily put crinoline in the back of her dress and trimmed the waist with violets, and Agnes put new sleeves in her gown.... It seemed to me that the military was an unusually nice one, it was very large, and the university girls were more numerous than the town girls. Every man that I had on my program was a good dancer and I was sorry when it stopped. [Ruth]

April 28, 1895. After dinner [Mr. Thomas] asked me to play for him so I played one of Chopin's waltzes. He did not bring any songs with him but Emily and I went over to Mr. Powers and borrowed some of his songs. I made an attempt at playing the accompaniments and he sang two of them, which he happened to know. While he was singing Will Shafer came to go out walking with me. We had made arrangements to go on Saturday morning when I met him on the campus. Will sat down to hear the music and while Mr. Thomas was singing again Mr. Kelly came to take me walking. I brought him into the parlor and was just getting ready to play Beethoven's Sonata Pathetique when Mr. Longacre and Mr. Tompkins came to take Jessie Capron and myself out walking. Jessie was not here and of course I could not go, so I brought them into the parlor to join the circle. We had some more music, I played, Mr. Thomas & Gertrude sang and then Eleanor recited. In the meantime Mr. Gordon and Mr. Lewis came to take Blanche and Emily driving and Mr. Northrup to go walking with Carrie Myers. So then Mr. Longacre & Mr. Tompkins got Eleanor and Gertrude to go for a walk with them. Mr. Kelly persuaded Carrie Laurence to go with him, and Will and I started, we four keeping together. We went through the tunnel and then walked out to Forest Home and back. Every girl in the house was off with a man, so you cannot say that Delta Gamma's are not popular. [Ruth]



Oct. 27, 1895. Saturday afternoon I went up to the library and finished a short essay in English. As I was coming out of the library on my way home I heard someone say, "Are you going home now." I looked around and it was Prof. Emerson. I had thought that I would go to Sage, but I decided that it would never do to miss an opportunity of walking across the campus with a Prof. So I said "yes" and we walked together until we reached Oak Ave. I had a very nice talk with him and I believe that I grow more fond of him every time that I see him. [Ruth]

Oct. 30, 1895. There is one thing for which I am profoundly grateful, and that is that there are no men in that class. I think that I would never have recovered consciousness I would have been too mortified had I fainted away before a lot of men [Ruth].

Feb. 9, 1896. I suppose that I would better tell you before you read it in the papers that there are two cases of scarlet fever on the campus, one in the Sigma Phi house and the other in the Kappa Alpha house.... The measles are also on the rampage.

Feb. 20, 1896. Will has asked me to exchange photographs with him and I don't know whether to do it or not. What do you think about it? I was glad that Will came after me [to go skating] as it is nicer to go with a man than it is to meet one after you get down there [at the lake] ... There were crowds of people down there, faculty, students and townspeople, old and young, rich and poor, in fact there must have been more than a thousand persons on the clear solid green ice which stretched unbroken down to McKinney's and from the east shore clear over to the west shore of the lake. It was warm with scarcely a breeze stirring and I skated all the afternoon without once sitting down to rest.... Will Shafer skates beautifully and just before we came home we skated from McKinney's over to the West shore, back to the pier on the east shore up to McKinney's and back to the pier, over to the light house and back again, in long slow strokes and stopped only twice. [Ruth]

Jan 21, 1897. I have christened my rainy day suit. Last night it snowed quite hard and then turned to rain so Esther and I decided to wear our short skirts today. I felt that I was much better off tramping untrammeled through the slush, than those people were who were tying in vain to keep their skirts dry. [Ruth]

Oct. 22, 1897. Last Thursday evening I was studying hard when I was informed that Mr. Otis was down stairs. I proceeded to go down stairs and entertain him the rest of the evening, and I am firmly convinced in my first impression of the gentleman, which is that he is a chump. I don't know when I have seen a man to whom I took such a violent dislike. I hope that he will never come to see me again for he gives me the jim jams. He isn't at all young, he must be at least thirty, is bald headed and homely.... Mr. Urquitha, the Spaniard stopped me and wanted to know whether I had any engagement for next Wednesday evening— the military. I did not think I cared to go to a mil. with the Spaniard so I said that I really wasn't quite sure. [Ruth]

March 14, 1897. Mrs. Elmer told me that associate professorships had been abolished here, and in their place there are first and second grade assistants. All the former associate professors have been raised to first grade assistants with a slight increase of salary ... Carla has the most elegant new outing suit. It is made of a new cycling material, which looks like corduroy only there is no rib in it. It is tan color, made with short skirt and waist with Norfolk Pleats, and she has high brown bicycle boots to wear with it. The material is narrow like corduroy and cost $1.25 a yard. It is really too nice for rough wear. [Ruth]

April 22, 1897. You should have seen us Jew the man down. O I tell you there is nothing like a college education to teach business management....We had a class meeting last Tuesday at which it was noted that the cost of the class pipe $2.35 should be deducted from the class tax for the girls, so they do not have to pay for a pipe they have no use for; however, if any girls want a pipe for a souvenir they can have one on applying to the pipe committee. This was done at the request of the girls. [Ruth]

May 6, 1897. The first news that I heard of the fact that I had been elected to Phi Beta Kappa came just as I was starting off to a nine o'clock when Grace and Faith came over from Sage to congratulate me.... When I went up on the campus everybody I met congratulated me, and when one of the girls brought up the mail she brought the formal announcement. I was utterly astonished and feel yet as if I must be dreaming. [Ruth]

May 9, 1897. There has been a great deal of feeling here among the girls against Pres. Schurman for the way in which he has treated Mrs. Hooker and a great many of the faculty are in sympathy with the girls. I think that there will be a new president here as soon as Hen. W. Sage dies. [Ruth]

May 14, 1897. We had a long conversation about Prexy and the way he has treated Mrs. Hooker etc. You have probably seen a good deal about it in the papers some of which is true, but most of it exaggeration.... Went down town and got my Phi Bet key. It is a tiny one and is very pretty. It cost $5. [Ruth]

June 3, 1897. I have just come home from my last examination in this university and with the exception of a lecture to-morrow morning my work is done. [Ruth]

# ADELAIDE TABER YOUNG

## CLASS OF 1899

Adelaide Taber Young entered Cornell in 1895. A science major, after graduation she taught for six years at Elmira College, then married and raised a family. In 1957 Adelaide wrote that "the greatest gains I had in my college life came to me, I believe, through varied worth-while personalities and places with which I was in touch." She mentioned "the times when I slipped into a back seat in the lecture room to hear Professor Hiram Corson read Shakespeare to his class," or "the Sunday evenings when a group gathered in Professor Burr's Barnes Hall room while he read to us from Kipling or some other then-modern writer." She remembered, too, the "welcome that always awaited us at the Comstocks' home." She noted that "my college years were happy, interesting and, I hope, profitable years. It is amazing that four short years, which make up only a little segment of a long life span should seem so important even now." She died in 1964.

Here, Adelaide writes enthusiastically about her classes, and her letters reveal a good deal about life in Sage College, where the women created a social life of their own. She is forthright in her opinions, especially about the faculty, although it is interesting to see her initial impressions change.

[Sept. 30, 1895] My dear People: One girl went home yesterday. She came here and started in and tried the Scholarship exams then had to go home because she didn't get the Scholarship. I think it was too bad. Everything goes nicely with me so far. To tell the truth I don't think I am very well prepared for Sophomore German, but

I think I shall get along all right. French seems to be harder for me than German was. The chemistry I think I shall find very interesting after I get into it more. That was what the $15 was for Papa. To cover the expense of instruments and chemicals, I suppose ... mathematics I like very much. Professor Jones makes remarkably clear explanations. One really can't help understanding.... We have begun Gym work although our suits are not done yet. Miss Canfield is our instructor. She is a fine looking woman so large and strong. She has a voice that it seems to me you could hear in Wellsboro if you tried. There is no fooling going on in her classes. The Gym work comes every afternoon except Saturday at half-past five. That means we'll have to hustle for dinner because the work lasts half an hour.

[Oct. 2, 1895] I got up sick with a backache yesterday then the first thing as I was starting out to recitations opposite the library my hat flew off. The wind was blowing quite strongly and of course on Cornell campus you have to chase your own hat no matter if there are a whole lot of men standing around. When I picked it up my hatpins were gone. I hunted until I found the silver one and then hurried to recitation.... Well all this just tended to make me blue and homesick.

Oct. 2 [1895] My English teacher Mr. Strunk I don't like at all and I am so sorry because I generally like that study so much.

[Oct. 7, 1895] Papa, I have a little pink card that says tuition ($40) must be paid on or before Oct. 5. How does that strike you? Like a cannon ball?

Oct. 20, 1895. My eyes have been hurting me some and I want to get to bed early, I am using my lamp tonight for I think the electric light may have something to do with it. While I was in Miss Gunn's room tonight she discovered that she had lost ten dollars. There have been quite a good deal (about a hundred dollars in all,) lost lately. Mrs. White said they should begin investigations tomorrow. The girls are getting quite wrought up over it. I have kept mine locked up and I haven't had my last check cashed, as I haven't had to use it. An unendorsed check wouldn't be apt to do any one much good I suppose.

The sophomores and the girls all looked so pretty. The thing [dance] broke up a little after eleven. I had as good (if not better) time, as I ever had at a party where there were men and where we stayed until one o'clock....

Oct. 24, 1895. Our Gym suits have come and they are lovely to behold! Lisle McCollum kindly informed me I looked like a picked chicken in mine, but I know I don't look any worse than she does....

[Oct. 28, 1895] There is one stunning gown here. A plain black skirt and sleeves and waist in black, plaided with colors, some yellow. But the girl that wears it is a very pretty little Jewess. It probably wouldn't be my style at all. Two or three of the girls have black gowns that they wear with wide, colored, collarettes....you should see me [on the] hills and stairs. I leave every one behind. I walk up and down to town without getting a bit tired. I really surprise myself. The only drawback is that I don't look a bit studious.

[Nov. 13, 1895] The bill for the term's room rent and the board for two months would be $52. It seems to me you are putting a good deal on me and I am getting all the good time out of it. It makes me feel rather conscience stricken.

[Nov. 18, 1895] Yesterday we ... won the Cross Country race of U. of P. The men had a big time last night, but I didn't see them for like a good girl I was in Agnes Binkerd's room studying. They came up to Sage too. Mrs. Hooker was shocked and thought it extremely insulting, because, as one of the freshman said, "they were all dressed in pure white."

[Dec. 2, 1895] Tonight I went to cut my cake and found that the red ants, the plague of Sage, had got on it. I have had to put it on the radiator in order to drive them away.

[Dec. 5, 1895] Well I went last night and had a good time, though it was quite a crush. I met a lot of men that I shall probably not know again. Danced every dance I think. Among my partners was my English instructor Mr. Strunk. He gave me a hint that I might cut his eight o'clock this morning if I wished but I didn't.

[Dec. 9, 1895] Well! Asking day is over, at last, and I got the invitation that I wanted. The Kappa Alpha Theta. I was so glad that I had talked it over with you and papa and knew that you were both willing for me to go there. Nelly Gunn, Friday night, asked me to take a walk with her Saturday morning and I knew what that meant.

[Jan. 6, 1896] I went to church ... after that I came up on the hill to hear President Schurman talk on "The Problem of the Book of Job." It was fine. I think the president is great anyway.... Friday evening I went to a spread in Miss Allen's room. She is a P.G. who lives on this hall. (In this case those initials may mean either "pretty girl" or "post graduate" for she is both.)

[Jan. 10, 1896] The men here use something I never saw at home. They call them skiis. They are about seven or eight feet long and they fasten one on each foot and with poles in their hands to guide them slide down the steepest hills. It is rather dangerous, I believe, but they say it is lots of fun. Perhaps you know all about skiis but they were new to me.

[Jan. 17, 1896] I talked some time to my charming instructor Mr. Strunk. I have heard a rumor that some one got exempt from English for the rest of the year, on a mark of 90.

Jan. 19 [1896] There is a mild case of varioloid reported among the students. Now don't be frightened, because there is not the slightest danger. I am only telling you because I was afraid you might get an exaggerated report of it through the papers. The man is a man in the Law School and he is properly quarantined. The University offers to give the students free vaccination. I asked Grandmamma and she said she thought it was unnecessary for me to be vaccinated.

[Jan. 21, 1896] Well I did get vaccinated after all. I didn't intend to at all but at the last moment I heard that some new cases were reported, and every one seemed to think it was the only thing to do, so I screwed up my courage and had it done. Since, I have heard that it was a false report and that there are no new cases. However, I suppose it is just as well to be on the safe side. It really was very funny to see the girls marching in to the ordeal. Imagine if you can the state of affairs when all these vaccinations begin to work.



Mar. 8, 1896. I went to hear Professor Nichols lecture on the X, Roentgen Kathod (whatever you want to call them) rays. It was a very interesting lecture, he made some experiments and showed some picture by the stereopticon.

Mar. 19, 1896. I got a note from Mamma this morning and a box of capsules addressed "Ithica." ... got an exempt in that [English] for which I am duly thankful.

March 21 [1896] I dreamed irregular French verbs last night.

[Mar. 25, 1896] I got an exempt in Chemistry so that I have one less examination and I know for sure that I have passed at least two subjects, that is some relief. I had my Algebra examination yesterday morning; it was neither very easy nor very hard. This morning I had one on the Chemistry lecture course. It was the hardest exam we have ever had in that subject. Tomorrow I have no work at all and shall spend the whole day getting ready for the two I have on Thursday, French and German.

[April 9, 1896] Several of the girls are going to take Photography this term.... My tuition this term will be $25 to be paid before next Saturday....My dear Mr. Otto the French instructor has been called back to Germany and I have gone into Mr. Segall's section. Mr. Segall is, if possible, a little more disagreeable than Mr. Otto.

[April 19, 1896] If this weather keeps up a week more I shall be a raving tearing crank. It is very bad on my temper. Everyone has come out in summer clothes, the men have even put on white ducks and straw hats.

[April 27, 1896] The men, that is, a few men, have just been singing somewhere up on the avenue. It sounded very pretty. I like to hear them sing Alma Mater and those other college songs.

[May 4, 1896] My dear People....A Wheel! Just think of it. I can hardly wait to get home and begin to learn to ride it....

This afternoon Mr. Haynes, (a Brooklyn boy, a Freshman and withal a very nice youth) piloted me out to Violet Island and around the Forest Home way. I got quite a lot of purple violets and a big bunch of cowslips. The woods are lovely now and I enjoyed the walk very much.

May 6, 1896. We came back across lots from the station to the campus. We came to a lovely, long grassy hill and I took a start and ran all the way down it—a proceeding I confess more befitting a "high school girl" than the "University woman" (that's Mrs. Hooker you hear talking). When I reached the bottom my hat was over one ear, and soon raised the familiar cry of "Side-comb lost." We went back up the hill but of course it was a hopeless task. There was a perfect horde of men behind so I thought that surely they must either have trampled on it and broken it, or picked it up, but I walked back and found it all right.

[June 1, 1896] I am going to have three examinations in German and they are coming next week instead of examination week. I am rather glad of it. My trig comes next week too. Oh woe!



[June 8, 1896] Billy Strunk with his usual thoughtfulness has gone and put an English examination (no examples) in on Monday afternoon. I thought we weren't going to have any at all, you may imagine it has somewhat the same effect on one's feelings that a douse of cold water would have.

Sept. 23, 1896. My room looks dreadful yet, and I want to fix it. I have been living in a perfect whirlwind since I got back. I didn't know I should be so glad to see all the girls again.... Everything is going nicely except that there are two more Miss Youngs here.

Sept. 24, 1896. My dear people.... The tuition ($40) is due before Oct 13. I have two or three fees for which I have enough money, but they will use about all.... I have elected a three-hour course in Mathematics, Analytics and Calculus. I suppose though that it is a very good thing to have, discipline for this mind etc. But I prefer German.

Sept. 30, 1896. Monday evening was the Christian Association reception for the young women.... I got my glasses yesterday and am dutifully wearing them for all reading and writing.... I am going to rent a wheel for an afternoon or rather part of an afternoon a week. The Sports and Pastimes makes arrangements to have them.

[Oct. 5, 1896] This morning I have no work until twelve that is no recitations. Then I have a Physiology lecture, which completely takes the starch out of me. I hate it.

[Oct. 10, 1896] I don't understand though why my money doesn't come. I begin to worry for fear the check had been sent and lost but as you say nothing about it, I take it for granted that it has not been sent. Tuesday is the last day on which tuition can be paid.

Oct. 15, 1896. The rain for two days was dreadful. I wore my short skirt to recitations. A great many of the girls wore them.

[Oct. 26, 1896] I was invited over to Mrs. Comstock's to dinner Thursday night. Gladys and I went. We were invited to meet a freshman friend of Mrs. Comstock's. We had a lovely (!) dinner and one so prettily served. Dark blue and white china to delight your heart mamma.... In the center of the table was a beautiful cloth embroidered in pink sweet peas and a tall cut glass vase of pale pink carnations and ferns. A little Japanese man waited on the table.

[Nov. 2, 1896] I took Miss Hemstead to the dance. I sent her some pretty bright pink chrysanthemums for it. I wore the dress with pansies. It really was a very pretty dance but I was too tired to enjoy it very much.... We had to stop dancing at eleven o'clock when the lights went out and after that we came up into Cornelia's room.... Last night too the men went on their regular Halloween cider raid. Somewhat before twelve o'clock they came back by Sage. They stopped and yelled and yelled. Then they sang Alma Mater and "Good night Ladies" very well and departed.

[Nov. 5, 1896] Somewhat after eleven the girls came to my room and told me that returns were in from most of the states. We all got up and dressed in our wrappers and slippers we paraded the hall to the music of combs. After the parade some of us went into Miss Peacock's room and made chocolate and ate wafers and marmalade. Emily Dunning opened her "McKinley jar of marmalade." We had several different returns and then went back to bed before one. Yesterday several of the dining room tables were decorated in honor of McKinley. One had a big flag down the middle with McKinley pictures and small roosters upon it. Then at each place there was a stick of peppermint candy tied with red, white and blue ribbons. One was trimmed with flags and "gold" chrysanthemums, and still another with a flag and between the two pillars a long line of whiskbrooms hung up. (Clean sweep, you know). Yes, the board is better this year I think, for one thing we have fruit every morning now.

[Nov. 12, 1896] Last night I went over to the Brooklyn Club, and had a nice time. Mr. Freund played his violin, Mr. Ransburg, a Glee Club man sang and we had mandolin and guitar, etc.

[Nov. 19, 1896] Such a funny thing happened in Physiology lecture the other day. As a general thing Physiology lectures are not funny. Am too much of an old maid to enjoy seeing cats cut up. Dr. Wilder has a cage of monkeys down in the basement and Tuesday we were very much surprised to hear a strange squealing in the lecture room, two of those monkeys had got out and pranced upstairs. The men got up and closed all the doors and windows and those monkeys had a fine time. I think monkeys are all right caged up but I do object to them at all close range. One of them got up on the back of a girl's chair and pulled her hair and bit her. At last by dint of much coaxing with grapes they managed to get the little beasts shut up in a little office, where judging from the sound they had a glorious time playing among the alcoholic specimens.

December 10, 96. The girls are all quite excited over basketball. Last night we had a challenge game.... I think myself I'm rather a chump but although I love to watch others play I haven't the slightest desire to play myself.

[Dec. 17, 1896] All Sage has developed into a mill, which is grinding day and night.... Every other door almost is adorned with a sign "Busy" and "Please do not disturb," are very common. One says "Please make your calls short." My room was filled with Mathematics students the other evening and we hung out, "Don't bother us, we're working." Bessie Avery put out the best one I think, "IBA very Busy Lady." Yesterday I spent a good part of the day studying for Analytics. In the evening, Faith, Agnes & I went to the Library where we could get quiet.

[Feb. 7, 1897] They all came as new women, in bloomers and blazers and little walking hats. They kept up the play the whole evening talking about their reforms, athletics, politics, etc. they were good actors and the whole thing was awfully funny. The food disappeared like magic. Half of the girls were men and the rest junior girls. The men were dressed in bloomers, shirtwaists and jackets, except a very few who wore real men's clothes. Then we divided into fraternities. Each of us took a girl except Bessie Drake who went "stag." The girls wore their prettiest gowns ... the girls who were men looked very natty, while those who were girls looked as pretty as could be. It made a pretty dance and we had a jolly time.

[May 2, 1897] First and foremost in my mind for the last week has been the [class] election business.... Forty-three girls voted, all except two in the class, and the tax we took in amounted to just sixty dollars. We thought we did well. The men hustled off to drill after counting votes and never came to tell us the returns, so at five o'clock Agnes and I put on our hats and went in search of a sophomore man. Having found one and learned of Miss Bickham's success we rushed back to Sage and spread the good news. You never saw a happier lot of girls. Later news told us that Miss Bickham had the highest number of votes 113 and that the four men elected were the ones whom we supported.

Mrs. Hooker announced today that this is her last year here. We are wondering now who will take her place. Some one with a doctor's degree they say.

[May 9, 1897] Would you be willing to give me a written statement saying that I have your permission to go on the lake? All the girls under twenty one have to have that. Of course, I may not have any chance to go and then again I may. I think you may trust me by this time to use common sense about going out.

[Sept. 30, 1897] Busy! It seems to me I was never quite so busy before. Eighteen hours a week is hardly going to be a snap. I have a good deal of afternoon laboratory work too. I have either lectures or laboratories every afternoon except Tuesday and Saturday. Wednesday I am hard at it from 9 A.M. until 5 P.M. with just time for lunch in between and Thursday I have from 9 until half past four. Saturday I have no work at all.

[Oct. 10, 1897] Friday were the class races in which our own '99 came out winner. Professor Tyler dismissed History so we could go down and see them.

[Nov. 14, 1897] I feel quite hurt at only getting one letter this week.

[Nov. 24, 1897] I have three hours of work this afternoon, but the professors whom at this moment I consider but little lower than the angels excused the classes.

[Dec. 15, 1897] I guess if you have not sent my money you had better and more than ten dollars after all. I forgot my CUCA dues.

I have finished two examinations this morning and came out of them with my life though I am afraid not with my honor.

[Dec. ?, 1897] Phi Beta Kappa elections were announced today and they were quite generally full of surprises. The only two you will be interested in are Gladys Willard and Mr. Haynes. The latter was especially unpromising at least to me for I didn't know that he stood any show, to say nothing of getting it now in his junior year. Aren't you ashamed of your ugly duckling? Never mind.



[Jan. 14, 1898] Monday night we all went to the debate. Miss Laughlin was the first woman to ever get on the stage and she won it and won it well. There was no one who even approached Miss Laughlin except Mr. Zink and he kept at a respectful distance. I am not fond of Miss Laughlin but [she] deserved to win and I was glad to see her.

[Jan. 24, 1898] Yesterday afternoon Miss Brownell gave a tea to the Juniors in her pretty room. You must see it, the walls are in dark blue canvas and such pretty little book shelves.

[Feb. 21, 1898] I have just joined a new club called the Tree Club. Con, in derision, calls it the Tree Toads. It is a sort of Botanical Club, which goes out on excursions on Saturday afternoons to study the trees and shrubs. We are to make a collection of pictures of the trees together with notes. Prof. Rowlee is at the head of the organization.

[Feb. 24, 1898] Yesterday morning we went over to the Memorial exercises. You will probably read about them in the paper. I was very, very glad I went for I wanted particularly to hear Judge Finch and Goldwin Smith. I admire Lyman Abbott very much too. Goldwin Smith talked in our History too on Monday afternoon.... Yesterday afternoon there was a faculty reception over at Sage.

[Feb. 26, 1898] Yesterday afternoon the girls went down to see the *Mikado*, which the Choral Club gave.

[Mar. 3, 1898] Tuesday evening Miss Brownell's friend Miss Walker talked on College Settlements ... I am so much interested in the work and in Miss Walker.... Miss Walker is a large and almost beautiful woman with fascinating manners, and having been intimately connected with the work she made her talk doubly interesting.... Tonight is the Cornell-Pennsylvania Debate. Of course I am going to hear it. I hope Cornell wins but if she does it will be entirely through Miss Laughlin.

[Mar. 9, 1898] Wasn't it great that Cornell won the debate? To me it seemed quite a one sided affair. This may possibly be due to the fact that I was a trifle prejudiced. I really don't think though that Miss Laughlin won the debate even if she was the best speaker. Any two of the Cornell people, I think could have won the debate. If I had time I'd tell you of some of the funny things that were said for the Pennsylvania men got somewhat rattled.

[Mar. 14, 1898] I know papa will think I am a beggar and wonder what I have done with my last ten dollars but I've got to ask for more.

[Apr. 21, 1898] Naturally war talk is the order of the day. Last night the students marched in a big procession with the Cuban flag at their head, yelling and tooting.

The Cornell yell was given time after time with "Cuba Libre" on the end and was often accompanied with the phrase about Spain, which is usually reserved here for Yale. Then this noon they had an immense mass meeting in the Library Lecture Room. There they had patriotic speeches and music. I was sorry I couldn't go but I had a committee meeting.



[Apr. 24, 1898] I wish you might have heard the little Hindoo woman whom I heard the other night. Pramdita Pamabai her name is. She had the most engaging smile and swathed in her white robes she was quaint enough to look upon. She is simply fascinating when she talks and her tale of her work for the Hindoo widows is both pathetic and interesting. You must know when I tell you that I joined the Ramabi Circle. The dues are a dollar a year and membership is supposed to hold ten years. Papa will probably groan ...

[May 1, 1898] Yesterday we went, that is some of the Tree Club and some other botanists out to Summit.... We ate our supper in the station and got back just in time so that I slipped into a back seat, short skirt and all, to see the play.

[May 9, 1898] By the way I had a bid for Der Hexeneras, the senior society, which I refused. It is made up of one or two seniors from each fraternity and one Independent and is supposedly very secret and somewhat of an honor. No one knows except Con & Brin that I was asked, but several suspect it. I thought I had perfectly good reasons for not going in. In the first place it wouldn't be much fun for me without Con and in the second place there were one or two girls who had been left out of some other things and wanted this very much and as I didn't want it very much I let it go.

[May 16, 1898] Verily, I am becoming a "greasy grind."

[May 30, 1898] ... I'm afraid I didn't make it forcible enough that I need money but I do need it very much. Fifteen dollars would I think pay my bills and bring me home. Lovingly,

[June 1, 1898] I have been in bed all the afternoon ... this is one of the days that I don't believe in the higher education of women.

[Oct. 14, 1898] Yesterday afternoon our botany class went down to Renwick and rambled through the marsh in search of grasses and sedges. I confess, I was quite as much interested in the wild forget-me-nots as the grasses and the nearness of water and boats was most tantalizing. This morning I have divided my time between botany laboratory and my especial bugbear French Conversation. This afternoon I spend in Invertebrate Zoology. That is very interesting; Prof. Comstock is, I think, fine.

[Oct. ?, 1898] Lest you might hear similar rumors, I hasten to assure you that small pox is no nearer us than McLean and that the Health Board don't intend to have it come any nearer.

[Oct. 23, 1898] Friday night was the sophomore dance and as I told you I took Margaret Bailey. I wore my high-necked organdy because there was a crowd and it was a horrid night. I was glad I did for as it was I tore the shirt some—not badly ... I don't like to lead very well and most of the freshmen dance very badly.



[Oct. 26, 1898] I am in a quandary. Mr. Haynes came up the other afternoon and in the course of the conversation asked me for both the Junior and Senior this year. I never thought that invitations to those affairs would bother me instead of delighting me. I told him I couldn't say yes on the spur of the moment, but must think about it and write home. I don't know what to do. Of course, I want to go to the balls themselves but I should rather not go with Mr. Haynes. I am pretty sure that I shall not accept both now. I don't see why he asked me to both. Oh dear, what do you think? But then you like him so well and you always want me to have everything.

[Oct. 31, 1898] I will go to the Junior with him. The Senior I can't answer for so long ahead.

[Nov. 21, 1898] Saturday evening we all including three or four freshmen went up to Mrs. Comstock's and sat around her open fire and then the Professor came down and made a delicious rarebit for us. It was all great fun.

[Dec. 2, 1898] Marcia went to the Sigma Phi dance last night and had a fine time. She and Miss Almy were the only University girls there. All the rest were city girls and out of town girls who had come on for the Assembly tonight.

[Dec. 15, 1898] Mrs. Comstock read to us two stories from a book of which I had never heard before, *David Harem*, is the name, I think. Anyway the stories were great.

[Jan. 6, 1899] Today has been the opening of the chapel, so of course we all went. The chapel is not changed so very much only it is larger and lighter. It was crowded this morning.

[Apr. 10, 1899] ... Friday night we went to a lecture on Folk song, which was very good. It was by Mr. Krehbiel, who is the musical critic of the *Tribune* and his wife sang the songs.

[Apr. 7, 1899] ... I must have spring fever, and I know I have a cold in my head and the two together manage to make me feel generally head achey ... I'm sure I don't know when this bore of a thesis will be done and when it is done I don't know what good it will be. If papa is going to be overwhelmed with time I think I shall send the thing to him to typewrite for it is going to be pretty long after all.

[Apr. 20, 1899] Yesterday I wore my cap and gown for the first time. Only a few people were out in them and we felt rather queer. I went to chapel in the morning and then in the afternoon I put on citizen's clothes and went down town.... Saturday night after chapter meeting we went to a Seminightly show in the Botanical Lecture Room. It was very funny and I should think could easily be copied or adapted. The curtain rose on a session of a certain debating society composed of different typical women. Susan B. Anthony, which Margaret Bailey did very well, being the President.

[May 4, 1899] Last night was the great Syracuse Basket Ball game. It was a great game but the result was hardly satisfactory, 6 to 2 in favor of Syracuse. The girls from Syracuse were larger and stronger than our girls and had had a man to coach them. They threw very much better than our girls.... The Syracuse girls wore very striking and, to my mind at least, not very beautiful suits of white flannel with orange colored sashes and ties.



[May 21, 1899] Well as I have already remarked quite mournfully, I guess I have gone to my last dance at Cornell. I had a good time at the Military Thursday night though I got very tired.... Then too, as always I got my foot stepped on pretty badly and my dress! I wore the white one and you know it is very long. I tried to pick it up, but in the second dance, a girl tried to walk up the back and literally tore my skirt off. That is she tore the hook on the band completely off, so that I simply had to gather myself together and flee for the dressing room. The maid fixed me all right but later in the evening I found that there were yards of ruffling dragging so that I had to carry the overskirt up over my arm the rest of the evening ...

Saturday afternoon we went on a Botany trip down to Renwick. The mosquitoes were thicker than the flowers and we had simply to fight our way through them by waving branches around. When we were coming home we heard the people yelling wildly down on Percy Field so we mounted a hill and watched a good part of the Princeton game. We got there in time to see the last part of the fourth inning in which Cornell made all her seven runs. The final score was 7 to 4 in favor of Cornell. But just imagine me hanging to a tree on a side hill watching the game, while, beside the botany class the immediate audience was made up of street urchins and colored gents.

# W. FORREST LEE

## CLASS OF 1906

W. Forrest Lee decided to keep a diary when he arrived in Ithaca in 1902. He writes about his progress on the freshman football team, his struggles with exams, and his work for Charles Howes, a local photographer. His self-doubt about his abilities and future is common among students of any era. Winifred is his girl back home. Lee was a member of the Zodiac and the Sphinx Head, and he rowed as well as played football. Lee graduated with a B.A. in the Arts College and later attended medical school. After practicing at the Clifton Springs Sanatorium, New York, he moved to Ithaca. During World War I, he was associated with the Aviation School in Ithaca, and during World War II, he was chair of the Tompkins County War Council. He was also a president of the Tompkins County Medical Society. He died in 1963.

Feb. 1, 1902. Been thinking quite a while of starting a diary so I am going to start today and try to keep it up the rest of the year.

Sept. 17, 1902. We spent the afternoon looking for a room. The cheapest we could find were about three dollars.... I have a fierce bump in the neck every time I think of Winifred. Shoot, I am just finding out how much I cared for her.

Sept. 18, 1902. Have put in a queer day today. Had breakfast with Roy then started out looking for a room. My goodness I hunted all over the town, couldn't find anything I liked. There seemed to be something the matter with all of them; about noon I was pretty homesick.... Corman he told me about this place. I liked it fine as soon as I saw it. It is on the third floor but light & airy there is steam heat and electric light here. Two rooms, single beds. I was out to see Mr. Rose the secretary of the Christian Association this morning. He is going to get me a nice roommate. Hope I can get a nice decent fellow in here. There is the finest view I ever saw from the front of the house, looks way across the town over to the farther hill. This is a mightily pretty place around here anyhow. Went down town this afternoon and had my trunk sent up. Went in and struck Howes the best fotographer in town for a job. Had a fine talk with him.

Sept. 19, 1902. I tried my exam this morning and don't know but that I got through but there is no telling. After the exam went down and called on Miss Gaskill at Sage cottage. I think she is a nice girl. Made a date with her for tomorrow P.M..... After dinner took a shave and put away a few of my things. Mr. Rose sent down a fellow and I took him in for a little while I don't know whether I shall like him or not. I have about made up my mind to chase him out tomorrow. Went down & put my money in the bank this afternoon.

Sept. 20, 1902. Walked around a while this morning up to Barnes Hall awhile and tried to make up my mind whether or not to keep this fellow ... I like him better tonight.... Went down to Percy field about ten. They gave me a football suit, jersey, pants, supporters, shoes and stockings. Had a whack at tackling the dummy, trying the machine, falling on the ball and bucking the coach.

Sept. 21, 1902. The more I see of this place the better I like it. My, but it was pretty along there. The woods are all wild and are full of squirrels. There is a path on each side of a big deep ... gorge at the bottom of which is a little stream running over rocks and little falls. It certainly is great.... When we got down to the Depot they were just pulling a dead man out of the Inlet. He had been in there nearly a month. He was fierce.

Sept. 22, 1902. I'm good and sore tonight. Went down to the field with Smith this morning. Moakley put me through a good stiff practice with the hammer. After dinner went down again and practiced football.... Am going to register tomorrow. Think I will take Mathematics, English, Chemistry, German and Drawing. There will be 17 hours all together. I don't know how I will make out as some of my work will come in the afternoon.

Sept. 23, 1902. Well I'm a regular bona fide Freshman now. Went up and registered this morning. I got 80 in my English exam, German only got 73.... Went down to Football practice this afternoon. Got it good and hard. I was on a team for scrub work for the first time, going through the signals. I got mixed up and ran into a fellow. Have got a fierce swelled lip and a loose tooth. We lined up against the Varsity today ... made quite a lot of gains on them. I was left guard.





Sept. 24, 1902. Am sorer than ever tonight, black and blue all over.... A Christian Association man was here and I pledged to join the association, two dollars by Nov. 1.

Sept. 26, 1902. We had our first recitations today. The Geom. isn't going to be any cinch, but I think I will like my German fine. President Schurman gave an address to the Students this noon. I was sort of sleepy but what I heard was fine.... Reed told me to be around tomorrow at the game. Wish I would get a chance to play for a few minutes. Went up to a meeting in honor of the crew tonight. My goodness it was grand. It was held in the Armory. They started out by all singing *Alma Mater*. It sounded fine to hear two thousand singing that. Schurman gave a talk. Courtney gave a mighty good spiel. He is a fine fellow. Capt of the crew gave a talk so did Reed and two or three other fellows. We ended by singing the evening song.

Sept. 27, 1902. Went to an English class; didn't have anything to do but were told what books were needed. Met Roy up on the Campus bought my books.... Went around to the training table on my way home and got a job washing dishes for my board. I am going to try it and see how I make out. There will be mighty good grub there. If I stick to that my expenses will come down a lot. Besides the incidentals my room will cost me 1.62 a week, so I will make it easier for the folks at home.... After dinner went down to the field and got my suit on. Reed gave the fellows a great talk before they went out on the field. Cornell had a pretty hard time making the score 5-0 against Colgate. After the game the scrubs had a lot of signal practice and scrimmage.

Sept. 28, 1902. Feel sort of sick tonight. I guess this water has put me on the bum. Went down to the Presby.... After dinner went up to a Freshman meeting at Barnes Hall. There were about 300 there and nearly everyone got up and said something. I got up and gave a little spiel for the first time. Came home and studied a little bit. I am not going to study Sundays if there is anyway out of it.

Sept. 29, 1902. Didn't have my lesson very well but managed to recite. Didn't have my lesson in German but didn't have to recite. Got started in Chem allright. In German composition the Prof. didn't say a word in English so I don't know much what he said.... After Laboratory work went over and registered for the crew.

Oct. 2, 1902. Didn't have my Germ lesson very well this morning but didn't have to recite. At 11 went over to Barnes Hall and read the Buffalo *Express*.... Had my physical exam at 11:45 got my card for football. After dinner went down to the field. Threw the hammer for a little while. Had about the hardest work in football I have ever had.

Oct. 3, 1902. Well I have just been through my first [class] rush. My goodness I am sweating like a steam engine and am shaking from excitement. Was up to a reception at Barnes Hall. Had a fine time there.... Went around and met a lot of people, coeds etc. ... a bunch of freshmen came along and waited outside. When it was over we all got in a bunch and marched down to the bridge yelling 1906. There the sophomores met us yelling '05. I was in the front four. First thing I know I was on the ground with about fifty on top of me. We got up and formed again and dug into each other. We did this a lot of times. I fell in the middle of the road once got my clothes all mud.

Oct. 4, 1902. After dinner went down to the field and got my suit on. Beat Union about 43-0. After the Union game we (scrubs) lined up against the Ithaca High School. Neither side scored. I played nearly all the time.... My board this week has cost me $1.10. If I can keep it at that I'll be alright.... The freshmen and Sophs had another rush tonight. I guess it was a pretty fierce one. I should have been there but I was too tired and felt rotten.

Oct. 6, 1902. Didn't have to recite in a thing today. After dinner went up and staid in the Lab till five. I think I shall like that work first rate. After Lab went over to Barnes Hall. Got my Bible study books and read the *Express.*

Oct. 7, 1902. This has been a pretty good day. Only had recitations till 11.... I read German a little then went down to the field. Fired the hammer a little ... Moakley says that 100 ft will win a place in the interclass meet. Just as we started football practice it started to pour. We were soaking wet and covered with mud before we got through. After supper studied and talked till eleven.

Oct. 8, 1902. I am on the Freshmen prayer meeting committee at Barnes Hall. Don't know how I got on. We had a meeting tonight.

October 10, 1902. Had another exam in Math this morning. Guess I flunked it.... sometimes think that I would like to be a farmer. I wish I could decide what I do want. I came home and went downtown on Nick's wheel.

October 13, 1902. Well I am eighteen years old now. Have had a pretty good day. Didn't have to recite at all this morning. In the Lab got through with the day's work about an hour early. Came home and printed Miss Gaskill's picture. There is a fine one of her with boy's clothes on.... We went up to Earl's.... We had playing in the piano violin and singing. We staid there till after ten.... The fellows took me down and spanked me.... Paid my Tuition today. I hope that I may be able to accomplish a little this year in many ways. Hope that I will be a better Christian and do what I know is right.

October 14, 1902. Flunked my Exam last Friday—38. I am not going to flunk another if I can help it. Went down to the P.O. this morning and got $20 also two registered packages.

October 17, 1902. Guess I passed my exam in math this morning. After Heine walked over to the Library.... The freshmen played baseball today with the soph's, beat them 12-4. The freshmen football team got together pretty good today. I was the only one out for Left guard. Went up to a reception at Barnes hall after supper.

October 18, 1902. Went down town with Smith this morning and hunted up a wash woman.... Went down to the game. It was rotten, Carlisle beat 10-6. Our fellows have got to wake up.... Walked up the hill with Moakley tonight.



October 22, 1902. I guess I have been too sleepy the last couple days to write this up.... Monday night we had our class election.... During the meeting the sophs came around and yelled and tried to break up the meeting. We had a great scrap getting the windows shut. One of our fellows got hold of a 1905 cap. After we had the window shut they fired in some stinking chemical mixtures. After the meeting we lined up and marched down but didn't see anything of the sophs.... We had pretty hard work at the field this afternoon. Worked hard from 2:30 till 5:40. Ran signals with the Freshmen, lined up with the scrubs.... The way things look now I think I will play in the Freshmen team Monday.

October 23, 1902. Was in the library and read a little about Photography as a fine art for English. Talked with Jane Chaney a little while then walked down with her. She is certainly allright.... Have studied a little for the Exam tomorrow. I want to get it. Went up and saw Courtney, a little while before six. He said it would be plenty time enough to get out for the crew after football. He seemed pretty well pleased with my looks (swelled head).

October 24, 1902. Think I flunked my Geom. Exam and didn't know any German.... Have been to the reception at the First M. E. church tonight. Had a pretty good time. Went home with a Miss Birdsell.

October 25, 1902. I have got to wake up and dig in. Have been thinking tonight that I would have done better going to a small college. I'm afraid that I am going to be a big frizzle. Lord help me not to be a disgrace and failure.

October 26, 1902. My leg isn't much good yet but if I get a chance at playing I'll play with all there is in me. I'm afraid I won't get a chance at hammer. Went to Bible study this morning. Didn't like it very well.

October 27, 1902. I guess I have struck about the biggest disappointment I have had so far. I didn't play this afternoon. I don't know why he put the other fellow in but I guess it's in account [of] my old good for nothingness. I think I had a swelled head. But by jinks I am going to brace up and not fail in everything this way. Think I'll get out and try with all my might for that hammer. We beat anyhow this afternoon.

October 28, 1902. Didn't know much today was a little late to Math. After English went over to the Library for a little while. Read a little about Forestry. I believe that I will take that up next year.... Went up and sang tonight didn't sing worth a hoot. I wish I could do something decent. I have got to look out or I will be busted first thing I know. Guess I better turn in.

October 29, 1902. Got back my last exam paper. Didn't flunk after all but came darn near it got about 63.... Went down this afternoon and tried throwing the hammer. I was rotten, didn't fire it more than 75. I never felt much better and never threw it any worse.

October 31, 1902. Am afraid I flunked my Geom. Exam this morning. Had an exam in Heine but I guess I got it.... After dinner went down to the track meet.... Saw several fellows on the football team. They said it was a measley trick that I didn't get on the team.



November 1, 1902. This afternoon went down and watched the game on the bulletin board. Princeton won 10-0. It was too darn bad.

November 2, 1902. Went down to the depot with four hundred others to meet the team. It was great. When the train came in the fellows gave a lot of yells and as the train stopped and the fellows got off and were carried through the bunch to the float everyone took off his hat and sang "Alma Mater." The football men nearly broke down.

November 3, 1902. Didn't know much today. Got 60 in my test in Heine. I ought to be kicked. Was called on about six times in Chem. When I went up to Chem. lab found that we were to have a test. First anyone had heard of it. Flunked to beat all. Got all caught up in my experiments and am a little ahead of some. Got a pretty good dose of Chlorine this P.M. which has put me on the bum. Went over to the Library and read a little.

November 4, 1902. Got 63 in the exam. I thought I flunked last Friday....

November 5, 1902. We certainly have had a great time tonight. After supper went up and had our rush. I was one of the five in our team to have hold of the flag at the start. I hung on too. We won two of the rushes thus winning it.

November 8, 1902. I feel like smashing everything in sight tonight. Am about disgusted with things and myself in particular.... After dinner went down to the football game beat Wash & Jeff 50-0. After the game lined up with the scrubs against Ithaca High ... left my specs and sweater under the bench. They were gone when I went after them. Swiped. It was the first time I hadn't taken them in but like a fool I left them out. I wonder if I'll ever get over being a fool.

November 9, 1902. Went down to the field this morning after chapel with Smith & Weiss. Found my specs laying on the ground but didn't see my sweater anywhere. I am going to keep my eye peeled for it.

November 10, 1902. I have had a bum time today. Went up without my lessons and was called on in everything. In Lab. this afternoon Root came around and asked what was the matter on the exam. I told him. Said that he had thought I had done pretty good work in Lab and was surprised to see me so bum in the exam. Went over to the Library and read a little.

November 13, 1902. Got my recitations all right.... Tonight was a swell one. The moon was great and it was as warm as summer out. Studied a little while then went up to the Library asked Miss G. to go for a walk but she had to study.... I am pretty scared of that exam tomorrow. I should have studied harder.

November 14, 1902. We didn't have the exam in Math this morning it is coming Monday. Had to say not prepared in Heine.

November 21, 1902. Flunked my exam in Geom this morning but got through the rest of the day pretty good. Went down to the field for our last practice. Took a picture of the team. They put us through signal practice pretty good.

November 24, 1902. Took my football stuff down and turned it in. A fellow sort of hates to quit the old place down there.

November 25, 1902. This has been a bum day. Flunked my final this morning and handed in my bum essay in English. Got a bid this morning to a party down stairs Thursday night.... Went up to the Library and read Deutsch for a while. Walked down with Jane. After supper went up and studied at the Library. I signed a contract today to be an agent next summer selling Chautauqua desk things. I am going to try them and see what I can do. The football team left tonight for Pennsy. They are going to win.

November 26, 1902. Finished up the last of Solid Geom this morning. Couldn't recite in Heine.... Went up to Barnes Hall tonight to a reception. Walked home with Jane.

November 27, 1902. This has been a pretty bum Thanksgiving. It was rainy and sloppy.... Pennsy beat Cornell too, 12-11. It's enough to give anyone a fit. The team has certainly had hard luck this year. This was Pop's [Warner] last game too. I have felt a sort of empty feeling all day today. I don't think it was homesickness but just an indefinite longing. I guess Smith and I will room together allright next year. That is if I don't go home next Feb.

November 29, 1902. Classes started again this morning. Went up to see Jones about my standing. He didn't have them yet but I saw two of my last exam papers they were 43 and 100. So I guess I got the stuff... Then went over to see Andrews. He said my essay was about the worst one in the bunch; got 40 on it. He said I could get through all right if I wished but if I didn't I wouldn't. Guess I better work.

December 1, 1902. Got a letter from Howes the photographer, this morning. He wants me to come down and help him print. Went down after Lab.

December 6, 1902. Haven't written this up before this week. There hasn't been much doing however. Lessons have gone pretty good. Got a mark of 75 in my Solid Geom. The algebra is fierce stuff.... I have been working afternoons [with Howes] ever since, got 75 cents a day.

December 7, 1902. We walked around the campus this morning a little. Went up to chapel this afternoon. The music was great. Miss Gaskill was there she certainly did look great.

December 12, 1902. I have been getting lazy about writing this up again.... Got 74 in my Algebra exam last Friday.... Went up and rowed yesterday. I never imagined there was so much to think about at once in that. Calson, Courtney, and Frenzel and Pop Leuder showed me about it. I am going to learn that stroke or bust. We had a fierce exam in algebra this morning. Hope I got 60.

# WALTER L. TODD

## CLASS OF 1909

Walter L. Todd's father was a Cornell alumnus, and Walter entered the university in 1906. He was a member and president of Zeta Psi and the Quill & Dagger, and a participant in Book & Bowl, the Sunday Night Club, and Kappa Beta Omicrom. He was also editor-in-chief of the *Era*, business manager of the *Cornellian*, chairman of the Ice Carnival, and chairman of the senior banquet—all activities he reports to his mother. A "machine," mentioned several times, is an automobile. Walter lives at his fraternity and is bound up with its social life and status. He writes about rush from the perspective of the fraternity, looking for just the right men.

From 1917 to 1919, Walter Todd volunteered in the Office of Naval Intelligence. He served on the Cornell Board of Trustees and was an active member of the Cornell University Council. In 1926, his brother also graduated from the university, and in 1937 the two established the George W. and Grace L. Todd Professorship in chemistry in honor of their parents. Todd also supported the university library, CURW, the Department of Ornithology, and the Cornell Plantations.

April 13, 1907. I have not had time to reflect that I am a MAN now, but can't imagine any brighter prospect for one than those I have. To be located in a big university on a twenty-first birthday is in itself, I think something to be very thankful for.

May 29, 1907. I enclose a menu of the Zeta banquet, which I said I was glad not to miss. It is always one of the big events here in the house and this year it surpassed all others I think. The tables were placed in the form of a T with the seniors across the end. The dining room as well as the tables was decorated with the fraternity colors and the cold weather we have had did not make the dress suits uncomfortable.

May 31, 1907. Excitement ran high and in the evening the freshmen burned their caps on the library slope.... Was exempted from the Greek History exam—the only possible chance to be excused but it will give me a little more time at least. Exams begin on Monday and I have one nearly every day during the week and one or two the following week.

June 2, 1907. Cornell is blue today over the defeats of yesterday but nevertheless a goodly crowd will meet the defeated teams at the trains—that's Cornell spirit for you!

September 6, 1907. I can't realize myself that I am here for another year but it is more difficult to think of the summer as come and gone.... Have my room all settled. The rug and curtains were just the thing. The latter needed no alteration and make the room look much better. Bought a small table and a bookcase—otherwise have things arranged about as last year—think now it is the best room in the house.

The "rushing" will engage our attention for some time. Several old brothers are back to help us and the house is full of freshmen most of the time but we have not pledged any of them yet. Will write you more about it a little later. A good many fraternities have machines here to meet the trains and the fellows want me to go home for ours but don't know what you would think about having it here.

Sept. 20, 1907. About all we do these days is to meet trains and sit around the house talking to the rushed men. Most of the fellows are all talked out and it is pretty hard being agreeable sometimes, after a few hours of it, but we have to do it to get the men we want. Zetas all over the country cooperate at this time of year to bring desirable men our way.

September 27, 1907. Yesterday I made a deal for an Ithaca phone so can talk with you from my room in a day or so.

October 4, 1907. Glad you think the courses are O.K. As regards the work I think I have about the same amount as last year though the number of subjects is larger. This is due to the fact that two of the courses I am taking without credit; that is in addition to the regular eighteen hours, which I have been taking each term. In "Money, Credit and Banking" for instance I am merely attending lectures and doing what reading I have time for but am not taking exams, etc.

We are having a dickens of a time with Ted Case—that is getting him back into the university and then keeping him at work. The upper-classmen have told him that he will either have to do his work this time or never, but it is another case of trying to make a student out of the other kind of a fellow. You might just as well try to make the other kind of a fellow out of a student—so I am beginning to think.

October 25, 1907. Last night we initiated Prof. Gordon. Wonder if you realize what it means for us to get him. He graduated from Cornell in 1904 and during his course had many chances to join a fraternity but could not afford to do so. We think we did well to get him for he knows all about the fraternities here from A. to Z.

October 27, 1907. All of the undergraduates in the order of classes marched to the field from the Ithaca Hotel in a line ten men wide and extending about four blocks. The "Big Red Team" and "Carnelian and White" came out a little stronger than when we try to sing them. In the meantime about twenty streetcars were taking people to Percy Field and I estimate that there were over a hundred automobiles in tow so that when 2.30 came around there were fourteen thousand people at the field including the four hundred from Princeton. New steel stands have been erected; four of them on the corners of the field were filled with Cornellians and one with Princeton men; and on the outside of the field they were crowded in three or four rows deep. To look over the stands it seemed almost like Junior week but the presence of so many fall hats and furs did not keep that crowd from making a lot of noise. From the time the team came on the field till they left it "Cornell I yell Yell yell" was heard from some part of the field and during the second half (neither team had scored during the first) they gave the locomotive yell continuously. One corner stand came out with a "Cornell" that it seemed as if you might have heard in Rochester, and then the one opposite answered "Yell Yell Yell" and so they kept going right around the field for half an hour. I don't believe you can imagine what it was like. Why, I saw some of these dignified Profs throw their hats into the air and act like a lot of kids—an example of the enthusiasm shown by everybody.

November 3, 1907. Was appointed chairman of the carnival committee—the carnival as you remember is the affair on Beebe Lake the first night of Junior Week. It is a big affair, posters are posted about town concerning it, and so forth. It gives the man in charge of it no little notoriety and is in a word a chairmanship of a Junior Week committee and a position worth having but the funny part of it is that I scarcely know the men who did the appointing, whereas a good many of their friends had tried all kinds of politic means to land it.

Also if I had had time I would have written you more about my work this term. It seems to me it is one of the best schedules I have had. Have made quite an advance in Spanish ... started in a small way to read Spanish works. Geology and Astronomy are very different than I imagined they would be—and very interesting—a lot more to them than I supposed. The history courses are about as I had last year but I find that the American History and History of French Revolution work along together very well, identical events coming up in each.

January 10, 1908. Tomorrow the University closes for Founder's Day celebration, which makes a little let-up in work and also gives me the first opportunity I have to write you.... In general you know that the carnival is held on Beebe Lake, back of Sibley College. Arc lights are suspended over the ice and colored electric lights, lanterns, etc. are strung up and down the toboggan and along the shores. An arena is enclosed in the middle of the ice, decorated also with electric lights, flags, evergreens etc. The bandstand, booths, and rink are erected within it, etc. The toboggans are decorated with flags, bunting, lights and so on. Everyone attends in costume. Last year it cost $700.00 to run off the affair, about 1500 electric lights of all colors, including Japanese lanterns etc. were displayed so I think you can imagine that it was attractive and hard for us to surpass. You can imagine also that a good deal of planning has to be done beforehand and the whole thing executed the day of and the day before the carnival because it is uncertain what kind of a day it will be—and executed during examination week.



February 7, 1908. I never saw anything like the way the faculty has dropped people this term. In all 650 bust notices were sent out—more than ever before. A large percentage of that number will get in again on "Probation," but a whole lot of them are required to leave town within five days. Two sophomores in our house will have to go, one of them has not done his work, the other deserves by all means to stay—just happened not to hit some of the final exams. It's so all over the hill—fellows are being dropped right and left regardless. The entrance requirements have been raised in all of the colleges. In medicine an Arts degree will be required hereafter, etc. Some of the fraternities have lost from five to a dozen men. Our fraternity had fifteen members bust.

February 10, 1908. Guess I wrote you about the "bust" notices. Tompson, Cornell's All American football player, the Captain of Track Team, and a number of the managers have had to go. Much excitement over the way people have been dropped on the slightest pretext.

April 3, 1908. You will be glad to hear that we have received word from two of our alumni to equip the house fully and immediately with fire-hose, stand pipes, escapes, alarms etc. at their expense. Steps have been taken to accept their offer and to do so right away.

April 5, 1908. Was invited to join a club called Book & Bowl, a description of which you will find in the Junior Week *Era*. It is a very young organization but has gained a good deal of prestige in the university and above all it has an object beyond the wearing of a pin and the possession of another shingle. You will see from the description that it will mean a good many enjoyable and instructive evenings.

April 26, 1908. Ithaca is beginning to take on its usual good appearance and to make you glad you are a Cornellian—more glad than usual.... Today the two memorial windows given by the classes of 1908 and 1909 are being unveiled in the Chapel but had too much work to do to go up there. I think I wrote you some time ago about the windows: to commemorate the death of the Chi Psi men who died in the Chi Psi fire.

May 18, 1908. A week ago I hardly anticipated having the good luck I did on Tues. to be bid by both societies at sharply 6.30, the only one in the house who made both. Quill & Dagger is so far the better.... The excitement ran high I tell you. The initiation is Tues night, then I will write you more about it. For the present it just means that the work I've done and the things I have given up etc., have been worthwhile. It was the culmination of two years of fairly steady effort.

May 25, 1908. There is a ruling in the University that no exams may be given the week before the finals and that crowded six prelims into the last week for me. Every day we had a *Cornellian* sale on the hill. Tuesday Night the Quill and Dagger Initiation was held. Wednesday Night a Book and Bowl Banquet, Thursday night I ushered at the "'86 Stage." Last night we gave our annual banquet to the seniors in the house and I was booked for a speech. It was about as strenuous a week as I have had.

The Quill & Dagger Initiation was by far the finest thing I have attended here but I won't take the time now to tell you about it only that it ... is the only thing I have had which didn't look smaller when I once had it.

May 29, 1908. I received an invitation to and attended the Cornell *Daily Sun* Banquet last Wednesday night.... My invitation came, of course, on the strength of the *Era*....Was elected Editor-in-Chief of the *Era*, "Alpha Phi" of the house, which will make me President of the chapter at Junior Week time next year, and at the organization of Quill & Dagger last night was elected Vice President of Q. & D. What the last means I want to tell you more about when I come home. It gives a man an opportunity above all to do more for the university.... A very successful and profitable year is over now.

October 2, 1908. I wrote you I came back to find six men with the white buttons and we all agree that the buttons never adorned six better freshmen. Yesterday we increased the number to seven by pledging another star who was "bid" by a number of the best fraternities in the University. No one has yet declined our invitation.

Do you know why this is? It's because right in this house we have some men that are not often equaled on this hill anywhere.... I'm always glad to get back here but this year brings an additional promise because it's the Senior year and the work, anticipations and uncertainties of other years are lacking. Personally I have some satisfaction in feeling that my share of the work had been about accomplished and most of my anticipations realized. Can you see that this year is different? 1909 men are at the head of everything in the university. Our class is running the house. We have no competitions and our associations are made. We feel that we belong here; everything and everybody is familiar.

October 9, 1908. A committee [of fraternity men] came here to the house yesterday afternoon and offered me the nomination for President of the Senior Class and I gracefully declined. It's a very hard position and would mean more work and responsibility than any of the ones I have had and they were bad enough. I don't think for a minute I could have been elected because it usually goes to a debater who can fill the public speaking requirements of the office well—anyway I did not want it this year.



February 3, 1909. I have registered again for as much work as I can take but just enough to keep me busy without outside affairs. Will not send list of courses because they are continuation of last term except for a change in Spanish, which I have made (in preparations for S. America).

February 28, 1909. ...being more happy & contented with life than at anytime since I have been in Ithaca. Have never had anything but good times here but now everything has turned out so favorably that I am enjoying these days more than any others. Each day, in some way, I am profiting by the sacrifices and work I have done before and this fact makes each day better than the one before it. I have come to believe in the things the University stands for, in all of these men I've known as well as anyone can, and I tell you it is going to be a sad day, in about three months, when we all say goodbye to the finest phase of life that was ever invented.

March 5, 1909. I have most everything one could ask for from the University, that is my share of so-called "college honors," hundreds of good friends, a satisfactory record on the hill, etc. This house with our new furniture & good cook is a palace to live in. The Zetas are good people to be with I tell you. Anyone who says this college game isn't a winning one has never had the experiences I've had in this university, in this town, or in a house like this one. I couldn't be treated any better than I will be when I am home with you again, yet I never expect to have four more years like these have been. I will be ready to leave when the time comes but between now and then I am getting all I can out of every day—the time remaining is short enough.

May 7, 1909. I'll tell you first about my petition, which I have just this morning learned was granted by the Faculty last night. It was if you remember to be graduated on my present credit and relieves me of any further exams—took the last one this morning. Will have no more term reports, no final exams and this minute my name is "scratched" for a degree.

# CHARLES M. FRENCH

## CLASS OF 1909

Charles French came to Ithaca in 1905 and began a diary in 1907. He mentions the classes he attended but writes mostly about athletics and his social life. Charles was member of the track team, Delta Kappa Epsilon, Sphinx Head, Dunstan, and Aleph Samach, and he was a class officer. Charles French graduated in 1909, took a job with Allis Chalmers, and in 1917 entered the Army, serving in the 34th Engineers in France. He spent two months attached to the Peace Commission in Paris. Upon his return to the United States in 1919, he set up the French Manufacturing Company in Connecticut, producing radio apparatus and novelty items.

Jan. 2 [1907], Wed. Left for Ithaca ... only a few of the fellows are back in the house

Jan. 3, Thur. Made first 8 o'clock of the year. Rained all day. Ran 10 laps on the broad track.

Jan. 4, Fri. Went down town; deposited money. Bought this diary

Jan. 5, Sat. Exam in Materials. Walked over on West Hill alone after dinner. Came back and ran 7 laps. Fellows all went to show *Gingerbread Man*. Stayed in house & read *Vanity Fair*. Bro. Somerville of the faculty was in for a while. Ordered a dress suit at Morrisons $65

Jan. 6, Sun. Had a meeting at night; 1st meeting as secty.

Jan. 7, Mon. On board track, 1/1/2 laps = 24 sec

Jan. 8, Tues. Ran twice today 9 in morning fast and sprints ... in P.M.

Jan. 9, Wed. Did not run strained back.

Jan. 10, Thur. Tried on coat at Morrison. Ordered 3 dress shirts & pajamas from Folger $12

Jan. 11, Fri. Founders Day. Holiday. Played billiards.... Studied in P.M.. Walked around 5 mile course

Jan. 12, Sat. Track meet in P.M. ... Rogers won 3 lap race. I got 2nd

Jan. 15, Tues. Worked Six hrs. in Forge; 3 hrs in Foundry; 1 hr Mechanics Rec. 1 hr. mechanics Prel[im]. Ran 10 laps

Jan. 17, Thur. Worked in forge 2 hrs. Drawing 3; Mechanics 1. Ran 7 laps with Townsend; he did 2:23. Went up to see Military Hop

Jan. 18, Fri. Working 6 hrs. in forge; Ran 5 laps with Coplitts, won by 5 yds 1.24 3/5. Meeting of Dunstan at Zincks. Went out later to Orient had a fine time.

Jan. 19, Sat. Worked in forge during P.M.. Had a track meet later in P.M.. Won six lap race from Townsend & Rogers. Colpitts second 1.56. Went to Soph Smoker with Chase, Bob Treman. Met at Zincks later. Fine time.

Jan. 27, Sun. Went down to see Kate Hoff in P.M. stayed; went to Church; Revival meeting; lunch;

Jan. 29, Tues. Hustled around getting ready for the semester. Got Kate & brought her up to the house in P.M.. Met the house party. Had an informal dance in house during evening. Danced all. Ran twice today. Exam in mechanical tomorrow.

Jan. 30, Wed. Party is on. Mechanics exam interrupts. Ran twice. Kate & myself took a walk. Masque in Lyceum in evening followed by Soph Cottillion danced until 4 o'clock. All came back together sat around the fire until 6 o'clock.

Feb. 4. Mon. Arrived in Ithaca 8 o'clock. Registered, went down to see Kate off and spent P.M. fixing schedule.

Feb. 5, Tues. Snowed all day.... Charlie Shaw is busted.

Feb. 8, Fri. Exams in Calculus, got 97 %.

Feb. 9 Sat. Ran 6 laps P.M..... Meeting of Dunston at Zincks in evening. Took in new men.... Bought class pipe.

Feb. 10, Sun. Walked up lake 6 miles

Feb. 21, Thurs. Ran P.M.. Sprints 100 yd. Chandler won 2 yds. 7 laps 3 easy 4 fast. Won 1.21. Went to Junior Smoker in evening.... Fire alarm went off twice last night.

Feb. 22, Fri. Wash[ington] Birthday, no school. Played cards. Ran twice.

Feb. 25, Mon. Ran twice; went to show in evening with Mac.



Mar. 6, Wed. Went up on Toboggan Slide.... Slide was great.



Mar. 8, Fri. Went to Soph Banquet in Evening.... Speeches, stories

Mar. 10, Sun. Went for walk with Bob Coit to Buttermilk in A.M.. Wrote letters & went to Presb. Church in evening with Tommy Thompson. First time for Tommy.

Mar. 16, Sat. Rush in P.M. near Armory.... Went to bed early. Freshmen are having Banquet lights went out.

April 2, Tues. Paid board bill 34.90/Room dues 60.00

April 5, Fri. Last Exam in Calculus. Ran at Field.

April 12, Fri. Ran at field. Took suit back to Morrisons to fix up. Going to infirmary for [tonsillectomy] operation to night. Slept in Infirmary. Dr. Beaman operated with Miss Reddington.

April 13, Sat. Got out of infirmary at noon. Stayed in house P.M.. Cornell 3, Niagara U. 2. Rarebit in evening.

April 19, Fri. Went down field saw Lacrosse game. Cornell & Seneca Indians. Cornell 2-0. Went up to Goldwin Smith, met [Ithaca] Conservatory girls.

May 3, Fri. Took Calculus exam.... Resting for Princeton meet

May 6, Mon. Went to field and got sore legs rubbed. Saw Lacrosse game: Cornell 3, Harvard 2. Muddy field. Studied late. Prelims every day.

May 17, Fri. Spring day. Big time on campus.... Went canoeing from 3 to 7 on Cayuga with Alice H. Fine time, water rough coming back.

June 5, Wed. Went to Physics. Got an exempt.

June 9, Sun. ... went to Renwick/ got on boat went to Taughannock Falls. Back at 8:30. Stayed until 11. Wore an Alpha Phi pin back.

June 10, Mon. Went over in evening to see A. H. walked in country.

June 16, Sun. Around house. Rained. Senior had Baccalaureate Sermon. Took some pictures of seniors & robes.

June 17, Mon. Spend day around house. Went canoeing in P.M. with Bob Coit & his brother. Broke paddle. Rained, in evening down in Dutch [Kitchen].

June 18, Tues. Went to exercises at Armory with Mr. Conover then to Campus to hear exercises. Spent P.M. alone on Lake Cayuga paddling in shade terribly warm.

Sept. 21, Sat. … down to Ithaca 8 P.M.. Fellows all back

Sept. 22, Sun. Went to Cong. Church with Doyle, Ray, Bob, met Bro. George afterwards. Fixed room in P.M.. Rushing freshmen all day.

Sept. 24, Tues. Rushing Frosh. Tompkins County Fair with Chas. Crowell. Fine time

Sept. 25, Wed. Rushing frosh. The frosh rush at Bridge fierce. Fence bent over gorge.

Sept. 26, Thurs. Registered 7:45.

Sept. 28, Sat. Went to game: Scrubs 6, Varsity 6. Rarebit in evening by grads. Fine time. Wrestled & threw.

Sept. 29, Sun. Rained. Went to meeting of Aleph Samach at Alhambra 11 A.M..

Sept. 30, Mon. Went to 1st rec[itations]. Went to Dentist in P.M. in chair 2-5. Seth had crowd around forming a literary society (seniors)

Oct. 1, Tues. Fine. Fowler's '11 funeral Sage Chapel. Spent P.M. fixing up Stunt books. Played Van tennis, won 6-5

Oct. 4, Fri. Went to Dr. Davis in P.M.. Teeth fixed 2-5. Went to field ran.

Oct. 6, Sun. H. See and myself with Olive H & B Watson drove in the harbor for Supper. Rained. Auto frightened horses, pole broke. Back 10 P.M.

Oct. 11, Fri. Went downtown in Even. with Buck. 3 Ginger ales. Van & Snider & Baird got tight.

Oct. 16, Wed. Worked hill in A.M. in P.M. went chestnutting with Alice Hutchinson, went up toward Casc[adilla] Field. Got apples. Fine walk back 6 o'clock.

Oct. 19, Sat. Worked cement test in Lab. Went to game.… Initiation at house 9 men. Bed 6 A.M.

Oct. 26, Sat. Worked Mech. Lab in A.M.. Exam in E.E. went to 1:20 train with Brinton. Met 9 Wells College girls.… Cornell 6 Princeton 5. Went to campus later. Downtown in Evening dance of Macabees with R. Treman. Fine time.

Oct. 30, Wed. Davy Hoy & wife here to dinner.…

Nov. 1, Fri. Flag rushes at Armory. Sophs won all three rushes. Worked EE lab with Hill. Walked to Enfield Falls with Harry Freeman 15 miles, started 2 P.M. back 6. Went to dance with Miss Lender, a friend of Polk's … fine time.

Nov. 23, Sat. Went to Game. Penn Frosh Cornell Frosh 26-0 with Chas. Shaw. Had rarebit in evening at house fine time. Bed 1 A.M..

Nov. 30, Sat. Went on hill worked Lab 8-11 & EE Rec[itation]. 12.1 Went to matinee with Bush.

Dec. 1, Sun. Got up late. Had breakfast. Snowing hard.... Went to chapel.

Dec. 3, Tues. Worked on hill all day. Snow. Skating on Beebe Lake.



Dec. 5, Thur. Worked on hill snow & fine skating. Military Hop tonight did not go.



Dec. 7, Sat. Went to Mech. Lab until 10 A.M.. Went out to Dryden in machine with Morrison as timer at the race 10 ½ miles. Got back 12.

Dec. 13, Fri. Worked on hill. Downtown to try on suit at Morrison's. Ran at track.

Dec. 14, Sat. Worked on hill. Viscosity Test of oil. They ran the inter Collegiate CC race 3 miles to day; snow 1 ft deep. 160 men ran.

Dec. 20, Fri. Finished work. Leave to night.... 9.15 went via Binghamton on the train with A.H.

# REILLY BANKS

## CLASS OF 1911

Ray Steeve "Reilly" Banks was born in Edmeston, New York, in 1889. He entered Cornell University in 1908 and received his DVM degree in 1911. Reilly was a member of Omega Tau Sigma fraternity and the Comparative Medicine Society, and he played on intercollegiate soccer and baseball teams. While he was at the university, the New York State College of Veterinary Medicine's campus was being built on the site where the School of Industrial and Labor Relations is located today. After graduation, Reilly lectured for a short time at Cornell, entered private practice, and then became a veterinarian with the State Department of Agriculture. He died in 1957.

Jan. 12, 09. My exams come rather bad so I will not be home for as long as I thought. They begin next Monday. I have examinations Monday, Wednesday, Friday and the following Monday. Whether I will be able to get through Monday night is at present a question.... The nice fall weather took a different aspect and it has snowed here all day. Makes things rather interesting. There is a veterinarian's convention in session here today and to-morrow. There was quite a large meeting tonight but I did not go up.

Sept. 29, 09. The boarding house begins its meals this morning minus my assistance as I turned my place over to Jay. I am going to board there. I am sorry that I did not put in my baseball toggs. The underclass play a series this fall and it is possible that I might win my numerals as I am in good trim ... I will numerate the articles so you will not have to worry that you haven't sent them all. Suit (shirt & pants), 2 pair of stockings, which were behind the door. Rubber apparatus known [as] jock strap. Shoes as they are. Round cap. The rest of material I will leave to you.



Oct. 19, 09. I have made my college team in Soccer Football, which is a kicking kind. Not as strenuous as the regular football.

Feb. 11 [1910]. I am somewhat lame from the strenuous practice that we are being put through. Another cut in about a week so then I will know how I stand (probably on the outside).... The Vets had a nice dance last Thursday night. Just a good crowd, good music etc. no refreshments. The bill was a dollar. I took it in. They have their banquet soon but I probably won't take that in.

Feb. 28 [1910]. It was some sacrifice for me as work is piled high here and I hardly know where to begin. But I expect to get everything straightened out before Easter. We missed the Junior Smoker and I missed the Vet. Banquet. Syracuse has Cornell beat socially but the spirit is not there that they have here.

March 7, 1910. The weather here is much like spring, quite warm about 65 yesterday. But I guess it is coming too early to stay.... The Junior Feed was last night and I took that in. It was fine. Will bring home my stein and Program Eastertime. It was held in the Dutch, about 175 there. There were about 10 vets went in a bunch and so we had a good time. Served Oxtail soup, steak with mushrooms, peas, shrimp salad, ice cream & cake, coffee, cigarettes. After this came the toasts, which were exceptionally good in my opinion. I have a prelim in the morning and another soon.

March 14, 1910. Yesterday the annual rush between the sophs and freshmen took place.... The Freshmen outnumbered the sophs which should not be according to rules. After the rush was over the captured ones were painted up and paraded around the campus. They were painted to represent something and some of the interpretations of characters were fine. Walter Page was in on the other side in five different rushes and captured as many Freshmen. In one instant, needing the help of another man to get his man, he tackled the wrong man when he tackled the Freshman quarterback. After this the Freshmen had their banquet in the Armory and the sophomores had their smoker in Dutch Kitchen.

n.d. 1910. The carnival took place yesterday and was very hotly contested. We should have won and ought to have been second yesterday but for some dirty work in the relay race. As it was Arts won, M. E. & C. E. were tied for second, 2 points ahead of us and we were fourth.

# FLOYD NEWMAN

## CLASS OF 1912

Floyd Newman, called "Flood," came to Cornell in 1908 and kept a diary for his first two years at the university. He attends church and participates in athletic events, but he does not much frequent the library—at least he never mentions going there. While at Cornell, along with thirty other students, he skated the length of Cayuga Lake. After taking a degree in chemical engineering in 1912, Newman worked in China. He served in the military during World War I and afterward founded Allied Oil Company of Ohio. In 1948 he cofounded the Ashland Oil and Refining Company, the largest independent oil company in the United States. He served on the Cornell University Board of Trustees and as a presidential counselor. Newman's gifts to the university can be found around campus. There is the Floyd R. Newman Laboratory of Nuclear Studies (1948), the Newman Annex close by, and across Fall Creek Gorge, the Helen Newman Gymnasium (1963), built originally for women and now open to all. There are also the Floyd R. Newman Arboretum and the Newman Overlook at the Cornell Plantations.

Sept. 28, 1908. Left C for Cornell at 7:11.... Pleasant trip.... Arrived in Ithaca at 12:30. Spent afternoon with Gib Wilson. Saw the "Big Red Team" go thro practice. Engaged board at Sage College. Unpacked trunk. Raining heavily.

Sept. 29. Went shopping in A.M. In afternoon saw the football practice. Over forty men were out. In evening attended a student's mass meeting on Library Slope.

Heard ... Coach Schoellkopf and Pres. Schurman. Sung the Alma Mater for 1st time.

Sept. 30. Registered. Started at 9:30 A.M. Finished at 4:30 P.M. Will take French, Math, Chemistry, & Drawing. 18 hrs. Finished settling my room.

Oct. 1. Registered for drill work. Rented locker and took a plunge. No. is 4-13-8. Reported for football practice but manager didn't show up. Watched varsity scrim.

Oct. 2. Started French and Math. Went down town. Got into football togs for freshmen team. 60 candidates out. Hard practice. In eve. went to a freshman athletic meeting in Sibley Dome. Pres. Lewis of Senior class, Coach Halliday, Trainer Moakley, and Caldwell Capt of B. B. team spoke. Pres. Schurman addressed undergrads at 12 o'clock.

Oct 3. Studied a little in A.M. but didn't succeed very well. In P.M. I saw Cornell defeat Hamilton 11 to 0. Freshmen were also out. Got a few bruises. In eve went to a meeting in Barnes Hall. Pres. Schurman and others addressed the freshmen.

Oct. 4, Sun., Went to Sage Chapel in A.M. Heard Dr. Lyman Abbott, editor of "Outlook." I studied some in P.M.

Oct. 6. Lost signet ring. Worked out at Percy [field]. Feeling very stiff and sore. One of the squad broke his collar-bone.

Oct. 7. Found signet ring. Attended 1st lecture in Chemistry. Enjoyed it. Rec'd 1st instruction in military drill. Liked it very much.

Oct. 8. Solved 1st problem in analytics. Registered in drawing. Drawed about 20 letters in 3 hrs. Hard work. W[eigh]t 145 (stripped)

Oct. 10. Went to two football games. 1912 beat Ithaca H.S. 15 to 0. Varsity defeated Oberlin 23 to 10. It was a very spectacular game.

Oct. 13. Rec'd A in analytics last Fri. Recited in chemistry for 1st time. Don't like the Prof.

Oct. 14. Went down to Percy Field. Gave up me togs and came right back.

Oct. 15. Hot day. Finished 1st sheet in drawing. It was accepted. [U.S.] Vice Pres. Fairbanks addresses a Republican mass-meeting tonight. Am unable to attend.

Oct. 16. Had a prelim in analytics—pretty stiff. In the evening went to a "frosh" meeting in Sibley Dome. A constitution was adopted. Then we marched down town. After about an hour, we were confronted by the Sophs. Dangers of a serious rush were averted by Coach Halliday of the football team.

Oct. 20. Tues. I went to Cong. Church with Gib W. to a supper. Met a few young men and older ones too. Also, three or four very cute girls.

Oct. 26, Sun. Went to Vesper service at Sage Chapel. Dr. Hulley of Florida gave address. Music was fine.

Oct. 30, Fri. Another "prelim" in geometry. 1st prelim in Chemistry. Soph-Frosh football game a tie, 0-0. It snowed about 10 minutes this P.M.

Nov. 5, Thurs. Went to football mass meeting in Sibley Dome and sung "We March to Victory" for 1st time.



Nov. 7, Sat. The students paraded from the Ithaca Hotel to the football field led by Cadet Band. In a hot game, Cornell defeated Amherst 6-0.

Nov. 12, Thur. At 6 P.M. went down to Lehigh Station to see the "Big Red Team" off for Chicago. About 1000 students were down. I put in the most strenuous 20 minutes of cheering that I ever did. Sang "Alma Mater" etc. and as the train pulled out we sang "Fight for Cornell."

Nov. 14, Sat. Worked in drawing for five hours. Finished 3rd sheet in lettering. Went to a football mass meeting at the armory to hear returns from the Chicago game. Cornell out played Chicago although the score was 6-6.

Nov. 21, Sat. 3rd sheet in lettering accepted. Cornell defeated Trinity 18-6. Cornell cross country team won the intercollegiate meet at Princeton. Capt Young of Cornell broke the track record. Penn freshmen defeated Cornell "frosh" 18-0.

Tues. 24. Undergrads marched from campus entrance to L. V. R. R. to give "Big Red Team" a send off to Philadelphia. Big gang.

Dec. 14, Mon. Rec'd 95% in analytics last week. Chances for an exempt are now brighter.

Dec. 18, Fri. Broke record again last night. Studied until 2:15 A.M. Rec'd 90 in last week's French prelim. Had a prelim in Chem. Hit it hard.

Jan. 5 [1909], Tues. ... arr. in Ithaca at 1:01. Mighty sorry to get back. Warm weather has been raining.

Jan 9, Sat. Went skating on Beebe Lake for 1st time.

Jan. 11, Mon. Founder's Day. No school. Still feeling bum.

Jan. 18, Mon. Feel mighty lazy. Very cold day. Block Week begins.

Jan. 25, Mon. Had French exam and got "stung." Mighty hard. Exams are now over.

Jan. 30, Sat. Registered and saw Columbia defeat Cornell 47-20.

Feb. 1, Mon. 2nd term begins. 1st lab in Chem. 7. No light yet in calculus. Went to 1st military lecture—uninteresting.

Feb. 2, Tues. ...am well nigh buried in work—calculus and French.

Feb. 4, Thur. Have discovered light in Calculus. Went to 1st lecture in sanitary science.

Feb. 9, Tues. Analyzed 1st unknown in Chem 7. Correct. Very interesting.

Feb. 12, Fri. Went to wrestling meet between Cornell and Princeton. Cornell won, gaining 2 falls & 3 decisions to 1 fall & 1 decision. Went skating.

Feb. 22, Mon. Explored Ezra Cornell's tunnel.

Feb. 24, Wed. Feeling bum. Went up to Ag. College for a little while—Farmer's Week.

Feb. 26, Fri. Went to debate between Pennsy & Cornell. Penn won. Cornell won at New York vs. Columbia, thus gaining 2nd place in league.

Mar. 4, Thur. Pres-elect Taft inaugurated to-day. Very wintry; worst storm of the season. Rec'd 100% in calculus yesterday.

Mar. 27, Sat. 1st prelim in integral calculus.... Organized underclass rush took place. Was captured and in parade. Attended Freshman Banquet in evening. Had a great time.

April. 16, Fri. Got stung on acids. Drilled out doors for 1st time this year. Played cards with Brice and Becker.

April 18, Sun. Heard Rev. Fred Courtney at Sage Chapel. Walked all the P.M. with Brice & Becker. Visited salt works [at Portland Point, Lansing] and Renwick Park.

April 20, Tues. Started baseball with chemists. Trying for out-field.

May 9, Sun. Parents and Ruth arrived on 1:10 train. Ate dinner.... Showed folks around.

May 12, Wed. Had regimental review in military tactics. Pretty classy.

May 13, Thur. Had an accident in chem lab and got a bunch of $(NA)_2S$ in my eye—pretty uncomfortable.

May 17, Mon. Began practical work in mathematics. Entered last two weeks—home stretch.

May 18, Tues. Annual inspection of cadet corps. Occupied entire afternoon. Enjoyed it.

Sept. 28 [1909], Tues. Trunk arrived. Unpacked it. Becker, Davis & I swiped about 2 bbls. of apples from ag trees.

Sept. 29, Wed. Frosh hats are appearing.

Sept. 30, Thur. Registered to-day. It required all day to straiten out the tangles. Am taking Chem 12 & 30 and P 1 & 10.

Oct. 8, Sat. Had 1st prelim in organic. Hit it pretty decent. The university was visited by a bunch of Japanese business men. Had 1st lab in physics 10.

Oct. 10, Sun. Went to Sage Chapel and heard Dr. Mott. Had lunch at A.Z. house and went nutting with Mac.



Oct. 16, Sat. For first time saw Cornell defeated in football. Fordham won 12-6.

Oct. 29, Fri. Got stung in organic prelim. Coldest day of season. 29 at 7:30. Sophs won flag rush. Went to big crew celebration in Sibley dome, hot time. Went down town with the sophs and had a little sport with the frosh.

Jan 4 [1910], Tues. Arrived in Ithaca at 1:20. Spent afternoon in getting ready to work.

Jan 8, Sat. Worked & Loafed.

Jan 11, Tues. Founder's Day.... Went tobogganing & skating.

Jan. 22, Sat. Loafed. Went to organ recital in Sage Chapel. Fine!

Jan. 31, Mon. Started second term. Re'd 85% in Chem 12, 75% in Chem 30 for last terms marks.

Feb. 22, Tues. Washington's birthday. Rec'd bid from Banhu.

Mar. 12, Sat. Underclass rush took place with ideal weather conditions. Caught four "frosh."

May 21, Fri. Spring Day. University closed from 11–1. Good shows.

May 23, Sun. Heard Rev. Francis McConnell at Sage Chapel.... Called on Prof. Bailey.

# ADELHEID ZELLER

## CLASS OF 1916

In 1912, at age twenty, Adelheid Bertha Marie Zoe Zeller and her twin sister Cornelia Pauline Hedwig Zeller entered Cornell. The following January, Adelheid began keeping a diary detailing her academic work, social activities, and friends. Adelheid and Cornelia were active in sports and excellent students; both studied German, and both graduated Phi Beta Kappa. Adelheid embarks on a number of sewing projects—a "waist" is a blouse or top of an outfit—and provides information about clothing, "spreads," and women's social activities, especially dances, in her pithy entries. "Block week" is exam week at the end of the semester. Surprisingly, although Adelheid and Cornelia roomed together, there is relatively little mention of Cornelia in the diary, not even when they are inducted into the honor society. Adelheid married and taught languages in several New Jersey high schools.

Jan. 6 [1913]. Classes re-opened.

Jan 10. Box from home; blue silk waist. Junior party at Sage for Frosh. Danced

Jan. 11. Founder's Day. No classes. Ezra Cornell's 106 birthday.

Jan. 17. Spread in Ruth's room. My chafing dish works finely.

Jan. 18. Sophomore's entertain in gym. Dressed as a baby.

Jan. 25. Reception at Sage to meet men of class. Danced in gym. Met several nice men, a friend of N. Baker. Chocolates, delicious cakes and ice [cream]. Pronounced a success.



Jan. 26. Grand exciting dangerous walk in tunnel. Turned over ankle. Pleasant afternoon.

Jan. 27. First prelims. Ankle hurt. Had lunch up at Sage. This is block week!

Feb. 5. Read "Mrs. Wiggs of the Cabbage Patch" aloud to girls. Started to embroider white handbag.

Feb. 7. Box from home, with candy and apples. Mending and sewing completed. Social at Baptist church.... came home with Mr. Hogg. Invitation to go skating. Prof. Needham's address to Short Course students.

Feb. 8. Registration. Skating on Beebe.

Feb. 10. Dean approved my choice of course which is not open to freshmen, generally.

Feb. 14. Received as valentines cookies, candy, cards and a pretty original design from Alvin. Home Economics building very fine. Deutscher Verein meeting in the auditorium. Prof. Erich Marks spoke on the historical relationship between Germany and America.... Dr. Andrew D. White spoke on the diplomatic relations. He added many personal incidents. He was minister and ambassador. A word of advice was that when in such a political position, never write letters discussing public or international affairs, to friends.... We sang a German version of Alma Mater.

Feb. 19. Tobogganing with Mr. Hogg. It is perfectly glorious! We may have made about ten trips and had only two spills without fatal consequences. A glorious moonlited evening on the lake. I enjoy Tobogganing more than any other sport.

Feb. 21. Received notice of an appointment to a State Scholarship.

Feb. 22. Chimes played national tunes. A reception for the men at Sage. Better time than at first one, altho' did not dance because of Lenten reason. Met quite a few men who are in various classes. Also Mr. Wall, who is very nice. Mr. McMaster came home with me.

Feb. 28. Went to Star [Theater] this afternoon. Performance was not particularly good. Got a dandy pair of skating shoes. Had a very pleasant time this evening. Mr. Castillo and his brother called and played guitar and sang for us. I think the Spanish serenades are very sweet.

Mar. 1. Invited to Ladies Night at the Cosmopolitan [Club] tonight by Mr. C. H. Ballow. I certainly like him. The entertainment was fine too. Half the members are foreigners. Some read selections in their native tongues. Met as many fellows that I could began to remember names. We were shown throu' the club house, it's a fine place to live in.

Mar. 3. Dean Hull consents to our taking German 10 instead of review. Skating was fine this afternoon, but fell down several times. Went tobogganing in evening.

Mar. 7. Compulsory meeting at Gym. for all girls will be held 1st Friday of every month.



Mar. 17. Lecture from China study class by Mr. Hu was very instructive.

Mar. 18. Invitation to Chinese Night at Cosmopolitan with Mr. Ballow.

Mar. 22. Cosmopolitan Club Chinese night was most interesting. I am quite proud of all my autographs. The refreshments were punch, nabiscoes, dried candied white fruit, compressed quince pulp, sugared dates, things like green plums and some raisin tasting nuts. All was very good. The musical numbers were very peculiar and the instruments were the strangest things!

Mar. 23. Attended services at the Catholic Church this morning, the first time I ever have. The decorations were beautiful and the music very fine. Went up to chapel in the afternoon. There wasn't an inch of space left, even in the aisles. Music was from the Redemption, perfectly grand. A window to the late R. S. Tarr was unveiled and was accepted in behalf of the Univ. by Dean Crane. It is beautiful.

Mar. 26. Biology field trip to the inlet. Such mud!

Mar. 29. The afternoon was the Soph-Freshman rush on the Armory green. It was fine and exciting sport and we could see very well. Then they had a grotesque parade, which was a "terror" because the boys were all mud splashed, and painted, not to mention the costumes and standards. We took a long tramp all over the campus and the heights. Went through the powerhouse. We rode back from Renwick on the trolley.

Apr. 13. Trip to Buttermilk falls. Was not very muddy, and just delightful.

Apr 18. Took our gym walk before seven this morning. Glorious weather all week. Sophomore dance was a very nice affair. Miss Pekary brought me flowers and was an ideal "man."

Apr. 27. This evening we heard Miss Rose speak at the Baptist Church.

Apr. 30. Got tickets for Boston Festival Orchestra, at Sibley on Saturday. This is my first treat to myself and I think it is going to be a good one. Biology trip to the woods this afternoon. I never saw so many violets.

May 3. Today the seniors gave a maypole dance. I had never seen one before, and shall never forget this one, for it was such a pretty sight. This evening we heard the Boston Festival Orchestra.... It was wonderful and too glorious to have missed.

May 8. Ag assembly was the last one this year. The girls' glee club and Mr. Whitney sang. Dean Bailey addressed the audience and read several of his characteristic poems. Then we went over to Domecon and had ice-cream on the cafeteria roof garden. That was delicious 'cause I had chocolate, which I like so much.

May 9 ... We had a long mass meeting at Sage tonight to adopt rules for next year. I think they will be more satisfactory, let's hope so.

May 10. This afternoon was the girls' athletic meet. The sophs won the event, but a freshman scored the greatest number of points. This evening I was at the Cosmopolitan club with Mr. Elting. The Argentine ambassador spoke, the whole program was fine and the evening the pleasantest I have yet spent there. The floral decorations were palms, ferns and tulips and in the dining room refreshments were served by a caterer in great style.



May 18. Heard Prof. Hayes at the Baptist church. We had quite a party of escorts home, but I *do not approve* of such actions. I want to be independent and I feel perfectly capable to walking up the hill, even if it is dark.

May 19. This evening we all who spent a few weeks studying China, were invited over to Mrs. Gilmore's. She has a beautiful home on the Heights. We spent the evening conversing and listening to Mrs. G's experiences. She has spent some years in Hawaii and showed us many beautiful pictures.

May 24. The cap-burning in the evening was gloriously exciting. Such a bunch of jolly frosh with fire and torches! And the huge bonfire and the shouts of glee as the caps went in! We gave a fudge party in our room.

May 25. Heard Dr. Hugo Black at Sage. He is an eloquent preacher ... Dean Crane paid a most fitting memorial tribute to the Sophomores who were in last week's lake tragedy [drownings].

June 2. Choosing of rooms took such a long time. We can reduce prices by $20.00 if we send laundry home every two weeks.

Sept. 24. Glorious day for registration, but line was very long.

Sept. 28. John R. Mott was preacher at chapel today. I have seldom heard a better preacher. He brought out the value and necessity of religion in a student's life and how study ... leads to intellectual improvement in all ways.

Oct. 10. Crew celebration was glorious. Everyone was out, red fire galore, and moonlight. About 3000 gathered on library slope above the fire. Yells, cheers & songs and speakers were on the program. The chimes played too.

Oct. 11. Saw "Dear Old Girl" at the Star this afternoon. It was acted here last summer. Views of Lib. Tower, chimes, President's Ave, Goldwin Smith & Sibley. D.L.&W. Station.... Only persons I recognized were "Pinkey" Williams and Lieut. Twesten.

Oct. 18. Girls mass meeting. All the new by-laws were read & discussed. I agree, with one or two exceptions.

Oct. 30. Comparative religion lecture today on Egyptian, Babylonia and Greek and

Mediterranean religions by Prof. Sill. Deutscher Verein meeting was very interesting. The boys gave musical selections, and caricatures of German university life. Miss MacNeal and I managed to speak German all evening, but as we didn't sign up [to be out of the dormitory], we had to leave early.





Nov. 4. Bid to the Star with Mr. Levy. Enjoyed it ever so much. Afterwards we stopped by an ice and also got some candy. I guess I'm quite fond of him.

Nov. 6. The CUCA comparative religion lecture was particularly good today. Mr. Hu was the speaker. His address gave the early development of the Chinese national religion, the methods & their idea of God. It is not Confucianism, Taoism or Buddhism. They worship Heaven, Earth, Spirits of the dead, and from that developed the worship of heroes, ancestors. The attributes of Diety are supreme, governing just co-equal with existence of Earth.

Nov. 12. Mrs. Hu spoke at Y.W. meeting. She is a dear. We didn't have time to stay through the entire talk. Another play rehearsal.

Nov. 23. Went downtown to church. Rev. Mr. MacIntosh accidentally said "The parable of the Sinner & the Republican." Few noticed it, but I almost destroyed my reputation by giggling.

Dec. 2. Went to the Infirmary to see Katherine Lyon. She had too good a time at Mary's spread, but will be back tomorrow.

Dec. 8. Heard a most delightful lecture on "Modern Persia" by Madame Ali Kuli Kahn, the wife of the Persian minister.

Dec. 18. Went down to Prof. Strunk's with Cornelia. I think he's very nice.

Jan. 7 [1914]. Cornelia woke me up at about 3/30 this morning and the smoke was pouring in quite uncomfortably. Everyone was hurrying about so we dressed quite respectably and went down. They didn't sound the alarm. The watchman and Mrs. Barbour had some time locating the fire, but found it was spontaneous combustion in a closet on the second floor where dust clothes etc. are kept. There is an order against keeping oiled clothes there, but someone disregarded it. The fire was soon out, but the smoke was horrible, so we went into Teresa's room for a while and ate crackers and chocolate till things were cleaned up. I was exasperated at having to lose two hrs. sleep. Everything was smoky smelling all evening even. I got along pretty well in classes, but was disgusted with the mark of my astron. prelim.

Jan. 9. We got to the Green Lantern where Dr. Parker had the most delicious refreshments for us. We all went home on the last car, but I didn't mind because we had a chaperone and there were quite a few of us.

Jan. 13. In psychology lecture it was only 46F but no one left the class.

Jan. 30. None of my exams were exceedingly difficult. Time will tell results. Went downtown today on a shopping tour. Had to state my age because I wanted to get 5 [cents] worth of alcohol at a drug store.

Feb. 1. The preacher in chapel was Rabbi Theodore Joseph of Allentown, Pa. He is very different from all we've heard. He read lessons from Isaiah and I Cor. 13 and his text was from Malachi "Have we not one God." He spoke for friendliness and fellowship as opposed to tolerance and prejudice. Gave examples of tendency toward fellowship and unity of feeling in religion. He quoted from some German writer.... He quoted German quite often. Was rather hard to understand at times; announced afternoon topic as the treasures of a snowflake. He is a Cornell man as one could tell from his reference to "our university" and as we heard him say afterwards. In the Lord's Prayer he omitted the clauses about trespassing and temptation. In the evening we went to the Baptist church & heard an illustrated lecture on the matter of the effect, mental & physical, of the liquor business.



Feb. 8. Went to Bette's at Prudence [Risley] for our India study class.

Feb. 11. Went to an illustrated lecture in Rockefeller A. on Chile and Strs. of Magellan, given by Mr. C. W. Furlong, a Cornell man who is an explorer of S. American regions, a lecturer and a painter.... The slides were grand and the lecture on the whole, the most interesting of its kind I'd ever heard.

Feb. 13. Went to the new auditorium and heard Mrs. [Carrie Chap.m.an] Catt and Dr. Anna Shaw, suffragettes who are here this week.

Feb. 15. The fellows were skiing on Buffalo street and on South Hill. It must be grand sport. We had some fun sliding down Buffalo St. on our way to church.

Feb. 27. Heard a lecture on the "present Situation in Mexico," by Henry Lane Wilson, former minister to Mexico. I think it was rather vindictive and sarcastic, but very important as regards knowledge.

Mar. 2. Prof. Davidson wasn't in class on time so all but two left. Saw him in the lib. and he said he was going to give it to us on Wed. They say he was furious when he found the class had left.

Apr. 18. The Soph-Freshman dance at Risley was a very enjoyable affair. Carrie King was a delightful partner. Everyone had a good time.

Apr. 21. This evening at 11:30 about we heard a youngster calling out an extra, telling all about the war! Prof. Karepetoff's Chopin lecture-recital was fine. He's such a witty, lovely man. Prof. Davidson told me he is one of the greatest geniuses here.

May 20. Astronomy: we saw a comet, which had just been discovered on the 15th of this month. Even saw the tail. It will probably grow enough to call popular attention.

Sept. 24 [1914]. First classes. Everything seems to be going pretty smoothly.

Sept. 26. First mass meeting. I liked Mrs. Martin's talk to the girls.

Oct. 8. The organ dedication concert was fine. I am particularly fond of the chimes & the echo. We had seats in the front row circle. The speakers were Prexy Schurman, President White and Andrew Carnegie, who is the cutest little man ever. It was 46 years to the day that the U. opened.

Nov. 11. Heard David Starr Jordan '72 on "Confessions of a Peacemaker." It was a treat and well worth hearing in spite of 3 prelims this weekend.

Nov. 23. Burned my left hand in lab with Bromine. Dr. Welsh was very nice when I went to him to have it cleaned. Got A in the second lecture prelim.

Dec. 2. Lecture by Miss Dora Keen, FRGS [Fellow, Royal Geographical Society] on her ascent up Mt. Blackburn in Alaska. It seems almost impossible to do the things she described.

Jan. 20 [1915]. Went to lecture by equal suffrage Club. Their speeches were very good and well given.

Feb. 13. Got my marks today.... Went to an illustrated lecture on Japanese home life, given by a Prof. from the Univ. of Tokio. This at 4:45.

Feb. 14. In the evening I chaperoned Arline and Mr. Baldridge to the Methodist church.

Feb. 15. This evening we heard Dr. Calderon, the minister from Bolivia, give an historical sketch of his country.

Feb. 25. Prof. Davidson's lecture on Tsing-Tao and the war was one of the best I'd ever heard at Deutscher Verein. It is getting colder again.

Mar. 3. Heard Wm H. Taft in Bailey. There were hundreds more people than the auditorium would seat.

Mar. 5. Mr. Ardell called about 9 o'clock. I had a good time at the dance & all the men I met were nice & good dancers.... There were but 4 or five co-eds there.

Mar. 6. We went up to Bailey again to hear Taft's last address here, on "the Presidential life, its limitations & obligations," etc. It was certainly good, & he gave us a good bit of his sense of humor.

Mar. 14. Jo, Verena, Mary & I walked to Buttermilk instead of going to church.

Mar. 18. Prof. Faust gave me a ticket for the Univ. Orchestra concert on Sat. evening. Sat next to Dr. Pumpelly during Prof. Andrews lecture on the Dardanelles, Constantinople & the Bosporus.

Mar. 21. Mr. Cobb told me "entre nous" that he and we two were on the list for Phi Bet', though Sue is considerably better than I am.

Apr. 20. Dance at the Country Club. It is a much smaller place than I expected. All the men I met, most of them that is, I liked very much & they could dance well, too. On the whole tho the evening was rather stupid to me.

May 7. The *Lusitania* is reported sunk by torpedoes near Ireland. Kathie Douglas sailed on it Saturday on her way home. No reports given of passengers.

May 8. Mother sent the most beautiful spring dress for me. We sewed & mended all evening.

May 9. Kathie Douglas' name is not among the rescued, so she must have perished, thus adding another name to the long "In Memoriam" list of the 1915 class.

May 22. We went to see the Spring Day parade. It seemed inclined to rain, so we didn't go to the Cayuga races, which by the way, I've never seen. Helen T., Lila, Sue & I climbed upon the TOP.M.OST roof of Sage & had our supper there. It was a glorious sunset & we could see all the [students] returning from the races. Harvard won. We had such fun getting up on the roof & the best time we'd had anywhere this year. Cap burning was not so nice this year. I finished my little blue striped waist in the afternoon.

May 31. Cramming, cramming, cramming!!

June 2. Exam in hist was terribly long. I wrote 2 books, each all but 3 pages.

June 8. Latin exam today was not so easy.

Sept. 27 [1915]. Got to Risley at 9:00 and helped with the freshmen.

Sept. 30. First classes. I liked the two I had today. In MHG [Middle High German] there are only three of us. Some talk of an advanced German composition course by Prof. Davidsen. Prexy Schurman's address was on "What is civilization" and perfectly great. Mary, Hypatia, Sue & I went to Six Mile and took several pictures, which I hope will be good. My head ached so that I couldn't go to our first prayer meeting. I lay on Hypatia's bed while she read me from the Finnish legend.

Oct. 2. Jo and I walked downtown and back and we were pretty tired. Mrs. Martin's address at the mass meeting in Sibley Dome was perfectly wonderful.

Oct. 5. I believe I will go out for hockey this fall.

Oct. 8. In the evening went to Bailey to hear ... wife of the Labor Party leader of Parliament in an appeal for woman suffrage and she certainly was fine. Mr. Graves, editor of the *North American* also spoke.

Oct. 9. At noon we all marched from the quadrangle up to the Stadium to the dedication of the training house and Alumni field. There were about 400 girls in line and we had section 1 facing the speaker's stand. It rained somewhat but we stayed.

Oct. 11. The Seniors gave the Frosh a party in the recreation room. We had the tea party from Alice in Wonderland, the band, Love's Labor Lost, Alimantary Canal, wherein I was the Zuzu gingersnap & had a great time getting over chairs & desks. It was a very nice party, tho.

Oct. 20. There were nine in our box party with Mrs. Weld chaperoning. Maude Adams was Babbie in Barrie's "The Little Minister" and she was a dear all the time.

Nov. 24. We had dinner & then cleaned for masquerade in the Armory. It was the prettiest party we've ever given. I should guess that about 400 girls were there. We had a stunt & a play & refreshments between dancing.

Dec. 22. Last classes today and everyone is leaving at noon.

Jan. 6 [1916]. Practically everyone is back and looks tired, esp. the girls. Ice was good today. Spent evening at the Library and am trying to get to bed at 10 every night.

Jan. 10. Debate stage in the armory… On the whole the debate was not so good as in former years. The speeches seemed to me to lack enthusiasm, conviction and "pep."

Jan. 11. Right after breakfast we went downtown and returned to hear the Founder's Day address in Bailey by Maj. Gen. Wood; he spoke on military preparations and gave a very comprehensive & interesting account of this since 1776.

Jan. 13. Mr. Wolferz gave a very interesting lecture before the D.V. on Student life in Germany. It certainly taught me a great deal I hadn't known. Snowing tonight.

Feb. 13. When I was awakened this morning at 7:30 some of the girls had been up since 6, for Morse Hall was in flames. I got over there at 8, saw the east end of the roof fall in and everything seemed doomed. After chapel we went over again. Many valuable things were saved. Several students lost their theses, 3 yrs of work. Hugo Black was the university preacher for today and he was especially good at vespers. When I went down to call for Susan after supper flames and smoke were still visible in Morse.

Feb. 16. We heard Prof. W. H. Taft today on "Our World Relations." He is very broad, and was enthusiastically received.

Feb. 18. My marks came today, two each of A, B, C. I've read the work for my Seminar report. Am going to tutor Miss Gale in Caesar and plane geom two hours a week for this coming term.

Feb. 19. Got my German 16 mark changed from C to A, which is more like what I expected.

Feb. 25. Today was "Quality Street" our first public appearance, at the Lyceum. It was a terrible night but every seat was occupied and many bought standing room. The play was well given and was beautiful in scenery etc., tho I didn't find the plot so interesting. K. Lyon was by far the best. The girls did the duty of ushers and were very pretty in colonial dresses and curls. We walked the last two blocks home because the car simply could not make the grade. The ice on all the trees made a veritable fairy land scene.

Mar. 1. Jo, Louise and I went up to Roberts to see the film The Spirit of Audubon, which had some of the finest bird pictures there can be, I'm sure.

Mar. 2. There is skating again but I have too annoying a cold to indulge.

Mar. 6. The address on "The Liberal College," by Pres. Meiklejohn of Amherst tonight was fine.

Mar. 11. ... Mrs. Sherwood Eddy was our speaker today on the Women of India.

Mar. 12. This morning, and at vespers in Bailey, we heard John R. Mott. I like a man of that kind, everything is sincere and deep and nothing emotional about his addresses.

Mar. [n.d.] This evening we saw the Portmanteau Theater in Bailey, with Mr. Heitinaun. I enjoyed it. They have very little scenery but unique & extensive lighting effects and the 1st piece was especially good for that. The second was clever and very popular. Nevertheless, it was called [not extended].

Mar. 25. This afternoon we saw "The Birth of a Nation" at the Lyceum. It was stupendous, a wonderful production and well worth seeing.

Mar. 28. This morning the ΦBK list came out and I was on it, also Frances Rosenthal and a lot of others. It was quite a surprise to me to have the elections out so soon. I never realized how many friends I had until they all began to congratulate me.

Apr. 2. Seminar today instead of next Wednesday. I went with the Davidson's to the Jewish Relief Orchestra concert.

Apr. 19. Today Pres. Wilson is to read his ultimatum to Germany. I guess it will make quite a difference to me this summer and next year. I never supposed that the war could excite me so that I couldn't concentrate on my studies, but that was the case in the Library tonight.

Apr. 25. I saw a ouigee board today which may seem strange, for I've long heard about them but never seen one.

May 11.... this is the fifth time I've been out with Mr. Urband within a week. It does sound most unusual for me, but so it is.

May 20. We wore our caps across the campus, had supper at the Silbey Dog [café], played on the Sage tennis courts and then marched through Sage and presented our caps to the Soph team.

June 6. Mr. Engelder took me out in his canoe... I found out quite a few interesting things about him. He thinks I'm quite German in many ways. I heard that Lord Kitchener & his staff have been lost. We saw the Thomas aero hydroplane make its landing on the lake; how it does fly! I hope I can go canoeing again.



June 17. Today was nice & sunny. At noon came the Alumni banquet at the Armory. We helped serve and enjoyed seeing all the classes back. The oldest I saw were some from '71.

June 18. ... The baccalaureate line formed, with all the officials leading, girls next, there were 90 of us, and then the men. We were seated in Bailey, filling the orchestra almost.

June 19. This morning dawned rainy again, however we went out to the organ recital, and then to the art exhibit. After lunch we met Prof. Durham, and visited the museum of casts, McGraw Museum, White Historical Library. Then at Miss Nye's tea the folks seemed to be very well pleased; they met Mrs. A. D. White & Mrs. Schurman, among several others. After dinner we all went down to the Star to see Mary Pickford in Madame Butterfly. It was pretty good.

June 20. This morning came class day exercises and rain.

June 21. Here we are graduating in the rain, as we came to Cornell in it. The procession formed about Goldwin Smith, and we marched all around the quadrangle, forming a complete rectangle. It was very pretty & quite solemn. I was sorry the folks couldn't see that part, but glad they were fortunate enough to get seats in Bailey. Many hundreds could not get in. Outside Bailey we formed two lines, and the faculty & trustees passed between. Andrew D. White wore his red Cambridge robe. There were many other beautiful ones. There are some good pictures of yesterday with us in it. It was very impressive. Lieutenant Thompson called out the candidates for degrees and we got our tassels safely over to the right side. Prexy's address was on preparedness of course, in the commonwealth and in the individual. We all thought it was the best he'd ever given in our days, and it was a really fine one too. The afternoon we spent downtown and packing our belongings. A number of the girls left in evening trains. How strange it will seem never to see them all again. In Bailey it was congratulations and good-bye. One could hardly realize it.

# KATHERINE LYON

## CLASS OF 1916

Katherine Lyon's letters home to her "dearest folks" are lively and extensive. She came to Cornell in 1912 from Hudson, New York, and joined the Social Service club, the YWCA, *Cornell Women's Review,* and the Junior Stunt. She starred in many dramatic productions for the Cornell Dramatic Club, and she also excelled academically, winning a Phi Beta Kappa key and other honors. She objects to Nathanial Schmidt's antifeminist ideas and misidentifies him as Jewish. Her letters are detailed and playful, set against the years of war and the final push for the Nineteenth Amendment, and indicate some of the ideas prevalent on campus concerning women's political activities. With the opening of Risley Hall, more women are on campus, and their regulation is an ongoing topic as Katherine details her life at Cornell to her parents. She married Arthur Mix, an instructor of English at the University of Kansas, where she taught creative writing and courses in Victorian literature. She died in 1990.

March 3, 1913. I'll now proceed to give you the latest news in the drama of the Insulted Freshmen.

March 10, 1913. So we are both engaged in the only pastime left to co-eds outside of studying—letter writing.... Then in the evening was the Junior stunt (the girls only of course) in Barnes Hall.... It was awfully good, very funny, and very clever. No men are allowed to see it except married or engaged ones and a few who have special dispensations by reason of their relatives being in it or something like that.... I must close this as all Frosh and Soph have to attend a Lecture on Personal Hygiene instead of taking gym today.



March 14, 1913. Tonight Catharine and I are going to a debate on Woman Suffrage. It is between two women, some Mrs. Owen, Cornell '10 on the affirmative side and some New York society woman on the negative. I imagine it will be interesting. I am getting to be an ardent suffragette, by the way, and Lucy and I have frequent discussions with May and Belle who don't see it our way.

March 17, 1913. Friday night Belle, Catharine and I went to the Suffrage Debate. It was very interesting and I enjoyed it immensely. Mrs. Owen had the best of all the arguments without a doubt, but Mrs. Scott was a good speaker. Mrs. Owen (affirmative) spoke thirty minutes. Mrs. Scott, forty and then Mrs. O. had a ten minute rebuttal. I took lavish notes on the affirmative speech as did Catherine and Belle but when it came to the negative I got so mad I didn't take one, nor did Catharine get more than two down. Belle, however, who is a strong anti wrote vigorously.... I was awfully disappointed in Mrs. Owen's rebuttal for she got sort of mad and catty at some of the things Mrs. Scott had said and while I did not blame her a bit it would have been a bit more dignified if she hadn't shrieked and shook her finger quite so much. Belle, of course, immediately said that was just like a woman and just what would happen when women got the vote. It was all quite exciting. If it was only this summer that the suffragists were going thru Hudson I'd go part way with them. Father dear are you in favor of Suffrage. If not—I'll take great pleasure in argufying you when I come home.

You see Belle and May are antis while Lucy and I are valiant progressives and we sure have lively discussions. Honest, anyone listening to us when we didn't know it would probably succumb to a nice polite fit but the joke is we mean it and are getting so excited over it. But we do get to saying killingly funny personal things. F'rnstance. Belle had been quizzing and pushing Lucy to beat the band and finally Lucy yelled in desperation, "Well, if you think I'm going to shine mahogany furniture, polish brass beds and wash windows all my life you've got another guess coming." It was so sudden and unexpected that we all simply rocked with laughter.

March 21, 1913. We've got a new instructor [in Biology] and he is the awfullest crank you ever knew. He's young and good looking and you'd think he'd be nice but oh my!! One lab report he gave me 55 on. He marks perfectly dreadfully except a couple of girls whom he likes and they get 80 or 85 while the rest of us humbly say thank you for a 60. He's some instructor.

March 27, 1913. Prof. Schmidt who is head of the Department of Semitic Languages here gave us a lecture on What is the Bible. It was one of the most interesting talks I ever heard. He certainly is a wonderful sort of man. Of course he's a Jew and spoke somewhat from a Jew's standpoint but never the less, he surely knew his subject. He did not let your attention flag a moment and he put things in such a peculiar and humorous way that it simply demanded your interest. We all wondered what Mary would ever think about it, but she announced (somewhat I fear to our disappointment) that she liked it, but she hoped her grandfather would never know it. I didn't approve of Prof. Schmidt's ideas of the woman's sphere however. He certainly is no supporter of votes for women.



April 14, 1914. Friday night there was a mass meeting of all the women in the U in Sage gym. Attendance compulsory. I was awfully mad to have to go as I was dead tired with classes in the A.M. till one, lab till four thirty, and gym after that. But I managed to get over there some how and listened to some very plain talk from Mrs. Martin and Dr. Parker as to what we were here for etc. Came home, read *Cosmopolitan* and studied.

April 22, 1914. Friday night was the Sophomore and Frosh dance at Sage. Leonora asked me to go and I broke then my rule of "no more dancing" to go this once. Each Sophomore asks a freshman to go and plays the part of a man, furnishing flowers etc., and some even got carriages. It was some classy dance all right. The Sophs wore tailored shirtwaists and skirts in very manish style, but Freshmen wore their very bestest and swellest creations. Of course I wore my pink gown and with white carnations presented by my man I felt real swell. Had an awfully good time. It was just crowded. Catharine, Belle and Lida went from the house here and they all enjoyed themselves as much as I. I guess. Met a lot of nice girls and it sure was good fun.

April 23, 1914. Election of the new dean of the Colleges of Arts and Sciences. There was quite a good deal of curiosity and guessing as to who would be elected. Sampson, our aug. professor was spoken of, and also Durham, the Latin Prof. It was thought the latter had an awfully strong pull because his wife is Pres. Schurman's niece and he is also a great friend of Andrew D. White, and it was understood that both men had recommended him. But strange to relate, neither got it, but Prof. Nichols of the physics Department. I don't know him even by sight, but every one seems to think him a good man for the place. I was glad any-how that Durham didn't get it … it seems to be generally agreed that while a wonderful scholar his morals and principles are rather loose.

Tomorrow they are going to take a panoramic picture of all the Students in the University. Five thousand of them. Can you imagine it? The picture will be six feet by sixteen inches, and cost three or four dollars.… I don't know yet whether co-eds will be invited down to be photographed or not and … have not decided whether I'll take advantage of it.

May 2, 1913. Went to the Freshman stunt instead of staying home and studying as I should have done.… It was awfully good, an awful take off on the men, by the way. The general plot was the prevention of co-education at a certain men's college. The girls were screamingly funny as college boys and their rage at co-ed was awful to behold. I certainly enjoyed it muchly.… A mass meeting of women at Sage tonight.

May 5, 1913. [two men came to call] they both had on ice-cream trousers and blazers, which only seniors are allowed to wear, and pumps, and looked stunning.... Mr. Wilson arrived at eight. He had on his tuxedo, with a flower in his buttonhole and looked stunning. I felt as tho' I were going to a dance with him instead of merely receiving a caller. We had quite a nice time. He is a little stuck on himself, like most seniors, but very nice.



May 13, 1913. In the evening there was a mass meeting of the women at Sage to vote concerning the rules for next year. It seems they have not been obeyed at all this year and they thought that by making them somewhat more lenient next year the results would be better. But it didn't seem to me that they accomplished very much for every time a more lenient rule was proposed some old fogey would get up and tirade against it and it would not be passed. It made me quite disgusted.

May 19, 1913. The University has been a somewhat sad place for the last two days. Probably you have read in the papers of the four students being drowned in Cayuga Lake Saturday night. They were all Sophomores, two men and two girls ... set out to take a canoe back to the boat house where it had to be by ten. They were coming back by land. When they did not return to the cottage, the girls thought perhaps it was too stormy and that they had gone home.... As soon as it was light they started a search and found the canoe floating bottomside up and one of the sofa cushions. They dragged the lake all day yesterday. But did not find the bodies. They are going to continue the search today but they do not hope very much to find them as Cayuga seldom gives up its dead. It surely is a horrible and hideous thing. At the last meeting of Sage women, which I told you about, they voted to allow the women to go boating until ten for they always had to be in before dark. I imagine that privilege will be withdrawn now.

May 21, 1913. Tuesday evening was the first night of Senior Singing. That certainly is great. From seven thirty till a little after eight, the Senior men sit on Goldwin Smith steps and sing. Everybody goes over and walks around on the campus or stands around in groups. The Seniors sing college songs and snatches of popular music and its very lovely and impressive and college like. We all went over.

May 26, 1913. Now I want to tell you about the rooms at Sage. They draw for them Wednesday and all lower classmen must room there or in Prudence Risley so that much is settled. But, the prices! Instead of paying so much for your room and so much for board as before, this year they have posted that room, board and laundry must all be paid in a lump sum and the lowest is $290 in Sage and $310 in Prudence Risley. That is a big increase of about fifty or seventy five dollars over the prices hitherto....May asked me yesterday to room with her next year. Curses. What shall I do. I certainly like her but it doesn't seem as if I wanted to have another whole year with her. I suppose that's horrid of me isn't it, but I can't help it.

May 28, 1913. Today at Sage they had a mass meeting and a committee was appointed to call on Dean Crane and the trustees ... the drawing has been postponed until

Monday. We did not go to the mass meeting as we did not know of it, but were talking with some of the girls who were there and they said that there was a very strong feeling of protest against the raise. Whether their action will do any good or not remains to be seen. The single rooms in Sage are all (with the exception of a couple at $310) $305. All the rooms in Prudence Risley are $310 apiece that is double and single. The rooms in Prudence are really much nicer than the rooms in Sage and have more light and bigger closets but of course it is off campus and means that you'll have to go for gym to Sage. Now in Prudence they have a few suites of four rooms that are very desirable at the same price. These are at the end of the corridor and shut off by a door, like a small flat. One room can be used as a sitting room and then two girls sleep in one room. Mary, Bell and Lucy want me to go in for one of these. Of course we'd never have a chance.... You see it would mean the bunch of us sticking together for another year and we probably wouldn't make many more friends. I don't mean to be snobby, but, ah gee, I don't know. Then again I might not make any better friends if I roomed alone in Sage or Prudence and of course rooming alone is lonesome.... Please advise me immediate.



June 2, 1913. Well I have a home for next year in Prudence Risley. But such a time as I had getting it. We girls went over to Sage at about two thirty and it was seven before we finally got our rooms. All this time I was standing up in an awful jam most of the time so you can imagine I was nearly ready to drop. We could not get our suite, which we were so anxious for but we got four single rooms quite near together on the second floor.

June 9, 1913. Now listen: Mr. Wilson wants to come to Hudson sometime this summer. What about it? I'd sort of like you folks to look him over for he is going to be back here next year, instructing, and I probably will see more or less of him. Of course I don't know a lot about him but his frat is about enough to vouch for him and he sure is some bug here in Cornell. He knows Paul too, belongs to Y. M. C. A. and *doesn't drink!* I haven't any desperate case on him but he's awfully nice to have for a friend.

October 2, 1913. Professor Titchener, who lectures is probably the greatest psychologist in America and he certainly is wonderful. He is awfully funny looking, big and large, with brown hair and an enormous brown beard. Honestly, it is too funny for anything; it's a great big bushy one and very long. He wears a gown to lecture in. I think he is about the only Prof. here who does. I sort of like the idea, it seems sort of "universitiyfied" ... some Senior in Ag, name forgotten, escorted me to Risley and I got rid of him in short order. You don't need to warn me about no fussing this year for I have made that decision for myself. I have decided to leave out men pretty much this year and cultivate girl friends. Have met some awfully sweet girls ... [the postman at Alumnae House] wished we were back at the old house—there was a great change now—"there's a sheeny frat there!" It was roaringly funny the way he said it. We all walked by there Sunday and they were out playing tennis and baseball.

October 8, 1913: Spent ten cents at the Lyceum. There were two Essanay Pictures which were acted in Ithaca. One was "Tony the Fiddler," in two reels, and the other "For Old Time's Sake." The former had scenes in one of the gorges, but the latter was the best. That showed Mrs. Comstock's front yard, the Chi Psi house, the swinging bridge and Professor Somebody's House. If it ever comes to Hudson, you surely want to see it.

October 13, 1913. Went to the Star to see the Ithaca pictures, those being the only times you could possibly separate us from our money with movies. They had a two-reel film, "Dear Old Girl," and as far as college scenes go it is the best of the bunch. It is a tragedy, however, and very tragic. You certainly must see it if you go to any. It shows the campus, Goldwin Smith [Hall], the library chimes, about which the story hinges, one of the fraternity houses here and the Lehigh Station. There are a lot of local college fellows in it, as a general background and it is a scream to watch them. Lieut. Tweston plays the important part of the hero's father and appears once. But he has his name on the list of characters just the same.

Oct. 27, 1913. After the dramatic Club meeting I went to the mass meeting in Barnes Hall and it was some meeting! As far as dramatics go, it had the dramatic club skinned a mile. It lasted from seven thirty till nine, so you can imagine how hot the discussions were about the new rules. Well, they aren't so bad as at first reported but they're rather strict at that, it seems to me the worst ones are that girls cannot go walking after eight o'clock, that is they must be in by then. Girls cannot go to the theatre unless accompanied by a chaperone (a married woman from those approved by the Dean) or an escort. In the afternoon two girls may go together without a chaperone but in no larger groups. There are a lot more of pretty bad freshmen rules, which, as they do not concern me, I will omit. I think the theater rule is rather arbitrary, not letting more than two girls go together. For my own part it would seem wiser to me to let more girls go for I think that I should rather sit with a lot of girls than have men on all sides of me. But we shall see. On Tuesday we vote on them and whether they will be passed or not is the question. One fool rule is that you have to get permission from the head of your house to go away for vacations.

Oct. 29, 1913. Last night the Epsilon Chapter of the Alpha Omicron Pi sorority invited Lucy and I to join their ranks! Isn't that great? Well, of course you can't realize how great it is, until you know more about it, can you? It is a national, with very good standing, has twenty-one chapters, included one at Barnard, Randolph Macon, Leland Stanford and oh loads of other places. The girls here are all lovely, well there is one whom I don't like an awful lot, but she is nice as far as that goes, only she lacks individuality, to me at least. The initiation fee is ten dollars and the dues after that, five dollars *per year.* But I must also state that there are various assessments during the year, as little things come up, which amount to about five dollars, so Clara said. The pin costs anywhere from five dollars to forty dollars, but none of the girls here have the forty dollar one, which is studded with diamonds. The one most of the girls have is partially set with pearls and costs seven fifty. I inquired somewhat minutely into the object of the society, for I didn't want to strike one which has no aims besides having a good time etc., and from what they could tell me without divulging any secrets, it is most high and uplifting. Clara said that it nearly killed her trying to live up to all its ideals, but it was making an entirely different girl of her and really all the girls are so sweet and charming, not snobbish or syruppy, but just lovely and gracious to everybody.... There's no other frat here that I'd rather go and it certainly means a good deal to belong to a frat here. I can't begin to tell all of the advantages but principally, you belong to some one, and somebody is interested in you.

October 30, 1913. Well, Lucy and I were pledged at six o'clock last night. I wish I could tell you about it, but I can't of course. It was all very solemn and quite surprising. I was pledged first, so I could watch the effect on Lucy. She came in with a grin on her face and when it was over, there was not a sign of the grin left.

Nov. 13, 1913. My dears, I didn't get to write yesterday on account of studying for Psychology and now I can hardly write on account of being besieged by despair at the thought of the mark I undoubtedly obtained in it. It certainly was a hard exam. I will send you the question paper next letter, but Clara has it at present. I didn't know quite what to expect in the way of a prelim, but this was pretty bad. It was not so much the difficulty of it, but the idea of knowing just <u>what</u> to give in answer to each one. I may have passed it would not surprise me, or I may have failed it would not surprise me.

Jan [6], 1914. There is to be a half hour's reception in the drawing rooms. Pres. White is going to address us I believe etc. They say that Mrs. Russell Sage is to be here soon. I will certainly want my gown then. The dining room is lovely. A great big affair. The floor is red tiles like bricks and the windows are very high and big. Up from the floor is a brown wainscoting in panels and the doors are all concealed. That is they are just two panels and do not show when closed. To see the waiters go out is like seeing the wall open and let them into a secret chamber. Miss Nye has a long table at the farther end of the hall and nine girls who are changed every week sit with her.

March 8, 1914. [in speech class a man rose to speak and said] "Lady and gentlemen." Hum, big joke.

March 18, 1914. Yesterday as you know was St. Patrick's Day and the Architects had their usual parade. We had Classic Myths at twelve but Durham, for once was mighty nice and let us out to see the sights. The Architects had their usual long green snake... all the men were much decorated with green crepe paper etc. And of course all the Arts and Sci men snowballed them. This year there was an added attraction,... for the Electrical Engineers had an Orangeman's parade. They all wore much orange crepe paper and other decorations and a large orange drum and horns to march by. For a time, when the Architects saw 'em coming, it looked as if there was going to be a hot time, but after exchanging a few snowballs they all apparently thought better of it and the Architects yelled for the Engineers and the Engineers returned the compliment, and everybody went home.

April 10, 1914. Catharine Bard has just dragged me into a suffrage lecture and so I am going to write to you during it and improve the time, if it grows too dull for my edification. I hope the lecturer will think I am taking copious notes. There are a great many very interesting people here, mostly women, considering that the subject is "Woman and her Opportunity," and likewise professors who I suppose are here to keep up their reputation of broad mindedness ... went over to Sage for meeting. We had quite a long and stormy session.... We have a new professor in Eng. 20 now. Prof. Strunk. I don't like him as well as Sampson, but he'll do at a pinch.

April 22, 1914. Last night we had fraternity meeting and after that committee meeting so that it was very late about eleven thirty when we, Lucy, Clare, and I started for home. The campus was all dark and gloomy and suddenly we heard this shrill cry of a newsboy. "Ithaca Journal Extra: Extra all about the war." Why it was the scariest thing. We got one and read the headlines and then were more scared than ever. Then a streetcar passed us filled with excited men all reading the papers and very patriotically inclined. They said there was a regular riot down town. The Mexicans here are all preparing to go home to fight against U. S. and feeling is very high. If the President calls for volunteers Lieutenant Bull, the Commandant here will take a regiment from here. Three hundred and sixty one had signed up until noon today and if the situation grows any worse, it is expected the number will be doubled. The chimes play "Tramp, tramp, tramp, the boys are marching" and everything is very patriotic and war like. I certainly hope the spirit is all we get.

May 27, 1914. At present we are having a hot fight with the *Sun* trying to get them to put a woman on the board of Editors. I'm sure I don't know how it's coming out, but they are mighty mean about it. They won't print any of our notices now, at all. I reckon we're going to boycott 'em, if they won't give in.

Sept. 22, 1914. Gladys' roommate was Bessie Goldstein! Of course that was enough for Gladys. She vowed she would never never room with her, nothing could make her, she'd go home first. Well, we all came up to Sage to see what could be done about changing rooms. They couldn't find out anything last night, so went down town for the night. This morning they came up again and finally this afternoon managed to have Bessie changed to another room with another Jewess and Evelyn Snow put in with Gladys.

Oct. 5, 1914. I have also joined a Y. W. C. A. study class, which meets Sunday at noon and discusses "The Working Girl."

Oct. 12, 1914. Thursday night was the dedication of the new organ in Bailey Hall, which was made possible thru Andrew Carnegie.... Mr. Carnegie is very interesting to look at and to listen to. He is so small that you want to pick him up, put him in your pocket and take him home to stand on the bookcase. But the program was very long and before it was over I fully expected to expire. Lots of people went out.

Oct. 23, 1914. Monday night Mary and I went to the Lutheran Club meeting and had a very nice time. There were only five girls there and about forty men so we were very popular. Mary was quite flirty, *drank cider*, and let a man come home with her. I was quite thunderstruck.



Oct. 29, 1914. This afternoon Mary and I go down to the Inlet to the Settlement to conduct a kindergarten class for the squatter's children and little "slumites." I imagine it will be very interesting, but rather trying at first.

Nov. 16, 1914. Well, I had my Policon prelim this morning and it surely was frightful. I shan't say that I don't think I passed, but I guess that was about all I did do. Everybody is wild about it. They asked you to think instead of asking questions you know and it is simply impossible to do that in an exam only lasting an hour. You don't have time.... Went to study class at twelve. Mrs. Shaw, the Police Woman of Ithaca talked to us. She was very interesting and is to help us in our organization of the Big Sister movement here. Next Sunday night we are all invited down to Dr. Parker's to supper.

Nov. 20, 1914. I am feeling very low. Have just learned that we are going to give our Thanksgiving Dinner to the Belgians!

Nov. 28, 1914. We are going to have our Thanksgiving dinner after all. The vote was not unanimous and so the authorities thought they did not have the right to give away the money. Oh joy.

Feb. 23, 1915. I saw my first aeroplane Sat. at a distance and had quite a near view of it yesterday. There is a new aeroplane factory in Ithaca, The Thomas Aviation Corp, and it has just completed a new military trainer which is very successful. Frank Burnside is running it and he has been taking it up every afternoon. Yesterday he established a new record for climbing, reaching 4,000 feet in seven minutes. It certainly is a bird. I'd love to go up in it.

March 3, 1915. William Howard Taft is here today and addressed the students at twelve o'clock, all classes being dismissed so everybody could go. Well, I had an eleven o'clock and as luck would have it, the man kept us over the hour, so when Catharine and I finally panted up to the Auditorium there was not a square inch of space left. We did not even get a glimpse of the man, tho I did manage to see some of the fresco work at the top of the stage, but only a small part of that. It made us so cross. But we were not the only ones, there were hundreds of others who went disconsolately and crossly away, murmuring that it was a fine state of affairs when the University couldn't provide a building large enough to hold all its students. Those who heard him said he was very good.... P.S. There were more people busted out than usual this year.

Mar. 12, 1915. Andrew D. White was here for the festive meal and later addressed us in the Drawing Room on "Some of the Traditions of Sage College." He is such a splendid old man but he is so prone to ramble. He began about seven o'clock and for some unknown reason began back in the B.C.'s somewhere discussing Universities in general. By eight he hadn't even got the charter for Cornell and we began to get desperate. The room was stifling hot, and most of the girls were sitting on the floor, which does not grow more comfortable with continued occupation. He finally got Cornell founded, but could not get Sage built till about eight thirty, and then seeing that he was really approaching his subject started a little side discussion of his mother's views on religion. At about eight forty five some of the girls who had engagements for eight, got up and went out, to Mrs. Barbour's intense pain, but I fairly think they were excusable. After a long time, he seemed to realize that he was still talking, and at ten minutes of nine apologized for taking so much time and sat down amidst tumultuous applause without having said one word about Sage traditions.

Mar. 27, 1915. Well, the expected has happened. I've had my pocketbook stolen, but not from my bureau drawer. It was in the lib last night. I had it on my desk under some papers and when I went up to get a book from the shelves some one must have taken it, for when I came to go home it was gone. I looked all over and asked people but could not find a trace of it.

Apr 12, 1915. Oh, I must tell you that I am out for the *Sun* competition.... Tex called for me and we went for a little walk. He doesn't approve of my going out for the *Sun* and we had quite a little argument.

April 19, 1915. Your reporter daughter is very busy but she will do her best to write you a little news too.

May 14, 1915. We are having a lot of excitement here concerning the Arts Association banquet. You know this is the first year that girls have been admitted and they are making it a dinner dance in Prudence Risley.... Andrew D. White is also coming to show that he favors it.

May 19, 1915. Had several [dances] with Mr. Velez, that Spaniard who went to Peddie and knew Clate. He's an awfully good dancer and very fascinating—tho he is reported "dangerous."

May 24, 1915. There was much excitement alright, so much that I was frightened. The Frosh all marched down after their annual cap burning and tried to storm the Dutch [Kitchen] etc. It was some fight, the best example of mob insanity that I have ever seen. It was enough to make one sick and disgusted with the masculine sex forever. Finally Frosty Speiden got up on the roof of the steps of the Dutch and made a speech urging them to go home and reminding them of the awful black eye exaggerated reports of this would give Cornell etc etc.... Today they are having Arts elections but as there is a man against me and so far I have not seen one girl voting, I think it is a pre ordained conclusion as to who is elected. I feel I have done my duty in running....

September 29, 1915. I must tell you that my grandchild is Mary Jackson, a young lady of color. I have not yet been able to see her but I must take her to prayer meeting on Thurs. night and to the Reception Friday.

Oct. 11, 1915. Tuesday being election day, oh yes, I forgot to add that I watched at the polls for an hour and distributed Suffrage literature in the good cause that went down to undeserved defeat …

Nov. 8, 1915. In the evening, Bert and her sister and I went up to Bailey Hall to a big Suffrage Meeting. Mrs. Snowdon, an Englishwoman and Mr. Graves, Editor of the *N.Y. American* spoke. The former was very good but the latter acted as if he were half intoxicated and certainly was not a very good specimen of the male of the species. Saturday was the opening of the Schoelkopf Memorial Field, the formal dedication, you know, and there was to be a … parade of all the students in the University. All classes were suspended and it was some big time. They invited "the ladies" to march too … there were about four hundred women in the parade, think of that, and then I don't know how many thousand men.

November 9, 1915. [at a Skip party for all those who did not go to the Military Hop] All the small girls went as men and took the big girls. I took Catharine Bard and everyone said that we were the prize couple there.

Mon. [Jan 14, 1916] The grippe epidemic is very bad here. The infirmary is full, there being 80 people there which is the record number since its opening. There is some talk of closing the University if a lot more cases are reported but I don't imagine it will be done. I surely hope not. There are a lot of girls sick here in Risley, but there is no room for them in the Infirmary.

[Jan or Feb 1916] The student government party was restricted to the Fair Sex alone with the exception of the Janitor.… We are quite self sufficient without any masculine additions (especially since we took to rushing the peanut) and such dances are much more fun without men.

Mar. 16, 1916. My hand seems to be getting better so I guess I can dispense with the $7.00 ex-ray photograph of it which the Dr. suggested. Imagine spending that to see the inside of one's hand.

Mar 22, 1916. I am very much worried about my future. As I can see it there are two alternatives at present for getting a job—either to go to N.Y. the end of Easter vacation and look and come direct up to Ithaca, or to wait like Mr. Macawber and go down in the summer. Mrs. Martin seems to think it would be better to go now.

March 27, 1916. In the evening went to see the *Birth of a Nation* with Mr. Guise. It was perfectly stupendous and simply beyond mere words of description but I don't think I should care to see it again. It was too harrowing and nerve wracking. The man in front of me wept buckets but I didn't even squeeze out a tear tho I came near it a couple of times.





Mar 29, 1916. I have just been elected class poetess for the Senior class. Now isn't that a little irony of life all right? Think of me being that! I shall certainly have to crib it off some old codger of ancient times. Of course I am rather puffed up about it for only two girls are elected for class day officers, the class essayist and poet.

Apr 28, 1916. All classes were suspended for the Convocation Hour at which time Charles M. Schwab, our newly appointed trustee, Pres. of Bethlehem Steel etc., spoke on "The conditions that create Success." Signe and I went to hear him but as he seemed to direct most of his remarks to male students taking M.E. we being females in Arts did not receive much encouragement. The only thing we gleaned was what we already knew, i.e., "money is not to be despised." He said it by actual count, six times.

May 2, 1916. It being May Day [yesterday] they [Sophomores] honored us by waking us up with a carol at 7:00 A.M. and hanging little May baskets on our doors. It is a very pretty custom but makes us feel like female Methusalahs, for they did the same at the Old Ladies Home.

May 4, 1916. First came the [Phi Beta Kappa] initiation in the Auditorium and then after we had been duly taken in, every one shook hands with us and we went down to the banquet in the Cafeteria. There were very few nice men with the exception of Jacob Gould Schurman Jr., son of the president, a Mr. Biefield, Editor in chief of the Annuals for next year and a Mr. Cantley, so Kate and I decided in fun that we'd have to sit with them.

May 15, 1916: On my way met Elsa Allen wandering around. Arthur was away and so she invited me to go to the tearoom for lunch with her. I accepted after some urging and we went out to Forest Home. Then ... took a long walk thru the woods. Elsa is a marvel about birds. She can just hear one about half a mile off give a faint peep and she knows exactly who he was, how he looks and everything about him. She is going to make herself as much of an authority as her husband is if she keeps on.

June 9, 1916: Kate and I were walking down to Eddy Street ... when Prof. Sampson passed. As he went by he said, "Perhaps you young ladies would be interested to know that you both received B in Eng 59." We both staggered in our tracks but managed to regain ourselves a bit and I said "Thank you," in quavering whisper while Kate gasped "How" and then stopped short.

June 12, 1916: Well I have at last severed my connection with the official blue book of the University—or in other words my last final is over and now there only remains graduation.

# HELEN BULLARD

## CLASS OF 1919

Unlike Katherine Lyon and Adelheid Zeller, who excelled at Cornell, Helen Bullard found herself in academic difficulty. Her diary entries detail her trials, but after four years she earned a degree. She became a landscape architect, worked for the New York City Parks Department, and was involved with the planning for the 1939 World's Fair.

Her college years coincided with the war that waged in Europe—a conflict whose effects reached the Cornell campus: two thousand students enrolled, special leaves were granted men going to fight, a unit of the Reserve Officers' Training Corps was established in 1916, and troops drilled on campus. There were even pup tents on the Arts Quad. Nevertheless, the war prints itself but faintly on the student record even though it thunders through the newspapers and on film. Helen's general disregard for current events gives the few comments that do appear more import. It is, of course, always so: college years are regarded as apart, and what happens elsewhere, in current student parlance, is "the real world."

Wednesday [November 28, 1917]: I work the majority of the day on Landscape. After a prolonged scolding the day before after which Mr. Montillon promised to meet me at ten he got around about twelve. I went to see Mr. Bailey and got a list of books for Kenneth to read and wrote home, felt angry with my roommate and blew every one up in turn.

Thanksgiving, Thursday, Nov. 29: This was a most peculiar holiday. I slept late, went up to Landscape to work in the morning and then went over to talk with Mary the money taker till D— who was serving potatoes was there. Then we ate lunch and went over to see Louise who was very blue about her brother. After we came home and worked. We went over to Dryden Road for tea and went to the first show at the Crescent [Theater].

Friday, Nov. 30, 1917: Though petrified at the possibilities, I dared to ask Mr. Wichelns for an appointment and got it. Work on Landscape all the rest of the day and night. Entertained Miss Baker at supper. Had a lot of fun.

Dec. 1, 1917: Dorothy went with me again to Public Speaking. The tall man we hardly noticed and still less did he notice us. I had to sit beside the man of horrors who always makes me shake and shiver. Work in the LA the most of the day. Got my problem in at six. In the meantime I had appointment at Mr. Wichelns. I told him I had little time to think of a subject and he told me I had the same twenty-four hours in a day that he had.

Dec. 3, 1917. We had what I hope is our last out of door surveying lab this afternoon. In the way of clothes I wore a gauze combination, a woolen combination, a paper jacket, a corset, a muslin combination, and a petticoat and corset covering shirt waist, suit, winter coat, shoes & stocking, golashas, gloves muff and hat. At 4 oclock we decided we were too cold to stay any longer.

Tuesday, Dec 4. Prepared for a prelim in Engineering tomorrow. This afternoon in LA 17 we went to the nursery and out to look at evergreens for the exam Thursday. In Polecon they returned our prelim papers. I got a B.

Wed. Dec 5. Took a prelim in Engineering—did not know enough about it to appreciate its difficulty. Then I went to the big lib[rary] to hunt for material on my speech "Why we need a variety of companions." I think I must be one of the forerunners in this subject for it was impossible to find any writings upon it. Then I came home, worked on my sweater and wrote home.

Thurs. Dec. 6. Today I went up to Landscape and started my new plate. I got so interested I cut Polecon. Mr. Bones decided my ideal nickname was pep. I proved to know very little about evergreens in the indoor test. Later in choir Mr. Dann called me down for my indifference. It was but a little time ago Mr. Wichelns raved in the same subject. How little they know me—another proof that I am somewhat of an actress.... We went to Sibley dog for dinner. Then I came home and got Ann's ideas on the speech.

Friday, Dec 7. Rushed all day.... Cut mass meeting, attended sorority meeting.

Sat. Dec. 8, 1917. Prelim was dreadfully long. At the end of the period up marches Mr. Wichelns and asks how many are through. No one was. He asked us to copy the questions off the board, take them home and answer them when we could. Then correct the papers with another color ink or pencil and hand in Thursday. From 8 till 12 I worked on the speech but at 12 I made an awful mess of it. I am to rewrite my outline.



Monday, Dec. 17. Started making our survey in Engineering laboratory today. We got about two lines drawn. Worked in LA at night. This was the story all the rest of the week till finally on Wednesday got my problem in.

Thurs. Dec. 20. Went to LA 17 in the afternoon and choir after that.... I fell down coming home and let a chink pick me up.

January 2 [1918]. I felt very sleepy this morning and must have showed some outward and visible signs for Prof. MacCurdy asked if I was very tired. I had only the one class so I came home, prepared some work for the next day and finished knitting.

Monday, Jan 7. I am starting in to work with a vengeance. I worked hard all day and spent the entire evening in the library. I wore the green suit for the first time to school.

Thurs. [Jan.] 10: I studied all day to day, very hard. Elsie Gutman returned my outline with a wonderful criticism. I worked in the library tonight marred by a great war between Mr. Bones & I on the subject of coeducation.

Sat. Jan 12, 18: I made a dreadful mess of my speech. I just got scared stiff. After P[ublic] S[peaking] I went up to the Drafting room.... Louise announced Olive's engagement with a five pound box of candy. Big pigs that we were we ate it nearly all. We stayed till twelve. Then we ran home. We had neglected to sign up and so had to ring the door bell and get Mrs. Smith up.

Tues. Jan 15, 18: We had a nice little party and about 12 P.M. when we were ready to come home we remembered we had not signed up so we ran to the drug store called the house and asked the girls to leave the door open.

Friday, Jan. 18. Today I was working in the drafting room except a few minutes which I was obliged to devote to appear before House Committee. They brought up numerous offenses and concluded to keep me in after eight o'clock for two weeks and after ten for a third. That will take me two weeks into next term.

Tues. Jan 22, 18. Today I took Engineering final in an ice cold room at Poultry. Then I took History of Architecture.

Wed. Jan 23. Mr. Ladd told me I got P in design and if I bust Public Speaking on top of that my heart will surely break.

Sat. Jan 26 ... went up on the hill to register. In the afternoon D and I went to sorority meeting. I was nominated together with Louise Brown as Vice President.

Mon. Jan 28, 1918. Today I began classes...I went to a Landscape construction class. After waiting around for some time Prof. Curtis found out for us we were not to have a class. In the evening I went to choir. But by far the greatest event was a talk given privately to me by Prof. Davis. He said my work had not been up to standard. They had merely passed me in junior design because they were so short of pupils. Although I have had mentions and mention 1st on all my plates they gave me accepted in the last and P for my mark in the course. He said the best thing he could do would be to bust me out and then unless I was real serious I would give it up. I told him I thought if I were not so tired all the time I could do better work, and another thing against me was the fact that I had not seen a great deal of Landscape work. I said I loved the work. He said it was one thing to be in love with the idea, another to be fitted for the work. He however said he would consent to let me continue with the work next term and if I made a go of it I could major in planting and probably get through the course.





Wed. Jan 30, 1918. Today I had my first Plant Path lab in the basement of Bailey Hall.... On my way back I stopped into Sage to see the two Betties. Betty Miller has been to see Mr. Betten about her misfortunes. He said Davis had previously called and asked if he would stand back of him if he should bust a girl out in the spring. I think that girl is me. He has it on me too. I am taking 9 hours under him. I feel that this should be attended to immediately but I do not know how to go about it.

Sat. Feb. 2. I worked in the drafting room till two except when I tangled with Cornelius Betten. He said he did not believe the bust threat was meant for me and advised me to stay on in the department. When I was coming home in the afternoon I heard a great amount of shouting behind me and two frosh grabbed me out of the way while a run away horse went dashing by dragging a snow plow. I was so startled that when it was all over I just said gracious, not even thank you.

Mar. 7, 1918: Today was quite a long one and after crew practice I was ready to go to bed. I got undressed and put up the windows. There was a wonderful Aurora Borealis in the sky. The highest part of the dome was green. Then there was red, then yellow and purple way down around the horizon. There were white rays radiating from the center toward all directions and the color in them flooded back and forth. It was a very wonderful display.

Leah Barad, class of 2007

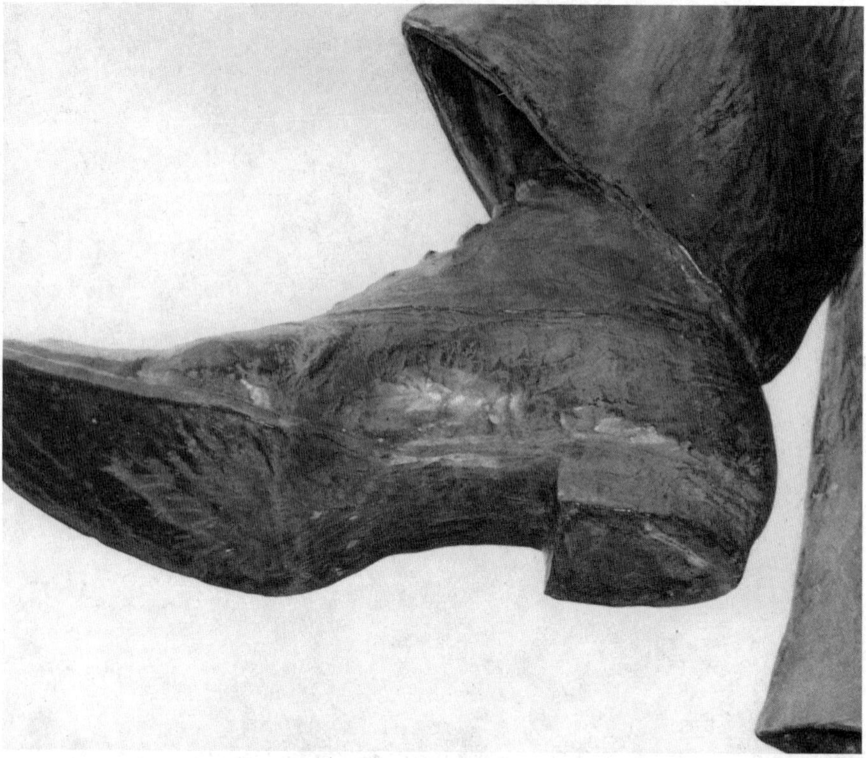

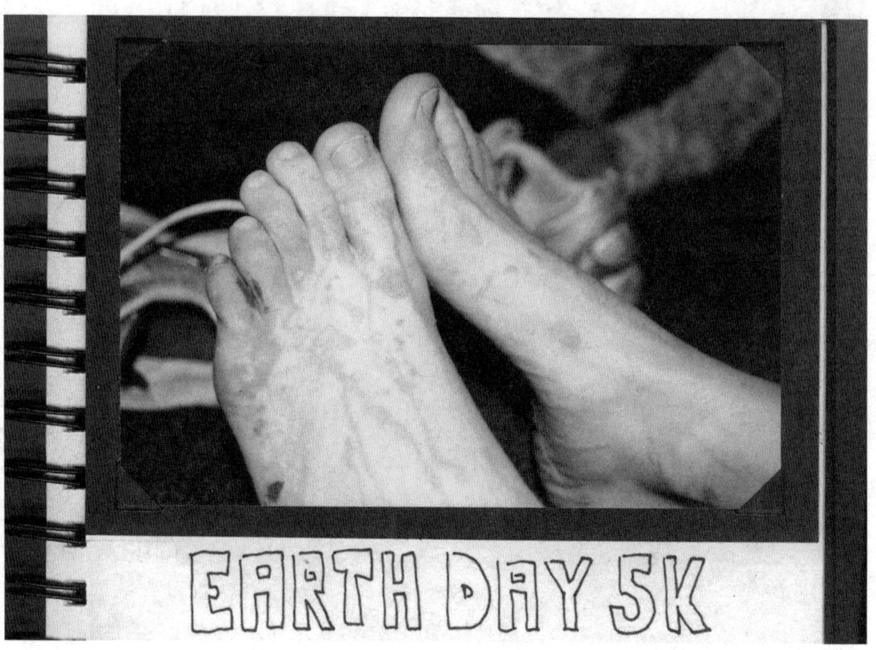


Leah Barad, class of 2007

*Above:* Devon Goodrich, class of 2007; *below:* Leah Barad, class of 2007

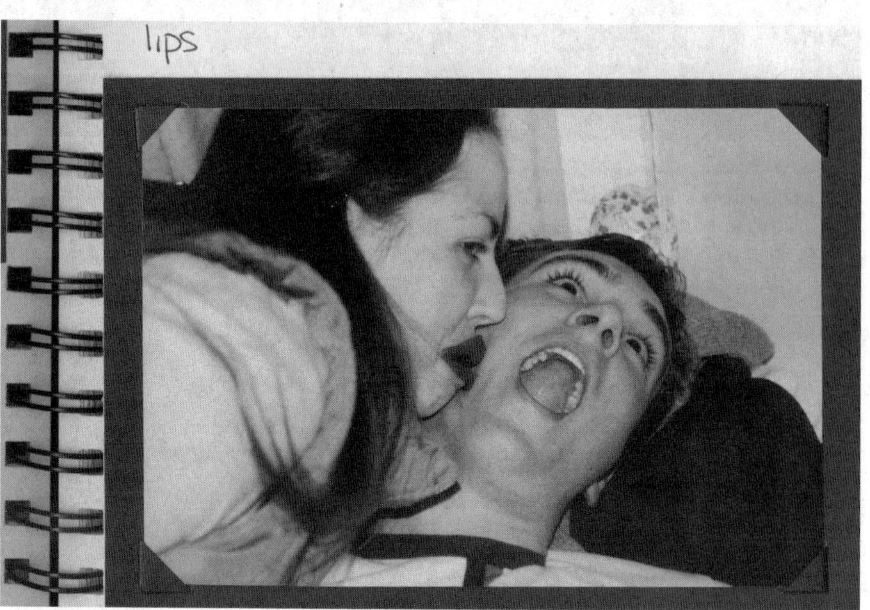


Leah Barad, class of 2007

Leah Barad, class of 2007

Leah Barad, class of 2007

*Above:* Devon Goodrich, class of 2007; *below:* Lou Robinson

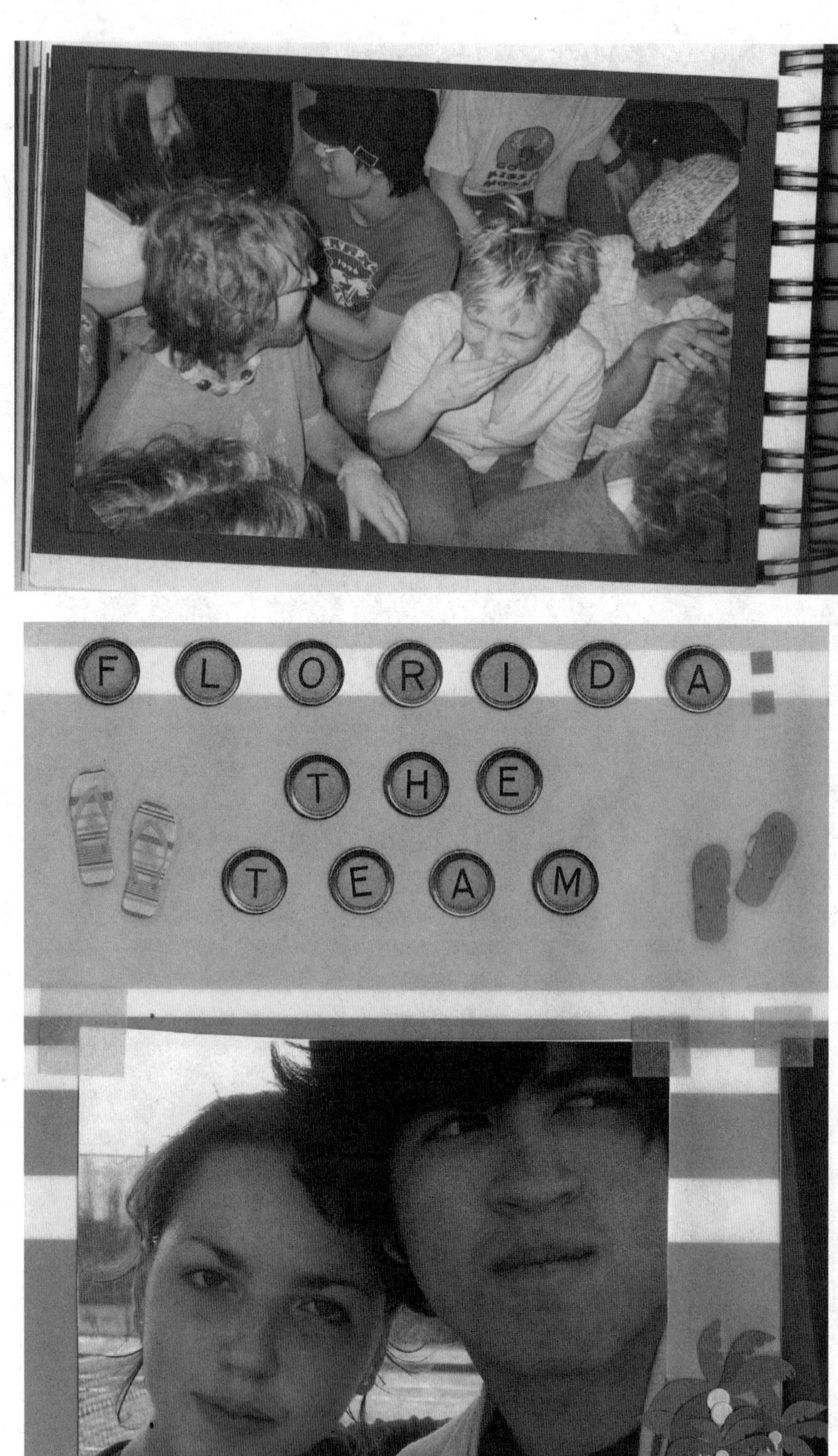


*Above:* Leah Barad, class of 2007; *below:* Devon Goodrich, class of 2007

Leah Barad, class of 2007

Leah Barad, class of 2007

# EVIE LEE CARPENTER

## CLASS OF 1918

Evie Carpenter, the granddaughter of slaves, was born in 1886 in Reva, Culpepper County, Virginia. She graduated from Manassas Industrial School and then Yonkers High School and came to Cornell in 1914 on a scholarship. Her diary entries are brief; money is scarce, and Evie works to support her studies. She graduated in 1918 with a B.A. from the College of Agriculture with an undergraduate major in chemistry. She taught at the West Virginia Collegiate Institute, was engaged in social work in Pennsylvania, and then taught at the Virginia State Normal School and the Cheyney Training School for Teachers in Pennsylvania. She taught "agricultural subjects," especially gardening and poultry management. She married in 1924 and raised three children, identifying herself thereafter as "housewife." Evie Carpenter Spencer attended her fiftieth class reunion but sent her regrets for the sixtieth. She died in 1984.

Sept. 21, 1914. Registered for Cornell

Sept. 22, 1914. Entered Sage college for R & B [room & board]

Sept. 28, 1914. Left Sage College because of lack of means to support myself there.

# HAROLD E. GULVIN

## CLASS OF 1930

Harold Gulvin came to Cornell in 1926. His letters are written to his hometown sweetheart, "Dear Alice," explaining college life to her and urging her to visit, which she seems reluctant to do. Alice was enrolled in nursing school, and it is unclear whether she ever visited Ithaca. Harold's letters discuss fraternities and his classes, and he includes interesting comments about wearing a freshman beanie. After graduation, Harold and Alice married. He taught agricultural subjects at the high school level for sixteen years, and then at the University of Rhode Island until his retirement. At his death in 1989, Gulvin donated six scholarships to the College of Agriculture.

March 6 [1927]. Willard Straight Hall is a beautiful building. It is the recreation center on the campus. It is only a little over a year old. It contains study rooms, reading rooms, clubrooms, card and billiard rooms, two large cafeterias, tea rooms and porches and a large theatre all in the same building. The whole campus is pretty these spring days.

I am taking English I this year and it certainly is deep stuff. We just finished Hawthorne's *Scarlet Letter* and Hardy's *Return of the Native.* They are both good books. We are now going to study *Nicholas Nickelby* and the second volume of *Beowulf to Hardy*, which is mostly poems. I have three prelims this week. We have prelims here most any time and not at certain times as in high school. If I take French next year I would complete an equivalent to your years work in one term here. They have a system here of cramming knowledge into you in a short time. Educating and learning is the chief object of the University.



[March, 1927] I saw a funny sight to-night and I am going to tell you about it just to show you something of college life and what the freshmen have to put up with. Well *he* was all bandaged up, fake bandages I guess, though. He looked like the remains of a wreck. He was walking across the corner when I saw him and I noticed a large placard which was about two feet square hanging in front of him. It had these words on it "I won't wear my frosh cap." Upon looking at his back I saw another similar card with these words in large size, "I am like this because I didn't wear my frosh cap."

This might not mean much to you or appear funny to you. It made me laugh. You probably have never seen a freshman cap. It is like a baseball cap only about one third as big. It is a problem to keep them on and in raining weather one thousand upturned brows are damped. This only goes to show how some of our college traditions are enforced. I have learned my lesson. I came nearer than I care to go again to a tubing with my clothes on once when I didn't wear my frosh cap when I went down town.

April, 14, 1927. We are studying the Trillium and the tulip in Botany now. The Trillium is the flower found so much in the woods ... with three white leaves or occasionally with red leaves. We have studied everything from a simple one-celled plant to a pine tree in Botany this term. In Geology a while ago, Prof. Rees mentioned Canandaigua Lake in his lecture. Sometimes the lecturers work jokes in their lectures and cause some fun, which makes them all the more interesting. Most of my lecturers are pretty good-natured.

April 25, 1927. I had my name in the *Cornell Daily Sun* last Wednesday as being one of the high men in rifle practice. If I keep it up I will shoot in the match on May 7th. We shoot three big army rifles. I came home last Tuesday with my face all black from the oil on the guns.... I have just returned from a field trip in Geology. It was a little bit windy and cold, otherwise we had a good trip. This is funny weather, this morning it snowed hard for half an hour. In the field trip we visited or walked about the campus, taking note of the stone used in the buildings. We walked along the Fall Creek gorge and noted the geological features. Next week we go to Portland Point in buses.

Oct. 12, 1927. I don't believe I told you that I am a member of the Varsity Cross-country team now.

[November 3, 1927] Now to tell you a little about initiating. You see my house [Alpha Gamma Rho] has pledged 7 or 8 men to become members and this is "Hell Week" for them. They have to stay & live here at the house for three days, tomorrow is the last. They have to enter the house thru the basement and then stand at the bottom step and yell "Hail thee, Hail thee, this lowly neophyte [his name] desires to enter the house of his noble lords." If he don't say it just right or loud enough he had to do it over again.

Each pledge or frosh has to carry a whiskbroom and a shoe shining set with him. He must shine his lord's shoes. (I had mine shined yesterday) Also he must carry cigarettes and candy with him. They have 12 rules in all and they must name any rule when asked. There is one lowly neophyte in my room. He is supposed to be the scum in the room. He has gone to bed now.... The pledges were lined up and eggs were thrown to them. The first one to drop an egg was to be tubbed. It wasn't long before one of them dropped one and us sophomores took off our clothes leaving only an old pair of trousers on. Six of us rushed the lowly neophyte, dragged him downstairs and into the tub full of ice water. He splashed around so that we all got wet and some one closed the bathroom door leaving us in there to get wet. It was great fun although it might seem unfair for six of us to pick on one scum but the more we have the less wet we get.

[November 9, 1927] Friday night was the night though. That was rough house night and it certainly was rough alright. One of the neophytes had to enter the house singing some song, he was blindfolded and was asked some questions and then plunged into the black depths of.... a blanket held by some fellows who tossed it up. From thence he undressed and was taken upstairs and put through some more torture as jumping on spikes, lying on an electric bed and singing and some other things which I don't believe I should tell you (seeing that you are of the opposite sex).

[December 2, 1927] Did you ever hear of the absented-minded professor who put his umbrella to bed and stood in the sink all night or the one who put the cat to bed and himself outdoors?

Did you ever see a Chinese piano? It is a small instrument with keys, which press on two strings. One of my roommates, Steve, can play it good. We spent several hours to-day listening to music. These are some of things you can't get anywhere but in college and what brings recollections back to you some day.

Jan. 18, 1928. I went to chapel last Sunday and the sermon was not very good. Cornell is supposed to be the godless college but a lot of students go to church. The chapel is non-sectarian, or anyone can go.

May 31, 1928. Well there is one other thing that I might tell you about. It was quite some time, referring to the Frosh cap burning. We put up a good fight for the number we had. About eight o'clock four sophomores from here went to a meeting of the sophomores on the upper campus behind some building. We could only congregate about 20–30 sophs while the Frosh across the road and in the field were increasing in the hundreds. Making things kind of uneven. They hadn't gotten any wood yet either which we could capture. We hunted through the Forestry & Poultry building for fire hose in order to extinguish the fire when they started it. Worse luck just as we had four pieces fastened together ready to take outside a policeman showed up, sat on it, and said he would arrest any one who touched it. Well we fooled around for a while, the sophomores on a little hill and the Frosh across the street. It was getting quite dark and they wouldn't quite see how few we were. They didn't attack at first but finally got brave enough to. Well in that first rush I lost my clothes unfortunately, and the sophs. who weren't stripped had to seek cover by running away to some of the buildings. I finally found my shirt and put that on but it didn't stay on. Then the Frosh lit their fire, sang songs and had speeches. Well somebody uncovered another fire hose and just as the Frosh were making another attack some other fellows and myself screwed the bore on the hydrant and turned it on, but what a time, the hose leaked badly, and streams of water came out of the sides as well as the nozzle. Everybody near got wet. The water from the hose made a big pool of mud and that's where several got a good cool muddy bath. We could strip the Frosh without fear of being stripped ourselves. We literally tore the clothes off of them. Fellows were running around without anything on and the upperclassmen and their girl friends seemed to enjoy it. There were plenty of cars around to make it quite light. The ground was simply strewn with torn clothes. Finally the frosh left.

Oct. 14, 1928. Went to the show last night just to hear all the noise. You should have heard it, I wish you could have. Of all the screeching, yelling, singing, clapping, hissing you ever heard. The manager appeared on the stage about seven different times and tried to speak but the noise would grow louder when he came on the stage. He wanted them to quit throwing things on the stage as it might cause an accident. The vaudeville was fairly good, it had to be, only you couldn't hear, just see. When one girl sang "now ain't she sweet" the whole student audience joined in and sang it. Between the shows we furnished our own singing. Once the manager came out and threatened not to go on with the show and he had the curtain pulled down for a while, when the whole audience said "I want my money back" and he had to go on with the show, although the two last performances were incomplete.

Dec. 9, 1928. Len and I went to the new "State Theater" downtown Friday night. It is a dandy theater. Something like the Rochester only of entirely different architecture. Part of the ceiling has about 60 coat of arms of universities. Then there are stars, which twinkle all the time like real ones.

Yes, I guess a college fellow in a co-educational institute can know quite a few girls, but perhaps about two dozen or so is about all that I know, which is very small when there is about a thousand in the University. I probably know about a hundred fellows I guess by name and sight.

Mar. 26, 1929. Had a make up lab yesterday and a make up prelim also. This psychology course is quite interesting especially the laboratory we have. French prelim Thursday and I bet I will bust it. I had one prelim coming tomorrow but it was postponed.... I haven't been working in almost three weeks at the Poultry building as yet. I think I will work there to-morrow afternoon. I haven't had a ultra-violet ray treatment [for tonsils] in quite a while either. I bought a new tie at S and Roebuck and just put it on this afternoon.

April 9, 1929. Well, I have started in studying already. Say, I got a C in French, which is not so bad eh? I didn't study at all for it either. I am having one in Psychology this Friday. We had a funny laboratory in it this afternoon. We had sixteen stars and a mirror. We looked in the mirror while someone held a paper over the star between your eyes and it and we had to draw a line all the way around the star between two lines. If you touched either line or crossed it, it was an error. The first two were with the right hand and it took me 2′10″ to draw around it and I had 21 errors. The eleventh one I did with my left hand I did in 30 seconds with only two errors. The last two were with my right hand and I could do as well with my right hand although I hadn't practiced with it. I think I will have you try it sometime.

May 15, 1929. Two Cornell students were drowned in Lake Cayuga last Saturday. Their bodies have not been found yet. They were paddling a canoe and it must have swamped with them. Cayuga Lake is awfully cold and very deep and they just didn't stand a chance.

May 21, 1929. I have a final on the 4th, 6th, 8th and 10th of June. One each day so I have a day to study between each one. Ah! say, I got a B in the French prelim I look that morning. I think my marks will be pretty good this term. I hope so as I want to graduate next year.

May 23, 1929. There was a "Battle of Ithaca" to-day here northeast of Ithaca. Cannons bombed and soldiers marched. It was a sham battle between two divisions of the R.O.T.C., I didn't take part as I am all through with drill. It sounded just like war probably would.

Sept. 21 [1929]. I have been figuring out a schedule of classes. I am afraid I won't have any afternoons to work in this term. I am going to have classes every afternoon and on Saturday. I hope, if I have a son that he won't have to work his way all the way. It is going to make this last [year] extra hard I am afraid, especially this term. I am ready to dig in though.

Say but it is hard trying to figure out what to take. Some things you can't take because it comes at same time as some other course. I would like to specialize in something.... What I need then is a job to get experience.

Then of course there is teaching, but I don't think I will have enough educational subjects if I follow out my present schedule. Then I could be a farm Bureau Agent but they only get $125 a month.

Sept. 25, 1929. The new girls dormitories [Balch Halls] are finished now, except for the landscaping. They certainly look good. The university is also building some new men's dormitories. A big new plant or Botany building is nearing completion also.

Sept. 28, 1929. Well I have been to all of my classes. So far I have got to buy five textbooks which will mean some money. One afternoon a week I have to go up to Trumansburg and get experience on teaching. I don't know whether I am going to teach or not but at least I am going to be prepared to. I got acquainted or tried to with the bacteria yesterday afternoon. In public speaking next Wednesday we have to give a speech on the country Church. I am afraid maybe I won't like that course although it will probably benefit me.

Sept. 30, 1929. I spent $9.20 for three books today. Gee at that rate it won't be long now, before I'll be broke. And that isn't a half of them.

Friday the 13th [December 1929]. I am really beginning to enjoy teaching agriculture, it is so different from ordinary teaching, there is so much to do that the time just flies. I help with the classroom work now and help in the field trips. I was up there to Trumansburg most of Tuesday and most of Thursday. I had a terrible time getting back to Ithaca that night. It rained on the windshield and froze and it would not come off or stay off and it was almost impossible to drive on that account and because the roads were so slippery. It took me almost an hour coming from Trumansburg to Ithaca, only 14 miles.

## J. S. FINCH

### CLASS OF 1931

From the very first, Cornell students created a rich student life, publishing journals and newspapers, producing dramatic and musical events, and forming clubs and Greek letter organizations. Some student clubs were open to anyone interested in joining, others were by invitation only, and a few were secret. The following is a typed invitation, received April 1929 by J. S. Finch, Cornell class 1931.

This is to inform you that you have been elected to the Majura Club and to make you ready for the initiation which will be held Saturday, April 20. You will observe the following conditions;

1. The initiation fee of twenty five dollars must be sent to J. D. Waterbury at the PSI U house before 4:30 Friday, April 10.

2. You will be on silence on Saturday, the 20th.

3. You will report to the Psi U. house at 3 o'clock of the 20th bringing the following articles:

1. A lantern.
2. A roll of adhesive tape.
3. A pointed stick exactly 3 feet long.
4. Three one quart cups.

Show this letter to no one.

# MARY ELIZABETH FESSENDEN

## CLASS OF 1936

Mary "Fessy" Fessenden came to Cornell in 1932 in a class of 1,214 students, of whom 292 were women. She types weekly letters home, which were collected in four bound notebooks. Mary is enthusiastic about her classes in math and chemistry, which she thought would interest her father, a professor of engineering at Rensselaer Polytechnic Institute. "Sister," as she was known in her family, is active in a sorority, in dorm life, in the Women's Athletic Association, and as a costume maker for the Dramatic Club. She has many friends but rooms primarily with Mary "Pony" Horsley, whose classes coincide with hers; they study together and join the same sorority. She mentions dating, though she takes none of the young men very seriously.

Mary Fessenden was at Cornell during the days of the Depression. She is careful about her finances. She and her friends earn money by developing photographs for other women; some students, she notes, have problems paying their bills. She also mentions the closing of the banks in February 1933. This was the era of Prohibition as well, and Mary describes having to sign a pledge not to drink the alcohol used in the chemistry lab.

Sept. 25, 1932. My roommate has just arrived and is now unpacking.... Allegra seems very nice on five minutes' acquaintance.... Finished getting my trunk unpacked and can't find room for everything. Went to church with some Lutheran girls for want of something better to do.... Somebody or other thought that the girls in Sage weren't getting enough ice-cream so she donated some money for the purpose, so we have a choice of ice cream or "what have you" about every meal. We haven't been assigned tables in the dining room, yet. We just sort of land somewhere.



Sept. 29, 1932. Registration was some jam, even worse than the Pan-Hell. We stood in line in the basement of Goldwin Smith for about three hours and then had to go chasing class assignments in about ten different buildings, as well as our faculty advisors. Mine is very nice. He teaches Economics and is really very patient and long suffering, considering the dumb questions I (and other '36s, I suppose) ask him.... Classes started this morning. I have German six times a week at 8 A.M! The professor is quite a lot of fun. Almost all our books are written by Cornell professors, so they won't be kicking about "what the book says" like the E[mma] W[illard] teachers like to do. We had Chem. recitation. I got along O.K. until he asked me to define kinetic energy. However, no one else seemed to know anything. He fires questions at you until you miss one and I disposed of about four. No one else withstood more than two. We had Hygiene this morning, too, but it seems to be more like Biology than anything else. I am taking English three times a week and it seems to be English Lit. all over again. We have to read Chaucer, which isn't so bad, because I always sort of liked him anyway: I couldn't get any French or Math in this term. Do you think one term of German would be enough? It's supposed to correspond with a two-year high school course. I have Chem. lab this P.M. Sports don't start till next week, but I've got my red rompers.... President Farrand spoke to us last night in Sibley dome. It was a pretty good speech. There [are] about 400 Freshmen girls and about 5500 altogether in the U.

Oct 10, 1932. As to the tuition, etc., I had to pay $137, including tuition for this term, lab fees, etc, etc. I had to pay $100 tuition because the $100 from the state scholarship comes from the state and has not yet been sent here. So when it does come, I'll just get $100 to put in the bank. I have about $20 now.

October 16, 1932. Thursday we had a W[omen's] A[thletic] A[ssociation] picnic on Cayuga Lake. Three of us from our corridor went, Pony (otherwise Eleanor Horsey), Ruth Sharp, and myself. We got ambitious and wore knickers, high shoes, etc. We had lots of fun, only it was cold. We ate hot dogs and doughnuts, mainly, sang songs and had stunts. Thursday evening, after we came home, I went to a Cosmopolitan Club meeting with Mary Tillinghast. It was very interesting. A very nice little Japanese girl is president. There are not very many Americans in it, but Mary is going to join and maybe I shall too. Mary is majoring in Government and is a very serious minded individual. I like her very much.

Oct. 31, 1932. I don't know about the posture picture; I had mine two weeks ago and have heard nothing of it since.... At dinner last night we had a baby party. I wore my white ducks and a middy blouse, which was supposed to be a small boy in a sailor suit. It was fun ... T[illinghast] and I have taken to going places together, partly because we are about the only "independents" (non-sorority) girls on the corridor and also about the only two without half a dozen male admirers hanging around—for which we are thankful.

Nov. 18, 1932. I got 90 on a Chem. prelim, which could be improved upon, according to Mr. Schofield. The girls had it all over the boys again.... Thursday night I went to Cosmopolitan Club with Tillinghast, and afterwards to a reception for foreign students at Barnes Hall. Some Germans sang German songs, some Swedes Swedish songs, etc. It was quite a lot of fun and interesting.... If you're fifteen minutes late [returning to the dormitory], you lose one night out, so we can't go anywhere after 9:30 next week. That isn't bad, because we weren't intending to anyway, and it's mostly vacation, but we do have to account for our actions before the House Committee on our corridor.



Dec. 4, 1932. I've gotten all my mid-term marks except German. I got B in English, 92 in Chem. lectures and 88 in lab. We all came through all right except Pony. She is on pro[bation]. And consequently hasn't been seen with her nose out of a book for a week. I found out last night that if you get 90 in Chem lecture prelims, you don't have to take finals. Hereafter I'm going to study Chemistry. Had another English conference with Marx, but he didn't say anything of interest, except to tell me that B was really a very good mark.

Dec. 10, 1932. Allegra and I have a new occupation. We take walks after dark and explore the campus. It's more fun. We went way up to the Ag. College, once and all kinds of places. Wednesday evening we went up the library tower where they play the chimes, while the chimes were playing. The tower seemed nearly as high as the Washington Monument. The chimes made so much noise we couldn't hear each other. It was very exciting and lots of fun.

Tuesday night I went to hear Amelia Earhart. She was good. She spoke very informally and not too technically. She didn't brag, either. She showed some moving pictures, both of her own flying and flying in general.

Jan. 14, 1933. Peggy Taylor, a junior and a sorority sister of Pony's, advises us to steer clear of all foreigners, especially Russians.

Jan 21, 1933. Pony and I decided to get up early and go to Sage Chapel to hear a rabbi, because neither of us had ever heard one. We woke up when the chimes began to play hymns just before the service.

Feb. 3, 1933. We had a new arrangement the other day—practically everyone more or less against Pony on the subject of the equality of the negro ...

Feb. 18, 1933. We were going skating this morning, but the red ball is down. In case you don't get me, I will explain. When there is skating there is a sign with a big red circle on it stuck in front of the trolleys, like movie notices. When the sign is up, we know there is skating. It was up yesterday, so we decided to go, but now it is down.

Pony and I are the only girls in our chem. Rec. section, but he wouldn't let us sit together. Wise guy! ... There are only eight girls in the whole U. taking Qual. this term, four of them being Pony, Mickey, Case and myself.... In the physics lab, they put all the girls in one section and in one room. We can pick out our own partners. But in chem. we all have the same lab. at the same time, but we are arranged alphabetically, with about six instructors each having a different section. So I'm the only girl in mine.

Also got my term marks! A in Chem. 101, B in 105, B in English, B in German, 73 in Hygiene, and 75 in Gym. And here I thought I was on the verge of busting German! Do you realize that's the first B I've ever gotten in a language as a term mark?



I have just begun to notice the large amount of walking I have to do to get to classes. I have every subject in a different building.

[At a lecture] I didn't notice that Mrs. Buck looked particularly high colored, but we were so far back that we really couldn't tell. She wore a rather bright blue suit and hat, and was a great improvement over Mrs. Roosevelt.

Thanks for the check, although I didn't need it after all, because the scholarship one came today. However, if the banks continue as they seem to be doing now, the extra fifty will come in handy. Anyway, my tuition is paid, which is more than some people can say. The paper says that they aren't going to make any particular provision for people from states where the banks are closed, although Pony managed to get an extension of time.

I think I have enough money to last 'til the end of May. I have about $12 in the bank (much good that does!), a $50 check from the university, and about $25 in cash. I told you the lucky break I had in being able to cash Daddy's check at the Co-op about two days before the banks closed.

Sunday A.M. [September 1933]. Registration was in the Drill Hall, which was a great improvement over Goldwin Smith basement. It took us about five minutes to do what took about four hours last year. Of course, we did come in the back way and land at the head of the line, and proceeded to chisel our way through a whole ten minutes before we were even supposed to start.

Pony and I are the only girls in the [Chemistry] class, and he stuck one of us at one end of the lab and the other at the other end. More fun!

Mary and I went to Cos[mopolitan] Club. The meeting was held to disband the club, so there ain't no sich animele now. There's no point to it, because there are no foreign students. So that's that.

Oct. 14, 1933. Thursday I enjoyed the chem, delightful experience of being the only girl in the chem. class, because we decided that Pony should stay in bed. I got pretty well on my way with the next experiment, which was very nice except that maybe it isn't right.

To return to the laundry, I can just as well iron it here, if that would help any. The point is that people here just don't have it done outside, because Student Agencies have charge of the whole business and gyp you like the dickens, and we're not allowed to hire outside laundresses (University ruling). So there you are.

Jan. 27, 1934. I found both Daddy and Uncle Charlie in an imposing volume labeled "American Men of Science" under the title of "Engineers." Just you wait, maybe I'll be in there someday too.

February 3, 1934. I figured that I got 76 on the [chemistry] final, but one problem that counted ten and that I thought I had right was wrong. Our cards came in the other day. I got 65 on the final and an 80 in the course, which is very provoking, as I must have had a 90 average before that. Pony made a 43 on the final with a 62 in the course, which, I am afraid, is some my fault. Anyway, I got 70 in lab., and she got 80, which has nothing much to do with it. And so that was that.... Pony thinks that we should take some education courses. You absolutely do have to have some 18 hours of education to teach in most states, including New York, under some new law or other. We don't want to teach, but decided that we had better be prepared for the worst. But that will give us twenty hours, for which Pony is going to petition because she's got to take everything else too. I can't picture myself teaching, anyhow, and hate to waste time on such courses any way, so I don't think I'll try it. I thought, that if absolutely necessary, when I finished here, and if I couldn't get a chemist job, I could get enough Ed. Courses in Albany in a year.... What do you think?



Feb. 18, 1934. Prof. Stephenson called me over to his office the other day. I went with fear and trembling, but all he had to say was that I could have an A in history next term, if I wanted it (oh yeah). And the nice part about that is that the second term's mark is the one that counts for the course, that is, the final exam in June gives you your mark for the year, provided you haven't done anything awful during the course of various prelims, so that would cancel out the 87. The same system works in French but the trouble is that my French instructor this term is a good deal stiffer than the one I had last term. Maybe you have heard of him; he wrote a book a while ago, and sometimes writes poems and things for the *New York Times*, and his name is Morris Bishop.... I have hooked myself up with Advanced Quant., and my old pal Joe is the instructor. I am the only girl in the class, and most of the others are grads or seniors.

Feb. 24, 1934. I sailed in[to class] yesterday alone in my glory, and one boy said, "Ssh, fellows, no swearing now."

Mar. 2, 1934. Tuesday I spent most of my time in chem. Lab. as usual. It is quite fun, as I am managing to keep well up by going one or two extra lab. periods a week. And the chief reason I'm taking this course, aside from the general fact that I like Analytical Chemistry, is because I got such a punk mark in elementary Quant. I decided that this would be good practice. I haven't turned in any results yet, but I have two tin oxide experiments that check within .015%, and if he doesn't like that I would like to know what he wants for his money. The boys all seem to accept my presence in the class quite philosophically.

Well, since yesterday was Thursday, I parked myself in the Chem. lab. I spent most of the morning chasing some alcohol around. First I had to go to the office, get a permit, get it signed by the first big shot I could find wandering around loose, take it back, get an alcohol book, trot it around to said big shot to get him to sign a ticket which says that you may have 100 ml. of alcohol if you promise not to drink it.

I have about come to the definite conclusion not to take any Ed. Courses here, at least not for some time. Peggy says that I wouldn't be able to get any practice teaching in chem here, as the boys get first choice, as they have to teach in Ithaca High.



Mar. 9, 1934. I shall start off in the middle of things like Mother did, and answer the charge about ski-pants first. Supposing the thermometer were wandering down around zero, and you had an eight o'clock class miles and miles away across of campus stuck up on top of a hill with all the gales in the state blowing across it and making drinks in your overshoes, and you had a nice warm pair of ski pants, what would you do??? Well, *we* would wear ski pants. No kidding, the freaks were the ones who didn't. Usually it would be warm by about eleven, so that people that started out then didn't wear them, although one morning I was waiting for a trolley at eleven, and counted twelve in less than five minutes. One 'specially cold day Pat Pennock said that the Sigma Kappa chaperon wouldn't let them out without ski-pants on ... Also, in this here college one can do almost anything one pleases, sorority or no sorority, without exciting comment. So there.

Sept. 29, 1934. It is getting harder and harder to major in chem. in Arts, and more people want to do it. Zoology is fun—so far. We had to investigate a frog, both dead and alive. Dr. Mekeel is the first woman professor I've had, except for hygiene. She is a good friend of Pony's aunt, so we ought to get somewhere ... Thursday: It was sort of exciting when a live frog jumped out of his jar, but Miss Mekeel persuaded him to get back in.... Organic chem isn't bad so far—all we've done is determine a few melting points. There are several other girls to keep us company for a change.... We have a new cook—negro—and is she good! Also we pay her two thirds as much as we did the one last year.

Oct. 7, 1934. Organic chem is pretty easy, I think, mostly memory and nothing much to figure out for ourselves, however, the prof. wears coral nail polish. There are about six or eight girls in the section, for a change.... Tuesday we had a physics lab. in which we had to measure the length of the floor of the physics lab. ten times, just to prove that we aren't as accurate as we thought we were, I guess. There are three girls altogether in the section, but there is another course, the elementary B. Chem, physics, which is in the same lab. There is one girl in that, a Hawaiian frosh Bio. Chem who is the granddaughter of the last Queen of Hawaii. We have been rushing her.

Oct. 21, 1934. I went to a two-hour education class with Pony, given by Kurt Lewin, who got kicked out of Germany by Mr. Hitler. He was pretty interesting, what I could understand, but I see where it's practically impossible to take notes, and since there is no textbook, Pony seems to be in a pretty bad way.

Dec. 8, 1934. Don't you think that something is wrong either with the marking system or the method of teaching when the class average is either busting or just above it, especially when the majority of people are taking the course because they want to, I mean as a major or related to their major?? Anyhow, I'm getting awfully tired of getting sixties and seventies, when there is nothing much we can do about it.

Jan. 26, 1935. Tell Eleanor [her younger sister, a student at Russell Sage College] and her gang that even here, where there are supposed to be fewer and more lenient rules for girls than there are in any other college, the Freshmen have to be in by 9:30 every night except for two nights a week when they can stay out until 12. And nobody, not even seniors, can stay out until 12:30 unless it is an informal dance, or until 1:30 unless it is a formal. Maybe that'll squelch them. And we don't think much of boys who disregard rules and won't get the girls in on time. Most people seem to find that they have sufficient time to enjoy themselves in as is.



Feb. 16, 1935. Monday morning I got a big thrill; I didn't get up until 8:30. This is the first term since I've been in this university that I haven't had eight o'clock classes every day, and now I only have three.

Mar. 3, 1935. Bill has come around every day after his lab. To help (?) me clean up—also to get Physics's assignments when he cuts class. Anyhow, what's the good of going out with a boy in the evening if you're with him all day in labs and classes, 'cause we do have to study sometime. As Pony would say, all our friendships are very "Plutonic." As I think I've said before, everyone who goes out at all goes steady, and the rest of us can't take the time and energy to cultivate one. Most of us don't even bother when someone wants a blind [date].

Sept. 29, 1935. Went to see Johnson [her adviser] and he informed me that I was eligible to graduate with honors, provided I took some awful sort of a comprehensive exam in the spring, and that I don't bust any thing this year, I suppose. I guess I'd better do it, but I don't like the prospect—of the exam, I mean.

Friday morning we had a phys. Chem. Lecture. It sounds as though we might have to do some work in that course. Also advanced inorganic. Then I had to cart all the drawing stuff up to the Dairy Building in the rain. It's only a mile from here. However, it is worth it, because it's lots of fun. I'm beginning to think I should have been an architect, maybe.... Yesterday morning we had a phys. Chem lab. And spent most of the morning attempting to measure the surface tension of water. For once there are as many girls in the class as boys.

Dec. 15, 1935. Tuesday we had microscopy lab, as usual. We arrived early, and Prof. Mason jumped on us, and asked us what we thought we were going to do along about next June. We told him that we would sort of like jobs as chemists somewhere or other. He tried to squelch us by telling us that they didn't want lady chemists, but it didn't work. In the course of the conversation I told him I knew Catherine Gallagher, which seemed to impress him considerably. But he reminded us that the nearest she was to getting a job in chemistry was marrying her instructor. He ended up by advising us to do likewise, only not necessarily an instructor. Maybe we should have taken him up on that, but he's already married.

Jan. 26, 1936. I went to see Prof. Johnson to get him to sign my petition to register in the graduate School next term. He signed it all right, but said that chances were pretty slim, since they have stiffened up in their entrance requirements since he told me he thought I could do it. The catch seems to be that I still have one term of Phys. Chem. to finish, and also they don't want a lot of people starting in who won't finish up their work for their M.A. right off. Anyway, the petition is in the hands of the committee now.

At present we are having another war with Mrs. Powell. On the very coldest day, she announced that we couldn't wear wool socks, over our stockings [or] even, sport shoes, or sweaters and skirts to dinner. Then she up and went to New York, leaving the poor Vice-Presidents to enforce rules they don't like any better than we do. It wouldn't be so bad if the meal was worth dressing for, but who wants to get all dressed up to go and eat a boiled dinner, consisting of one cold boiled potato, 1 cold carrot, 1 ditto turnip, 1 large pile of cold boiled cabbage with a piece of partially corned beef that would be a disgrace to any cow draped over it?? However, since people are continuing to wear sweaters, flat shoes, and socks, I guess she will have to back down.

Feb. 2, 1936. The big excitement around here now is that Gil Dobie has resigned, which you've probably read about in the paper by now. Now we'll see if it's his fault or the team's fault.

Feb. 9, 1936. I went over to see Prof. Browne, whom you may have heard of before, anyhow he teaches inorganic chemistry. He had called up the day before when I wasn't around, so I went to see what he wanted. It seems he had gotten a letter from the next-to-the-head of the Chemistry department at Smith College, a former Cornellian, stating that there were some vacant assistantships there, and asking him for suggestions. Prof. Browne suggested that I write to him if I were interested, which I did. I figured that a mere Senior should not turn up her nose at anything. At any rate, it would give me a chance to get started on my M.A., if nothing else, oh yes, tuition and $600.00 I don't particularly relish the prospect of teaching in a girls' school, but probably nothing will come of it anyway.

Feb. 16, 1936. Thursday. I decided that we would go and hear Mrs. Roosevelt, which we did. It was so crowded that they put some chairs on the stage and let us sit there. We almost expected to be asked to speak too. The only trouble was that after Mrs. R. got through about eight other women, presidents of the W.C.T.U., Woman's club, Parent Teachers, Grange, etc. etc. etc. had to speak and we couldn't get up and walk out like most of the audience did. That night we went to the Armory to swim in the new pool.

March 1, 1936. I know you fellows don't like to make up your minds so far ahead of time, but people are already making reservations for graduation week. Commencement is on Monday, June 15, so any time you decide definitely when and how many of you are coming, I'll try and get something better than the Clinton House.

May 17, 1936. Not a sign of a job for next year. The boys in Chemistry are making out pretty well, but the girls are all in a bad way. One, a Phi Bete, has a job at the experiment station in Geneva until January, but she lives there and knows all the people. Another applied for a job somewhere and was told that they would let her work there for the experience, if she could bring her own microscope, because they didn't have one. The rest of us, as far as I know, haven't gotten that far.

I finished up in foods lab, and checked out, after assuring Prof. Cavanaugh that it was a very nice course, at which point he said he was very happy. He is a funny old duck. He graduated from here in 1889 and has been here ever since. He has much more fun telling us about how they used to run the university than he does about chemists.

# ARTHUR K. WESSELS

## CLASS OF 1941

Arthur Wessels's letters provide full accounts of his life at the university, his work for his fraternity, and his relations with his family. He pays relatively little attention to world events, nor is he overly concerned about his finances. His language echoes the era, as if from a 1930s movie; he uses "swell" and other current slang liberally. His comment on All-American football player Brud Holland is particularly interesting. Arthur reports on class rivalry, and the riots he describe mark the end of that tradition. Wessels graduated in the top ten percent of his Cornell class of 1,464. After graduation, he took a position with Union Carbide and was exempted from military service because his work was deemed "essential to the war effort." In his letters Arthur mentions Barby Hamber, whom he married in 1942; he also mentions her sister Janet Hamber, whose letters appear later in this collection. Arthur Wessels died in 1993.

September 28, 1937. Monday morning started a day I shall never forget. At 8:00 A.M. rushing started. There must have been twenty boys at my door and I spent an hour in interviewing them and making dates for their frats. Then I went up to register. Dad, you sure got me in one H--L of a mess. I'm not in the college of engineering at all, but am in Arts and Sciences. I had to get a transfer and I was running around the campus from 9:30 until 5:30. Even then I had to go back again and finish up this morning. What a time I had!

October 1, 1937. Rushing is practically over. There is one fraternity that I think is tops. I'm not going to mention the name until I've given you a fair idea of the financial part of it. The initiation fee of $100 is not due until June if need be. I think that $100 is average for this fee. As a Freshman I would eat both lunch and dinner at the house, and the charge per month for those meals is $32. In my budget you allotted me $360 for meals. This would come to $256, leaving over $100 for breakfast through the year. Also as a Freshman I pay dues of $8.00 per month. Another thing—these monthly installments of $40 (32 board and 8 dues) is paid only for eight months of the year. Lastly there is a social fee of $25 for the entire year. They say only $20, but probably an extra five would be added, so we counted it as $25. So my total expense for my Frosh year would be $445 including board, dues, initiation fee, and I would be free to use the house from 7 A.M. to 8:30 P.M. If you wish any further idea of the financial standing of the house just call up Harold Gilmore, because it is Sigma Chi.... There are several other frats that have bid me...Alpha Tau Omega bid me tonight. I like the fellows immensely, but the house is slightly dilapidated.



October 14, 1937. Last Monday classes started and everything went well until, at the end of math period, Mr. Galbraith informed us that we would have a prelim Wednesday. Mr. Cooper next period announced Physics quizz, and not to be outdone by the others, Mr. Newkirk assigned a test in Chemistry. However, all that is a thing of the past now. When that horrible Wednesday came I was about ready to die, because there were to be my first tests in college. However, I weathered the storm quite well, for I pulled down an 85 in Calculus prelim, a 100 in Physics, and an 80 in two Chemistry quizzes. Also I was put in the upper section in English. However, I'll only have to work harder now ...

Today in Chem. Lab. we had to experiment with a highly explosive gas—hydrogen. Mr. Burke called us together before going to the lab. And gave us a pep talk which amounted to nothing more or less than if we blew up any part of our apparatus, we would be dismissed from lab. So we all with quaking hearts and trembling fingers marched into what seemed certain doom. Luckily no one blew anything up, although there were numerous explosions.

October 16, 1937. Well, everything went wrong today. The Cornell campus is not as boisterous as it was a week ago. I have no excuses for offer for our defeat. However, Peck's retirement has broken our team up. I've never seen such a complete change over last week. Baker was lousy, Holland wasn't any good, and we just didn't have the fire, the pep, and the spirit we had in other games.

October 20, 1937. At present I'm just emerging from a major crisis. Starting Monday I have never seen so little time to do my work in. I've been working like a dog and I'm still not done. I've fallen behind in Calculus, but will make up this afternoon, which is free. All of a sudden for no apparent reason all of our teachers began to pile on work.... I am beginning to realize that college is no cinch, and that all who said Chem. was the hardest course were right.

There's one boy pledge who comes from Colorado Springs. He has a slow, drawling Southern accent. He was told that he would be called on in the near future to sing a song in Jewish dialect. The poor guy didn't even know what a Jewish dialect was like.

October 28, 1937. The last two days have been dreary, damp, and foggy, rainy, misty, wet days. I can put plenty of feeling in those words. I have to walk all over campus in the rain. No wonder so many fellows have colds up here.

As you know we have a dance next Saturday night. I have gotten a date from Wells. That seems to be the only place to get dates around here. Every Saturday night there is a general exodus of Cornell students out of Ithaca to Wells.

November 3, 1937. Last Saturday we had a great celebration in Cornell. Our pledge dance was a great success. However, several of the wilder boys got drunk and had to be put to bed. That seems to be the common thing to do up here. After 10 o'clock Saturday night nearly every person you see is slightly happy, and by 12—well, they're dead to the world. I pity them.

November 9, 1937. I am in the depths of despair! Just as everything was going smoothly, and I had everything under control, all of a sudden I busted a prelim.... I have a hard time in class. I can't recognize different parts of sentences and tell why they are what they are, their definitions, etc.

December 1, 1937. Last night six fellows got paddled over at the house. They had been caught drinking which is against the Frosh rules. All the pledges were lined up and the guilty six had to take one step forward. Then everyone turned around. We weren't allowed to see the massacre. Each fellow got two hits, and boy, they were hits too. The sophomores do the paddling, and they swing out with all their might.

December 8, 1937. It doesn't feel any different when you're 18 than when you're 17.

December 11, 1937. The calculus prelim Wednesday drew me a 75, a mark I'm not kicking about. Larry, when he saw the test, did not know one single thing. So he sat and drew pictures in his exam book all period. At the end of class he just walked out without handing his book in. Now he is entitled to a retake. Pretty clever, I calls it.

January 7, 1938. Today I was made proctor in Calculus. That means that I supervise the work of the members of the class and show them what mistakes they make in their work. There are about four or five proctors, and the rest of the class has to work.

January 28, 1928. I have finished all my classes except a physics lab this afternoon. After that, well, you know. Already the fever of study has gripped Cornell and for once everyone is staying at home instead of going to see a show or sitting around bulling for several hours. I found out that my English mark is 75 instead of 60 at mid-term. I had an average of 80 in themes, but the first prelim 48 pulled my mark down. Calculus is 77, and I stand about sixth in our section.

February 12, 1938. What a wild time we've been having. It's junior week, and the bands are playing and the liquor flowing. Thurs. night I went to six dances, saw six orchestras and got home at 4 A.M. Among the orchestras were Claude Hopkins, and my favorite, Artie Shaw.



February 19, 1938. The work this term is much harder than last. Chem. labs. last anywhere from 3 to 4 and one half hours. And the greatest accuracy and care is required, which makes it very difficult. I notice that the ranks of the Chem. E's have been greatly depleted since the last notices were sent out. Boy what an English class we have. I think English is one of the hardest subjects we have to take.... Yes sir, the first week in March marks a great free-for-all between Frosh and Soph. During the week, commonly known as Hell Week, the sophs usually take the beating.

February 25, 1938. I'm sorry not to have written sooner, but things are happening fast right now. Two important things are foremost. First—I've stopped smoking, and second—I'm competing for management of the football team.

March 1, 1938. We have just gotten over a severe blizzard. Yesterday there was a very high wind, and the temperature was 5 degrees above zero. Believe me, it was cold. The wind drifted snow in some places over two feet. Coming to class in the early morning we had a hard time climbing through drifts, and my nose froze. That is, there was ice inside of it.

March 22, 1938. I haven't written for a long time. I guess you know why. Initiation ended on Sunday at 6 P.M. and believe me, all the initiates were plenty worn out. I passed out twice, once Sat. night and once Sunday morning. I'll tell you all the horrible things we had to do when I see you spring vacation.... I lost five pounds last week, and feel terrible right now. Work is harder than I've ever known it to be. However, I offset a beautiful zero on a physics quiz by an 88 on an Eng. Prelim, an 83 on a Physics prelim, and a good mark in calculus.

April 15, 1938. Last Wed. night we had a terrific riot in the dorms. I guess the holiday spirit carried over, and the boys all gathered outside in the warm spring night to vent their restlessness at ten thirty. Three boys broke in to the fire hose on our floor and turned the darn thing on. Water went everywhere. Everybody yelled "Fire," and soon other hoses came forth. Then there was a real battle.

April 20, 1938. This week is one week during which little studying will be accomplished. Starting last Thurs. the Freshmen had riots and the class spirit and rivalry was climaxed last Sunday night with the beginning of the Frosh-Soph week.... On Friday the Frosh went one worse by marching up to the girls' dorms and turning in a fire alarm. The resulting melee of fire engines, policemen, and curious onlookers, together with the mob of about 200 Freshmen did anything but put favor in the eyes of the University faculty. Saturday night was more or less a vacation. But Easter night the real battle began. The Sophomores kidnapped our class president. However, we were tipped off, and a hastily-raised gang of Frosh piled into 5 cars and tore over to the house where he was being held prisoner. We stealthily crept up on the unsuspecting kidnappers, then suddenly crashed into the house, freed the president, and grabbed one struggling and very unlucky Soph. Up to the dorms we led him, then in full view of several hundred eager and blood thirsty Frosh, we cut a nice wide stripe right up the middle of his head. The poor fellow looked plenty funny with that bald streak and did we laugh at him!

Rivalries were resumed last night when a band of forty Sophs attacked the dorm. We in the court had rigged up a big siren, and at any emergency it was sounded, and the Frosh turned out for the battle.

April 25, 1938. The riots have ended—suddenly, dramatically. Last night two Sophs were severely injured. Some Frosh were chasing a Soph over the Gorge bridge. He, trying to escape, ducked into the bushes at the side of the road. However, there was a nice rocky cliff behind the bushes, and the poor fool dropped sixty feet before he hit the water below. He was a bloody mess, but they say he'll live. Then a Soph was being taken for a ride. However, he got unruly, so he was actually thrown from the car, which was moving at high speed. The doctors say he might live.... No one knows who the Freshmen are who did the deed. The car used was stolen and there are no clues whatsoever. Because of those two accidents and other severe riots, the Board has absolutely put an end to all class rivalry and even abolished the Frosh banquet, the Soph smoker, and the annual flag rush.

May 24, 1938. Well, I am no longer a Freshman. Last night we held our cap burning ceremonies and just to celebrate today, we all walked on the lawns and smoked on the campus.

June 1, 1938. Today we had the President's review. All the Frosh and Soph R.O.T.C. boys turned out and we all looked quite snappy in our "Park Guard" uniforms. We all marched into a large field and stood at attention by platoons of battalions. Pretty soon a big black limousine tore up and three Army officers and President Day alighted. Day was in top silk hat, formal cut-away and gray striped trousers. He decorated about twenty senior officers. Then we all marched past in review.

June 4, 1938. The year has passed quickly, and it has been a most wonderful year. I have had lots of fun and have made a lot of very fine friends. Altogether college life has proven a vast store of fun as well as work.

September 25, 1938. The wild excitement of getting back is over. Now the even wilder excitement of a week of rushing is about to start.

November 7, 1938. Everything is going wrong. Expenses are terrific. I have to cut down on everything. I guess I'm lucky to be here at all, so I can't kick. I wonder if it wouldn't be better to give it all up and quit school, but what can one do with an incomplete education. All you do is study, all the time. I'm so darn sick of books and Chem. Labs and prelims I could scream. We have averaged three prelims every week for two weeks, and are not looking forward to three more. I wonder if they will ever end.



November 14, 1938. You certainly gave me an awful scare by calling me up.... I suddenly thought something might have happened. I rushed to the phone and called you up. There was no answer so that made me worry all the more. I was sure something was wrong, and was practically tearing my hair out trying to find out what to do.... Please don't mind my horribly pessimistic letters. I very often feel low, but it is only natural, so don't worry. I think I have all under control again.

March 10, 1939. We had our first prelim today—Org. It wasn't too bad. Everything is going very smoothly scholastically. My tuition this term was not as bad as last term, but unfortunately fell due last Mon. at the same time my house bill fell due, which did a fairly complete job of draining the bank. If my figures are correct I have had deposited to date $1190. If I take it easy as I fully expect to do, I will keep down as much as possible.

April 25, 1939. The schoolwork is very hard now, because I'm a little behind in Org. lab and drawing and making up is plenty tough. I got sadly gypped on an Org prelim last Wednesday. Only got a 67, but the marks were all low, and besides they marked harder than any time I have ever known. I am going to object to Johnson tomorrow and maybe I can get back 6 points which I truly believed I was swindled out of. The way those darn guys mark is something awful: 100% correct or nothing! They just don't give you a break or a chance even.

May 24, 1939. Sat. night I was downtown when I ran into Dusty Rhodes. Now get this. I thought he was going to bawl me out because of low grades when he stopped me, but instead he said he had heard a rumor that there was a "White man's Club" being organized in the Soph Chem E class. I replied I knew nothing about it, and asked him what it was. He replied that it was a club for the "10 or 12 real boys in the soph class.".... That means one thing. The ten or twelve real boys in Dusty's language are those fellows who do not necessarily get wonderful marks, but are socially set up, and who are regular guys. Those are the kind of boys Dusty graduates—and moreover—I am included in those ten or twelve! In short if I can maintain even a half decent average, I am as good as a chem. Eng. Doesn't that sound good?

May 30, 1939. Barby and I went to my 305 lecture together. All the boys were rather surprised to see a girl in a purely boys' class, but didn't mind at all, and all cast very speculating and pleased glances now and then.... After the prelim Barby and I went down to the Straight and had a coke. Then at twelve we went to German class. Again she created quite a hit with the boys ... Barby has invited me to come to the graduation dance on June 26 and stay a few days at the World's Fair.

September 30, 1939. This term I'm taking the hardest work I've ever had. My schedule consists of mechanics, materials, minerology, Physical Chem. and Advanced

Quantitative Analysis. It is going to be a difficult grind, but I'm ready for the worst. Rushing has been a terrible headache to me, but everything is rosy now. We have pledged six wonderful boys.



October 9, 1939. Last Monday, Bartlett and I drove to Cortland and each of us bought a second hand shot gun. I paid five dollars for a neat single shot 20 gauge. Then we got hunting licenses and went out after crows. We had more fun. There is a regular fad of hunting sweeping the house. Everybody is getting a gun and a license and going out.

October 11, 1939. Dusty Rhodes wants to get to meet some of the "good boys," the possible "white men" of the class of 42. So Hathaway and I are undertaking the job of co-organizing the party.... We'll have about 25 boys or so, and three or four professors.

October 31, 1939. On Sunday at 12:30 we had a gigantic rally at the station to welcome home our victorious team. There were 2500 students there and I've never before seen a mob go as wild as that one did. We had a parade up main street from the station up to the Straight. The marching line was over a mile long. The city was a wreck. Hysterical, jubilant Cornellians tore the town wide open. At 11 P.M. Sunday night, the band returned. Another rally started and again thousands of boys downtown and blocked traffic in the center of the town for over an hour.... our prestige at beating Ohio State has made us one of the most formidable teams in the country. We're undisputedly Ivy League Champs already.

November 6, 1939. Do you remember how I was saving Phillip Morris wrappers all summer? Well, right now we are first in the contest. Fraser, John Boyle, and I pooled all our wrappers, and entered the contest together. Each week we guess the scores of two games. For each correct score we get 100 cigarettes free. But that isn't all—the group putting the most wrappers in the contest wins a great big RCA victrola and radio combination. The set costs well over $100, and we are first! If we win Frase and I will have it for our room. Isn't that wonderful. But, we need every wrapper we can get. Mom, could you send me all the wrappers you can lay your hands on in my laundry? We want to win so very much.

December 3, 1939. Thursday night I really burned into the work, as I had two tough prelims on Fri. I didn't get to bed till 1:30, and got up at 5:30 to study some more. I think I hit the prelims pretty well.

Dec. 11, 1939. I got my bid to Al-Djebar today, I am going to accept tomorrow. I never before realized what an honor it is to belong to that club. It is terribly exclusive, and only the very best guys in the class got in. It certainly means a lot to me.

December 17, 1939. For the next two days I am going to just sleep and rest ... Wasn't the Graf Spee incident thrilling? I guess old Hitler was plenty annoyed. Well, that finished 33% of Germany's battleships. It looks bad for the Nazis now.

Jan. 6, 1940.[To his father, but unsent] I want to tell you. I'm in love with Barbara. I'm afraid it's the real thing. I have waited for over a year to make sure that I'm right, and I know I am.... I fully realize that I have to finish college and get a good paying job before I can ask Barby to marry me. You needn't worry about my making any foolish moves along that line.... Last Sunday I met Mr. Gormely, vice pres. and Gen. Man. in charge of electro-chemical metallurgy. He was very kind to me and took great interest in me. We talked for an hour and a half, and he invites me to come down to the office on Tuesday to visit some of the other big boys.... They all agreed that the technical fundamentals are all important, and that I can easily learn business principles from those of company I work for. They thought that the radical college ideas might be a definite setback in learning the principles of some conservative firm. Another thing, when I get a job, I [shouldn't] consider pay, or what I do. All that matters is interest in what I do, and I can work up from the lower end. I got an application blank from Mr. Endicott, head of employment.



January 14, 1940. The weather up here has been horrid. The cold snap is over, rain is falling, and the snow is a messy slush. No tobogganing. This is the time to beware of colds. However, I think I am very well fortified. I am taking 3 pills a day, three glasses of milk and a big glass of orange juice every morning which is costing me about $3.00 a month extra.

Feb. 13, 1940. It will now be mandatory, it appears, to get a 75 average for this next term. All I can say is, I'm not licked yet, and I'll get that 75 or wear myself out in the attempt.... I know it is a disgrace, not only to me, but to you, my parents. However, the fact remains that my work is not satisfactory, and by God, it is up to me to clear myself and wipe that disgrace away.

Feb. 19, 1940. Being placed on Pro[bation] is only an indication that I'll have to work even harder, put more time, more concentration on this present term's work.... I had absolutely no idea that I was in a precarious position. I had no warning. I was in perfectly good standing when I started on my finals. And it was the result of those finals that pulled my average down to where it is now.

March 3, 1940. Last night, Frase, John Boyle, and I took a little vacation and went up to the Straight Theater to see "The Big Parade." How the motion pictures have improved since that day! But, nonetheless, it was an excellent picture, and all the way home Boyle, an infantry man, and I, an artillary boy, argued the relative merits of the tactics used in the picture.

April 10, 1940 ... Isn't the war news terrific! Things have pepped right up and it doesn't look too good for Germany. I hope they take the grandest beating it is possible to give. If only Hitler would die or get killed, events would shape out much quicker.

April 17, 1940. I want your O.K. on something. As Juniors each member of my class is entitled to get a Junior blazer. All the boys are going to get one. Would it be all right for me to buy one also? They are tailor made, of white flannel with red piping and the Cornell seal on the left top pocket. The cost is slightly less than $10.



September 30, 1940. Classes started Tuesday and together with intensified rushing, time has flown like nothing. Every one of my courses is reputedly TOUGH! I am taking (hold your breath) 1. Advanced Physical Chemistry, 2. Advanced Inorganic Chemistry, 3. Special topics of Chemistry, 4. Unit Operations of Chemical Engineering, 5. Chemical Engineering Lab, 6. Heat Power Engineering, 7. Mechanical Engineering Lab!!! I bought seven pairs of much mended socks—at a wonderful bargain. I got 4 pairs for $2.00. I also had to buy some collars, but now I'm all set for the fall and winter.

Jan. 20, 1941. I started work on a 710 report on Distillation. We have over thirty graphs to draw, besides computations of data and complete discussions. From 7:30 Friday night till 2:30; from 9:00 Sat. morning till 2:00 Sat. night; from 9:30 this morning till 10:30 this evening I have been drawing, plotting graphs. Nothing but graphs with co-ordinates so fine that 25 of them make about an inch.

March 13, 1941. It is hard to believe that only three more months are ahead of me.

April 7, 1941. I have a bill from the infirm[ary] for the rather amazing sum of $4.19. The statement reads: $1.00 for X-ray; $3.19 for medication. I will pay the bill tomorrow.

April 29, 1941. T. L. and I went to see a show which was a superb "Lubitch" comedy.

[n.d. 1941]. Tonight we listened to the President. It seems quite evident now that we will be in a war soon. Since I must register for the draft on July 1st, it seems logical that I should register with the Board that will not take me first.... At present I am rushing through to finish up work. I have three prelims and several reports to do. Graduation is on Monday, June 16.... Please give me some advice on this new war situation. Gosh—I'm all upset now. All the boys are in an uproar about Roosevelt's declaration.

June 1941. In [three] hours I will take my last final.... School is dead. Everybody has left, and the campus is deserted.... Everything is under control here. I got a letter from Duffet at the Co. this morning telling me it was unnecessary to report for work before June 3rd, and I could get properly organized.

# JOHN HUNTER DETMOLD

## CLASS OF 1943

John's letters to "Dear Mum" are wry and engaging. "Broker" is his car. In 1943, while working for the *Alumni News*, Detmold created a dictionary of current university slang in which he defined absent as being "home in bed"; co-ed as a "sweater-girl in saddle shoes"; lecture as "a system of education whereby the professor talks while the students do the *Sun* crossword puzzle, read alien textbooks, sleep, write the next hour's assignment, discuss past, present, and future dates, comb their hair, catch flies, knit, and, as a last resort, take notes," and up as "Dirt; the latest scandal—as in, 'What's up?'"

9/25/40. The apartment has lost none of its charm. I have finished going over all my drawers and the closet, and now everything is in order and where I can get at it. The kitchen works beautifully; we cook both breakfasts and lunches. The latter consisting of a many fried-egg sandwiches.... The milk and the *Sun* come regularly, and are a comfort. You're really living in a home, somehow, when a quart of milk and the daily paper greet you every morning. The thing we need most, and that not badly, is a chair for me to sit on.

Well, this is still the most beautiful place I've ever seen; and now and again, when I'm walking on the campus, and looking at the trees and the lawn, and the hills across the lake, and down the valley, I remember to think how lucky I am, just being here, and get the humble elation of an airplane trip. Other times, driving Broker around, and looking a third at the road and two-thirds at the girls, I just feel good. A less complex emotion, but no less satisfying.

... for the rest, there are my courses, which excite me hugely. I'm all registered and ready to go; and have I ever got a program. No classes before ten o'clock, and none at all in the afternoon! I work three hours, beginning at ten, on Mondays, Wednesdays, and Fridays. Two hours, beginning at ten, on Tuesdays, Thursdays; and on Saturdays just one class at eleven, which, you will admit, is deloverly.... I've got a drama course, with Bob's favorite, Henry Myers. We read some fifteen representative classical and modern plays, in one term. Sounds good. And had some trouble about a second English course, which I needed, since I'm majoring in the stuff. Louis MacNeice, the eminent modern, has had to return to England to fight the war, so there is no poetry course available until next term. I tried to get into an upper class section handled by Adams and Bald, but Adams thought I better start more broadly, and specialize later.



And then there's a famous course with Lane Cooper, in his department, the Comparative Study of Literature. Rapid reading in the best translations of Greek and Latin classics. This should be fine, for he's one of the best men on the hill ... and there can't be more than eight or nine in the class.

And for French, which I like to keep up with, ere I forget all I've acquired, there is one called the History of French Literature; which covers a lot, and should tie in with my English. Next year, if I'm still at it, I can have Morris Bishop.

Finally, a course in public speaking, called, strangely, Public Speaking. This is the standard foundation for lots of things, such as dramatics. And radio, maybe. Oh, I'm going to have a lovely time this year. Everything looks good, and there are no flys on the horizon.

9/27/40. The coroner decided it was suicide, which of course it was. She seems to have been a nice girl; graduated with highest honors, and a tennis champion. Shirley Charlotte Slavin, a freshman, and probably scared. She sat on the bridge for more than an hour, before she jumped. And she jumped, all right. Gave her purse and books to a passer-by to hold for a minute. Well, every year someone jumps into Fall Creek; usually a freshman. Maybe the quota is filled for a while.

9/27/40. Broker is fine. I don't use her much, walking to and from classes every day. Which is quite a walk, and one of the loveliest I've met. All along Cascadilla gorge, under the trees, in a Wordsworthian profusion of Nature.

And I've been to all my classes, and have them lined up. The Greek and Latin classics is still my favorite, mostly because of the professor. And the Chaucer next, though I feel awfully stupid. And French, an enormous man, with more in his head than two John Kierans, scares me. Already, in the first section, he has assigned a report to me. But this should be fun, and I'm sure I like Chaucer. The drama course also looks good, but it's a huge class, which isn't for the best. Myers gave us an excellent lecture on drama, in general, this morning: Its elements, and such: intensity, a reversal of fortune, et al. And the other two courses are not so hot; at first glance, that is. Public Speaking is presided over by a nice, but a rather effeminate young man;

and we all have to make a speech on "My Pet Peeve." O, Lord. I'd hate to tell him.

French turns out to be the old circus course. They've got a room packed to the rafters, and most of the sardines asleep. The lecturer stands there and reads good poetry poorly. He's an old man, with the funniest haircut you ever saw, and a caricature of a voice. Well, right now he's well into *Le Chanson de Roland*, which is nice, and I'll probably get interested before long.



The Book and Bowl ... most marvelous banquet. Everyone there, and the guest, David Daiches, a little twinkling, brilliant Scot, was tops. Morris Bishop started things off, after an hour or so at the cocktails. (I waited until Bob had nearly completed his first, and then I took it and held it for a while, to look professional. Then there was the steak dinner, and then Morris.) He gave a short and witty resumé of the history of the club, reading the names of all past speakers at the banquets. The best speech, he said, came in the middle of the prohibition era, when one of the guests turned up with two gallons of applejack, which was added to the already potent punch. By the time of the address, everyone was high, (not drunk: the definition being "when you fall to the floor and hold on"). The speaker got up, told one dirty story, and fell over backwards. Coming to, a half hour later, as two of the strongest undergraduates were putting him to bed at the Straight, he murmured, "God! Wasn't I wonderful!" and relapsed into oblivion.

9/24/41. I've spent a rather stupid morning in between Mr. Cooper and Mr. Adams. These two gentlemen dislike each other and give me contradictory advice, mostly about a Dante course of Mr. Cooper's. He thinks I should take it, and Adams does not. They insult each other to me, Mr. Adams coming off in better grace. And I'm not taking the course, since it conflicts with two others, and since Jack Adams is my adviser.... Adams teaches the Shakespeare; Harry Caplan, the Greek; Ed Nungezer, the Drama course; and Cecil Bald, the History of English Literature. It's not as good a program as last year's.

12/7/41. ... [a] stag really has all the advantages; most of them just stand around miserably, though, and content themselves with the lion's share of the refreshments. Not your John. A real fine dance; good orchestra; and all the pretty girls looking much prettier in—or nearly in—evening gowns. I didn't bother with suspenders, since Bob had the extra pair. I started tripping at first, when the pants slipped rather too far; but I fixed that by buttoning the top button-hole to the first left suspender button—if you can figure that one out.

It has snowed steadily for just twenty-four hours. Cars piled up all over the place; the temperature down around your ankles. Wonderful weather. Rehearsal all afternoon, now. And then, oh Lord, you work! Two prelims next week, two papers due. I love it. Bye Mum.

12/10/41. ... people up here are nearly as crazy about the war as they are in New York. With reason, for there's no denying the seriousness of our pickle, and it's difficult to keep one's mind on the ordinary pursuits when the Japansies are knocking hell out of the world's two finest navies. That a few planes could sink the "Prince of Wales" is absolutely incredible, as is nearly everything about this war. If there is one thing I was sure of, along with Lindbergh, it's that we could never be attacked. I've known all along that we'd get into this mess, and it made me sick to see us come closer and closer. But I kept waiting for the denouement; we'd have to get into it by protecting somebody, much as Hitler protects the underprivileged nations. About the only clean way to go to war is in self-defense, and we've been lucky enough to have that method presented to us.

None of which hides the ugly truth. Parker Fennelly and I are all for Jeannette Rankin. I would never, I think vote for war. But if you grant that we were bound to get into it some way, it's heartening to be able to feel noble about it. (I wonder, did Frankie bribe the Japs to start the works?) I guess he didn't, but I still don't understand it. In spite of the amazing Japanese successes, naval wars are always nice (irony); I hope this stays in the Pacific for as long as possible. Which I take to be a matter of weeks.

It's rather a stimulating catharsis so find yourself so wrong. I can't help being thankful for so many things I've scorned; the draft, National Defense—however botched; an enormously increased navy and air force. And though you won't agree with me here, I think Franklin is and will be a good war president. I never wanted war, and never wanted him. But having one, we may be lucky to have the other. His whole philosophy of government is right for war, as it is wrong for peace; a strong central government; most of the power in the hands of a few. It may well be true that another man would have kept us out of war, in which case we are scarcely lucky in our president.

Well, everyone thinks of little else. Classes are strained. Ed says he doesn't really see much point to Pre-Shakespearean Drama in these times. Yet Jack Adams spoke eloquently for a re-dedication to the arts of peace. In a mess like this, nothing is so important as keeping them alive. Shakespeare has outlived many wars.

January 22, '42. Registered Monday afternoon: in place of Greek, which I have dropped, I shall take a two hour biology course given in the main library, and three hours of informal study under Jack Adams. Bob says this last is a racket, but nice. There are no classes, no exams, no final, and no papers—unless I wish to write them. I simply read, at my own convenience, books suggested by Jack; mostly eighteenth-century novels, which I seem to have skipped. About one a week. A lot of ground can be covered in this fashion; no lectures to sleep through; rather in the Oxford tradition, where the student pursues his own studies, seeking advice when he needs it. I also signed up for the entire summer session, eighteen hours, through September. But they must figure out how I can get all my scholarships, or I won't play.

Saturday night "Mike" has invited Peter and me to come to Sage to dinner with her. Is not this nice? I've never been in Sage, and this will complete my circuit of the Cornell co-ed dormitory dining rooms. Saturday nights are fun, too, for they linger after the meal, to sing songs. Any table may start one, and the rest join in. Then they all stand up, in a circle about the room, and sing the alma mater. Masculine voices are much appreciated; and you may be sure that I try to be heard.

1/27/42. I must say they make it nice for the overworked students. Every afternoon, after the last exams, from four-thirty to five-thirty there is dancing, coffee, tea, and cookies free for all at the Straight. I stopped in yesterday, after Greek, had two cups of tea, with five slices of lemon and four lumps of sugar, eighteen assorted cookies, and more than a passing glance at all the pretty girls, looking none the worse for their labors.

March 13, 1942. [At Book and Bowl] Sampson read a fine paper about Ithaca Folk-lore, which turned out to be mostly funny stories about queer people in these parts, and especially about the eccentric and bygone members of our faculty. We all had our own stories to add someday.

August 16, '42. Jane and I went out last night. First to see and hear Sabela Wehe's "148th concert"—which was an absolute riot, and which I must see more of in the future.

# KATHLEEN PIERCE PUTNAM

## CLASS OF 1944

Katie Pierce came to Cornell in 1941 and started keeping a multiyear diary on January 1, 1942. In only a sentence or two for each entry, she records what it was like to be at the university during the war years: experiencing blackouts and rationing, marrying in 1943, setting up an apartment, and returning to dormitory life when her husband goes to war. Katie writes about her classes and her friends, working as a waitress, and—reflecting the importance of the film culture of the 1940s—going to many movies. After graduation, Katie Putnam and her husband moved to McGraw, New York, where she taught and raised children. Retired, she lives in McGraw today.

Jan. 7, 1942. Took B.J.'s books back to the Libe for her. Classes were lousy as usual. Had gym in afternoon & studied.

Jan. 8, 1942. Prelim in Psyc wan't too bad. Cut H.G.&D. to study for it. Pete came over & we studied over at J[ohnny] P[arsons]s. I really helped him with his calculus.

Jan. 13, 1942. Had gym & posture test in afternoon.

Jan. 16, 1942. Had fire drill at 6:15 A.M. Prelim in H[uman] Phys[iology] & Algebra were terrible. Lab was OK but I didn't complete it. We went to S[traight] play, "Across the Continent." It was swell.

Jan. 21, 1942. Finished registering. Got Hurwitz's signature. Didn't file study card.

Pete & I were over at J.P's during Black-out. I should have signed out.

Jan. 23, 1942. Checked out of Chem lab & brought home a lot of glass. Saw "Dumbo" & went to the Dutch [Kitchen]. I had muscatel & Peter had 2 Tokays

Feb. 4, 1942. Had to give an autobiographical speech in Public Sp. at 8:00. Came home & studied.

Feb. 12, 1942. Had classes all morning. Got marks. Had Chem lab. this afternoon. Went up to Home Ec. with Janet & met Mrs. Roosevelt.

Feb. 27, 1942. Went to the Sq. dance up at Warren Hall. Had swell time.

Mar. 6, 1942. Prelim was OK. Came home & did H.A. Then back to Psyc. Got 83 in the prelim. Saw Pete before Chem lect. We went to "A Yank on the Burma Rd."

Mar. 7, 1942. Went to see "Blondie Goes to College" & "Roy Rogers."

Mar. 9, 1942. I overslept & cut PSJ. Had to wait on a regular table. Slept from 9:45-12:00. Studied all afternoon. Pete called up twice. Went to Mass Meeting. Bed at 11:15.

Apr. 8, 1942. Pete came over & we went to J.P.'s to study only we didn't.

Sept. 24, 1942. Packed this morning. Got to Risley at 2:30. I'm family waitress again! Straightened room a little. Letter.

Sept. 27, 1942. Went to picnic at Balch with grandchild. Pete came last night. Went out in P.M. & eve.

Sept. 28, 1942. Took my grandchildren to register.... Class meeting in the afternoon. Went to "Voice of Terror"—Sherlock Holmes.

Oct. 1, 1942. Today was the first day of classes. It was fun. I had an awful rushy time [waiting tables] at noon. Pete didn't come over so I went to bed at 9:30.

Oct. 6, 1942. Had classes & what a rat race. We canned pears & tomatoes in F.N. lab. Went up to Home Ec after supper & Pete met me up there at 10:00. Coke.

Oct. 8, 1942. Had classes per usual. We did beets & meat in the pressure cooker in F.N. lab.

Oct. 12, 1942. Mom & Dad took me to the Chinese-American place [Asiatic Garden Restaurant]

Oct. 20, 1942. Went to libe at 8:00 & stayed all day. We dried foods in lab.

Oct. 22, 1942. Had classes. Went to AOD house.... Cooked dried foods in F.N. lab. Went up to Pete's apart.

Nov. 3, 1942. Typed paper & got it all done. Classes were OK. We did something in

H.A. for a change. Had class meeting & rolled bandages. Then studied.

Nov. 5, 1942. Had classes & got back FN prelim—86%!! Highest mark was 88%. Went up to the Libe & Pete came up & got me. I'm so happy about the F.N. It's a wonderful world.

Nov. 9, 1942. Had classes & studied. Went over to Balch & got caught in a blackout so I decided not to go to Libe.

Nov. 10, 1942. Went up to Ag. Libe & did Ed Psyc. for prelim tomorrow. Rolled bandages until 8:30 & then Pete went up to the Libe with me again & we both studied.

Nov. 12, 1942. Classes as usual. Made cakes in F.N. Ours burned.

Nov. 17, 1942. Had classes. Made angel cakes in FN lab & also custard & mayonnaise. I rolled bandages. I'm a monitor now. Pete didn't come over cuz it's raining.

Dec. 2, 1942. Classes. Prelim was easy in R[ural].Ed. Came home, slept in between R.Ed & FL. Had to do sleeves again in TC. Grrrrrr.

Dec. 3, 1942. Classes were fun. Had a demonstration of yeast & quick breads by Mrs. Snyder of Chicago. Went over to Music bldg. & heard *Mikado.* Blackout came.

Dec. 14, 1942. Was awfully embarrassed in RE 100. What did I learn today? Fooey. Almost finished blouse & cut out jerkin. Went to chorus. Studied FN. Pete didn't come over but he called 3 times.

Jan. 20, 1943. Had last classes. Worked on shirt & jerkin & almost finished them entirely. Had chorus.

Jan. 23, 1943. Got up at 9:15 & went over to music bldg & finished *[Princess] Ida.* Went to clinic & had blood test, JP's & to music building.

Jan. 23, 1943. Got up late ... went downtown & bought wedding dress & Janet's & made plans. It's to be at noon.

Jan. 24, 1943. Registered, etc.... Got ring but no license. Also have to fix Wasserman test thing.

Feb. 6, 1943. Got up at 8:00. We all went downtown ... I dropped the cake. Wedding was at 12:00. Pete & I went to Syracuse by train for the night. Hotel Jefferson-Clinton. Passion!

Feb. 7, 1943. Ate b'fst. at Hotel. Took 12:00 train home. Came back to Ithaca in the afternoon.

Feb. 8, 1943. Had classes. Studied in dead hours. Went to chorus, etc. Studied & stuff in the evening. Made a luscious chocolate pie, which the boys ate at once. Fun.

Feb. 19, 1943. Classes were a relief to get through. We saw "Star-Spangled Rhythm" tonight. It was so funny & I'm glad we went.

Feb. 21, 1943. Had to work all day. I'll never work another Sunday if I can help it. It was awful. Did some overtime. Studied in P.M.

Feb. 24, 1943. Had classes. Got sugar ration book #2 at 10:00. So did Pete. Fixed tan skirt. Studied in the evening with Pete. I love him so much.



Apr. 7, 1943. Had classes. Am going to write on "Working Wives" for P.L. 270. Went to chorus for a change. Came home in the afternoon. Studied in the evening. Bed early.

Apr. 9, 1943. Came home after 2 P.M.. Got some hamburg & cooked supper. What a ratrace! Studied a little.

Apr. 14, 1943. Had very interesting lecture on digestion & the genitals by Papez in Foods. Started typing term paper.

Apr. 20, 1943. Bact[eriology] was fun per usual. Studied foods from 11 [to] 12:20. Came home in the afternoon. Pete & I went down to see Dr. [Esther] Parker & got a diaphram.

Apr. 23, 1943. Pete had two shots for the army & doesn't feel good.

May 25, 1943. Commencement is all over. I slept until 10:00. Sewed, made stuff out of felt. Made supper for Pete. He went to work today. Went to bed early.

June 16, 1943. Saw Pete go.

June 30, 1943. Got stuff to register with from Home Ec.

July 2, 1943. Worked at Old Armory for 6 hrs. today. Had a letter from Pete. Was on desk from 7:30 to 10:30. It was fun. Wrote to Pete & read stuff.

July 21, 1943. Went downtown & donated my blood.

July 28, 1943. Had FN lab & fixed the meal all by myself. Went up to a meeting about food preservation. Read some Ag. Engineering & stuff. Had KDE initiation.

Aug. 4, 1943. Got 1st Army check $50.

Aug. 11, 1943. Had a blackout that lasted for a whole hour tonight.

Sept. 7, 1943. Classes as usual. Quiz in Ag. Eng. Again. Prelim in LL120 next week. We learned about mustard plasters too. Went over to Risley & rolled bandages until 9:00.

Sept. 28, 1943. Went to classes all day. Wasted time in TC200. Home nursing—we saw a baby bath with a real baby.

Nov. 1, 1943. Registered, etc.

Nov. 2, 1943. The ["practice"] baby is coming Thurs a week, we hope.

Jan. 3, 1944. Our first day of school. We mostly observed but answered a lot of questions too. Met faculty & people.

Jan. 5, 1944. I taught my first lesson today & it was wonderful! I wasn't scared at all & I loved it love it love it.

Feb. 10, 1944. 3rd grade was loads of fun as usual. Miss C. observed.

Mar. 4, 1944. I registered in 15 minutes. It took Janet 2 hours.

May 16, 1944. Michael Tseu asked me to go to the Spring Formal & I accepted! What will Pete say? I'm going to wear Chips' dress. I'm so excited.

May 20, 1944. What a wonderful day. Mike came at 10:00 & he, Chip, Sami, & I went to parade & carnival. Then ate w. chopsticks downtown. Then baseball game & crew races. Home for a rest. Then the formal! Swell time.

June 21, 1944. Took my last final. Saw "Gaslight" with Michael.

June 25, 1944. Graduation.

# ELIZABETH SEVERINGHAUS WARNER

## CLASS OF 1950

Libby Severinghaus's letters home are buoyant and good humored. She reports to her parents about her classes, her finances, and her satisfaction with being at Cornell. She makes a yearly request for her parents' signature on a permission card so that she can leave the dorm on weekends. Libby mentions her posture pictures, which were taken of men and women at several universities at the time, and she joins a sorority. She is also a member of Ivory Tower, an organization founded in 1943 as a "steam blowing off" society for women; she joins Octagon House and puts on musical productions; and she participates in WSGA, the Women's Self-Government Association. Libby's Cornell experience is different from that of Katie Pierce, but both women reflect the importance of current film. Libby also comments on the physical expansion of the university, which escalated during the years when Deane W. Malott was Cornell's president. Libby graduated with a degree from the College of Architecture.

October 16 [1945]. To begin with I have no homework tonight.... You see, the same class here is held only every other day. Tomorrow I have five hours of art and I can hardly be expected to study for that. At least that's what I say.... Today has been lovely. It was actually warm enough to go without gloves.... To catch you up on the news of my short stay in Ithaca I shall begin with my arrival. I don't believe you've had an elaborate account of that momentous voyage. We arrived about six and no roommate was apparent. Since then, though, she has become quite so. The following day, Pop being still here, we went to Willard Straight Hall to get my A[thletic] A[ssociation] book which enables me to attend athletic contests at a considerable discount. I was quite lonely and thought I would never see a familiar face.... On Saturday I went by myself to the Cornell-Colgate game in the pouring rain ... this Saturday I expect to see us beat the living daylights out of good old Eli.

March 28 [1946]. I've been freezing up here for ages and I gaze thoughtfully at six-foot icicles on the falls.

[no date] Spring's here! It's a beautiful day and I'm sitting on top of the world. I got an 80 average for a half term mark in English, an 80 in both my lit courses, and the other two marks I don't know yet. But isn't it a Terrific time to be alive? And to be going home in four days? If that's not a set-up, I don't know what is! We had a mad blizzard all day Sat. and half of yesterday and that is hardly conducive to a suntan. I went to Chi Psi Sat. night with Bill Kinsolving—everyone had a roaring time and I drank my two ginger ales and had a time although not nearly as roaring!

May 15, Thursday [1946]. I have thought at great length about your introduction to social life on the Hill. I am sorry that the circumstances greeting your arrival were soaked in alcohol. I don't know whether it's up to me to apologize or not, but if it is, I will. I was awfully glad you came and terrifically proud of both of you.... Last but not least—I'm running a bit short on sheckels—sheet music, tickets for the show, house dues, etc. have kind of cleaned me out this week—so—uh ... well.

---

October 13 [1946]. Here it is Sunday and I'm just getting around to writing. I've just been too distracted to sit down. We registered yesterday and they had given me the wrong registration blanks. They were for the college of A. and S. instead of Arch. I thought they were wrong to begin with but they wouldn't listen to me. Consequently I went back and forth between Barton and Goldwin Smith three times, which is not one of life's shortest strolls. We finally got that straightened out and just missed the kick-off. I don't know whether you read about the game or not but it really poured rain. People left after the first half but I stayed 'til the bitter end. I was soaked to the skin, underwear and all in spite of raincoat, bandana, and umbrella. Cornell barely won because its passing attack was ruined by the rain, naturally.

Friday night I went to the freshman rally at Bailey with that guy who yelled at me the night we got here. I can't stand him & last night I went to the Colgate Hop at the Straight with Carrow. We went down to Jane's first and played bridge. He's really very nice.... You have to write a letter direct to Mrs. Wilvert, Balch III. I wish you would do that as soon as possible. That's my permission, which they have to have in their files. There are no required freshman activities that weekend as the team is at Princeton so there really isn't any reason why I shouldn't go [to Princeton]. But please drop Mrs. Wilvert a line.

I am still horribly homesick and today is ghastly. This morning I missed church because of a two hour posture exam in which they silhouette you stark naked against a screen and take your picture. Then this afternoon we have the regular physical and really I think it's a little extreme. They poke you to find out if you have cancer of the breast and test you for venereal diseases. I think that's rather a difficult thing to go through. They also give the tetanus shots and I don't think I'd better have one so soon. I just had one last month. Would you get a statement from Dr. Taylor certifying that I had one and send it to me.



Wednesday afternoon. It's a gorgeous day today although I thought it was going to snow this morning, and I am sitting here watching the many little passing Cornellians from my window. I can't understand why none of them have any work to do ... Luce and I are having the most horrible time trying to concentrate on work with homecoming out of our mouths every time we say a thing.

November 4, 1946. Life around here rolls along at a great rate and I wouldn't be any other place for all the money in the world! Our football team is wonderful, the campus is beautiful, the girls are swell, classes are awful as they always are, and there's not enough food. It's raining dismally today and there is no rain in this world as wet as Ithaca rain.

I got back a biology test the other day with an 85. Or did I tell you? There's not too much scholastic news because you're kept completely in the dark as to marks most of the time. I love my figure construction class with nude model better than any other class I've ever taken anywhere. Really, it's fascinating. We had to draw the head of a colored girl model the other day, a really careful study, and the next class period he had all 40 of the pictures up on the wall with the four or five that he thought best at the beginning. He was telling who did them and mine was at the very beginning. He said, "Severinghaus's is very good!" Aren't I conceited? But, Dad, I was so pleased that I had to tell you. It's really quite something to get credit because the class is full of veterans who are really good.

The social angle is terrific. Saturday afternoon we listened to the first half of the game here in the room, and during half-time Kitty and I ran all the way down to the Straight where they had the game being broadcast in the Ivy Room with free cider and doughnuts. It was really something to see the spirit down there. And then they announced the score of the Penn-Princeton game and the mob went mad. We will beat Penn or die trying. Having Princeton beat the Red and Blue has really changed the color scheme up here. It's going to be a really marvelous game and I wouldn't miss it for the world.... Saturday night I went out with Bob Becker, Phi Gam, who is divine looking and very popular in the house.... I went to Sigma Chi yesterday for Sunday lunch with a horrible creep but they say that Sigma is a good fraternity on campus so I thought I'd look it over. A very dull time.

November 12, 1946. I have just finished struggling through the essay, "The Good Duke." I thought it was lousy. I don't know when I've ever seen such foul big words. Good Lord, I had to use the dictionary eleven times.... I have a History of Fine Arts prelim on Thursday in which we have to identify with name date and country, 40 slides of all ages. The Museum of Casts where we take this course is a regular morgue with horrible statues from the Greeks hanging from every imaginable place. Just the atmosphere is enough to scare anyone.

December 6 [1946]. This weekend—if you can call starting Sat. noon a weekend—rushed by me much too fast. Friday night Jim LeBarr (a Phi Gam pledge) and I went to the huge pep Rally (2000 plus) on alumni Field. Ed McKeever ... introduced the team—we had an ungrammatical speech from Joe Martin—the band played while we shrieked "Cornell Victorious" ... and I swear if they couldn't hear us in Hanover, they're deaf. Then we bolted to the other end of the field where, with great ceremony and all excess of war whoops, we cast the immortal Dartmouth Indian on the fire. This was followed by a series of snake dances around the pyre.... Following that we went to Zincks. Finding Sigma Chi monopolizing the place we moved to the Dutch (a place like Zincks in the Hotel Ithaca). Here Phi Gam had the situation well in hand.... The Dutch ran out of beer so we moved en mass to the Lehigh Valley House where we again loudly condemned the Pennsylvanians. 1:30 loomed ahead and meant deadline so I returned to the dorm—sadly. Incidentally I indulged in NO alcoholic beverages. When I returned we found out that the Dartmouths had painted the statues of Ezra Cornell and Andy White on the quad quite green and added quite a few large green "D's" to the classic fronts of some of the main buildings. They also kidnapped the students from the campus broadcasting system and broadcast "As the backs go tearing by."

Saturday morning I went to my drawing class, which I adore. I again received very favorable criticism from my instructor.

December 9, 1946. I have just returned from an evening at the library and I feel extremely intellectual.... And life around here continues as planned. I have an appointment with Mr. Hartell (You remember him: the frowsy-haired so and so) to plan out my schedule for next term.... I reaped another 85 in an English theme last week—that makes three in a row—and I must say, I'm quite pleased with myself as I did not do too admirably in the subject at school last year. My accumulated average for the first six weeks was a 73, which is nothing to write home about, but it's not bad.

January 6, 1947. I'm pretty low in spirits and I can't put my finger on the reason why. I'm horribly restless and there's no one around to talk to—not that talking to people around here would do any good anyway. They're all so different. Yes, I know what you'll say. They're different but they're the type that make up the backbone of America and I ought to know some people besides my own snooty friends on the Main Line. But still, they're different. I feel as though I were just marking time waiting for something to happen—Lord only knows what it is. Sometimes I wonder whether I'll ever get through four years of this away from home. Then I decide that maybe I will, maybe I won't and that time will tell. There's not too much I can do about it.

I no sooner walked in the room last night than the telephone rang—a Phi Gam (not Bob, darn it) and a Si U. Both wanted dates this Sat., one wanted one next Sat., and the other wanted one the 25th. I just didn't feel like making up my mind or even thinking about dates so I told them I just didn't know and they could call later. Boy! How to make enemies and alienate people.



January 19, 1947. Today I have to go down town and have my picture taken. It seems that I am one of the ten girls nominated for Freshman Beauty Queen and we have our pictures taken and they are sent to John Robert Powers to be judged. The first is queen, and the second and third are her court. Frankly I think it's just one big joke because I'm not one of the world's most gorgeous girls and I photograph horribly besides.

[Jan. 27, 1947] Your mail appreciated muchly but you must send the permission directly to Mrs. Wilvert—they are afraid of forgery—sorry you went to the trouble but I thought I had made it clear to Dad the last time. The permission cannot come through me.

[Jan. 31, 1947] I've committed the most amazing feat of my career. I turned down all Saturday night dates and I'm going to work on Biology! How 'bout that?!!

Friday, February 21 [1947]. The only final exam mark that I have found out is English and in that I got an 87 of which I am quite proud. However, I guess Dad has told you about my average and it is not bad at all. I don't know any of my other exam marks but they don't make any difference now as all the marks are averaged in. 66 in Fine Arts, 67 in Biology, 78 in English, 80 in Figure Construction, and 82 in painting and composition. That gives me a 75 cumulative average! I must go to class now—it's snowing to beat the band and we have about a foot.

Monday [Feb. 24, 1947]. Rushing is underway at full-speed. The bids come in the last night and I got ten out of the eleven sororities on the hill. We have to narrow it down to four this week and I chose Theta, Alpha Phi, Tri Delt, and Kappa Kappa Gamma.... This is all a pretty awful throat-cutting business, and Luce didn't get a bid from the one she wanted. I feel so terrible about it but there's nothing I can do. There's loads of work to be done and I've got to do it ... about getting me transferred to Arts and Sciences from Architecture. For Pete's sake, no! This present set up with Fine Arts under Arch. is perfect. The Fine Arts under A & S is all history of art courses and very few actual art work courses which is what I want. So, I'd frankly prefer to stay right where I am. Apparently it's terrifically popular and everyone from Fine Arts in A & S is dying to transfer to Arch. So please may I remain? Please?

March 17 [1947]. Yes, I was pretty thrilled about Theta. It is supposed to be the finest house on the hill—even the other sororities admit to this—and its scholastic average is high. Not unusually so, but a great deal better than most, and undoubtedly higher than all the fraternities.... Saturday night I went back to Phi Gam under still newer colors: Tex Bratton. That makes Phi Gam no. 8 and I'm about ready to check out of that house. Tex is a wonderful guy with a heart of gold, and everyone is crazy about him because he'd do anything for you—however, in addition to his heart of gold, he had with him on Sat. night, a fifth of whiskey of which he partook freely during the Dartmouth basketball game, to my utter disgust. We went back to the house ...

Tex proceeded to indulge in more and more and it's not one of the nicest things to dance with someone who keeps losing his balance.... All my friends are falling in love around me and thinking of getting married or at least engaged. So far I haven't come within a million miles of the thought.



October 13 [1947] ... out in a field by Taughannock Falls. We played "Infiltration." It's a game where you have teams and two goals. Someone yells, "Go" and you try to get to the other team's goal. If a member of the other team recognizes you he yells bang and you have to go back and start over again. Of course it's pitch dark and you run into people crawling along the ground—but it's all awful lot of fun! Yesterday I went to church and last night Willard called up and asked me to go to dinner with him. He brought his buddy along and we went downtown to dinner and saw "Cross-Fire," that new anti-Semitic movie, which is excellent ...

Wednesday. We have no classes Friday morning—Tom Dewey is opening a new State School building here on the campus and we're all supposed to go hear him—don't know whether I will or not—I will!

[1948] We just finished dinner. Dean Allen was here—she's a conceited, swaggering bag if I ever saw one. Just looking at her annoys me. A bunch of us sat at the farthest table from her and roared all through dinner. We shot water and spitballs at each other and had the best time. College life is making real ladies out of us ... I never knew there could be so much snow in a place.

February 23 [1948] School is moving along, but my grades this term are not going to be any where near what they were last time. Rushing is going full blast and that is just death on studies. We go to the house every night at seven and don't ever get home until ten-thirty at the earliest and some times later. By that time one is just too tired to study. This government course has me floored. I never was one to show a vast interest in legal things and dry material which that certainly is, and I just can't seem to grasp it. But I honestly am trying. Then there is my Lit. course which is very interesting but in which I often disagree with the instructor. Sociology is fascinating, and not too difficult. We are now studying Chinese customs and I am enjoying it very much ... there are also my three courses in the college of Arch. I am thinking very seriously of transferring next fall to the Arts school. The only trouble is you have to have an 80 average to transfer and I doubt very much whether my average will be what it was this last term. I don't seem to be getting what I want where I am and some times it seems like a waste of time. I have a two and half hour lab this afternoon, then volley ball class until quarter of six, run back to the dorm, throw down some dinner, and over to the house until ten-thirty.

March 9, 1948. I had a date with Wally Ainsworth who is an Ace (that is the new term for some one who is something around here) and we spent rather a peaceful evening with two other couples down town at the movies and then at Zincks. This is the first time in my existence at Cornell that I have spent a Saturday night down town. As a rule, Sat. night is Fraternity party night.

May 14 [1948] To-day has been a bad day. I don't know when I've ever been so discouraged ... I'm so darn tired all the time and there's never a chance to go to sleep. I have to stay up until all hours studying because I've got such a fierce schedule during the day, and I'm just too exhausted to study well.... It's been raining steadily for the last four days and all in all I'm pretty low ... I got a 62 in the Govt. prelim—and I knew that stuff.... The Govt. course I'm taking next year is taught by Einaudi ... his father has been elected president of Italy.



Monday, September 27, 1948. School is rolling along as expected. I'm really going to have a rough time of it this term I'm afraid because I have an awful schedule and I'm really going to have to work. This political theory course gives promise of being very interesting but there is a 5000-word term paper due at the end of the term. However it is the first lecture I have ever sat in on that my little mind didn't wander. My art courses are good and the drama and theater course could be interesting except that the instructor would do better coaching a football team. Enough of the academic, for I don't have much time and I want to catch you up on the other things in life before dashing to my 12:00 o'clock.

... We all went to a party at Psi U Sat. nite and Wally and I came to a parting of the ways. It was very unhappy but I think it was the only way out. I've at last decided that I'm not going to go around with anyone steadily until I'm ready to marry the guy!

Tuesday, September 28, 1948. Herewith find enclosed the blanket permissions card. I don't think they've made it very clear by listing "hostesses," etc. but don't bother with that because I have no idea who the hostesses might be. So you can just leave that blank. If you would, please check "weekend" and for transportation I guess you'd better check "train" and "car." I guess the only way I'd ever go anywhere would be in one or the other of those fashions. I'm not pulling a fast one or anything. It's just so much simpler than having to write home for permission to go to the Syracuse game or to Tigertown or what have you. However, I shall always ask before I go and if you all say no, here I shall remain. About underlining specific places ... you might check "out-of-town houseparties," "other campus residences," (I'll be staying at KAÐ in Syracuse) and "private homes with any hostess or hosts."

Tuesday night October 5, 1948. To-day has been wild. My lecture this morning was very interesting as usual and I just made it by the skin of my teeth having slept through the alarm. After this followed Drama and the Theater, which is deadly and to the library to study until lunch. This afternoon to lab.... Remind me to tell you about the skit we put on at the WSGA meeting last night. Very funny, and quite clever. President Day spoke and I ran into him backstage while wearing my black strapless evening dress over red flannel underwear—long sleeves, etc. Leave it to Lib—she always looks her best.... P.P.S. I'm running low on money—well, not really low. I have about $90.00

Monday, October 25, 1948. For the rest of the season things look blue. Sure, Army looked good, but we looked horrible. I've never seen us look much worse. But the whole team is so banged up after the Syracuse game that there's hardly one who doesn't limp on and off the field—Joe Quice, Bobby Dean, Pete Dorset, Hank Drost, Paul Griolamo, Harry Casset—it's awful. But we have hopes for the Ivy League. Without Hilly, tho' I dunno! By the way, *Life* flew up a staff of photographers and writers for "Life Goes to a Football game" in the next issue. I don't know whether they'll print it since we lost, but maybe!

November 17, 1948. I have decided to write my 5000-word paper for Mr. Einaudi on some phase of the Catholic church. I haven't yet decided which phase, but I'll keep you posted. Work is really tough this year and I'm just a wee bit weary. It isn't social life that's doing it either because I have eliminated Fridays and Sundays from my social calendar. Last Friday night was the exception because I ushered at the Savage Club concert—which incidentally was terrific—but other than that little Lib is at the books.

February 17, 1949. For the latest news: I have had my right arm in a sling since Monday morning. Something seemed to be sort of slipping and grinding in my right shoulder so I went down to the Clinic. They told me to keep my arm in a sling, not to use it, and to report every afternoon to the clinic for heat treatments. I have faithfully done so and today the pain is rather bad. It has gotten steadily worse and I am just about fed up with the clinic. I am going down this afternoon and demand an x-ray, because I can tell even if they can't that something is out of place and the heat treatment is not doing any good at all. All the sling is doing is giving me a stiff elbow and doesn't keep my shoulder still at all. It seems to me that there is no excuse for their not having x-rayed it in the first place. It's not that I propose to be a medical authority, but you can feel when something is grinding and out of place. Other than that things are roaring along.

Yesterday and the day before the temperature was 55 and we nearly died of the heat. Today we are having a blizzard, a gale and the temperature is 14. Lovely place, Ithaca. Matter of fact, I'm rather fond of it.

Now for some scandal. Proctor Manning the Univ. proctor who is an awful man and always on drunken binges when he is supposed to be keeping the students from doing same was finally arrested. Enclosed is the clipping from the *Sun*. I think this looks very bad for the University, and I take a very dim view of its having kept him this long.... Would I were President of Cornell ...

April 15, 1949. They changed the system of grading in Fine Arts and it is really grim. All our designs are being judged by the entire faculty rather than by the particular professor of the class. I'm working on the window displays at Rothschild's for the Octagon show. They've let us have the two front show windows. That has been taking up considerable time.

May 25, 1949. I don't think you realize how much time extra-curricular activities take up and I don't mean social ones. This idea that everyone has to be a wheel is something and it grabs everyone up. I mean CURW, Octagon, Dorm social chairman, etc. It's just meetings all the time and never time to sit down.... I have just spent the afternoon in Cortland ordering 1500 cokes at the Cortland Bottling Co. for the dance during Freshman Orientation ... I'm in charge of a dance up at Barton Hall. This is just an example of things that have to be done.



September 23, 1949. I am hereby writing you my first letter as the old senior at college—it seems impossible that three years have come and gone since that ghastly physical exam freshman year.... Classes have finally gotten into full swing and I am crazy about my art professor in my main and afternoon labs, not to mention Mr. Washburn for sculpture who was written up in *Life*. The European Lit course which I am taking is a scream. The prof is Joe College personified and half the university is in the class. Pop, it is given in G[oldwin] S[mith] B. and all the seats are filled so you can imagine the size. I am ensconced between Wally and Dave with John Phillips behind and a million other people you have met at one time or another. My music course should be fascinating but will take immense powers of concentration in which I know full well I am lacking. Activities have also gone into full swing—for some strange reason I have been appointed to the Rally committee for the rallies Friday nights before football games. I don't know when I've enjoyed working on a committee more!

9/27/49. We've just gotten out of a long and boring chapter meeting. The first one after the summer is usually long and they're all boring. But this living in the house is great. It's so nice and sort of homey!

October 12, 1949. I shall elaborate on my Tigertown excursion when I see you—but ... I had a marvelous time and, both of you, you were right—I should have gone. Lord, what a time I would have missed! George was an enchanting host—we have a really great time together and we fully intend to see more of each other in the future. There are no life-long commitments involved—we just have a good time. As for other affections—I am not maintaining that I am less fond of David. However, we are not about to get pinned—that is for me, I'm afraid, too committing.

November 9, 1949. Work rolls along and I find myself doing okay. My art courses are shaping up beautifully and I went to see Prof. Morris Bishop this A.M. about getting jobs through the Institute of International Education and teaching English in French schools—it might prove interesting.

[12/2/49] I tear into my room, heave my books on the desk, and then hold my spinning head until I think of what I have to do next. And that's how it's going to be from here right up until Christmas, and as a matter of fact, probably until June of 1950.

[1949] Right now I'm going over to ask Prof. Morris Bishop if he'll waive a language course prerequisite and let me take French Lit next term. He will, but this is a required formality! Incidentally, yesterday I filled out my last university registration coupons—gee, it doesn't seem that four years have almost flown by. It seems rather awesome to write Terms Completed: 7, Terms to Go: 1



[1950] There seems to be a jinx on ye old universitee for the Capt. of the Lacrosse team, Larry Woodworth, who is also president of his fraternity and an honor student in engineering was found dead in one of the gorge's Friday morning. The coroner's ruled the death "accidental" as he had no motive for suicide and there was no trace of liquor on him.

Here is my house bill for the third quarter. Make the check out to Kappa Alpha Theta. This is my house fee, as a matter of fact so I'll keep the bill. Make check out to Kappa Alpha Theta for $250.03. And enclosed is my university bill for $340.00—make that one out to Cornell Univer. Many thanks.

February 28, 1950. Dave and I went down to the Straight tonight to hear Dr. Bethe lecture on the H-bomb. (I might add it was Dave's idea, not mine!) It was interesting but not very detailed. And now we're back at the Theta House.

May 26, 1950. As to our conversation of Saturday night it'll probably be years before I forget it—maybe I'll know what to say when faced by my children.

# DAVID S. KOGAN

## CLASS OF 1950

David S. Kogan came to Cornell a thoughtful, curious boy so alive to the collegiate world he was entering. Kogan was a Reconstructionist Jew—a sect whose members accept modern culture, value education, and believe in individual interpretation of the laws—and called himself a "Jewish scribbler." He was that for sure, and of the very best kind. He mused about Cornell, Semites and anti-Semitism, the strange and exciting world of women, his ability to "gafoodle," or waste time, and what he might make of his future. His diary spans his four years at Cornell, though the entries taper off in his final year, when he was diagnosed with a lymphoma and began a series of treatments in both Yonkers, his hometown, and Ithaca. Kogan graduated in June 1950 and died in March 1951.

Yonkers, September 11, 1946. Kogan luck (?) did it. I was awarded the State Scholarship and a Cornell Scholarship. The latter of course admits me to the University.

October 3, 1946. I went shopping with Dad these last few days; he loves to wardrobe-shop for his Cornell son. Suit, snazzy sports jacket, my first man's-type hat, gloves—O yes, my first bow tie and also collar stay. I could use a nice tiepin. Asked Mom to get me one with SDK on it.

Wednesday, October 9, 1946. My first full day at Cornell! In which I start off as a parent-pecked anxious boy without a place to sleep—am then placed in a fine dormitory at the University's heart as the unwelcome extra in a large room already occupied by a likable, talkative blond from Forest Hills, old stock with plenty of chips, and another fellow, sneakier and shrewder. I was shorn of a desk but retained a favored bed—we'll get along.



I also joined the band today. It is part of the R.O. T. C. (Reserve Officers Training corps) and football, and spent five hours marching and playing.



Was surprised to see Morty Weiner walking around Cornell this morning. He takes physics at Ithaca College and is jealous as hell of Cornell and quite lonely. We had supper in Willard Straight cafeteria, which serves fine food.

Friday, October 11, 1946. In which I am a day closer to my death—how did that enter? I write in my diary trying not to be discovered by my two roommates. Why is diary-keeping considered effeminate?

Saturday, October 12, 1946. Saw my first football game today under adverse conditions to say the least. The stands were uncovered and a pitiless rain unceasingly shamed itself on the field. Then to top it off, we took off our red coats for the spirit of it all, and shivered to death as we marched down the field. NOTE: I'm still alive.

Registered at last. My approved courses are English, Physics, Logic, Government, Psychology. Also received were chest x-rays and tetanus injections.

October 13, 1946. President Day delivered a thrilling, meaningful, and humorous welcome speech to the assembled Frosh today. He spoke of Cornell's tradition, "Freedom and Responsibility."

October 14, 1946. In which I am thrilled by my first college classes and meet a girl. I discovered these professors are personalities—their lectures quicken and embrace the learning experience.

October 19, 1946. There's a lot of neck going around in these parts. And even more serious activities. Ah, the Spirit of Co-Education.... Crossing the Bridge of Sacred and Profane. First Hillel Service was not particularly impressive, being about seventy-five percent Reform and twenty-five percent Conservative (that is merely hats, no organ, a bit of chanting). Nevertheless it is a necessary compromise.

Went to my first Cornell dance—taking the stocky girl from Rochester I met last night. I can't understand the morals of her position. We dance so closely—I am continually hot—the dips and hand-holdings are breathtaking. We then go out—I kiss her and it falls flat! She then fed me a line about she "didn't think I was that type." I devoted the next ninety minutes to brilliantly talking—at 12:29 I had completely won her heart! I've come to the conclusion (a) either I don't know the art of kissing or (b) I am not emotionally responsive to it or (c) both.

October 20, 1946. Went to Chapel this morning for an inspiring service. Heard Reinhold Niebuhr—he's terrific, a neo-orthodox Christian, he lashed out against fascism, communism, and state-ism; says every man should feel himself wrong.

I had thought that my courses would present an opportunity to distinguish myself. This is not so, as I would have to steadily grind to climb from good to excellent. Competition is too keen. I used to say "gafoodle"; here the expression is "goof off," and boy do I do a lot of it ... Sally found out I was Jewish today by watching me write a Hebrew letter (no words were exchanged); we just looked at each other.



October 25, 1946. I've been studying the Jews here on the campus. Of the approximately fifteen hundred, about one hundred are truly tied to Jewish values and traditions in the modern sense of the term. Then there are about sixty who are Orthodox and do not have anything to do with conservative Hillel House. Another one or two hundred enjoy going to services and are sympathetic to Jewish tradition. A factor almost unknown among Yonkers youth are the three hundred-odd radicals who work for the P. A.C. and the Negroes and Russia, but have nothing to do with anything Jewish, even refusing to come to Hillel House for social activities. Nevertheless they hang together at the "Universal" meetings where Jews predominate. The remaining nine hundred are in between; some come to occasional services; most going to Hillel House, but not at all really concerned with Jews and Judaism.

November 20, 1946. The Band was reviewed by a General today. In my contacts with Barton Hall I learn to detest militarism—the sharp disciplinary cries and the endless marching with rifles is abhorrent.

My English instructor, Mineka, wrote a long book on Unitarian Periodicals from 1790 to 1815. Anyone writing a thing like that could not possibly appreciate the talents of David Kogan as a writer. Seriously though, I can't understand where the others in my freshman class learned their grammar, for I certainly did not. The intrinsic dullness of grammatical principle.... My physics instructor wears long hair, is a shabbily dressed young man about twenty-five, doesn't know how to teach and smiles, giggles, or laughs after every word. (It is more of a course in abnormal psychology.) Colleges never pick or promote instructors on teaching ability. They are solely concerned with the amount of original research or the degree of the man in question.

November 23, 1946. In which I learn of the powers of song and dance, become a good friend of Walter Jaffe, take out sweet Alice, and do not in any way make time.

December 14, 1946. Cornell is becoming Christmasy with cards, signs, trees, and lights all over the place. Old gray alumni from various classes come here every weekend.... We are to begin preparing a term paper based on the reading of three books on related subjects. I secured approval for Kaplan's *Judaism as a Civilization*, *Judaism in Transition*, and Steinberg's *Partisan Guide [to the Jewish Problem]* as a trilogy for the Reconstructionist philosophy.

January 12, 1947. Ithaca is clothed in white, and snow is about eight inches deep continually. Some students ski to their classes. Life here is a constant variation of icy walking with muddy walking, slipping and wallowing.

I gathered up a textbook—perhaps as a lame excuse—and trudged over to Jaffe's. After the weekly steak dinner, much of the time was devoted to a bull session discussing what percentage of Cornellians of each sex are virgins on entering and leaving after four years! Naturally none of [us] was armed with statistics.

January 31, 1947. Attended yesterday a debate on Fraternities. As I see it, their chief points in favor are house parties, especially on the big weekends, conventions, more secure friendships. I would somewhere thrash out segregation, basis of choosing.

Joined the Cornell Rhythmic club, a group devoted to the appreciation of the best in Jazz, or as the white-bearded music professor at its head says, "Indigenous-American music."

February 1, 1947. Just received my English term paper on Reconstructionism, and found that I received a B. I had belatedly realized that my topic was a difficult one to set down on fifteen pages, that it was vague, non-factual, partisan, argumentative. Nevertheless I learned a great deal. I am in college for knowledge, not numerical ratings. In spite of a great deal of mechanical errors Mineka liked it, because perhaps, he's interested in modern religious subjects. (We Jews don't realize how interesting our peculiar existence is to the intelligent Gentile.)

Attended a meeting of the Hebrew-speaking club. I find that I can speak the language fluently, but my word range is not very wide. Half a dozen of the members are obsessed with maladjustment and nationalism, and want to go to Palestine to be "normal."

March 14, 1947. After services I went back to the United Religious Building and saw one hundred fifty Jewish students listening to the entertaining talk of the most lovable professor on campus, Thompson, the head of the American literature program here. He's a roly-poly cheery man with twinkling blue eyes—a third generation American of Irish descent, and his specialty is studying man's folklore. He spoke on Yiddish folklore, playing rare Jewish records from his private collection, telling about his walks in the East Side during the summers ten years ago with a Jewish friend, picking up legends and songs of the immigrants. He told touching stories he got from refugees at the Ontario Camp near here. Read the words of Yiddish songs in English (they sounded so funny) and read other song-titles in Yiddish with English letters (that sounded funnier). The audience loved it. Sunday night the little man is giving a presentation of Irish-American humor at the Browsing Library and I can't wait to hear him again.

April 29, 1947. A group of journalism majors are planning a weekly Sunday newspaper for next fall, and have asked me to be one of the founders. *The Cornell Daily Sun* does not present the human side of Cornell, nor does it evaluate campus life. We, with the sponsorship of the University and with their blessing, are launching this enterprise to fill such a need. The struggle for interest, subscribers, publicity, advertisers, writers, material, printers, is an exciting one. Have been working on a number of feature ideas.

May 1, 1947. As an example of conspicuous consumption and as an indication of the return of the University to the gay and flamboyant normalcy, a group of Cornell Beauty Queens select the Apollo of the Cornell men on the steps of Willard Straight. Some of the criteria of this hilarious contest are points awarded to the boy with the longest necktie, engaged to the most sorority sisters, the richest costume, teller of the best jokes, good looks, etc. It is a colorful, entertaining spectacle, Cornell's answer to May Day. And meanwhile, inside the building, members of the Marxist Discussion Group were holding a May-Day celebration. That's life.



I could write books on what I see. Am called a Communist for getting *In Fact* and a reactionary for subscribing to *Time.*

September 22, 1947. Rushing days—the stuffed shirts are all out, the missionaries of fraternities seek the right boys. They cautiously approach Temporary Dorm three—dozens. I suggested hiring a uniformed flunky to show them.

October 18, 1947. It is just before the Navy game for which, in this country town of 20,000, 34,000 tickets have been sold. Why?—because of the annual homecoming week, when all the successful fraternity Cornellians and their wives take their new cars and come back to face their classmates after ten years.

November 13, 1947. *The Observer* suspended publication for the time being. I am glad there was an *Observer.* It enabled me to meet a bunch of swell people, to study the promotion of a new enterprise, to witness some of the shadiness of the firms with whom we have dealt, and to generally get an insight into journalism and publishing.

November 24, 1947. What are my wants: to study the Jewish heritage—to be well-groomed and in the best physical health—to catalogue my faults and correct them—to satisfy sexual desire consistent with an honorable character and wholesome personality—contemplate, evaluate, and improve my living—to successfully pursue Cornell studies—to read wisely and record the reading—to plan and complete the action which make me a better being ... to honor my father and mother ... and perhaps more ...

February 25, 1948. In which I was formally taken in by Phi Sigma Delta in an impressive candlewick ceremony.... This evening to the Palestinian Protest Rally. Newman was excellent as chairman in the packed room. Konvitz is a great lawyer and thus talked. Ernie and I telegrammed White House.

March 9, 1948. My fraternity brothers—all kinds. It is hard as yet to discuss individuals; of the fifty members, twenty-five have cars; on the other hand, about ten are in a smaller or larger measure working their way thru college. We are the only group where all the waiters are also members of the fraternity.

May 4, 1948. Initiated into college horseplay yesterday. Pledges got into the spirit of situations so similar to the canons of college novels. They circuitously carried me far up Cayuga Heights Rd.—I called from a farm house (inhabited at that time solely by a young professor's wife, whose blouse was half unbuttoned down front) and asked Mel to pick me up—he came immediately. We all tried to tell our own stories as often as we could, and tried to avoid hearing the boring tales of the others.

With Ernie and Richard studying American history. It is most easy for me to get along with these "independents" (am beginning to understand the full wonderful meaning of the word—nevertheless, I am still glad I'm a "Greek").

A big event—I walked into Professor Cushman and asked him to be my adviser—he said yes. This will give me the best man in Government for adviser, someone whom I've euphemistically called my ticket to Law School.

May 6, 1948. Heard an excellent lecture by Enaudi on Marxian economics—theory of Labor's value, and of the dilemma of Capitalism—I confessed to Mel I was a mild Socialist.

May 15, 1948. I am thrilled about the formation of the Jewish State. Last night the beautiful Cornell chimes played the songs of modern Jewish Palestine for a full half hour.... This weekend I was elected president of the Hillel Foundation for the coming school year.

December 1, 1948. A fraternity brother, X, was caught stealing from another brother; the red-handed victim admitted to about 30% of the six instances of theft in the house this year—including $1.00 from me which I'd never missed. This enabled me to participate in the meeting, which was to decide what to do with the guy. I had talked with him, and liked to believe he took what he said [he] took, and we should give him a chance to re-establish himself. But more vindictive heads prevailed, and, under threat of divulsion, he left. It was a nasty business, and a fascinating one.

December 15, 1948 I'm terrifically run down. Am tired, oh so supremely tired feeling brought me to cutting most of the day's classes.

March 8, 1949. LAW SCHOOL APTITUDE RESULTS came in today—putting me in the 98.9 percentile. I consider this phenomenal.

March 30, 1949 [in Yonkers]. Mom saw I had some fever this eve—I've had such for some time. She called Dr. Wilenky ...

March 31, 1949. Will have to have an operation tomorrow to find out what is in the neck.

February 6, 1950. A fraternity meeting—the discussion concerned whether or not to admit a boy who has been pledging for four months, and refuses to completely subordinate himself to the group. We discussed every one of his character and personality traits, his actions, his potentialities. The line-ups on each side produced some beautiful speeches.

April 16, 1950. Hauser and myself get to be closer—based upon a healthy appreciation for each other and a knack for both being good audiences half of the time. We are both seniors who sampled the rich man's area of Cornell University. He however has the advantage of non-intellectuality, handsomeness, business ability, and the remainder of practical virtues. And what is worst—I am a shade more faced with the vagueness of the path. My anxiety over the future stems from the conclusion that I won't be making much of a living, or ever amount to anything much. And yet, I know how to live—so I'll be a successful failure. Enough pessimism for now.



April 19, 1950. A two-hour-long bull session with Nelson on anti-Semitism and prejudice toward minorities. My position is that we must fight prejudice by not consciously, or worse, self-consciously doing so. The Jews are in a fine position to study technique, falling as they do between whites and Negroes. The solution is a basic realization of the importance of treating an individual as an individual—and then doing so, with as much play and insult, as a married person would treat his better half.

April 26, 1950. Dad's phonecall—visiting. We had breakfast together at the Straight. Dad's a great guy, and I play his heartstrings wonderfully, giving him as much pleasure as I know how. It's mostly surface, as I withal neither work, nor plan, nor save, nor carefully conserve health. Talk was of present health and rosy future, Judaism, the wonder and glory of being at Cornell.... The guy brought up some pills, which will postpone the next attack past finals week and past graduation—and happily left for home.

April 28, 1950. Began itching today like hell—and this is an important symptom of lymphoma.

June 11, 1950. The pomp and circumstance of the Baccalaureate Service procession was beautiful—and a forerunner of the events of tomorrow. Marched with Sharon and Winn—in our caps and gowns—in a jovial mood.

The speaker was a divine, Sizoo, with a tremulous Scottish accent and forceful delivery—but with a sad lack of artistic use of the hands. He "burred" the tragic lack of faith in our time.

June 12, 1950. This day. Graduation—the leaving of a wonderful way of life—make-believe battles and leisure and golden times and girls. Paradise—for an uncertain future—and yet I'm not sad, and it feels momentous only on reflection.... We sang *America*, heard God invoked, and Day receive the title of President Emeritus. Some receive commissions, and, piecemeal, each segment in the hall gets graduated by having its representative and the proper Dean exchange words. De Kiewet, in his English brilliant academic costume—spoke for work against moral indifferences, and for use of our education to forge a discriminating instrument. Alma Mater and benediction.

# ANITA ADES GOLDIN

## CLASS OF 1950

Anita Ades came to Cornell in 1946 and wrote weekly to her parents, not just letters but also postcards, which were a popular way of keeping in contact. One of her letters brims with excitement at the larger world she was encountering at the university.

[Nov. 23, 1947] This has been the most wonderful weekend. Yesterday was one of the most stimulating Saturday's I've spent up here. I joined a club called the One World Club of C.U. R.W. (Cornell United Religious Works). Joanie joined also—and yesterday we went to the first gathering. We ate lunch at one of the cafeterias (in a side room) and ate at a table with one Frenchman, two Indians (India), and a Chinese. I was so busy asking questions I didn't even know what I was eating. Then Mrs. Sherwood Eddy (Eddy was sick and couldn't come) gave the most informative inside picture, well-delivered speech on the "Marshall Plan and Russia," that I have ever heard. Folks—it was absolutely out-of-this world. I guess you know about Sherwood Eddy. He and his wife just returned from Europe where they spoke to all the "big shots" in all the countries. The Chinese at our table took Joanie & my number and is going to invite us over for a Chinese dinner (he'll cook it) some time. He's just been here two months & wants to learn Eng. better. Most of the members of this club are foreign. The president is a *handsome* Dutch boy and you should hear the different accents floating around. It's very exclusive as far as American membership is concerned. You have to be affiliated with either U.N. or N.A.A.C.P. to get membership. I'm on U.N. and plan to join N.A.A.C.P. so I qualify. By the way a committee is being formed to arrange for a Cornell delegation to Europe this summer (school & camp work) and Joanie & I are trying to get on the committee & perhaps finally as exchange students. Wouldn't that be the most wonderful experience in the world?







We went to Hillel for square dancing, then to Tau Delt where they had a terrific Private Party and then down to Z. B. T. I wore blue jeans and was told I looked very cute. I cut my bangs some more & they really look smooth now.... Today I'm studying—tomorrow I have a basketball game at 4:30 (on A.E. Phi team) & tomorrow night J & I are going to hear a wonderful speech on Russia (I'll tell you more about it when I go). I can't tell you enough what tremendous strides I am making in the business of becoming informed (and world minded) ... I am being so stimulated.

... I guess I am just about one of the luckiest girls in the world. If I had gone to a school like Wellesley or Skidmore I doubt if I would have made such leaps and bounds. Wisconsin might have done the same—I'm very included to think I would have led an equally stimulating life.

# JANET HAMBER

## CLASS OF 1951

Janet Hamber arrived at Cornell in 1947 in a class of almost twenty-five hundred students. Her first letter home is reminiscent of John Davis's letter of 1868, although she does not actually measure her room's dimensions. Other letters to a high school girlfriend and her family reveal her impressions of the university. Janet discusses smoking in a most casual way and notes receiving a gift of cigarettes on Valentine's Day. In addition to selections from her letters, which are mostly about her academic work and joining a sorority, there is an entry from a notebook she kept for Rural Education 107.

September 15, 1947. I got a booklet about what we do orientation week. Science, math, French and achievement test—Oh, also a lot of teas, meetings, etc. We have to wear Freshman hats and buttons till the end of November [when] they have a cap burning ceremony.

Sept. 20, 1947. I arrived at Ithaca at 6:45 after 7 1/2 hours of creeping through New Jersey, Penn. & New York. I've never been on such a slow, hot, dirty train. I found out later that there were two air-conditioned coaches. I got to Clara Dickson about 7:15 and since dinner had already been served I didn't have any. Now I just have to describe my dorm. It's beautiful. Much nicer than my room at home. The walls are a light natural color, the bedspreads and rug are green and one lamp is red and the other eggshell. The closet is big enough to sleep in, has 2 shelves, a rack for shoes, rod for clothes and numerous hooks. The furniture consists of a bookcase, desk (very much like your one at home), a chair that has cushions, a dressing table and bench and a single bed. I also have a private telephone. I can't get over how beautiful it is.... The Straight is beautiful but then so is the entire campus. They have dancing, a library, game room and restaurant there. Gosh so much has happened. What I like most about this campus is that the people are so friendly. We had an aptitude & science test yesterday which were pips. The boy who sat next to me met me at Bailey Hall when we were officially welcomed to the University. After we walked down to College Town and all around. What hills they have here! I got my books yesterday at the CoOp for 18.15 which isn't too bad.



Sept. 22, 1947. I don't think I've ever had so much fun in my life. I went down with another girl and after seeing a play, I found Henry B. I started dancing with him and then the fun began. The Straight was jammed. Since there are about 5 boys to every girl I kept getting cut in on. I'd just about find out the name etc. and there'd be someone new. I met a lot of nice fellows that way—especially Frank Field. He took me to the Ivy Room, that's the restaurant in the Straight and bought me a coke—which I spilled on him. Oh well. After a while they started singing all the Cornell songs and it was wonderful. They have a way up here of making you feel as though you belong.... He asked for my telephone number so I'm hoping. I saw him again Sunday at Sage Chapel. Imagine I went to church. It isn't any denomination so I like it very much.

Sept. 23, 1947. I'll give you my finances. I'm going to the bank this afternoon. Arrived Cornell with $33.30 cash. Spent $2.00 class dues; $18.15 books; $3.03 alarm clock; $.85 paper, ink; $1.05 soap, shampoo etc. Now I have $8.22 left. Please send my fur coat as soon as you can. It's freezing up here! I'm really having a wonderful time up here. We have Senior privileges till tonight. That means we could stay out till 12 week nights, 12:30 Fri & 1:30 Sat. tomorrow we go on Freshman hours 10:30 week day nights. The people up here are very friendly and consequently so am I. I've met millions of people so far but I can't remember their names.

... I can't get used to having classes at all different hours of the day.... It's a pretty tough schedule since I have 3 8 o'clocks, no afternoon off and Saturday classes. So far I like all my classes but some of the Profs speak terribly and it's hard to concentrate.

October 7, 1947. Walked over to the Cornell orchard and I got a bushel of apples for the girls on my corridor. The boys carried them home so it's lucky I brought them.... My classes are swell except for a couple of dull professors. My Zoo prof is swell but Bot and flor. just about put me to sleep. They never change the tone of their voices and it gets very monotonous. I have to learn the Latin names of 15 plants for tomorrow's Flor. Lab. Went to Dean Allen's tea and it was very nice.... I think I would like to join a Sorority. I've met a lot of nice girls in Tri-Delt.... There are so many girls it's hard to get to know anyone real well. We all just go around with everyone, which is nice but doesn't lead to lasting friendship the way a Sorority [would].

Oct. 7, 1947. Well, my classes have started and I'm up to my neck in work. Just finished my first theme. This is theme paper in case you didn't know. Got a 5 on my first Chem test.... Like my labs a lot which is lucky since I have four of them.... I haven't started to work yet and it worries me. There are too many interesting things to do up here. The weather is beautiful. All the trees are changing and the gorge is beautiful. I can't get over what a swell campus they have here.



Oct. 16, 1947. I'm sitting on the grass in front of Clara Dickson smoking and eating an apple. To look at me you'd think I didn't have a care in the world and I don't—except for Chem (I got a 50 & 60 in my 2 tests and I just handed in a horrible theme). All my other classes are going along OK except that my average is about 79. That's just enough to stay in. Oh life. It's wonderful. I'd really be blue but there are so many nice things here to take my mind off studying—that's the whole trouble.

I just went to my first Frat party last Sat. on a blind date. It was Alpha Sigma Phi and after I got there I found out that it had the reputation of being a drinking house. I've never seen so much hard liquor in my life. I had a highball and some sort of very smooth punch. The boy I was with had five mug fulls (a mug holds 1/2 of a quart) of punch & 2 highballs. He didn't get exactly drunk but he was pretty high. He took me into the library (all lights out) as I turned them on with "Lets see what kind of books you read." He turned them out again and tried to neck with me (a blind date!) I kept turning my head and he kept saying Burrrr. Finally I gave him a shove and said No so he said OK you're the boss. Everything was OK until we came home, in the rumble seat of a Ford coupe. He said that I was going to kiss him goodnight & I said no (getting monotonous). He just about had me when I pushed him and said "We've hit civilization," (we were back at Dickson). I jumped out of the car and ran since I was late. Made it with 30 seconds to spare. What a night.

Oh, the Cornell traditions. You've heard about the suspension bridge but the tradition goes on to say that a girl isn't a true coed until she has been kissed on the suspension bridge. Another has to do with the statues on the Arts quadrangle. Ezra Cornell sits facing Andrew D. White. There are footprints on the path that connect them. The story goes that one night a virgin Cornell coed passed between them and since it was such an unusual occurrence they got up and met each other in the middle of the Quad. And, so the story goes, they've never done it for a coed since.... Some more traditions are if you walk around Beebe Lake & climb the Library tower or sit in A.D. White's lap (the statue again) and you're with a boy, you're supposed to marry him. We do have Frosh Rules. They consist of 1. All Freshmen must wear their Frosh hats (little red beanies), 2. Freshmen may not smoke on campus or visit Zincks or the Dutch Kitchen (local Ithaca hangouts) and, 3. all Freshmen are to learn the Alma Mater, Evening Song and Song of the Classes.

Oct. 15, 1947. I've as yet no date for the big formal dance Syracuse Weekend. Everyone seems to be having their girl up for it and the coeds are stuck.... I went to a couple of Fraternities (you don't say frats up here. It's too high schoolish, so I was told).

There are a lot of girls in most of my classes since some like Zoo, Bot. Chem & Flor have anywhere from 50 to 150 students. I'd say that there are about four boys to every girl but still there are plenty. The only one is Zoo lab in which until Mon., I was the only girl. On Mon., two more came in so I felt better. The only foreign student I've met is a Chinese girl who lives about three doors away from me. She is very nice and all the girls in my corridor are crazy about her. College work isn't so difficult but it is discouraging, especially Chem.... My best class is Zoo. since I have a lecturer that gives organized lectures and a wonderful lab instructor. Bot. Lab is swell but the lecturer isn't too good; same with Floriculture.... The work wouldn't be so bad if you knew what they wanted. I've talked to a lot of girls and they all have the feeling they're not going to last so I guess I'm not the only one.

There are 11 sororities (not counting the two Jewish) and I've eliminated two already, KKG since its too expensive and Alpha Xi Delta since I've seen several of the girls from it and I don't particularly like them. So far I've met the nicest girls from Tri Delt and Pi Beta Phi.

Feb. 19, 1948. I just got back from my first set of open houses. Rushing started today and we were divided up into groups and I visited five sororities. We only stayed at each house for 15 minutes but we met so many people that my head is still spinning. Of the five I visited I like Pi Phi and best and Tri Delt but we'll wait and see. On Monday we get bids. Tomorrow I still have to go to six more houses and I think a perpetual smile and I'm so glad to meet you will be my expression for the rest of my life.

I got some more of my marks. Starting at the worst, Chem 76, Eng 80, Flor 83, Bot 84 and I don't know my Zoo or Orientation yet. I don't think a report is sent home so I'll tell you my other marks when I get them.

March 4, 1948. I was going to fly today ... with the Pilot's Club but after four beautiful days, it rained. "Piper," a girl on my corridor has her Private's license so I was going with her.... We were going at 5 but found out the dorm doors are locked till 6:30. Just like a prison.... I joined Kappa Delta sorority and I'm crazy about it. The kids in it are swell. Am I glad rushing is over.... Well, one period of my life has ended. I no longer see Robin. It's funny, I knew after Junior Week that I didn't like him any more and evidentally he knew it too since I haven't heard from him.

April 19, 1948. Jeikki ... from Finland (that's why the name), tall 6'3" or 4", blond hair, blue eyes and terrifically nice. Check, he and I used to go ice skating last winter. Last Monday he asked me out for Saturday so naturally I went. We double dated with a boy who owns a jeep. First we went down to Ithaca College and saw their production of Holiday.... After that we went to Joe's for Pietza pie. That's the first time I've ever had it and it's wonderful. Afterwards we drove up to Theta Delt for awhile.

April 30, 1948. I just got back from the Waiter's Derby. It's a race sponsored by the Hotel School. Some of the students race, in rather peculiar costumes, down the road by the Straight carrying trays with dishes on them. More dishes got broken but it certainly was a howl.

Nature Notebook: Rural Education 107

May 1, 1951: Beautiful clear, cool, sunny spring day. Today I begin keeping my nature notebook of my experiences.

May 2, 1951. I was up early this morning, five o'clock, to go on a bird walk. It was dark when I arose which surprised me.... I ate a quick breakfast and joined the others behind Fernow at five thirty. It was beginning to turn light and every thing had a pearly gray color. The birds were out in full song and we stopped by a bush to catch the bubbly notes of a House Wren.

May 3, 1951. I walked home through Fernow Woods with my eyes and ears alert. A rustling on the path beside me caught my attention and I look down at a garter snake. His bright red tongue was flashing in and out and as I knelt down beside him he pulled back and froze. I watched him for awhile and then continued on my way.

May 5. 1951. This morning in class we went over to the Fish Hatchery to see what we could find in the ponds.

May 7, 1951. Our nice weather disappeared today and we had a cold cloudy May. After ornithology lab, I walked home through Fernow Woods. I could see that everything had advanced over last Thursday. The leaves were unfurling on the elms and maples so that the woods was filled with the gray green mist of the new leaves.

May 9, 1951. Tonight for the first time I went on a Peeper hunt with the class. We drove out to Sapsucker Woods at 8 o'clock.

May 10, 1951. This evening Hank and I took our first ride in our new car, Ferdinand, a Chevrolet Carryall Suburban. We drove up the road to Taughannock State Park. The trees are really coming into leaf now and the whole countryside is nice and green.

May 11, 1951. Up at five o'clock again to be bird walking. We headed west around Beebe Lake in the early morning light.

May 14, 1951. Since the end of the term is rapidly approaching, I was indoors all day trying to complete innumerable projects and term papers.

May 15, 1951. As the big migration wave is late this year and the birds just arrived this last week, I got up at 5.00 am this morning so that I could begin to learn them before the final.

May 16, 1951. Up again early this morning and down to Renwick Sanctuary. We saw and heard most of the birds we saw yesterday and even added a few to our list.

May 17, 1951. Today was a busy day so the only opportunity I had to observe nature came on my walk home from school along Triphammer Rd.

May 19, 1951. This afternoon we all went out to Dr. Gordon's for lunch. We picnicked out at her home in Brooktondale. After a delicious lunch we waited to see if we could see the Pileated Woodpecker. They have built a nest right near the picnic area in an old dead tree. The nest hole is about twenty feet off the ground. After waiting patiently for a short while, we were rewarded with the thrill of seeing the Pilleated feeding the young.



May 24, 1951. I walked down the road behind Fernow Hall to the Poultry building, looking for items usable on a Scavinger Hunt. Although there were many things to choose from, I finally decided upon 1. Bring in a winged fruit: the Box Elder is covered with new Maple fruit; 2. Bring in a leaf that can be used as a salad green: wintercress or dandelion; 3. Bring in a part of a plant which has the name of an animal or part of an animal: there are several, Staghorn Sumac, Horsetails, Chickweed; 4. Bring in a fragrant flower: Honeysuckle; 5. Bring in a flower which has a girl's name: Violet.

# ANN MEIGS GHENT

## CLASS OF 1961

Ann Meigs came to Cornell from Bernardsville, New Jersey. In her casual and enthusiastic letters home, she reports on Sputnik, Tripod the three-legged dog, and gossip about Vladimir Nabokov, professor of Russian literature. Ann also writes about a Cornell that is changing: there are panty raids on the women's dormitories and protests over the rules regarding women at parties in apartments. She married Ralph Ghent in 1961, and after a stay in South Africa for research, they settled in Australia.

[September 1957] Hello and all that rot: Would it be at all possible to send me my map of London? I really need something interesting in my room.... We have been having all sorts of boring meetings, and since all the speakers seem to say approximately the same thing, it seems rather silly. My Frosh hat is too small, but they only had small ones left by the time I got there. Also, (hint, hint) I think I shall go MAD without a record player. The only radio stations anyone can get clearly are the ones around here, and all they have to offer is rock-and-roll (perish forbid).... We had a jolly Class Convocation or something last night at which we were welcomed to Cornell (for the umpteenth time) by Malott, the Dean of Men, the Dean of Women, and assorted other dignitaries. Did you know that one of the assorted dogs, which always seem to be around is known as "Tripod"?

[September 1957] Well, I've registered and all that rot, and my bank balance is now down to $139.75. I've paid my tuition, bought a C.U.A.A. ticket ($16.50) and books ($18.75), although I haven't gotten my English History book yet, because the co-op was all out of them. Don't get me wrong, this is NOT a request for MONEY! I just thought you'd like to know.

There was some sort of Activities Fair at the Straight to which I went and spent the whole afternoon at the Savoyards booth, listening to Gilbert and Sullivan. I think that that's what I'll probably go out for.

September 30, 1957. Did I tell you about Tripod? He is a sort of a cross between a chow and an Alaskan husky, I think, and he has, as you may have deduced, only three legs. He sits outside the Straight, like a Library lion, and when the chimes ring, he puts back his head and howls. He's real friendly with all the other dogs around here, except when they come near the Straight or the Library. Then he fights, and usually wins, too.

October 4, 1957. Incidentally, the current expression up here is "fabulous." Be glad you were spared that at least.... Did I tell you that Alice is teaching (or trying to teach) me to play the alto sax? Also, I might be able to take Elementary Hebrew one night a week, I don't know yet. Lessons are being given by the local Jewish Y.P.F. (only that's not what it's called), and I think it's open to Gentiles too.

Marcia and I went out for dinner (courtesy of her parents, since there are a lot of rules and junk about "Sorority Women" spending money on Freshmen), and that was the first ride I'd had in a car since you left.

October 15, 1957. I went to the Savoyards meeting the other night. Very jolly. They listed it as a "folk sing" on the calendar in an attempt to lure some of the raffish Bohemian element, but most of those drifted out after a few minutes, T. G. [Thank God].

Yes, I have walked downtown and back several times. I have also walked up and down the Library Tower and stood up there while the chimes rang for ten or fifteen minutes. Have either of you done that? I went to Dean Brooks's tea the day before I went to the Infirmary, so I think I infected a lot of people. Goody, goody. She has a jolly collection of books—*Winnie the Pooh*, most of Dorothy Sayers' detective stories, and, I think, all the Angela Thirkells.

Boy did we lose the Syracuse game! (34-0, in case you hadn't heard).... I have signed up for fencing. I don't know whether they will have it though, since they're still trying to get a fencing coach.... Incidentally, Cornell certainly is a liberal school. There were two dogs mating in the main reading room of the Library the other day.

October 17, 1957. Well, nothing much has happened around here. I actually saw Tripod lift his leg today and keep his balance. Also, I had an Astronomy quiz today—I think I busted it. We're having a History prelim next week, but good old Freddie Marcham tells us exactly what's going to be on it, so that should be easier than the Astronomy.

October 31, 1957. I went to church last Sunday. They have a jolly little routine with the collection plates and the bread and wine. The two boys bring the plates up and they are followed by two girls, carrying the bread, wine, and water. After the collection has been blessed or whatever they do to it, the priest comes down to the rail and takes whatever amount of wafers, wine and water he needs. It reminds me of the quartet in the "Gondoliers" where each person steps out of the group to sing his verse and then steps back in again. I half expect them to start singing "In a contemplative fashion."

Have you finished (or started) my green sweater yet, mom? If you're still working on it, don't make it any smaller than the red one, because it seems that the bigger they are, the more "ivy" the wearer is, and we must be "ivy" at all costs.

November 6, 1957. We had a panty raid last Thursday night. All the boys (Freshman boys, anyway) stood outside the dorm yelling, "We want panties, we want panties." They even got the bars off one of the downstairs windows, but it turned out to be the Head maid's room, and she scared them away. It is rumored that the raid was led by the Campus Patrol, and had been planned as a consolation prize for not having a Fall Weekend. They knew about it around eight o'clock that evening, and they wouldn't let anyone out of the dorm—not even me for my Astronomy Lab, but that didn't matter, because there were no stars anyway. All of us were watching out the window at them, even though we had explicit instruction not to. Unfortunately, they didn't get anything. The girls on our corridor want to have a BVD raid. Don't you think that that would be a good idea?

February 4, 1958. I had my last exam today. History. I thought it was easy, which probably means that I busted it. I discoursed at great length on the rivalry between king and pope, from 1066 to 1660; the importance of Henry VII; and the feeling of unity prevalent in England during the reign of Elizabeth. My Russian grade for the term is 75, slightly below average. I didn't know yet how I did in English or whether or not I exempted English 112—I suspect not.

February 7, 1958. Rushing starts tonight and everyone is perturbed over the fact that it's raining and snowing and they have to walk to five houses tonight in their good clothes and heels. Sooner them than me!

Did I tell you that when we heard that the U.S. got its sputnik up I stayed up all night (until 3, anyway) taping news broadcasts and replaying them because my astronomy exam was the next day and I wouldn't have put it past him to stick a question or two about it on the exam. The exam was at eight o'clock, so I only had four hours of sleep, and of course, he didn't ask anything about sputnik. The rat!

February 17, 1958. History is going to be harder this term than last. First of all, we're having fewer prelims and recitations are going to count more. Secondly, my recitation is at 8 am, which is not an hour particularly conducive to thinking. Thirdly, the instructor is one of these large, hearty, Wodehousian bags who tries to adopt Marcham's rather dry humor and fails lamentably. And fourthly, and worst of all, we're expected to read the book and may be quizzed on it at any recitation.

Feb. 18, '58. Guess What? I have measles—German, I think. They've turned the Recreation Room into a Pest House and I'll probably be out by the time you get this. I got my grades today: Russian 75; English 78; History 85; Astronomy 65.

February 19, 1958. You know what I need? Another laundry bag. The laundry was late in coming back this week, and therefore I have no bag in which to send this week's stuff. So I'll have to take it upstairs and do it in the machine. Don't you feel sorry for me?

February 23, 1958. Everybody around here has been all clutched because rushing was drawing to a close. Peggy, who thinks, at times, that she is God's gift to Cornell was quite surprised when Kappa Kappa Gamma, which is one of the Big Three or so sororities (and also dear cousin Marcia's) did not ask her back for the final rushing parties. Miriam made it through, and Ann deForest and Ellen Loosli both got into the sororities they wanted, so nearly everyone is happy.

March 21, 1958. That History course is not a gut any more. There's an old proverb around here that a good gut only lasts three years, and this one has been a gut for four now, so they're cracking down. We have to read the book, we get quizzes; he doesn't tell us the prelim questions before hand. Rough life! Sociology is a bore.

April 24, 1958. Modern dance is the stupidest, most inane, pseudo-intellectual activity I have encountered in my whole eighteen years. Today we were required (out of class time, mind you,) to go see some asinine modern dance flicks, narrated by a couple of women. One of them kept babbling about how hard it is to be "a dancer," and the other recited some crappy modern poetry (you know, like "the sky is blue, and a voice is calling me in the wilderness to the arms of an octopus" sort of thing) and dance to it.

May 2, 1958. There were rumors of a panty raid last night, so when Isobel and I got back from rehearsal, about three minutes before closing hours we found the door locked. They let us in on time, though, and soon after, the campus Patrol called up to say that everything was under control. The boys only got as far as Comstock, and didn't get anything there. If they would organize decently, and keep quiet about it beforehand they could get into the dorm before the Campus Patrol knew anything about it but they never have yet.

May 19, 1958. Spring Weekend was evidently as jolly as could be expected, considering the fact that we now have a Social Code. Most of the freshmen seemed satisfied, but those who remember the Good Old Days kept telling us how much better they were. Friday, Isobel and I went out to Taughannock (or however it's spelled) with John Ashby and his roommate (or apartment mate), (also John) and afterwards he and I went to see "Around the World in Eighty Days".

[Included with these letters is a letter addressed to Miss Meigs from the Office of the Dean, dated June 25, 1958, saying that "you failed in the last term to meet the requirements of good standing. Accordingly, the faculty committee that reviewed your record placed you on probation."]

September 26, 1958. My dear, sweet, little adviser is a jolly sort of chap. He told me that I was the only person who failed to qualify in Russian, and consequently, there would be no 103 class. However, I was supposed to register for 103 anyway, and take 201. So, I am.... My tuition ($625) is due by October somethingth (12th, I think). This letter is simply a thinly disguised request for money, in other words.

October 4, 1958. Isobel and I went to our first legal apartment party the other day. It was given by some Kenyan friend of Isobel's. He's doing research in Plant Pathology, and knew Ashby and Peter Hunt and piles of other people that were here last year. While we were there Nick (the one giving the party) and some of the others had an informal committee meeting for the International Organization's monthly dinner, and Isobel and I got signed up to help cook it, so you see, I am getting to cook after all (goody, goody).

October 13, 1958. I just had a thought. I've got to see my adviser first, but it might be possible for me to major in linguistics here if, in addition to the pure linguistics courses I also took the Russian and French linguistics courses. There might be enough of them to constitute a major field.

October 27, 1958. I rather doubt if I'll major in Linguistics. All I could do with it, besides teach, would be to join some idiot anthropological expedition and study obscure African dialects and what-not, or else write witty little articles for magazines on the peculiarities of English, and devise a "logical" type of English in my spare time. I could switch to English Lit, or Classics if I'm desperate ...

I assure you I'd like nothing better than to get Nabokov to autograph a copy of "Lolita" for Marjorie, but the word is that he's not autographing any. The only person I know of who has an autographed copy is a girl who somehow acquired a copy in French when it was banned in France, and Nabokov was so impressed by her enterprise and what-not, that he condescended to autograph it. Our Russian teacher told us that he's also doing some sort of Pushkin translations that he's been working on for the last eight years and which will preserve the original rhyme and meter of the poetry (Eugene Onegin, etc.). He was giving us the original, letting us translate it and then giving us Nabokov's version. It made ours look pretty poor.

November 6, 1958. Did I tell you that they had to get rid of Tripod? We dissected frogs in bio. lab. this week. They were freshly killed—in fact, they weren't really quite dead, it was just that the brain had been killed, or something. The heart was still beating. There were only about three of us in the lab that would touch them at first, and I had a crowd of fat, feeble-minded, squeamish idiots with New York accents clustered around me saying "Ohh, she's cutting it!" and "No wonder *he* was so fat" when I took out the eggs. The people in that lab make me sick.

December 12, 1958. My English class was cancelled yesterday, because the prof. cheered too heartily at the Dartmouth game, and had laryngitis.

January 6, 1959. It's freezing up here—mostly wind (great gusts of it). With a couple of sweaters under it, though, my coat is warm. I seem to be the only person up here who was glad to get back. Everyone else is stir-crazy or something and several people are thinking seriously of transferring.



February 19, 1959. Tuition is $625—enjoy it—it's the last time it'll ever be *that* low.

February 28, 1959. Tonight is some sort of big weekend—can stay out until three—I think I'll go over to Risley and help Isobel sit desk.... They've started tearing down Boardman. I've got film and hope to get pictures of it in varying stages of decay, but I may not be able to.

March 13, 1959. They're really at it now—tearing down Boardman. I'm trying to get pictures for you and posterity, but one can never count on the weather. They've put up a big board fence around it, and last night somebody got at it with a paint brush and wrote all sorts of things, like "Mene, mene tekel ... " [Daniel 5:24] "Boardman razed, tuition ditto" and similar witticisms.

April 17, 1959. The weekend of 30th April is Hotel Ezra Cornell Weekend (all sorts of hotel-type people around) as well as being something called "Sub-Frosh Weekend (probably for prospective victims), besides which I have a prelim on the 2nd in a course that I'm so far busting.

---

September 21, 1959. Guess what? The classics department is absolutely full of nice little old scholarly men who look like Cardinal Newman; and none of them want to give me Latin or Greek exams. They all think I will do quite well and they're going to watch over me paternally for a few weeks, to make sure I'm doing okay.... When I went in to see Prof. Caplan (who's teaching my Greek course) he asked me if I were any relation to Bob (so they must be on first name terms, how jolly!) and he seemed quite encouraged when I told him he was my uncle.

October 11, 1959. I've been reading the neatest book on university (British) slang. Apparently prelim has been in use at Oxford since 1883 (at least that's the first written citation found for it, which means that it was probably in common use before then). Also a fascinating chapter on the coining of words by the addition of -er or -agger, -ugger, etc., leading to such words as wagger-pagger bagger for waste-paper basket.

November 7, 1959. Fall Weekend was hell. I didn't have to work Friday night at all, but Saturday was definitely poor. Mrs. Webster had said something about she and I relieving each other, so that we could both sleep for a few hours, but we both stayed up the full time. Isobel got a couple of hours off and came over to see me and Mrs. Webster fed us both Sanka (so as not to keep us awake!). There were two kids who were 18 minutes late (which, when they could stay out 'til four, is inexcusable)—one of them deliberately sat out there with her date in his car for fifteen minutes (after which time it becomes a more serious type of lateness, but her watch was apparently slow) until I banged the window shut, when she finally came in. Then, to top it all off, there was a girl (one of Marcia's sorores—ex-sorores, I should say, because she resigned a couple of weeks ago—this girl, not Marcia) who was an hour and a half late. She *says* she fell asleep in the car—with "two" Dekes—which actually makes her story a bit more plausible—if there had been only one, I'd be inclined to doubt it—and of course, no story sounds "too" good at 5:30 A.M., but we had the campus patrol out looking for her and they drove back with her in one patrol car with two patrolmen, the two guys following them, and another patrol car with two more patrolmen behind them—jolly. And the first thing Mrs. Webster said was that she was very inconsiderate, keeping her and me up like that.





January 12 [1960]. I was in the Law library yesterday—it's neat. The women's lounge there looks rather like a Victorian drawing room, complete with fireplace and piano.

March 4, 1960. Yes, I got to church—7 am—and there were a lot of people there who didn't seem to know quite what was coming off at first. I looked in the *Sun* and they had announced the R.C. masses as being held in the chapel, which might account for the large number of people at ours, since we were in the chapel and they were in the auditorium. Usually when that happens (and they don't realize it until Fr. Stott has started and they realize they can understand what he's saying) they just sort of slink out, looking horribly sheepish, but I guess they didn't this time.

April 11, 1960. I really think it's sort of stupid to spend money for me to stay up here when I could make more than enough as a lab technician or something to support myself. I don't really want to take German, and summers in Historical Squaresville are about as exciting as old dishwater (to coin a phrase). After all, I am nearly 21.

April 21, 1960: Room and board for the summer session is $168, and tuition is $30 per credit hour. The minimum number of hours one can take is 4 and German is 6. Do let me know about this ...

June 27, 1960. I think Ralph [Ghent, graduate student in entomology, to whom she is pinned] was right—it is nice up here during the summer. Everything is much more informal and the people are nicer. My room isn't too bad (even after the luxury of Balch). It overlooks the tennis courts (better that than the garbage platform). Lots of space—more than I need—two closets, desk, bureau, bookcase, etc. I paid my room and tuition bills today. There was also a general fee of $24.... Classes are five days a week at 8, 10, 1 and 2, which is nice because I can meet Ralph for breakfast at 9.... There are lots of high school kids in the dorm—National Science Foundation type people, and a bunch of nuns.

July 8, 1960. It's a horrible dorm—fifty million people at meals (because of a bunch of National Science high school kids) and all of them from New York City with loud, screeching voices. I could be collecting material for a master's thesis in linguistics on the New York accent. Speaking of Linguistics, I found out from one of the guys who was in my Sanskrit class that Fairbanks is giving a course in Indo-European next term. One of these grad seminars that's not listed in the catalog. I hope Kirkwood will let me change my schedule and take it.

Ralph and I went to the fireworks up here. Apparently it's a regular thing and people contribute every year for the next year's show. They spend around $4000, and fill up the interval between when it starts and dark with marching bands and things. They had a pipe band this year, which was nice. 



September 17, 1960. The [Thurston Court] head resident and husband are very nice. She said that it's okay for Isobel and me to have Ralph or Ken or someone here to talk with when we're sitting desk. Also, hotplates are pretty much allowed. No one seems to know what the official ruling is, nor will anyone ask in case it happens to be "no." The kitchenette has a little recessed window, which will be a good refrigerator when the weather gets colder.

October 7, 1960. Gamma Alpha is having a beatnik party sometime in the next couple of weeks—probably just for Ralph's and my benefit. Should be interesting, if nothing else. Ralph and I are going to a folk-sing tonight.

October 12, 1960. Ralph and I are going somewhere (we don't know where yet) to watch the Kennedy-Nixon debate Thursday. Last week's session was preceded by a spaghetti dinner and ended up with beer.

November 5, 1960. Ralph and I and everyone are going over to Bill Brown's to watch television on election night. If Kennedy doesn't win, I shall probably acquire a few new words for my vocabulary.

February 3, 1961. Isobel was working late in her lab (to finish up a course) and had signed out to a married couple's apartment. She then decided to come back to Thurston because she finished early and the people she had signed out to really didn't have enough room for her. So she came in our window around three a.m. and was there at seven-thirty when the maids barged in, thinking that the room was empty. Apparently one of the maids (probably the one that we found kicking the cat) told Mrs. Nugent, who sent Isobel to Dean Cross (for sneaking *into* the dorm, of all things—probably since who sneaks in can sneak out) and Isobel gave her an earful—about how the rules encourage people to do things that they wouldn't do otherwise. I don't know where she slept last night—probably in someone's apartment on the sofa. This university ought to have it's collective head examined.

Feb. 9, 1961: Tom has offered me a few other little jobs, like hunting up journals in the library (at $1.25 an hour) for which he will get me a stack permit, which has its advantages, since I got caught without one and was severely reprimanded by some little squirt who worked there (probably a freshman) and didn't know his way around as well as I did.... Triphammer bridge and the new library are both open now. The library's nice. I don't know how the bridge is since I never get over there anymore.

10 February 1961: Katy Payne said she wrote a paper in Soc. 101, describing the social structure of a Mexican village where she and her family spent a summer, and

since she hadn't gone to too many lectures, or read much of the text, she wrote it in clear, un-technical English, and the instructor was absolutely thrilled over it and they wanted to publish it, but she wouldn't let them. She did rather badly on the final exam, too, but got a decent grade on the reputation of that paper. A good racket if it works.



H. D. F. Kitto (an eminent classicist, of whom you may have heard) is lecturing here next Monday on Greek and Shakespearan Historical Drama. Unfortunately, Roger (Katy's husband) is talking on the hearing of owls (which is his thesis, and which I've been helping him tabulate data on—at $1.50 per hr), which I'd sort of like to hear too. Can't decide which to go to.

16 February 1961. I went to Roger's lecture. It's owl's hearing. Right now he's trying to keep one job open at Tufts, which he can have if he wants it, while he finds out about a couple of possibilities open in the Zoo. department here. They were also going to go to Costa Rica this summer, only Katy may be pregnant, in which case they probably won't go.

March 17, 1961. The architects were running around with green paint today—missed me, though. Also a paper dragon, and eight green chickens in a completely walled-in courtyard of the library—took three men a couple of hours to get them out.

[4 April '61] A small wedding seems much more desirable to both of us in any case, and would occasion fewer headaches all around.

June 17, 1961. I've written all my thank-you notes except to aunt Doris for a $5 graduation present. Warped sense of values, what? $50 for getting married; $5 for graduating.

29 August 1961. We paid for our tickets today [to South Africa]. Only $211 each. Once you get there the living expenses are cheaper than here, so if you stay long enough it probably evens out to what you spend at home. We still don't have reservations from Southhampton to Capetown, but they think there's a good chance of a vacancy, and if not, the Union Castle line will still take our luggage and pay BOAC fare above what ship would cost.

# ALVAN BRICK, JR.

## CLASS OF 1969

Al Brick, Jr., attended Cornell's summer school as an advanced placement student in 1964. His letters reflect his awe and his enthusiasm for his course and for Cornell, to which he returned as a member of the class of 1969. He earned his Ph.D. from Cornell in 1981 with a specialty in entomology. Today he is a blueberry and cranberry farmer and environmentalist in southern New Jersey.

[July 3, 1964] Today is Thursday or should I say that tonight is Thursday for it is now 11 o'clock. We arrived at Cornell at about 2:30 on Tuesday and Vinton and I immediately went to the main office of the dorms to get our rooms, post office boxes and instructions.... From the office we went to the rooms 1st to Vinton's. It's rather small and it's up under the eaves, the typical scholar's hide-away. Then we looked at mine, no kidding its probably the biggest in the entire place. My roommate and I ... each have separate bedrooms which join a lounge-type central room in which are two desks; two rather old, leather easy chairs; rugs and 2 bookcases. Vinton is green with envy. We did very little except get settled on Tuesday. We were shown the eating places and after dinner attended a meeting of the entire advanced placement group.

Wednesday came and with it registration. I handed over all the loot and most all those pink forms. Previous to the time of registration Vinton and I rambled (that's uphill all the way) to the Plant Sciences Building, the site of all my classes. Mom you should see the garden in front of that place; it contains an astounding number of different plants all of which are giant sized for this early in the year. It's funny though of all the plants I saw in the garden none surprised me as much as some Dahlias growing near a cottage on campus. The stalks on those things must have been well over 2 inches in diameter. I never dreamed they reached that size.



I don't know whether you are familiar at all with the Cornell campus so I'll tell you a few of the most outstanding points. It sits atop a very high hill overlooking Lake Cayuga and abounds with deep rocky gorges. Over one of these gorges is a very small suspension bridge (small that is in comparison to the Ben Franklin etc) at the end of the gorge is a dam which forms Beebe Lake. My classes are on the agricultural campus, which is a good 15 min. uphill walk from the dorm. By the way, my roommate is also taking Botany. Directly between the dorms and the plant Science building is Willard Straight Hall, this is where we eat breakfast. It is the Student Union and also the Information Center. Clara Dickson Hall is the name of the building in which we eat lunch and dinner. It too, is a long uphill walk from the dorms.

After we registered yesterday we went to buy books, mine cost $11.40 excluding the price of paper, pen and ink which raised it another 3.00. In the afternoon we went to a picnic off campus to a place called Enfield gorge. It rained but that didn't ruin any plans, they still barbecued the chicken and served a big meal. Pat and I explored the gorge, a beautiful place very similar to Watkins Glen, while V. "mingled" with a girl.

This morning we started classes at 9 o'clock. We went to a lecture. Our professor seems like a terrific guy, he reminds me a little of Mr. Cover only not so much of a screwball. His name is Dr. Grierson. After the lecture we had a 2-hour lab which consisted of tramping all over campus classifying trees. We returned to class at 2 o'clock and were lectured again. It's funny our lectures were in the lab and our lab was outside. The workload is pretty rough, we had to read 3 chapters this evening and get acquainted with certain other areas of our study. It rained most all day today, a real good day to get started. I'll write again soon.

Love, The summer Ivy Leaguer

[July 10, 1964] Things are going exceedingly well as far as my grades are concerned. So far we have had 4 quizzes and my overall average is a 99 (darn that 99 I got yesterday messed up the whole deal). Now, I don't want you to get the idea that this course is easy so I'll tell you 3 rather interesting facts: 1) each day's work is comparable to the work of a full week during the regular school year (according to Dr. Grierson) 2) one kid has already left the course and gone home, and 3) we have three teachers who are taking the course and just barely making it. Actually the best way I can explain my extraordinary good fortune is by saying that that studying I did before I left home has been a real blessing. From it I gathered a rather extensive background and many scientific terms, which have enabled me thus far to keep well up on my studies. The only trouble is my present position is subject to change. The real test comes Monday with our preliminary scans. I'll be sure to write you again when I get the results from it. I finally found out what the situation is up here as far as credits are concerned. I am actually taking two 3-credit courses. The first started July 2nd and ends the day after my birthday. The other then starts and continues until the 14th of August. Unfortunately we have a different instructor during the 2nd course, a Miss Thomas. That could be dandy couldn't it.



Now let me see where did I leave off. Oh yes, with Thursday night. Well, as you know by now Friday's quiz was a relief. The lecture on the other hand and the reading assignment weren't. Pat and I spent most all afternoon and evening working toward our doctorate.

Saturday morning bright and early Charlie (my counselor) dragged me and the rest of the 10 boys on our floor out of our beds and off on a little picnic. It was known as breakfast in the gorge. The two of us and Charlie went up to Willard Straight Hall, picked up 2 cans of pineapple juice, 36 hard boiled eggs, 36 glazed doughnuts, 4 tired Adv. Placement girls and two more counselors. From the "Straight" we walked about a half a mile to a secluded muddy gorge-ledge overlooking a wonderful body of green water they called a stream. Actually though, the stream was rather nice but at 8 in the morning it didn't seem to appeal to me. That afternoon Pat and I strolled into Ithaca and went to see *Cleopatra*.... That night after supper we went to the Straight to see how preparations were coming for the Advanced Placement get together dance. We arrived early and helped put up the decorations and stayed until it ended.

Sunday morning I went to church and afterwards devoted my time to the study of heartwood, sapwood and annual rings. In general the pattern of this week has contained little else but study time. We take a break now and then in the afternoon and as a rule we finish our work by about 10 each evening.... Classes are very informal. In other words I can wear sneakers everywhere I go. Dr. Grierson gives us all personal attention when we need it and will answer any question during lectures. Right now I can't help but think of all the baloney my dear friend Mrs. Bowman handed us this year. For the most part any fears I had about college are gone. As for the weather it has been cool ever since I got here with a thundershower every now and then. As for my use of green ink—I am now in the process of developing a color chart which will correspond exactly to my different moods when it's completed.

[July 17, 1964] ... as to the questions you asked, let's see. My radio can't pick up any stations except those in Ithaca ... the pool is only open while we're in class and it's actually been too cool to go outside. We do get in a game of tennis every now and then.

Saturday evening was the time of our first trip to the washing machines. We spent half the night running around trying to find change ... Monday morning bright and early our time came. The test lasted about an hour and 20 min. and wasn't bad. I handed my paper in and as usual remembered something I had overlooked.... On Tuesday classes went as usual, studies too then at about 10:30.... Yesterday after lab we got our Prelims back. My average dropped a little due to that... I got a 98 that lowered me to a 99 average. Boy if I can only keep it up—we've got another Prelim Monday. Today wasn't unusual but tomorrow promises to be something. Dr. Grierson is taking us on a field trip. We're instructed to wear old clothes and sturdy shoes. No shorts because we might bleed to death from wounds. Our lunches are going to be packed up by the staff at Clara Dickson so that we can take them with us.

Our field trip was really neat. I think more of Dr. Grierson every day. You should have seen the way he led us through the back woods searching out specimens, up rocky stream beds through tunnels and over "mountains." The lunches we took weren't worth the cook's effort, even as little effort as I'm sure it was. Pat and I rode in Dr. Grierson's car and got to know him a little better than we had before. The trip ended at 1:30 and we were free for the remainder of the day.



[August 10, 1964] Sorry I couldn't write sooner but as I said in my card I had to study constantly. I got an 86 in that Prelim and we had another today. Actually I didn't do quite as bad as I thought. The highest mark in the class was only 88. Pat got a 63. It's too bad but I think he has almost given up completely.

The first week of our new course was harder than anything else I've had to contend with. One day was mitosis, one was meiosis, one was spent on Heredity, one on DNA and the last on algae. All five of these subjects were new to me. Mr. Garrity skipped them to keep up with the other classes. Heredity was the worst by far. The worst part was that the majority of the class had spent a great deal of time on it in high school. Besides new subjects we were hindered by Miss T. and our Lab instructor. She may be a great person but her lectures are slow and for the most part uninteresting. Most everyone else in the Botany department dislikes her. When she taught this course in the spring there was almost a civil war between her and 8 lab assistants ...

Guess what? Tomorrow (Saturday) we have a field trip. But guess who with: Dr. Grierson. I told you he is a terrific guy. He and Pat (last times lab assistant) are going to take us out from 9 until after lunch. They're even bringing the lunches. He's doing it to help us with this course but I don't think, in fact I know, Dr. T. doesn't know anything about it.... The final is Friday morning at 8. Next week should be a real blast. I may have less free time than I had this week. Almost forgot: tomorrow night there is an A.P Banquet at the Straight.

# STEPHEN E. APPELL

## CLASS OF 1965

Reflecting the problems in the country, Cornell students in the 1960s encountered considerable turmoil. Issues ranged from civil rights to political positions and tactics and, of course, the war in Vietnam. Appell describes one of the protests and the response by the university president, James Perkins.

May 17, 1965. It is now 10 fifteen in the pee-emm. Tonight I am working on a term paper, and have gotten a good deal of it written already. Imagine—an Appell term paper on time! It's due Thursday.

Today was a sight to see. We have had some very hot political weather at Cornell for the 1st time in my 4 years here, concerning the international situation, particularly over Vietnam. These very radical types have been demonstrating all over the place, including at a Centennial ceremony a few days ago at which [Governor Nelson] Rockefeller spoke; a few nights ago they interrupted a program featuring Averell Harriman and a speech defending US policy, in which he was heckled, booed, called a liar, etc. In return, Harriman called the demonstrators Communists.

Today was the ROTC annual Presidential Review. The "Ad Hoc Committee on Vietnam" announced that it would hold a sitdown demonstration on the floor of Barton Hall, to obstruct the ceremonies (marching, presentation of awards, etc.), in protest against foreign policy and against ROTC as an instrument of indoctrination for war which has no place in an academic institution.

When I was in the Presidential Review 2 years [ago], hardly any spectators came to see it. (The President in question is the Cornell one, who is now James Perkins). But today, everyone was there, it seems, to see how things would turn out with the demonstrations. And indeed, the whole thing was quite a performance and a demonstration of some of the best qualities in the American existence.



First, Pres. Perkins requested the demonstrators to leave, acknowledging their right to dissent but not this way. Of course, they stayed put, sitting arms locked right in the center of the hall so that the various companies could not march around, to pass the President at the reviewing stage.—Finally, the ceremony began, with presentation of awards. When the band played the Star Spangled Banner, it was quite a sight to behold. Here were all the ROTC troops, with the colors flying, standing at attention, with all the people in the bleachers coming to express their support of ROTC and to disapprove of these demonstrations—and in the middle of it all, up rose the demonstrators in the middle of the hall, to partake in the observance of the playing of the National Anthem. It was quite a thrilling and chilling spectacle. In Russia, in South or North Vietnam, these people would have been clubbed, imprisoned, and God knows what. In this country, even at an official military event, they could demonstrate in peace, subject at worse to catcalls and egg-throwing by a few idiots. Americans one and all, soldiers, conforming citizens, peaceful dissenters, all honored the flag of their country. Again, it was quite a sight.

The university and ROTC handled the situation well. Usually, the troops march around, but today they did not. Instead, Perkins made the rounds of all the troops standing at attention and thereby averted a confrontation with the jerks in the center of the floor.

When they played the Cornell Alma Mater, it was evident that the commissar leading the demonstrators had not given orders to rise for it, and one of them rose. Instantly, everyone booed and hissed (including me) and finally they arose.

When it was over, President Perkins left, and received a standing ovation. He was certainly magnificent in handling a very difficult situation. Then the Campus Patrol ringed the demonstrators while the crowds left. I'm sure they would have been messed up otherwise.

Of course, the American way is not so perfect. The CP's took the ID cards of all the demonstrators, presumably for disciplinary action. That's okay in my book. What disturbs me is that the FBI will no doubt attempt to get hold of their names, and boy are they going to be in trouble. People were taking pictures all over the place of those kids. Whatever they are, communists or what not, they had guts. And although they are idiots, and going about their protest in the wrong way, one must certainly say they have more guts than the jerks who throw eggs at them.

# KNIGHT KIPLINGER

## CLASS OF 1969

Knight Kiplinger followed his father to Cornell. He was active in a variety of student activities—Campus Chest, Glee Club, Sage Chapel Choir—and president of Quill & Dagger. The events at Cornell in April 1969 served to focus and also divide the university, and the occupation of Willard Straight challenged not only Knight's convictions but also the means being used for ends he supported. As we see in excerpts from two letters written to his father, violence, obscenity, and threats are antithetical to his ideas of civil rights, liberty, and democracy. For more about the protest, see Donald W. Downs, *Cornell '69* (Ithaca: Cornell University Press, 1999). Knight Kiplinger eventually joined the Washington, D.C., financial newsletter and magazine publishing company founded by his grandfather, of which he is now publisher.

March 1, 1969. Last night I was a spectator at one of the ugliest incidents I've seen at Cornell since I've been here. The occasion was supposed to be a speech on South Africa by Allard Lowenstein, former [Eugene] McCarthy chieftan and now Congressman. Just as the speech was to begin, the stage was seized by several black militants. Two of them stood at the ends of the stage at Statler auditorium, holding two-by-four boards in their hands. A spokesman at the mike said they wanted President Perkins, who was present in the audience, to come to the podium and go through the university's rationale for the South African investments decision that your committee took last spring. He complied, and in the middle of a very direct and balanced account of the issue, was grabbed by the collar from behind by one of the goon guards. The place almost erupted, but the blacks on the stage took off. Then a black South African took the podium, and launched into a very eloquent and impassioned condemnation of violence. He made the point quite forcefully that these American blacks had denied President Perkins the very right of free and dignified expression that the oppressed blacks of South Africa were fighting for. The irony of it all was numbing. Lowenstein, when he finally rose to speak, junked his prepared talk and spoke very briefly and effectively about the same question—mutual respect and cooperation among all peoples. Do you remember that line from "A Man for All Seasons": "If you cut down all the trees in pursuit of the Devil, where will you hide when he returns?" Civil liberties, the young radicals have got to learn, must be applied across the board. The truth will only be found in a totally free exchange of opinions, in which, hopefully, sound attitudes will show their superiority to hollow half-truths.

May 5, 1969. Things are pretty quiet here now. The SDS, which seemed to have had so much backing during the crisis, has cheapened the legitimacy of some of their more reasonable programs by pushing such ludicrous ideas as "open admission" for the sons and daughters of the "working class." The Trustees' positions and guidelines were greeted well by most students here. Especially appealing is the statement that the campus is "no sanctuary from the law" of society at large. There might be some fireworks tomorrow at Barton Hall during the President's review of the ROTC group. If the SDS is strategically foolish enough to make a big deal of this, they will probably experience further erosion of their following. Of course, there is the "martyrdom factor" in student dissent, too. The arrests that came a few days ago after the scaling of the ROTC cannon in Barton have elevated those eight into sacrificial glory as the "May Day Eight." It's all rather absurd.

# DAVID RICHARD BEAN

## CLASS OF 1971

David Bean came to Cornell in the fall of 1967. After graduation, he accepted an opportunity to join a team as part of the Ocean Floor Analysis Division of Naval Oceanography. On the trip out of San Diego, he died of a combination of seasickness and diabetes, which had been diagnosed when he was fifteen. His parents published a small volume of his letters and drawings entitled *David: A Collection of the Letters, Journals, and Artwork of David Richard Bean* (Wichita, 1972).

September 19, 1967. Initiation was a very trying time, which mostly served as a "self-examination" period (since I was in a room alone for the best part of two days).... Last night we had our first big chapter meeting, and it ran on and on for three hours. In the course of the meeting it was decided that Dave Bean should assemble the brotherhood and teach them to sing the Sweetheart song in a manner reflecting on the brotherhood and tradition!

February 22, 1968. This week has been, at its least, distracting! Sunday, of course, was the speech by Ted Sorensen. Monday was a symposium of Cornell government professors. Tuesday was Mark Hatfield on "The Role of Dissent." Tonight was Wyche Fowler on "Southern Politics." Thursday will be Detroit Mayor Jerome Cavanaugh on "Politics in Urban America." A fabulous sample of government peoples!

March 7, 1968. Every day I look forward immensely to drawing classes in the afternoons. Every time charcoal touches my pad the result is, in a sense, discouraging and confusing. With a little bit of luck I will one day begin to search for something (form, proportion, light/shadow) in each drawing. At that point they will arrive (hopefully!) works of art—and not just exercises.



April 1, 1968. Today I decided to major in government. Pre-registration for me is tomorrow and next fall I've decided to take Introductory Philosophy, American History, American Political Philosophy (Rossiter), Constitutional Law (that with Prof. Berns, Dad), and Sophomore Drawing. Wise choices, I think.

September 24, 1968. You ask if I am happy—really happy—at Cornell. I must answer that if I weren't I'm sure I wouldn't be here. It's a *wonderful* place to be *educated.*

November 18, 1968. I think that lack of sleep is the only thing that keeps me going. It's beginning to snow outside. I don't think I told you about the 18 inches that snowed us in last Tuesday and Wednesday. Ithaca was caught off guard and it took all of Tuesday before roads were salted and plows were operative. In spite of all the annoyance of the deadlines and general inflexibility of society, school, etc., it was just fantastic to sit and revel in the fact that for so many weeks we had all ignored nature's changing face.

December 3, 1968. I got back my preliminary exams in Constitutional Law and Political Thought. As you remember, I didn't think that I had done well on them. I didn't. I failed the Con. Law and barely passed Clinton Rossiter's exam. In short, things don't look bright. I imagine the first thing that comes to mind is the car. Either that, or apartment living itself. I wish I were lucky enough to have something to put the blame on squarely. Part of the fault lies with the fact that I have been studying about the same as I was last spring. The difference, though, between that term and this one is staggering. My courses this fall are much harder—and I believe that's true of all my courses except Art. Where I was learning from books and lectures and regurgitating for exams last year; this year I find myself lacking not so much in work as in ability to think and order my ideas. In history I'm doing fairly well and should make a B without trouble. Art, of course, is a solid point, too. Where I'm falling down is in the government courses—my major, no less! On to this bad note, let me add quickly though, that it isn't unsalvageable. Three weeks remain till Christmas and most of those three will be put into short history papers and a 15-to-30 page final paper for my seminar on Technocracy. In Con. Law, two projects yet remain: 1) the final exam and 2) a term paper, which consists of writing a decision for a case now on the Supreme Court docket. For Rossiter's course all that remains is a final paper due during exam week. On top of that there is my History final. That, briefly, is what lies ahead.... Dad, I need your advice badly. I can come home [for Christmas break] and probably blow the chances of making decent grades this term. Or I can stay here during those 18 days before exams and do my darnedest to catch up. I can't promise any great results, because the work before me, as I have said, is staggering. But at the same time I can't show you and Mom and even MYSELF a report of less than a B- (2.7). I'd want to kick myself especially since the courses themselves are relevant and terrific.

January 19, 1969. My papers are finished. You will be interested to know that the seminar paper on technocracy and democracy which necessitated missing my plane home got an A.... Yesterday was the Con. Law exam and I didn't do too well. Our 50-point question was to write an essay, which in a sense, summed up the entire semester's work, under the rubric: "Write an essay on the compatibility of judicial review and democracy" ... a subject which has never been fully explored and which has never been applied with much agreement. It was a tough exam.



January 27, 1969. Went up today and found out my grades this term: Art: A–; Con. Law: C–, Rossiter: C, History: A–, Seminar: A. The average should be somewhere near B.

February 12, 1969. As I see it now, it's time for a perspective [really a backward glance at best] on the year so far. Academically I shouldn't complain, but I am still puzzled at how I manage to get involved on so many time consumers. Pledge committee work promises a great deal of effort-eating opportunity. Then there's always spring. And I'd like to take advantage of my week's free rental at Fall View Ski Shop before the season is through. I'm afraid that the bit part in the musical will, AGAIN, have to be sacrificed. Studies in the fall were marvelous! Each class suddenly seemed to have a real bearing on the real world. The same is true of my courses this spring. All at once I realize that over 5/8 of my college life has passed. Now THAT is a sobering thought.

The greatest challenge of the year has been apartment living. As I consider it now, I have learned a great deal about people—not just some people, but people in general. I have been disillusioned with much, including myself.

May 20, 1969. Professor Berns gave a speech this past week to concerned moderates [Students for a Democratic Alternative] in which he again voiced the one fear that pervades all the statements he has made; that the semblance of success in the ranks of the left will be invariably followed by the equally militant, awesome (and yet much more far-reaching in its effects) reaction by the right. Where, in the '50s, the universities were able to build (or remain) a sanctuary from the outside pressures to conform, the question in the 60's is whether the universities will be able to counteract the forces and pressures from within. Berns' point is that the university's role has always been (despite divergencies from that goal) irrelevant to the society.... Things have quieted down as the majority of students feel that things can be settled by someone else during the summer before the fall term begins.

January 30, 1970. It was wonderful to get back to Ithaca and the house. I have moved in with Rich Schneider way up on the third floor and plans are under way for a resurrection of the old jug band if time and studies permit.

I just read a *Look* mag article ... on coed dorms that claims the participants don't even alter their study habits considerably. It says they only study and eat together, but bathe and sleep separately. It says their grades have actually improved. It says that it offers a much more mature and valuable approach to living. And I say: DON'T YOU BELIEVE IT!!!

February 24, 1970. Things have slowed down—or speeded up, depending on view—

for me now. I am doing considerably more studying than even last year, and first round of preliminary exams is starting very soon. My courses are interesting—art most of all—but there has been still time for intramural basketball, bowling, and of course Ned Harkness and his hockey team. In art we have momentarily left watercolor and leapt into acrylics—I say "leapt" because our first project, being experimental, quickly became a somewhat sedate version of "play Jackson Pollack." What fun it turned out to be—throwing paint on canvas, dribbling, slopping, texturizing—altogether different from what I conceived oils to be. Record snowfalls in Ithaca this winter.

April 8, 1970. Latest news from Ithaca is on the order of "another spring"—referring to the events of last year and their commencement again now. You knew that "320 Wait Ave."—what everyone calls the African Studies Center—was burned (arson suspected by all emphatically shouted by the blacks) during vacation. Two days ago, in order to "be repaid," about 50–60 blacks went into the (brand new) campus store and proceeded to break a couple plate glass windows, and push over bookshelves, display cases, and finally to walk out with armloads of records, sweaters, and other merchandise. No hand was raised to stop them. So far the university had done quite a lot to meet their demands (which include armed and black protection at all times—Corson has just assigned the Burns Agency to it—special buses to take them to campus, amnesty for those involved in the Campus Store vandalism, and a new center built to replace 320 Wait fully operative by fall, 1970). We'd be foolish to think that the campus store would be the end of nonsense rather than the beginning. Sho' 'nuff, today some whites have occupied Day Hall. Mass rallies have been held in support of the Black action and demands. I am trying to keep up with my courses (paper and prelim coming soon) as well as my tennis as the weather continues to turn.

---

September 17, 1970. Much seems to have happened in this one short week. After the call I was sure that I could handle work and my classes, but your premonitions were fulfilled the following day. After having attended my government courses, there was little I could admit short of, "you're right." My schedule includes the rather ambitious prospect of reading at least three books a week. Thus I have terminated my career as waiter extraordinaire at the Boxcar; where, I might add, I was making $1.50 an hour wage and clearing $2.00 an hour tips. In all of Ithaca, it is the best work of its kind. I shall finish out this week—then I shall concentrate on schoolwork only.

My classes have inspired me anew, as I had hoped they would. Italian is a joy!... History 483 was the big surprise since I was expecting Southern history and found I had in fact, "The Southern Literary Renaissance: Origins, Dimensions and Achievement," with an impressive list of books and an able lecturer. My Government 354, "Political Authority in a Mass Society," promises to be fascinating; and my last course, Government 250, "The Crisis of Industrialism" puts me back with Professor Brenner who has provided me with great political insight. He also plays tennis and we have a match lined up for the weekend.

# DONNA FULKERSON LAVALLEE

## CLASS OF 1977

Donna Fulkerson LaVallee kept a tiny diary during 1976, when she was a junior at Cornell. She records her sorority activities and a good deal about her active social life.

Jan. 18. Back to Ithaca; Corky spent the night; snow!

Jan. 19. Rush workshop

Jan. 20. Rush breakfast workshop

Jan. 21. Rush open house; dinner at Lum's

Jan. 22. Rush open house; Dominos for dinner

Jan. 23. Registration; grades 2.97! Apartment hunting

Jan. 24. Baked 800 cookies for rush; added 1 class; Hockey game vs. Yale 0/ Cornell 8

Jan. 25. Rush party 1:30–3:30, 4–6; rush meeting 8:30

Jan 26. Classes start! Chapter meeting

Jan. 29. 1st invitational-coffeehouse; drink-off w/ATO

Jan. 31. Nutrition career day at WSH; *Deliverance* on TV

Feb. 3. 2nd invitational; Wizard of Oz

Feb. 4. Wine & cheese party w/cork

Feb. 5. 3rd invitational-Fiesta; membership vote disaster

Feb. 6. Corky tucked me in early—sick

Feb. 7. Getting ready for final party; slept all night; bad cough

Feb. 8. Final parties; medieval theme

Feb. 9. Pledging

Feb. 11. 6 stiches in my leg; exchange dinner with ΦΚΣ; hockey game Harvard 8-4 us

Feb. 12. Pan-hel plant sale; ice cream at Friendly's pledge-open house

Feb. 13. Wake up at SAE; west campus dating game

Feb. 14. Afternoon by the fire at ATO; dinner at Asiatic Gardens; daiquiri at Simeon's

Feb. 17. Dinner at ATO; movie, *Grapes of Wrath*; fireside at DDD w/ pledges

Feb. 19. Letters for jobs; dinner (steak) at ATO w/ Cork; study w/ Corky, party at DKE with DDD; Mike called

Feb. 21. Apartment hunting; Hockey game Brown 7-CU 3; cooked dinner for Corky, played Scrabble

Feb. 22. Wake up w/ my love! Pork chops for lunch; library all day; dinner at Straight

Feb. 25. Study for exams

Feb. 27. IFC weekend; ATO Prohibitions costume party & dinner

Feb. 29. Walk in the sun; officers council

Mar. 2. Library

Mar. 4. Dinner at ATO; marketing project meeting

Mar. 9. Phone duty; house meeting

Mar. 16. Dinner at ATO: Prof. Polenberg

Mar. 19. Movie *Clockwork Orange*

April 6. Coffee cup ceremony

April 10. Military Ball; dinner at Old Port Harbor; dance at Risley

April 11. Rush workshop; alumnae pledge tea

April 16. Spring fever; Cayuga's Waiters' concert

April 17. Tried to sleep out at Treman [State Park] too cold; errands; balloon sale on Commons; Doug Henning magician



April 19. Cornellian picture taken; party at the Haunt

April 20. Animal Science field trip to Rochester.

April 28. Phone duty.

April 29. Corky here for dinner; play "Brecht on Brecht," Corky was sound man.

May 2. Studied. Tried to lay in sun but it got cloudy; goofed off

May 4. Date night barbeque; Corky came over; hamburgers & hot dogs

May 7. End of classes! Spring Weekend; dinner at ATO: watermelon, baked Syrian flat bread, shish kebob, corn, cherry cheesecake; dance

May 8. Mom & dad came up; picnic at Lower Buttermilk; hike to Taughannock Falls; Mrs. Nelson's tea for Seniors; my Birthday dinner at Pierce's

May 9. My 21st B-d; gave mom tea & donuts in bed (almost); wandered in the Plantations

May 10. Pansy champagne breakfast; kidnapped seniors to Balch; drank too much Champagne

May 17. Study

May 18. Food exam

May 19. History exam

May 21. Corky & I out on the town: ate at McDonalds

May 22. Meat's test

May 23. Packed up

May 24. Drove home

# CORNELL GAY LIBERATION

## OFFICE NOTEBOOK ENTRIES

## 1976–78

Cornell's Gay Liberation organization opened an office in Willard Straight in 1976. Members took shifts at the desk and recorded their experiences in a notebook, which became a forum for the workers to talk to each other. The comments are in several different hands.

4/23/76 Why has there been no publicity for this office? I've seen nothing in the *Sun*.

4/27/76 A Visitor! A young gentleman wondering if it were too late to join a fraternity this year. I informed him our membership was not only unlimited but free. He seemed impressed. I then casually let drop the name of our organization. He retreated to the door. He then blushed at the possibility of having offended me and explained that he had simply been given the room number by some benighted secretary. I smiled as warmly as Arlene Francis. He stumbled out. And so another one slips through our fingers.

5/19/76 K. is the victim of a new disease which defies characterization by Gannett Clinic's own pathologists. However, they want another shot at it, and, even in the midst of my final examinations, my thirst for life is such that I feel I must try anything, even a third visit to Gannett. Au revoir.

[9/31/76] A young man visits, accompanied by a pair of folded arms and a steady gaze. Wants to talk of things sexual. He seems relieved at my enjoyment of the subject. I enjoy his relief.

5/12/76 Some ♂ with dog in again.... I leave for a "straight" break to coin a phrase.



Book II

2/7/78 Em stops by. The sign in the Straight lobby keeps getting turned to the wall: we put posters on the back.... a Chinese fellow came in towards end of evening looking for someone to talk to. Said he already had a "gay notes" when asked if he wanted one. "If" he can find a date, he'll be at the dance. Nice kid! Grad hotelly.

2/8 Man called, wanted the address of gay bars in Ithaca. Sent him to Purple Turtle. Man in for counseling. Set him up with B.

2/16 B. counselee calls; mentions that B. called him earlier but his question was related to possible difficulties he might encounter by talking—specifically he is concerned with B.'s association with housing office—he was reassured that everything he might say to B. is strictly confidential and seems reassured.

2/20/78 Note to Bob: There is no way we can offer free drinks to "Straights." A. Who can tell? B. What about Anti-Gay discrimination C. Who would pay for them?

[later] Can't decide if the poster of the woman on the wall is tolerable or not—in a Gay lib office one must reevaluate one's accusations of sexism, but perhaps for you gay guys this is sexism in a different sense—in any case it's not the best way to attract dykes to the office.

[later] On counseling: the alternative sexuality counseling group has expanded from 6 members to 10.

3:10 ♂ wanders off muttering "I'm so embarrassed."

2/24/78 Snowball through window

2/25 2 counselees this week have been fake. Oh well. Mardi Gras exists!

2/25/78 ♂ who knows me from the Floriculture department! Another one. They're everywhere!

3/6 Got a question for you guys, just having gotten out of my philosophy class, where we're studying (discussing) "Moral responsibility." Today's discussion regarded the manner in which society deals with those persons whose impact upon society is harmful, even when/if their impact, or qualities producing it, were "determined" in some manner over which they have no control. I of course got upset with the assumption that "genetically" (or physiologically, anatomically, psychologically etc. ad nauseum) determined traits different from social institutions are necessarily harmful to society, and asked, if we were talking about moral responsibility who had moral authority to decide that people should be imprisoned or sentenced to a psychiatrist. My question is this, since I was asked if I had a particular example in mind but didn't have the guts to say yes: what issue can be used in such an instance, that is strictly analagous to the gay rights issue? I thought of abortion but that didn't help because we were discussing determined factors, over which we can exert no control (everybody knows about our mad, lustful desires ... ) and abortion is a decision.

Maybe I'll just get my guts together and come out to my philosophy class, but for occasions such as these when points are wished to be made but discretion must be used, it would be nice to have in mind some convenient example that can be used to enlighten the informant without scaring them all away (homosexuality being as revolting as it is, it belongs in the bathrooms, not in Goldwin Smith 248!!)

3/9 Just stopped off to leave a Chrysanthemum plant that I got from the greenhouses ... it was going to be thrown out. I could [not] believe the way people were looking at me as I carried it across campus ... you would think I had 3 heads! First: I admit it's a pretty eye-catching thing, but instead of making people smile & chuckle, they try to make you feel like an imbecile. I really have to laugh at them. Second: I'm a guy. Boys never ever should carry, hold, smell, touch or slightly admire flowers: OR You're a Faggot!!! Sorry for my outburst, but people are sooo Fuck-up that I can't believe it! Us greenhouse boys tend to need to voice our grievances occasionally, too.

*Message: ♂ in need of someone to talk to. Would like counseling.

3/13 I would like to announce that today I found out that dear Anita [Bryant] has been voted *Good Housekeeping* magazine's most admired woman of 1978.

3/15 What's next? Hand-painted frescoes of Anita, impaled on a citrus tree adorning cathedral ceilings? A new hymn entitled "A Mighty Citrus is our God"? A revision of the Holy Sacraments to include not only the Body and the Blood of Christ, but the Juice of Anita as well? Oh God, where does it end?

3/19 One "fuckin' faggots" caller

3/27 Am working on how to pass non-discrimination policy statement. Have contacted the Vice-provost of C.U. for aid. He thinks the best way to go about it is to work through the Campus Counsel. If they recommend that it should be passed as University policy, the Faculty Committee of Reps. and the Trustees shouldn't give much resistance.

4/3 Anita has done it! She 1) gave an interview to *Playboy!!!* 2) said that homosexuals should be imprisoned for 20 yrs; 3) stated that all Jews, Moslems & other Non-Christians will go to HELL!! So much for her credibility.

4/7/78 [I propose that we] advertise in something as Gay women or Lesbian, in order to draw other women into the organization by first organizing something for women. I feel that considering this office's reputation as gay male (chauvinism being another issue entirely) a lot of women who would otherwise get involved will not respond to something simply sponsored by gay lib, regardless of everybody's terrific intentions. What I mean is that to catch the attention & interest of other lesbians the office will have to overcome its reputation, and the most efficient quickest way of doing that is to direct one's advertising to lesbians. I don't want the event (if we organize one) to be all women ...



4/8 Some mostly naked D.U. frat. boys running arrived in the building drew my attention for a few minutes. Only at Cornell!

4/11 The Trustees will be considering changes to the non-discrimination statement on May 9.... This is a very good chance that sexual orientation may be considered.

4/23/78 Bad news: Dad might come up with Mom on the 28th, and you can safely bet whatever you hold dearest that I'm not taking Dad to any gay lib pot-luck dinner. Cowardice reigns!

29 April 1978 Mom had a good time at the dinner.

Later: a nice looking ♂ closet case outside. I gave him my most reassuring smile but to no effect. He ran away.

5/2 I'm back. Oh its great to be back in Cornell's one and only and very special Gay Lib office. I've been in Boston and let me tell you that city can't begin to compare with Ithaca.

6/28 Sara from Cornell Cinema ... would like a complete listing of the most likely spots in town where gays in general can be reached—for purpose of publicizing a Gay Film Series soon. Please add places that I have left out: Smedley's Book Shop/Blue Angel/ East Hill Depot/ Mainline Growth Center/ Ears/ Women's Center/ Gays Affiliated with the Alternative Center/ Alternative Sexuality Counseling Services/ Being Ourselves/ Feminist Art Studio.

9/26 called about reps. for dinner w/ Rhodes; gave 3 names ... (only wanted students). We'll be invited sometime in the coming week. Rhodes is doing this w/ many stud. orgs, according to Mick

[later] I wonder if Dinner w/ F. Rhodes will be a piss elegant affair. No doubt we will be scheduled with Youth for Christ & IFC

12/21/78 Done at Last! Thank God! I've passed everything!

# "JILL"

## CLASS OF 1984

The following letters to a male friend were written by a female student who graduated in 1984. Her letters reflect society's obsession with thinness as she struggles with her weight; she also discusses her and her friends' attitudes about their parents. Whitby is a co-op living unit. The writer prefers to remain unidentified.

Thursday, 9 June 1983. My parents and I had a couple of run-ins during the vacation, mainly about my weight. I'd been lying to them all semester, claiming to be 115 when I was less than 110, and they found out. Not pleasant.... Enough of these weighty matters.

Life in Ithaca has been entertaining. Whitby is quite a home already.... The house people themselves are nice, both easy going and dynamic. Work, on the other hand, is far from peachy.... I went to complain to the chiefs yesterday. "Give me work," I begged. The outgoing Student Coordinator was there, wishing to show that he still had a little clout, he waved his arms grandly, "Show up at 12 tomorrow," he declaimed, "I'll give you hours." I smiled. I laughed. I danced, leaped, and cavorted. I thought and grew serious. "What will I be doing, John?" queried I, soberly. "Folding napkins." And this after a 4 hour napkin folding shift.

On Monday, I was a steak runner at Barton. I was briefed first. "Your job is very simple," said my mentor. "Get meat from pit. Bring to table. Understand?" I nodded, chanted "get meat. Bring here." To help myself remember, I developed alternate chants. "Dead meat, dead meat," "cow carcass, cow carcass," I muttered. My co-workers socked away, wide-eyed. When the time came for the actual steak-running, no-one stood in my way ...

Next week I start my other job at Hughes. The one-week training period for this job consisted of a one-hour orientation session, and I am more than a little nervous about spilling soup ... I wonder how long I will last.

June 26, 1983. My waitress job has turned out to be interesting and not nearly as terrifying as I'd feared.... Our patrons, whom I'd initially dubbed "The Burnt-Out Businessmen," are actually a rather peachy crew ... and remind one of little boys at summer camp, away from the strictures of home and indulging in their new freedom with childish abandon. Last weekend, we served them a buffet dinner with wine and they got quite inebriated.... I am doing a lot of recorder playing and reading; plays by Bertolt Brecht and Eliot, biographies and critical studies of Thomas Mann. Two nights ago I went to a party at Beta Theta Pi, where 2 or 3 friends of mine are boarding. They served an incredible punch, three-grain alcohol and vodka. Not being a drinker, I did not partake of it, contenting myself with picking out the fruits that had been floating on top. These had become saturated, and were potent enough to make me weave a little—or so I told myself.

23 July 1983. This is the evening of the Big Whitby Party. We've all finished debauching ourselves on 6 varieties of Pizza. The most memorable was a Fruit Pizza, well grounded in a sunflower seed crust and cucumber sauce. Much of Risley will be congregating here later on. The Whitby element will be well represented also. Whitby is rallying its granola-head core, preparing for the new year. Already, there is talk about the New People.... The famous Cornell Reservoir, however, is enjoying wonderful popularity this summer. To swim in the Reservoir is illegal; to swim there nude (which is really the only way it's done) is doubly so, and fines are heavy and embarrassing. Nevertheless, the primordial lure cannot be ignored. The risk, I think, just adds to the attraction.

August 7, 1983. One gets quite an interesting idea of parental relationships at Whitby. Parents are seen as stubborn and difficult people, whom one must visit and placate every so often. Through their ineptitude, they will inflict pain, but one is magnanimous and endures. If one is exceptionally perseverant and fortunate, one may be able to enlighten the old codgers a bit. After the requisite weekend or week of filial obligation, one returns to the Enlightened back at Cornell, where one is greeted sympathetically, praised, embraced.

# MOLLY DARNEIDER

## CLASS OF 1998

Scrapbook entries, 1994. Athletes tend to be especially superstitious individuals. Rituals and routines become a part of nearly every athlete's life. Ice hockey players seem to be particularly fuzzy about their routines and rituals. Hockey great Ken Dryden is famous for the dressing routine he used before practices and games. He would put on each piece of equipment at a specific time, always beginning with the left side. As a hockey player, I know very well some of the persnickety things that hockey players keep on their regimen of superstitious activities. The Cornell Women's Ice Hockey team has many rituals and routines, which can be effectively grouped into three categories: personal, team, and food.

The consumption of specific foods before games is very important to the members of our team. One player eats a turkey sandwich and two bananas before each home game. She claims that it brought luck to her during tryouts and that the luck will now pervade the entire team. Another player eats a jar of baby food immediately before each game for the simple reason that she hates being hungry during a game; baby food is easy to digest and won't upset her stomach. The entire team chews Big Red gum in the locker room before games. The food items are very important to the members of the team because without them, the individual or team feels out of sorts because they have become traditions.

Personal rituals and routines make up most of the superstitious activity on the team. One member of the team always taps the goalie's helmet, blocker, glove, left pad, and right pad, in that order, immediately before the first face-off of the game. One player didn't shave her legs last year until the team won, and with a 2-16 record, one can imagine what they looked like. Many players tape their sticks before each game, regardless of whether or not they need to be taped. There are many superstitions that are kept secret as well. For example, no one knows the meaning of the initials written on my stick for good luck. One can only imagine how many undercover rituals are taking place. Most of these rituals serve as a comfort to calm players before or during the game.



The most important superstitions that take place are those practiced by the team as a whole. Most importantly, no one ever says the word "shutout" until it happens. Other team rituals are to listen to the same tape in the locker room and do a cheer before leaving for the ice surface. Every time we leave the locker room we do so in numerical order, ascending from number one or descending from number thirty, depending on which goalie is playing because she leads the way. The team gathers around the net, not at the bench, before each period to talk and do one last cheer. These rituals and routines are never broken and are crucial to the team's belief in superstition and luck.

# MARGAUX NEIDERBACH

## CLASS OF 2000

Scrapbook entries, 1996. Sitting in that sticky room in Schoellkopf Hall on that sweltering August afternoon, surrounded by nearly eighty other girls, many of whom were nearly six feet tall and all of whom had extremely athletic builds, we listened to our coach, her voice booming at us about weight training and running and circuits and ergs and tanks and Yale and Princeton and Radcliffe and Dartmouth .... I don't think I've ever been so intimidated in my entire life.

I remember the meeting for the prospective members of the novice women's crew team like it was yesterday. I sat quietly in my seat, amidst a sea of unfamiliar faces. My fruitless attempt to make small talk with the enormous girl seated next to me had failed miserably, and so I sat, silent and waiting. Members of the varsity women's team handed out cards for each of us to fill out and then retreated to the back of the room. I nervously scribbled away.

Height 5/2 Weight 115

Previous rowing experience: none

Previous Athletic Experience: 4 years Cross-Country and Track, captain of both teams, varsity letters, all division

My original dream was to row. Although I had never rowed before, I knew that I had the drive and determination to learn. I could accomplish anything I set my mind to do, right? Well, I soon ascertained, much to my dismay, that in order to row for Cornell, I would need to grow about eight more inches before the start of training, which happened to be the following afternoon. It was then that I decided to learn how to cox.

At first, I knew nothing. I began completely unsure of myself. I was not even sure if crew was the sport for me. I had a long road ahead. ... My coach talked the new coxswains through practice until we had learned enough to start speaking ourselves. I learned the commands one by one. I learned the difference between port and starboard, between bow and stern. I began learning the intricacies of steering and docking, skills which take quite a while to master.



In the fall, we had two head races, or distance races. In the first, the Rochester Regatta, we raced three boats. The coxswains were chosen through evaluations and rankings by the rowers. I was nervous that I wouldn't be picked. Out of eleven coxswains, I was chosen to race and given the second boat. The feeling of adrenaline flowing through every vein in my body that day is a feeling that I will remember always. The second race, the Schwartz Cup Regatta, was an all Cornell home race, for which I coxed as well.

Next came the challenge of winter training, during which I became all too familiar with the inside of Teagle Hall. In indoor training, if there were not enough seats in the rowing tanks or there weren't enough ergometers (rowing machines,) the coxswains remained on the side so that the rowers could train. During this time, I asked question after question to the rowers and to my coach in order to learn as much as possible, which did, in fact, help to prepare me for our winter training trip to Florida. At this point, seven coxswains remained and five were invited to train in Florida. I was one of the five. The trip was a phenomenal learning experience. I coxed mainly for the novice women, although I was fortunate enough to experience coxing for the varsity women and novice and varsity heavyweight men.

More than anything I wanted to cox the first boat. I had worked hard all year, and this had become my dream. If not the first boat, I at least wanted an eight which would have put me in the second boat. When it came time for Charlotte to announce boats, I was not the first cox. I was not the second cox. I had received the third boat, which was the four. There are not words to describe my disappointment. I had failed myself.... All of my friends were in the eights ...

My crew had quite an interesting season. In terms of racing, our season was terrible. We didn't win a single race. Our times, however, did improve, and the five of us became the closest of friends. By the end of the season, we showed considerable potential for faring well at Eastern Sprints, our final regatta.

# HOWARD GOLDSMITH

## CLASS OF 2000

Scrapbook entries, 1996. Upon arrival I thought that I knew the exact direction I wanted my studies to lead me. A life of saving the environment via either a scientific or political alleyway seemed like the sort of life I'd enjoy. My major, Natural Resource Management in the College of Agriculture and Life Sciences, seemed as though it would afford me the opportunity to explore the humanities while, at the same time, learn all the policy involved with natural resource management. As I near completion of my first semester at Cornell I've learned that, while I still love the environment and wish to protect it, my aptitudes and my academic loves do not coincide with the subject areas studied in the Natural Resources department. Instead, the world of the humanities has captured my imagination; changing my hopes, dreams, and desires for the future.

As soon as Chemistry 103 started this fall I discovered that I did not have the scientific aptitude or fascination that I'd thought I had. At first, this did not scare me since the policy side of resource management interested me the most. I soon discovered that my major would require not only another semester of chemistry but many courses in field and wildlife biology as well. During an information meeting in the middle of the semester, career specialists made it clear that an entry level position in Natural Resources consisted mainly of field biology, something which does not interest me in the least. As time progressed I came to the realization that this major did not fit my needs academically or vocationally.

At the same time, my psychology class captured my imagination. The variety of theories presented each day allowed me to view my behavior and the behavior of my peers in new ways. Spontaneous discussions started in the dining halls concerning the validity of this theory or that theory. Needless to say, I never once discussed any chemistry in the dining hall. My Cornell history class taught me not only about the founding of the school, but also about the history of education and women's rights. This kind of interdisciplinary work makes me enthusiastic about my studies.



I love to think. I love to write about what I think. Discovering things that interest me and relating them to one another makes me tick. Ideas inspire me to go for it. To live life to the fullest. Ideas let me challenge conformity of thought. Ideas allow me to stretch my mind and constantly redefine what I know about my life, about others and about the world in which we live. Only through studying people, cultures, the past and the natural world can we possibly hope to progress in any way, scientifically, philosophically, or politically. I love knowing answers when people have questions.

I love to teach. Nothing brings me more pleasure than seeing a light go on in someone's head. When a person achieves understanding in some topic he gains a new perspective. With each new perspective a person's vision becomes clearer and clearer. People have told me that I have a knack for explaining things. I want to give people new perspectives and hence, vision.

I wish to spend my life studying and teaching things I love. I have discovered that working with people, giving them perspective, must lie as a corner stone in my life. The academic world stands poised at the beginning of the new millennium. This semester I have decided to join it.

# KAREN KLINGELE

## CLASS OF 2001

Scrapbook entries, 1998. Besides the drinking . . . college is about learning. It's not as simple as learning whatever it is that's being taught in your required gen-ed classes, though. It's about learning how to listen, how to speak, and how to think. Learning who you are, who your friends are, and the type of people you want as friends. Learning how to trust your innermost feelings, and how to find those feelings in the first place. It's about learning what's really important to you, and learning what you really don't give a damn about. College is about learning how to tolerate, how to accept, how to like, and how to love. Learning how to give as well as receive, and how to trust that everything will even itself out on its own (you buy a pizza one night, your roommate will the next night). It's about learning that your mom and dad actually do have the right answers sometimes, and that your kid sister isn't such a dumb little kid anymore. College is about learning how to treat people as people, not as stereotypes. Learning that sometimes a kiss isn't just a kiss, that sometimes it means more, and that sometimes it means less. Learning how to achieve, how to succeed, and how to accomplish. It's about learning how to not come in first place and still be proud, and about coming in last and learning how to admit that you could've done better. College is about learning that loud parties don't necessarily mean a good time. Learning that loneliness doesn't go away in a crowd, and that sometimes it's okay to be by yourself on a Friday or Saturday night. It's about learning that your lunchtime crowd doesn't constitute your popularity, and that popularity is all a matter of perspective. It's about learning that boredom is simply laziness of the mind, and that watching three hours of Thursday night NBC is not quality relaxation time. College is about learning how to pack a bag, how to pack a car, and how to pack a room full of way too much stuff. Learning that people probably like you a whole lot more than they'll ever tell you, and that it's your responsibility to make sure your friends know how much you appreciate them. It's about learning that simply doing what you're supposed to do isn't enough, you need to put forth twice that much in order to fully grasp whatever it is that's sitting in front of you. It's about learning how to make people smile. College is about learning how to miss people enough to not stick them in the past, and how to not miss them so much that it keeps you from moving into the future. Learning how to motivate yourself and how to motivate others. Learning what the phrase "make do" means, and how to use it to make it seem as if you're not simply "making do." It's about how to swear in all the different languages of your class/floor/dorm/housemates. College is about learning. Learning how to live.

# ABHISKEK MATHUR

## CLASS OF 2004

Scrapbook entries, 1999. Coming to college is like starting a voyage. In Hinduism, before starting any new endeavor there is a religious service that takes place to pray for good luck and fortune. Consequently, before coming to Cornell my family prayed for my good fortune at Cornell and a string was tied around my wrist. This string is not to be taken off the wrist but allowed to fall off the wrist. It is supposed to protect the wearer to a new place and provide good luck until the person is comfortable in the new situation. It is a symbol of my family's support and encouragement, but it also symbolizes the hope of my family that I will work my hardest and succeed. I am the first person from my family to attend an Ivy League University, and so it represents the hope that I will succeed and lead the family to greater success. The string is representative of the hope that someday I will be successful no matter what I shall choose to accomplish. It represents the reason that I strive to work hard: to be happy and to make my parents happy.

Coming to Cornell is a big step from high school. It will be hard to achieve as good grades as I received in high school. More studying and harder work will be required, yet college is not just about school. Increased independence at Cornell means better time management skills. I will have to determine how much time needs to be spent on one project, on studying, and on partying. No parents will be around for moral support or a hug during a tough time. Cornell is a great change from high school, and this string has provided the support needed to continue through the toughest part of it.

---



During most of high school, I had worn glasses. In my mind glasses were not attractive; consequently, I had gotten contact lenses during my senior year. All throughout my senior year, I wore contact lenses, which I thought made me appear attractive. At college, however, I decided not to wear contact lenses as much as high school. I made this decision because I didn't want get involved with anyone for my first two years at college. Therefore, I wear glasses most of the time to appear not as attractive as I could be if I wore contact lenses. Though I rationalize my decision to wear glasses by saying that I like taking naps in the afternoon and read a lot during the day, which is hard to do with contacts, it is hard for me to admit that the real reason that I don't wear contacts as much is because I don't want to be involved with anyone during the first two years at Cornell.

# DAVID LLOYD

## CLASS OF 2003

Scrapbook entries, 2000. Last weekend, my parents came up for "Parents Weekend" from Detroit. They arrived in Ithaca after driving most of the day on Friday. Right when they arrived, we headed off for dinner at Danos', which is just off the Ithaca Commons. At Danos' we had a lovely dinner that was certainly a nice break from the monotony of the food at Robert Purcell. The next day, I met my parents down on Ho Plaza and we went to an informational session about housing in the sophomore year. The presentation was very well done and informative, but was unfortunately interrupted by a fire alarm. Everyone hurried outside as the fire trucks arrived, but it appeared as though it was only a false alarm. My parents and I then went to meet one of my dad's favorite professors who came to Cornell while my dad attended classes here, and his wife. We had a nice lunch with them at Banfi's in the Statler Hotel, where we discussed the upcoming presidential elections and expressed our mutual hope that Al Gore would win. After some touring around the campus, we went to Madeline's for dinner and had another nice meal. At this dinner, as well as the previous night's, I realized how much different the conversations I had with my parents were compared to those with fellow students. We talked politics much more and had generally more sophisticated discussions. Finally, on that Saturday, I took my parents to Wegman's. I have discovered this is one of the great tourist attractions in all of Ithaca, and sure enough my mom was very impressed. On Sunday morning, my parents left to drive back to Michigan. The goodbye was not exactly tear-filled because I am going home next weekend. I think all of my friends had the same feelings that I had about my parents being here. It was strange to have my former life back again for a little while, but I knew it would not last, and, I must admit, I was not all that upset.



In late October, one of my suitemates, C., had a girl, whom he insisted was not his girlfriend (afterwards we did not believe him), stay with him. Nothing was really wrong with this, except that it did create a rather uncomfortable situation for his roommate, J. It seems that prior to her arrival they had made few, if any, arrangements about how to handle her presence. For example, they had not arranged a signal to indicate when it was safe for J. to enter. Because of this awkward situation, J. spent a lot of time in my room either waiting for C. to come out or trying to figure out if he was even in the room with her. In order to relieve the tension, I suggested that J. and I go out to dinner at the Indian restaurant in Collegetown. Afterwards, we came back and sat around in my room for a while trying to discern whether anything was going on in his room. (We thought about putting an ear to the door, but we thought it might be embarrassing if we were caught.) C. eventually came out, and all four of us watched *The Shawshank Redemption*. Throughout the movie, J. and I felt uncomfortable because of the high level of affection C. and his girlfriend showed to one another. Following the movie, I went to bed and woke up around 10 a.m. the next morning. At about 11:30, J. came out of his room and told me that he had been awake for over an hour, but felt trapped in his room. Evidently, C. and his girlfriend were again showing a lot of affection towards one another and so J. had pretended to still be asleep—the cot had been put away in favor of the same single-sized bed. In hindsight, the entire affair is rather funny. Nonetheless, next time either one of them is planning to have a guest of the opposite sex, I think, and hope, that they will discuss the "rules" beforehand.

On Friday, October 12, Dan, Cramer and I went to watch "Monty Python's Life of Brian" and hear comments from its star—and Cornell Professor at Large—John Cleese. This was very exciting for me, because "Life of Brian" is my favorite movie. Its uniquely British satire is much fresher than most comedies, and its commentary on religion is hilarious. The screening of the movie was in Bailey Hall, a particularly awful venue in which to view a movie. The acoustics are so poor that the lines, which were delivered with a thick British accent to begin with, were extremely difficult to hear. After a short period of time the chairs also became unbearable. They were so close together that there was no room for your shoulders. The seats were also made of wood, and quickly everyone squirmed around in discomfort. There was also little foot room for those in the audience over five feet tall. Despite the inhospitable nature of Bailey Hall, the movie was very funny. Afterwards, Cleese came out clearly showing that he has aged a great deal since the late 1970s. He then proceeded to take questions from the audience. His answers quickly made evident his sharp wit, but also showed a more serious side. He talked frankly about how he cheered up his dying mother with comedy and also went into some of the more particular elements of making a film like "Life of Brian." After someone asked how the group came up with

# MAEVA CURTIN

## CLASS OF 2004

Scrapbook entries, 2000. I went today to see the Blackness in color Exhibit at the Johnson. Predictably I did not see many other students there, it was early on a Saturday morning. But I did get to see the most adorable little girl, there with her mother, who twirled around the gallery and decided that I was a better thing to look at than the art on the walls. She came over to look at me and would then imitate me, considering whether or not to view the artwork as I had been doing. And then she ran away, and soon returned again. And before long, I decided that she was a better thing to look at than the art on the walls.

I am homesick for privacy. I used to have my own room; a space that I had created. I could escape there and know that I would be alone, with only an occasional knock on the door. I no longer have that. My roommate and I do get along, superficially; I do not trust her. I cannot talk to her about personal matters, what I do know of her life I know only from overhearing conversations she has with others on the phone. She is always on the phone. As a very private, independent person, I am uncomfortable overhearing her conversations and avoid talking on the phone when she is around. She and I are not as similar as I had hoped early on. The fact that we each have busy schedules keeps us farther apart. As does the fact that I feel the need to go out on weekends and have a good time, to escape the intensity of my studies, to be silly and fool around, while she goes to bed early almost every night. Even on weekdays, I am up studying long after she has turned in for the night. I find myself resenting her more and more and wanting to piss her off. So I leave my bed unmade, I have clothes strewn across my side of the room, and I come in late at night and turn the lights on. She says she doesn't mind, but I know I would. I want my own space back; I want privacy.





On Saturday, I went with Sarah to the Pyramid Mall. She spent what I believe to be much too much. Simply having that thought scared me—it sounds too much like my parents. Anyway, I bought a few things including some nail polish that matches my favorite, pink grapefruit juice. I just thought that was fun.

Yesterday, my studio section went down to the shop in Rand Hall for our first shop tour. We have to go through a series of little sessions like this one and demonstrate some techniques in order to use the shop for our materials projects. Anyway, the supervisor, Brian, really turned me off. He made a joke about Justin's shirt—a high school t-shirt with a football helmet reading "flames." Brian asked what kind of mascot that was? Your team was a bunch of GAYS? The joke alone would not have ordinarily offend me too much, though the tone of his voice, the disapproving nature, the mockery disgusted me. He went on to play up his own hard work in contrast with the professor's vagueness and lack of understanding, then to poke fun at my height (I'm five foot even). I hate going into things like this with such a bad impression of someone. It just makes everything more difficult.

Brian is growing on me. Last night I had the first test of my shop skills. It went better than I had expected, I always get so worried about things, wish I could stop that.

I received my voter registration card today. I almost felt like cheering. I've been hoping and dreaming of having it in my hand for quite some time. As soon as I was accepted to Cornell, last December, I was ready to register to vote in New York and vote for Hillary. Unfortunately upon my arrival I met doubts from my New Yorker friends as to whether I was really eligible to vote. I was sure of myself at first and I remained outwardly so. But I began to have doubts myself. Even as I filled out the form and read requirements over and over again, I doubted whether it would work. But I figured I had little to lose and sent in the form anyway. And in less than a week, a surprisingly short time compared to my previous registration in Chester County, Pennsylvania, I had a card in my hand. Things like this make me feel independent and strong. They help me to realize I can do things on my own.

I finished with shop tests, well; I still have the written exam on Monday. But I'm very glad to be this far into it. I got a little scared somewhere in there; I didn't think I could take it. We were shown gruesome pictures last week to scare us into respecting the power tools. Instead they just plain scared me. I was afraid of the machine as if it would come out and grab my arm and just eat it off. Oh well, I did it anyway, sucked up my nervousness and completed my tasks. The wood was worse than the metal though. The saws scared me and the metal is just something new—bending. It and wearing big (too big for my little head) welding masks. Exciting stuff all this is.

I have come to enjoy my study lounge at RPU. It's quiet, relatively, and has nice couches. But the most important thing is that there are other people there who are working just like I am, or should be. It's not the best for all my work but I really think it helps to be around other people who are doing similar things; it's motivating. I just get sleepy when I'm in my room with my roommate who, for whatever reason, can afford to go to bed earlier than I can. And certainly it's better than our unit lounge that is really more social than study in nature. It's much too loud and distracting. I like RPU though.



I hate reviews, and especially final ones. Other students hear the word review and think I am studying for an exam. It's quite funny, because I know most of them couldn't take one review, let alone one or two a week—they're either terribly boring or terribly disappointing and depressing either way.

I had to go second. I felt like I stumbled over my words, though I had planned and rehearsed them. I failed to get across my concept clearly. And the critics caught me on everything that I had expected and much that I had not. I try my best to simply take it all in, absorb the criticism and save the digesting for later. But our guest critic called my model effeminate! How am I supposed to apply that?

My sister visited me; I thought this would be a good substitute for going home over fall break. I showed her all of campus, finally getting the chance to be tour guide for a day. I told her stories and pointed out significant buildings. I gave her a feel for how much walking I do, only I made sure it seemed much harder than it actually is. I made her go tromping through the woods just to show her a beautiful bend in a gorge or a bright red tree set in among the green and yellow ones. I hope I showed her my love for Cornell. Because for whatever reason, with all the work and all the walking, I do love Cornell.

Rob called me today. And when I picked up the phone I knew it was he. Everyone has gone home for break, but he actually cares enough to call and check on me. He asked me how I was doing and made me laugh. Our conversation was much more segmented and rushed over the phone than normal. It's usually the other way; my phone conversations are usually smoother than those in person. He makes me feel loved, and I wonder if I'm alone or whether he does this for everyone. In either case, I hope I let him know he's appreciated.

I went out for yet another walk today, just after waking up. I headed out to Beebe Lake to take some pictures of the changing foliage and the gorges beyond. I accomplished my goal and then, just as I began walking across the footbridge heading back toward my dorm, it began snowing. It was absolutely beautiful. Streams of little white flakes floating down from a stormy sky. It made me smile and it made most other people smile. A few very old-at-heart people looked disappointed, cold, or bothered, though they were very few.

Just before opening my eyes this morning I believed I was back at home in my own sun filled bedroom. I could feel the warmth of the light and was well rested, a feeling I have been missing here at Cornell. And for a moment I could hear my parents down in the kitchen talking about politics and listening to NPR while cooking waffles and arguing about who made them better. I was ready to jump out of bed, run downstairs and tell them they were being silly, that they both made good waffles. Then my eyes opened to make out my roommate's lifeless belongings.

I went out to dinner with a number of people from my [studio] section. It was the first time I had eaten exclusively with architects since Summer College. We were stuck at studio, and had been for quite some time because we needed to put together a set of site models for the studio. The pieces were scheduled to be finished at four-thirty, and then six, and so on. We sat at a table between one group who were debating politics and one who were bragging about mountain climbing. And we laughed about Stupas, Basilicas, and the like. And toward the end of dinner, the group began calling me "god" and saying that if I had been in charge of our studio-wide construction of site models, they would have been done hours ago. And I realized that they considered me a leader and someone to go to when they didn't understand or know the measurement or some aspect of the assignment. And that meant the world to me.

Sarah and I went for a walk together. I showed her a path down near college town that I discovered when my sister was visiting. We walked and talked about things, cleared our heads. And then just stood and watched the water. It rushes over the rock in a clear geometric pattern cut concisely over the years. To see it traveling by is really quite therapeutic, that's why I go. Church never worked for me, but just being outside with time and space and air to think always does. Then Sarah and I remembered our work and walked back to central campus picking up leaves and arguing about which ones were more beautiful.

I had not slept for days leading up to my review; well a little here and there but really no more than an hour or two in any twenty-four hour period. I had work consistently without taking breaks except when I needed to cry out of frustration or from being overwhelmed. And I tried to avoid my non-architect friends. They simply could not understand what I was going through. I explained to them that I had worked from one in the afternoon Saturday until eight in the morning Sunday, went to the dorm to sleep and shower and then returned to studio within an hour and a half. They told me everyone was working hard and I shouldn't think that I'm doing anymore than other people. But I don't believe them because when I do run home for a nap and shower or when I come back to get an extra sweatshirt, they are sitting around chatting about guys or more trivial things. And I can't do that. And then they talk about the parties they attended the night before, when I had worked in studio with sixty other architects. And I look upset when I come home, as if all the energy and strength had been sucked from my body and mind, because it had. And they tell me I don't and that I ought to "get some sleep tonight."



Family weekend began today, and though I told my parents not to come, I feel a little homesick. It's been so long since I've seen them, and my dogs. So instead of showing our parents all the wonderful stuff one can do at Cornell, I went to dinner with Sandy, a girl whose parents, like mine, will not be participating in the fun-filled weekend. And we laughed about all the things we could do to make a bad impression with all the parents—to dress as homeless people and beg for change on the steps of RPU, to rudely push through the crowds and knock people's trays at dinner, to obnoxiously hand out political propaganda. But we could only joke, cause neither of us wanted to make a bad impression. I love this place too much.

Last night I started crying because I feel like I don't have the time to think anymore, about myself and about my life. I feel like I am changing, growing, adapting to college, but cannot sit down and consider how and why and in what direction. And I love to do just that. I would love an entire day to just sit down, or walk somewhere and think—think about anything and everything. I feel guilty now if I am not thinking about our latest studio problem or some paper I should be writing, and I spend all my down time thinking, unwillingly, about what needs to be done.

I spent my morning at the library, and then all day reading books, except for that short span of time I spent in studio. But instead of feeling bored, I feel satisfied in knowing that I am closer to finishing my workload. Because I know that if I were to sleep late, have leisurely meals, and then go out partying at night, I would have a miserable time through all of it, because I would be worrying about all that needed to be done and all that I could be accomplishing. And if I avoid wasting time, if I work consistently I cannot feel guilty and will be a much happier person.

My new studio TA has labeled my "scheme" as a "pinwheel," which I find degrading, this along with his little lesson the other day on how to cartographically use color. He even showed me how to make a simple key! He just opens his mouth and stupid things come out. I think he might make a good kindergarten teacher, but he'd probably treat four year olds like newborns. So I've started nodding and smiling and zoning out when he gives me desk crits. He has said that I'm a good self-critic, so I'll rely on that for a few weeks and make him think that I'm taking his advice. He'll probably fall for it.

This morning after class I went to the Johnson. I desperately needed a break, a moment away from studying, drafting, and modeling when I could do something of my choosing without feeling guilt. I arrived before the museum opened for the day so I waited in the lobby reading brochures while the security guards swept around the building, opening up roped stairs and passageways. And by the time I had finished reading, they had finished as well. I walked down the stairs to the bottom floor of the exhibit space. I recognized the name of one of the exhibitors; he was a recent graduate of the B. Arch program whose thesis I had read through days earlier. So out of school pride, I watched his film and gazed respectfully at his sculptural piece. Then I continued through the rest of the exhibit of recent graduates and then college faculty. And after I had finished looking, I reminded myself that Cornell could not be spectacular at everything and that I am here to study architecture, not art.

I continued up another flight of stairs to the Tibetan exhibit. Which was far more satisfactory. I had the opportunity to look at centuries old representations of mythic beings while hearing the chants of local monks, and then to see and hear the same monks creating their own visual expression. And I was amazed at the skill and precision with which each of them scraped their funnel-like tools to lay down piles of colored sand. And I walked outside to a crisp November morning thinking how lucky I was to be here, studying and absorbing knowledge.

# ELIZABETH CHASALOW

## CLASS OF 2003

Scrapbook entries, 2002. 4:29 am. It begins. The magic of sculpture in the moonlight, under the streetlamps and BlueLights. The thrill of creation in the inky predawn. The difficulties in joining nature and manufactured adhesives.

My plan was to build a massive semblance of a spider's web between two trees on the Arts Quad—the two largest trees nearest the main paved path through the Quad. I'd start as far up in the tree as I could get and I'd build the web down to the ground, thus effectively closing off the path. I had hoped to make people think, and observe, and pay attention, otherwise they would become trapped in a very large, very sticky web.

All this I had hoped to accomplish sometime between four and five in the morning, with permission to do so, and without arousing the suspicion of any roaming authorities.

With a tall friend on a ladder, we were able to begin the web fairly high in the tree. We wrapped the tape around the tree several times. Apparently, packing tape was not designed to stick to nature; we had to make sure there were layers of tape upon which to stick the next. After the main frame was up, it got both frantic and fun. Rolls of tape were flying through the air, I was climbing through a massive tape web while clad entirely in black, and we were hacking furiously at tape with a knife.

With two people working, we finished sooner than expected and returned the borrowed ladder and knife where we had found them. We stopped on the way back home to admire our creations, and watch, amused, as several people stopped just short of the web, baffled. (Just what these people were doing roaming the campus at nearly five in the morning is beyond me, but I wasn't in a frame of mind to consider it at that time.)



Some people touched the web, others walked around it a few times.



The irony arrived—drunken and stumbling—just as we turned to leave. A group of four or five hardly cognizant boys walked directly into the newly finished web. One got stuck there briefly and laughing, called to his friends. The whole group of them proceeded to stick to, and consequently rip, the tape from the trees. A half an hour's work demolished in minutes. I wasn't entirely disappointed, though—the sculpture had, after all, served its purpose.

I was never really interested in sororities. Not that I didn't like them, I just didn't know anything about them, and had no interest to learn. When it came time to sign up for rush, however, I decided that I might as well see if all the stereotypes I hear about them is true, and registered for formal recruitment.

After the first day of rush, I'd had enough. I dropped out, and didn't want anything to do with sororities. I hadn't thought of informal recruitment, though. I had a whole bunch of friends at Chi Omega, and was invited over to dinner there. I figured I might as well go for dinner if nothing else, just because it was free food and I'd never really spent time in their house. (Freshman girls aren't allowed in sorority houses until after formal recruitment.)

Before I knew it, I had a bid, and then I was pledging, and soon after I was initiated. I had forgotten to enter the housing lottery, and figured I might as well join – the house was in a good location, and I knew some people there.

I don't know that those are the best reasons to join, but being a Chi Omega has its perks now and then. I really like some of my sisters. Granted, I can't stand some of the others, but that's sorority life, it seems. I like the activities that we do: formals, apple-picking, hiking, and movies. Living in the house gives me an entirely different perspective on some things, and forces me to at least try to get along with the other girls. It also has the potential to be useful in career situations later on. It's an interesting experience if nothing else, and I'm not disappointed that I joined.

Go figure, I decide not to go Greek and then wind up double-pledging in one semester. I went to an info session for Alpha Phi Omega, a co-ed service fraternity, solely because one of the brothers was also in the Big Red Band and had told me I should check it out. I figured I might as well see what they were about if nothing else. After the info session, the whole concept actually seemed interesting: you do community service, hang out with cool people, have fun. I decided to pledge the fraternity.

Now that I'm a brother, I think sometimes I have more fun with the people at APO than I do with the girls at Chi O. It's probably just because they're not all girls, which makes things much more interesting, and must less typically girly .... We have all kinds of fun traditions, too. We're not a traditional fraternity, so we don't have a house, but we do have big brothers. Everybody in the fraternity is a brother, regardless of sex. There's a semester of pledging and quizzes. At the end of the semester, we throw our pledgemaster in the lake .... We sponsor fun things like Ugly Man on Campus, and Condom Rose and Green Carnation sales. The condom Rose sales especially have a tendency to be quite amusing, because people don't quite know what to make of that.



Ugly Man on Campus, sponsored by APO, created an interesting Tuba tradition. The event is usually a week-long fundraiser wherein people vote on pictures submitted of the "ugliest" people on campus. The one who gets the most monetary votes in the cans on Ho Plaza is declared the Ugliest Man on Campus, and the money is sent to a local charity. Or that's how it's supposed to work—sweet little democracy.

The tubas of the marching band have decided to make it a little more difficult for anyone else to even think about winning. Every year on Halloween they head to the chimes for a joint concert at the top of the tower. The tubas lean out of the tower and play a few songs, accompanied by the chimes. Then they head down to the ground to an anxiously waiting crowd of bandies, jingling change.

This part of the concert is a band tradition, albeit a mildly dangerous one for the tubas. People usually come armed with cans full of change to throw into the bells of the tubas. All the money goes toward UMOC. After they had enough change in the tubas last year, they played Tea for Two for tubas, and added a little dance where they made a tap-dancing sound by shaking the coins in the bottom of the tubas. It was cute.

The tubas are usually the only ones to do any fundraising outside of telling friends to put money in the cans, and so bring in a phenomenal amount of money compared to the others. It's a distinction that they've proudly upheld for the past several years, and I'm sure they will continue.

---

The art department is, I believe, the smallest department in the smallest school here at Cornell. As a result, the Art Majors Organization (AMO) was started a few years ago to try to unite the artists. Since there are so few of us, it was figured that we might as well get to know each other.

I joined sometime my freshman year because it sounded like an interesting concept. It has been my experience that most of the art majors only tend to know people within their year, so the very fact that the organization was run by sophomores attracted me. After a few meetings, though, it became apparent that AMO was a good idea mostly in concept only. A handful of art major friends who were sophomores at the time sat around and didn't do much more than plan one art show. It didn't really seem worthwhile, and I stopped going.

# JUSTIN MANZO

## CLASS OF 2003

Scrapbook entries, 2002. Sept. 15, 2002: I just don't believe it. What are we, circus animals? I try, I really do, but sometimes there's really nothing you can do to make any difference. I mean, come on, how do they expect us, as Ivy League students, to use a sink with two taps!

That's right, there are bathrooms on the engineering quad that have sinks with two taps—a hot and a cold. How does this work, I ask? Explain how we are possibly supposed to wash our hands comfortably with either exclusively hot water or cold water. I demand to know, oh civil engineer of Upson Hall! What was running through your mind as you put in two taps, and no drainage plug, in a building dedicated to mechanical engineers? Obviously, no water was running. Or perhaps, water was the only thing running through that person's head.

I wouldn't typically devote time to such a trivial subject, but this is just the last straw. I've been hanging around this school for four years, checking out all the bathrooms (men's only!), and I have to say that there are some serious problems with these sinks. There is only one cool bathroom around campus, and that is the one at Willard Straight, with foot operated water valves. Other than that, it's like the freaking dark ages....The point is, though, that we are sophisticated people at Cornell, and we need some more up-to-date faucets. Come on, even let the mechanical engineers design a decent faucet—I'm sure all of the aggravation over scalded or frozen hands would inspire us to come up with something to amaze us all.

October 4, 2002: I'm way too old. It's easy to tell that I'm old: I now think that frat parties are stupid. There used to be a day when I was all about drinking, feeling the music, and dancing stupidly in somebody's dark, dank basement. Even my own fraternity, which I am comfortable setting foot in, throws parties that I don't even want to be reminded of, let alone attend. Especially now, as I approach 21, I just can't bring myself to go to parties consisting almost entirely of my friends and drink, which lets me know that I'm getting way too old for my own good.



I'm not entirely sure when my party apathy started, but I know that it's been going on for at least a year. I joined my fraternity in the fall of 2000, at a time when I was dead set against the Greek system. I hadn't been to more than 2 parties before joining my fraternity, and suddenly found myself thrust into an environment where I was required to attend parties every week. Taking everything in stride, I came by every week for the rest of the semester, until I graduated pledgeship and became a full brother. From there, there were no requirements on my head, so I was free to attend if I chose to. I came by, but the magic was fading along with my liver.

Over the 2001–2002 school year, I came to realize that I wasn't a fan of drinking. It was a nice novelty, but didn't have the stamina to just sit around and drink, and I didn't much care for the taste of alcohol. But without drinking, there wasn't much else to do at parties, or any reason to attend. The music was too loud, and it was too dark to see anything. At the beginning of the 2002 school year, I finally saw myself as a senior who could decide to pass on whatever activities were not exciting, regardless of what people expected me to do. The brothers wanted me to come and drink with them, but I was in a position to decline, and read or watch television. I suddenly became aware of the fact that I was too old for my own good at the fraternity—the good bonding activities that bring the house close to each other are dependent on your willingness to succumb to peer pressure, which I wanted no part in. And, being old enough to rise above silly drinking games and hanging around with alcoholics, I started to drift away from the fraternity.

In retrospect, I see that the freedom inherent with being a senior at college may come with a price. Some activities that bring people close together are based on going with the group mentality, at least as was the case with my experiences throughout school. Now that I am old enough to be able to break from the group, being in a position of supremacy over a younger generation of brothers, I am starting to drift away from the people I live with. This is a dangerous position to be in, because my newfound individualism is causing a rift between me and my housemates. Oh well, only a few more months until I graduate and simply become a crotchety old alumnus.

October 25: So now I'm 21. I broke the barrier on Wednesday, and I've been recovering ever since. Apparently tradition is for the newly-turned 21-year-old to be taken to the bars at midnight on their birthday, and to drink until last call. If that weren't enough, they're expected to go out again the next night and do the same! Oh man, I wish my liver were that strong.

Truth be told, it was a rather unproductive birthday. I spent all of Wednesday trying not to be ill, encompassing my trip to the 'clean room' on the Engineering Quad. I was all gowned up in a plastic suit, in a facility where you have to use plastic paper because regular paper has too much dust, and I had to fight off the urge to be violently ill all over the equipment. I could hardly stop the irony from leaking out, however.

I must say that the transition from 20 to 21 is hardly more than a relief. Now that I'm legal, it just feels like a weight has been lifted off my back about circumstances involving alcohol. I don't have to feel out of place near bars, or be limited in cooking involving wine, or be scared away from parties where you are carded. I hadn't been looking forward to 21 like some people, nor do I feel older now. Life is just more simple.

Honestly, I'm just hoping to stay this age for as long as possible. 21 seems like the high point of life in the immediate future—you're finishing school, you don't have many responsibilities, and you have the world at your fingertips. I just hope that this isn't the best time I'm supposed to ever have; I wouldn't be able to cope with life being downhill from here, though I suppose that's something I'll have to determine or find out for myself.

---

I have a notebook made entirely out of plastic! Why, you may ask? Because I'm clean room certified! Oh yes, I can go manufacture semiconductors if I so chose (which are not quite like halves of train conductors) which I don't. What I can also do is waste time with much more expensive equipment than previously possible, which I'm looking forward to. And apparently, in this highly regulated clean room, I can get suited up, put on my lab goggles and safety gloves, and then almost throw up all over myself.

Indeed, I almost experienced what the staff would have considered a major faux pas ... I somehow make it to this training session, and get myself suited up and into the facility with my partner. It is just the two of us and the machine advisor, so it's not like I can hide in the back or anything. I had been feeling ill, but slowly progress from bad to worse as the lecture goes on. Suddenly, I break out into a sweat in the room, and start feeling sick to my stomach. The best decision—call it a day, and go sleep off the damage. However, realizing that people actually expect me to make something of my time at Cornell, and that I should stay at this training session, I instead sit down with my head clasped in my hands, over a garbage can, in the changing room ... Many engineering nerds find the concept of so blatantly breaking the whole 'clean room' concept absurdly funny, though they're probably just glad not to have been in my situation. Strangely enough, my partner had a stomach bug the day before, and was also almost ill in the clean room ... Our boss was so proud to hear that both of his trainees were of this digestive caliber, and congratulated us both on not getting ourselves banned from the facility. In the end, I guess there's something to be proud of ... if not, at least I still have a plastic notebook.

---

November 9, 2002: I'm definitely such a nerd. For my birthday, I got a new computer and printer, finally getting the opportunity to upgrade my out-of-date equipment. I was excited—perhaps too much so—at the prospect of a new printer. My original printer spat out maybe a page a minute on a good day, but not before gnawing on the pages a bit first. Everything came out crumpled, garbled, or missing half of the lines of text. This, after having to hold the pages into the feeder manually, because the printer would jam if I didn't. So, a new printer was looking like a gift from the heavens, especially now that I'm enrolled in a technical writing course with 30 page reports.

My Mom and I went to Best Buy when she got into town, and we asked for the best printer they had. I was like a kid in a candy store as we rifled through the technology they had, and came up with a printer capable of outputting 18 pages per minute, with a reasonable price tag. Having jumped up from one page to 18 in any given minute of printing time, I was quite satisfied. We quickly ran the printer back to my apartment and hooked it up, and it was a beautiful thing. Crystal clear resolution, fast, and not dependent on me to baby it through printing. Satisfied, we ceased thinking about printers for a while, until Mom left town.

Two days later, I'm browsing around online and I notice that there's a faster printer. Same brand, same product line, just that the printer output is 22 pages instead of 18 pages, same quality, with another 50 dollars on the price tag. Not to be outdone, I immediately needed the faster one. To me, it was just the principle of the thing. Why buy the fast one if it's not the fastest? At that point, what was once fast became tolerable. Mind you, we're talking about a difference of 3 seconds per page in printing time—not that big of a deal, right? Wrong. I am an engineer, and it's the principle of the thing.

So I took the printer back, having great difficulty in explaining why I needed to return a printer with nothing wrong with it. Basically, I found someone whose inner nerd sympathized with my claim—you always need the best one of whatever it is you're buying, or else there's no point in spending lots of money. I swapped the printer for the more expensive, and immediately convinced myself on first use that it was a huge improvement in speed and performance. I mean, we're talking about 4 seconds per page versus 6: that's huge. I think. Unless, of course, I realize that there's not much I would actually be doing with 2 more seconds. But that's not the point.

Now here's the irony, and hopefully the end of this paper. After wasting my time, and 50 bucks, on this other printer, it turns out that the longest papers for my technical class are over and done with, and that I will need to print a total of 5 more pages over the next two months in that class. Just days before I even got the 'slow' printer (18 pages per minute), I had to sit through a 33 page bonanza of manual feed-in and unjamming the mechanism, which was a point in my life when I regretted not becoming a chef. Though I can now print a full page in 4 seconds, I have nothing to print; and by the time I do, there will be an even faster printer available, somewhere. Oh, engineering school, why must you be such a cruel mistress?

November 20, 2002: the power of suggestion is truly remarkable. That is why I think that inventing a slang word and getting it circulating in common diction is not very difficult to achieve; and if I were actually motivated, I would actually try it. Based on the hundred-monkey concept, any slang word, such as 'shizzle', could be meant to represent something in modern college slang with a creative use of the word and enough exposure.

As remarked in class, the hundred monkey concept is something I heard about from my friend in high school, whereby theorists predict that getting 100 monkeys to do something is the threshold number above which any particular behavior can potentially propagate through the whole species, and below which a behavior will fail to spread ... if I could get an equal proportion of humans to start using a word as if it actually meant something, then it has the potential to find its way into slang dictionaries of the future. Obviously I am taking this idea literally, but I think there is a certain validity to the theory. If only a catchy description for 'shizzle' were apparent to me, I could quickly spread it around. This indicates the second point in making a slang word stick—its cleverness. The word is already humorous, and widely used without meaning. With a smart usage of the word, it could get a great deal of exposure, and potentially enter popular diction. Of course, the main problem is coming up with something clever for 'shizzle': it could mean crappy weather, or heavy drinking, or anything that is widely talked about and may be a variation on something similar to the word 'shizzle'.

Honestly, though, I've had enough of saying the word 'shizzle' After the slang lecture in class, I tried using the word a few times, and quickly got tired of trying. It was hard even to get me to stick to it, which probably means I won't be able to make it into a common slang word. Alas, I won't go down in the history books as the inventor of a word, nor will I be able to say, "Hey. That's my word, I'm going to sue!" Rest assured that one day I will figure out some kind of good word, and you'll all be totally shizzled that day.

December 5, 2002: It is early in the morning here in Ithaca, and I'm very tired. For the past few days, I've been winding down work in a busy semester—a semester that will continue to be busy right up until I leave for break, and then start anew as soon as I get back. I'm amazed at how much I have done this semester, as compared to what I have accomplished any other semester. At the same time, I'm shocked at how much free time I have had since August, which indicates that I must have had an abundance of time left over in any of my other semesters, which weren't nearly as fruitful as this one.

What have I accomplished this semester that I hadn't before the fall term? Well, I finally got fed up with not being involved in any extracurricular teams, so I decided to start my own. My Battelbots team is now a fully funded, Cornell affiliated organization, with aspirations of making a television debut in the near future, and a team base of some 30 students. My research work has taken me to the clean room, and shown me some really nifty gadgets that I would otherwise never have gotten a chance to see. And I'm cooking high-class meals in my spare time, just for fun. Seems to be a pretty nice setup.



Yes, it certainly seems that way. But how is it possible that I can just sit around and hang out most of the time? How can I be so overwhelmed, and yet so under-worked? Most likely it's due to procrastination, something I can't escape even in my senior year at school. In three and a half years, Cornell has only taught me to refine my procrastinating skills, not to reduce them. I can also 'crank out' papers—just sit down and start typing, and not stop until whatever I need to write is done. I don't think I am comfortable with this, but I seem to be on schedule for graduation There is little room for complaint in that.

My time at school has been interesting, and not without bumps along the way. A first year in architecture was a rough start to my college career, but the inevitable switch helped me cope with school much better than I could have in the AA&P college. Since then, there has been a great deal of complaining, but nothing so unbearable that I ever had to stay up all night or even study hard to learn something. At Cornell, I have been able to take the attitude that I either will pick up something on the first try or not at all, very much like my approach to high school work. Not much has changed in those 8 years, a fact I am unsettled by. For, if Cornell is just an extension of high school, what has been the point of spending so much time and money here? As I round out my scrapbook pages late this Wednesday night, I cannot help but be reminded of this fact; however, for now I must move on. Another semester awaits, and I must take a break from my somewhat exhausting, but often sparse workload. I cannot, as the University knows, be expected to dive straight into another semester of doing far less than I am capable of without being given almost a month off. So, let the holiday season begin, and I'll be back for my last chance at undergraduate productivity soon. Perhaps they can squeeze something intelligent out of me before I get out of here.

# ANGELINA ANG

## CLASS OF 2007

Angelina Ang writes her blog on xanga.com.

Thursday, September 4, 2003: o gosh, im so tired from last nite. i can't believe i actually pulled an almost all-niter when it's only the first week of classes ... ya see, this is what cornell does to you ... actually, i didn't even need to pull an all-niter ... i could've just MADE myself write the essay in like 2 hours or so ... but no ... angelina is just the biggest queen of procrastination in the whole universe

Friday [September 26, 2003]: classes ... pyramid mall with brian, leo, and alessandra ... got my printer!! Then went back to lily and victoria's ... wtched movie that wanzee's dad was in ... soo funnnieee ... went back to room

Friday night pat came over ... woke up at like 11 am

Omg ... we went to this stupid pre-party cuz we felt bad for the guys ... (cuz they woulda looked like losers if the group was just all guys) ... we went down to meet at balch arch at 9:30 ... but they had some acapella group there ... so it was packed ... we went all the way around to the front of the arch ... then johnny (the apt dude) took us to the pre-party at some apt in college town ... the gurls went first cuz we couldn't all fit in the car ... so yea ... we got there ... went up to the apt ... and omg ... it was just like mad drinking game there ... okay ... this is the part where it starts to be unpretty ... i was sitting with andy in the corner ... and then he said sumthin to me, and im like ... wut did u say? And then he threw up right in front of me ... okay ... so lesson learned … since i got to cornell: NEVER DRINK PAST YOUR OWN LIMIT!

Thursday, October 2, 2003: Wowzers! i don't think i had ever studied SO much in my whole entire life, today (well, yesterday—technically) was definitely a mad studying day. i didn't come back to my room until about 1.5 hours ago and why?? Because i had to study for my 192 prelim! Omg! i swear i had never been sooo worried about a MATH exam before … and even right now i still feel like i haven't studied enough even though i did all the krzy problems with kev. Ugh=x

On a happier note, i think i've found my two new study "buddies": the cocktail lounge and the balch unit 2 lounge. it's sooo nice in there … and oh oh! Come to cocktail lounge when the sun sets … cuz u can see it through the glass window and it's SOOO pretty! J and yea … balch is nice too … plus we can actually talk in there … it's so funny cuz everyone was there and we don't even live in balch =P

# NICK NIEH

## CLASS OF 2007

Scrapbook entries, 2004. For our interview paper, one of the questions asked was, "What Cornell traditions do you know?" One of my answers was traying down Libe Slope. Once there's enough snow, which there always is during an Ithaca winter, students go sledding down it. The easiest, cheapest, and most popular device used to sled down the hill is a dining hall tray, hence the term traying. Some people buy innertubes or actual sleds, but that ruins the experience. A student must sled down on a tray at least once.

My friends and I went once or twice during the winter. It was a blast! There's a little bump at the end of the run which launches you into the air. A few times, all of us linked up and went down the slope as a train. When we hit the ramp, we broke apart and flew everywhere. Climbing back up the slope is a pain. We kept slipping and sliding back down the hill. Once we finished, my pants were frozen solid! I ended up getting sick afterwards, but it was worth it. Traying is one of the few good things that results from all the snow.

The Red Carpet Society was a perfect opportunity for earning Tradition hours. I could earn 40 service hours by hosting five prefrosh. The training for this was quite easy; it consisted of a half-hour information session. Hosts should try to stay with the prefrosh at all times, take them to dinner, and give them a place to sleep. Obvious rules apply: no alcohol, no riding in cars, no parties, etc.

I turned 19 on February 21, 2004. It was one of my more memorable birthdays. I got creamed, literally. My friend hit me in the side of the head with a plate of whip cream. It got all over my shirt and inside my ear. The worst part was that the cream smelled horrible. I had to wash up and change shirts to get rid of the stench. Other than that, my birthday proceeded peacefully. I played some ping-pong, ate some cake, and opened some presents. For presents, I received some alcohol-related items, a poster, and a miniature pool table. My friends know me well.



This little ceremony was conducted in Court Hall, and afterwards, we all moved to Dickson to my friend's room. Here we played video games until the early hours of the morning. I couldn't have asked for more: chilling with friends, video games, cake, and presents. It doesn't get much better than that.

Collegetown is the social hotspot for Cornell. It's crazy on Fridays and Saturdays. Drunk people are always running around causing scenes. It's entertaining to watch. I can't wait to live in Collegetown next year. I have an apartment with four other guys right in the heart of Collegetown. We're going to have a lot of fun. Collegetown is great because every person who's walking around or who lives there is a college student. There are no kids, no adults, and no old people. It's like a college utopia.

Everything a college student could need can be found in Collegetown. There's plenty of restaurants and food places. Every genre of food is offered; there's Chinese, Korean, Japanese, Vietnamese, American, etc. If you have a craving for something, you can find it in Collegetown. Eating there is a good break from dining hall food. My favorite meal that I've had was at Plum Tree. It's Japanese food. It was so delicious, but so expensive! I'll probably only be able to afford to eat at that place once a month next year.

Four friends and I will be living in the heart of Collegetown at Eddygate Park Apartments next year. I can't wait. It's going to be so fun to have a place of our own. I have a double which is unfortunate because I wanted a single, but at least my rent is cheaper. We're going to stuff five guys in a three bedroom apartment. The place comes fully furnished with free DSL, which are major pluses. Also, the apartment is closer to the engineering quad than North Campus was. There are definitely downsides though. One, there will be no one to clean up after us. We're going to have to do all of the cleaning, including the bathroom. Also, there will be no more meal plan. Either I'm going to be eating in Collegetown a lot or I'm going to have to cook for myself. This is a problem since I don't have the slightest clue on how to cook. I'm going to have to learn over the summer. Right now, we're working on getting a person to sublet the apartment. I don't want to be paying for an empty place over the summer. If we can't get a sublet, then hopefully we can at least store our stuff in our apartment over the summer. I'm looking forward to next year. It should be quite exciting and fun.

One of the major reasons why I chose to attend Cornell was because I heard it had some of the best college food in the nation. I did not hear wrong. Cornell's food is terrific. We are definitely spoiled here. My friends at other schools hate their dining hall food. They get jealous when I tell them what we have here. We have dim sum, Korean BBQ, Mongolian grill, etc. There's such a diverse genre of food that I never get sick of the food in the dining halls. I had a terrible experience with college food before when I attended the Harvard Summer School. That slop was nasty. Cornell food is leaps and bounds better.

Cornell dining offers so many choices. Many eateries dot the Cornell campus. During the first semester, I ate all of my meals on North. Now, with my schedule the way it is, I have tried other dining options. The Terrace and Mac's Café in Statler Hall are great places to eat. The Ivy Room and Okenshield's are two other good options, though the food at both is not as good. The two best eateries are Trillium and Bear Necessities. I love the cheese quesadillas and Philly Cheese Steaks at both. No matter where I am, there is always a place to grab food within a 10-minute walk.

I eat at Appel most of the time because my friends like it better, but I prefer RPU. It has the Mongolian grill, and dim sum and Korean BBQ on Sundays. The freshmen on North Campus are lucky to have two great dining halls in Appel and RPU. Upperclassmen are always telling me how they wish they had both dining halls when they were freshmen. I'm definitely going to miss the all-you-can-eat food next year when I'm in Collegetown. Students should not complain about the food here at Cornell. Cornell dining is ranked among the top 5 in the nation. I've already put on the freshman 15, and this was only possible because I enjoyed eating the high-quality Cornell food.

Lambda Phi Epsilon Rush Spring 2004: Freshmen at Cornell can only pledge for a fraternity in the spring. Fall pledging is not allowed. I came back from Winter Break too late to rush for the traditional fraternities. Minority fraternities run on a different schedule, with a later rush. I knew I wanted to rush for the Lambdas. I knew some of the brothers from first semester, and they were really cool. The events were a blast. I went to every event except for the paintballing and slope takeover. I regret not going paintballing; everybody said it was the best event. My favorite was the ice skating because I had never done it before. I met a lot of people during those two weeks. Rush is very hectic but very fun. I enjoyed it immensely. Now that I'm a brother, rush seems like it was so long ago. Next semester, it will be my job to rush potential pledges.

Lambda Phi Epsilon played a large part of my second semester. Their rush in the beginning of the semester drew me into the fraternity. I decided to pledge, knowing little about what it entailed. Those were two very difficult months. But now that it's over, I feel like a new man. I feel like I can do anything if I set my mind to it. Nothing is too difficult to overcome. And now, I have 20 other brothers here on campus. Brotherhood is hard to put into words. It's a deep respect you have for another person. You don't even have to like them, you just have to respect them and know that no matter what they'll be there for you. Becoming a brother of Lambda Phi Epsilon is one of my greatest achievements. I will wear my letters with pride. I am now part of something bigger and better here at Cornell. It will help me participate more in campus organizations. I have three great years left as an active. Along with my brothers, I hope to improve the fraternity and make it a larger presence on campus.

# ELIZABETH BENNETT

## CLASS OF 2007

Scrapbook entries, 2003. I love being a hotelie, but the comments about hotelies anger me. Most people would claim that the Hotel School is the easiest school, and that its students don't do any work. But these people don't know anything about the school, the courses, or the work required. There *are* students who don't do much work, but there are students like that in every school. I don't know that the proportion of slackers is that much higher in the Hotel School than in the other schools. Non-hotel students only know that the Hotel School is easier because that's what they've heard, and that's what is passed down from the classes before them. I'm not saying that the Hotel School is the hardest school, because it isn't, and I'm not saying that it's not the easiest. My problem is that everyone automatically assumes that it is, without supporting this assertion with knowledge of the school. Non-hotel students hear class titles like "Intro to Food and Beverage Management," and "Intro to Wines," and assume that these classes are easy. ("This is wine and this is cheese, very good. Now fold these napkins," they taunt.) My food and beverage class required a group project that managed a simulation restaurant. In one week alone, I spent sixteen hours on this project (and that's only twenty percent of my grade and doesn't include time spent reading, doing other homework assignments, studying, etc.). I know that teasing of Hotelies is never going to go away (I'm even amused by some of it, "Hotelie Eye for the Engineering Guy," as performed by The Hangovers, for example), but I'm offended when people automatically judge me when I say I'm a Hotelie. I look around at my classmates, and some of them fit the stereotypes perfectly, but I don't! I work hard and I get good grades. I could be in any of the other schools at Cornell and doing well, but I know that I want to work in the Hospitality industry. I came to Cornell because it has a world-renowned Hotel school, and I don't appreciate being teased for that decision, thank you very much.

I can understand why Hotelies are teased when we have homework assignments that require us to eat at Banfi's. For the record, we did have to write a paper afterwards, and we also have to work fourteen unpaid hours in the hotel restaurant services. On Thursday, October 9, 2003, Crystal and I dined with four other hotel students and Mr. Chris Allen, the food and beverage director of the Statler, at Banfi's. I had the shrimp cocktail, the Catskill Trout stuffed with blue crab, and the warm chocolate torte along with hot chocolate. The food was delicious. I love our dining hall food, and I eat my fair share of it, but an upscale dinner was an appreciated break. The service was perfectly acceptable. However, since we had to write a paper on our experience, and we had been instructed in proper service techniques, we were analyzing the service and found a few faults. For example, when I arrived my water glass was on the left side of my place setting and some sort of small insect was flying around me. I heard the waitress respond to a request with "no problem," which is slang and therefore inappropriate according to our service practicum packet. Additionally, I had finished my water, as had someone else, shortly after the complimentary appetizers were served. However, our glasses were not refilled until after the bread was served and the appetizers were cleared. Furthermore, two of the ordered appetizers were given to the wrong people, and they had to switch plates themselves. Finally, both entrée and dessert plates were cleared from the finished members of our party before everyone was done with those courses. However, there were many good and impressive aspects of our service experience. For example, the backpacks belonging to Crystal and I were stored for us so we didn't have to deal with them. Additionally, with the exception of my first appetizer, everything was served and cleared correctly, and the water service improved as the meal continued. The arrival of complimentary appetizers and the appearance of the restaurant manager, Mohan Nair, the general manager of the hotel, Richard Adie, and a sous-chef was impressive. The dessert course was also spectacular as our waitress took our orders from memory and arranged for Arthur and I to have cheesecake and hot chocolate, respectively, even though both items are not mentioned on the menu. Thus, the failures in service were really just me being picky. The good aspects of the dinner certainly outweighed the occasional improper technique, as I didn't take the latter too seriously. I am afraid, though, that I will never be able to eat at a restaurant again without analyzing every aspect of the meal.

The flip side to getting a free dinner at Banfi's was having to work two unpaid shifts in the Hotel's restaurant services as a different homework experience. Our first practical was in banquet services, and I did mine with Crystal and another girl in our class, Dana. Our shift was on a Wednesday from 3:30–9:30pm. The first hour or so was training. We had received a service manual that we had to read over; it covered everything from pouring water to wine and carrying trays. We went over the manual and actually carried a tray and set and cleared a table. Then, we took a tour of Banfi's and the banquet services facilities. We ate a free meal at Mac's and then got to work shadowing employees and doing what they told us to do. There were only two events going on, and they were both low-key, so it was a boring night full of menial tasks, like polishing silverware. Additionally, watching all of the food being carried around, especially the chocolate cake made me hungry, even though I had already eaten dinner. The night dragged on and on. We finished everything there was to do, so we got to leave an hour early. Even though we weren't doing that much, if I had had to stay the extra hour I probably would've passed out from exhaustion.

We had a choice of working in Banfi's, the Regent Lounge, or Room Service for our second practical. I was originally leaning towards Room Service or the Regent Lounge as I didn't want to have to waitress, but when I saw the sign-up sheets I chose Banfi's for Sunday Brunch as I only had to work 4 hours instead of six for the same credit. Yay for effective time management. Unfortunately, there was only one student per time slot, so Crystal and I were separated by a week. I reported for work at 10:45 in my standard issue collared white shirt, Banfi's tie, and my own black pants and shoes. I was met by the Hostess, Clara, who proceeded to tell me that they were understaffed by three people, and then the details of her caffeine addiction (but not to coffee) and how she had forgotten about daylight saving's time and woken up at 3:00 A.M. instead of 4:00 A.M. She then gave me to my student trainer, Billy, who gave me the task of making place settings for the tables (inserting silverware into a folded napkin and then putting it in a water glass). Then I got to polish water glasses. Then I filled some water glasses. Then I cleared trays in the back and sorted the various items for the dishwasher. I couldn't believe it had only been an hour. Then I cleared tables and I reset them. I also carried a tray to the back, and then another one – these were much heavier than the one in training, and after my second one I stopped. Clara hinted to me that she had just gotten new glassware and didn't want them broken, although she was the one that set me up with a tray in the first place. Then I filled water and juice. Then I cleared and reset more tables. I was pretty busy, but I couldn't believe how slow time was moving. At about 3, when my shift was over, the last party left the restaurant and we were allowed to eat from the buffet. The food made it all worthwhile!! I had some garlic pasta with crab-stuffed Sole, Eggplant parmesan, some potatoes, and some mini pancakes. I also had chocolate mousse in a chocolate cup. Clara and my trainer, Billy, told me I had done a good job and encouraged me to take some desserts home to my dorm. They didn't have to ask me twice. I took a mousse cup, a mini pumpkin pie, and a slice of carrot cake. I felt slightly piggish, but figured I should take advantage of free food when it comes my way and besides, they were probably just going to throw it away anyways, right?

# GEOFFREY KOWALSKI

## CLASS OF 2007

These email conversations between a Cornell student and his mother were written during the 2002–2003 academic year. The style is modern, with its use of lowercase letters and casual spelling, but the topics hark back to earlier student letters home, with discussions of money and how it is spent.

Geoff: i have less than 200 left
Mother: do you not eat on campus
Geoff: i do
Mother: i put 1000 in your account on Friday
Geoff: laundry/groceries/rent/hockey tickets/crew boat club
Mother: welcome to the real world
Geoff: i have yet to deduct that 130/ so i have less than 50
Mother: have you rowed since you joined the club
Geoff: ah/its only twice a week but im learning to skull/its ok so far
Mother: that sounds great
Geoff: not as intense as last year/not as reliable for a great workout

Geoff: got your message and just finished reading it. Got up this morning at 9 ate some breakfast then took that math exam. There were 11 problems in 2 hours. i new [sic] how to do 7 of them, 2 i once new and with a little review they will be easy, the other 2 i had no idea how to do. Really advanced stuff. After that i went and met a kid for lunch and we rollerbladed around campus before my technology meeting at 2:30 i just set up all my internet stuff so that now i can e-mail and surf, all the cool stuff. i have so many packets with times and meetings. Tonight i'm gunna get some dinner and watch space balls the movie somewhat. Talk to you later.



Geoff: i've gotten your messages but i've been very busy with all the course stuff. i had to pretty much write my own schedule. The one i got in the packet didn't have the right engineering intro. So when i switched that i had to switch my calculus and then switch from Physics first semester to Chem. Making fit was a royal pain in my ass. Especially because i was complete on my own. i wasn't even sure what classes i was supposed to be taking. i got it all stra[igh]tened away at two in the morning the day of registration. i got up at six to go stand in line early to make sure i got all the classes i needed, because if you can't have one then the whole schedule is shot to hell. However, i couldn't find out if i was signing up for the right classes until i met with my advisor again at 10 am. So by the time he told me i was alright i had to wait in line for three hours to add and drop all of my old and new courses. i got the last space in Calc, but I'm taking 192 not the next one higher. i agreed with my advisor that its better to get a solid grade to start off then jump right in a third semester engineering calculus.

i wanted to sign up for tennis gym but there was no way i could take Calculus 192 and tennis. … For gym I'm taking karate. Its only twice a week and its in the gym, however its an extra 70+$. It fits my schedule. i bought books today ready for this total (in US $) $398.07. My engineering intro book is only a few hundred pages and it cost 100$. i handed in my writing seminar ballot as well. My first choice that fit my schedule was a class about NASA and the Apollo & Shuttle missions. My next choice was bruce lee films followed by Sex, society and race in Star Trek.

i ordered 25$ worth of posters on the Amex card. i needed something to cover the bare walls. i would also like to get a membership at the gym. i met a kid that wants to work out, as if the hills weren't enough already. It's cheap though. That's all i can think of now. Talk to you later.

Geoff: Hi Dad and Mom: i got back my essay on Aristotle and The Usual Suspects. i got a C+ on the paper which pisses me off. i tried to follow all of the comments in the assignment and took all of his advice. i talked to him after class and he thinks that i am being too general and assuming too many things. i told him that i believe that i would rather cover all the things possible and do it generally then focus on a few things and leave out examples. However i now know that this is not how he wants it. i will have to take my paper fix a few grammatical things but i want to pick the biggest points (one or two of them) and elaborate on them. i told him that i took the approach of making a point out of each of Aristotle's chapters, hence five different points. i will pick two points use quotes, elaborate, etc. i am emailing you the scanned copy of my paper. The number at the end is the pages number. When you have time please look at the comments and maybe think of the two ideas you think i should develop and maybe where you think i could elaborate and put a quote. i have my Labor Economics Prelim at 7:00 to 9:00 tonight so i won't be in after around 5:00 because i am going to the library then. Thanks again.



Geoff: Things are going good, rush yesterday was fun, i may be interested in some of the houses, but it is only the beginning of the week so i have a lot more time to figure it out. Skiing is good it isn't as cold as last week but the wind is brutal. Time trials for giant slalom are tomorrow so i hope i do good. My car is fine and i will be more careful on those turns. i will let you know more as it happens this week. Can't want to see all you guys Friday night and this weekend. P.S. What does the word kitsch mean. i think it is important for my writing seminar.

# NIIAMAH ASHONG

## CLASS OF 2008

Scrapbook entries, 2004. I love Female Orgasm: I was given advice by senior students at Cornell that one of the most important things about college life was to experience all that interests you and will be difficult to engage in later on in life. When I heard about the presentation of *Female Orgasm*, I knew that this was one such opportunity. A group of at least 200 students, essentially equal in gender, filled an all-purpose room on the second floor of Robert Purcell Community Center. I brought five girls from the floor below (Dickson 3-5) to accompany me. Part of me wanted to show that I was a considerate partner, and the other just wanted to get to know them better. The presentation was in a very laid-back setting as a couple explained the myths and mysteries of the female orgasm. Topics discussed were the more intense pleasure spots of a female, the long, and sometimes longer, road to female sexual climax, and vibrators. It turned out that a very popular vibrator was actually a Harry Potter broomstick complete with vibrating action to simulate flying. From the presenters, it seemed that for some female it at least *stimulated* and pleasure was shared by both children and parents alike. The genders split up to really try to discuss more questions about the female orgasm. While most of the guys were "confident" in their organs tactics, they (we) still wondered how to make it happen quicker for females. The girls later responded that communication was a key element. Shirts and buttons were offered at the conclusion. I purchased both and came home with some free condoms. (Free is good!)

A Capella Auditions: After the first time I heard Last Call sing during POST, I knew that I had to join the group or participate in A Capella at the very least. I quickly became a groupie and could be found "grooving" in the audience at most of the group's orientation arch sings. The auditions were held on the second floor of RPCC and I was comforted by other auditionists that claimed that I wouldn't just be A bass, but rather THE bass. However, as I had no formal voice training (I hadn't sung since fifth grade and at the time I was a Soprano!), I was quite scared. I also decided to audition for other groups in case I did not get "called-back," which basically is round-two of auditions. I also tried out for the Class Notes, Key Elements, and The Chordials, all co-ed groups. By the weekend, I had found out that I had gotten called back to three of the four groups (all but the Class Notes).

The Facebook: I think I'm going to end up failing out of school. Not because Cornell is too hard and not because I can't keep up, but I have just been dragged into the greatest website ever. It's called thefacebook.com, and it is essentially a huge network of people in college. I've actually known about thefacebook since mid-summer, but at the time the schools were limited to just the Ivy League, and I knew no one. Things are so different now! It keeps track of my own personal information such as my birthday, hometown, major/concentration, and old high school. It has this great feature that reminds me when a "friend" of mine (someone I've decided to connect through the site) has a birthday coming up. Now I know last names of friends and can show and be shown the cute girls that have caught the interest of my hall mates or myself. Political interests are chosen by everyone, and the site even goes as far as to allow members to post whether they are in a relationship, if they are looking for anyone at all and exactly what they are looking for with selections including but not limited to "random play," dating," "friendship," and "anything I can get." The reason I'm scared is that although it has no actual purpose toward school, I find myself spending more time looking for friends or trying to join different groups, than I do with my homework. I know a lot of people though. I'm not the only one caught up in the epidemic. For some reason as "pointless" as it is, few students here can stay away from it. It's the perfect way to be distracted from all the work we are responsible for.

My First Prelim: It just dawned on me how far behind I am in my studies. I took my first prelim the other day and the results were not good at all. It was in Math 112, $2^{nd}$ semester Calculus, and it was one of the hardest tests I have taken in my life. The main problem stemmed from my own personal lack of study skills. My intention at school was to make as many friends as possible, participate in as much as possible, and pass my classes. Up until then, the first two things were accounted for. However, after I left the testing site, I knew that the third one was far from being reached. This was a big step in understanding the transition to college.

Halloween: Halloween was quite an interesting holiday at Cornell. Actually, *this* Halloween seemed more like an interesting holiday. The 31st was on a Sunday this year, but the "good times" began on Thursday. It was on this day that everyone started bringing out their costumes to show off. It was also then that Halloween-themed parties began. Although many people find this to be an ample opportunity to dress in their most seductive clothes and get away with it, I personally did not find much of that happening on campus. Still, almost all of the party-goers stayed true to the spirit of the holiday. An interesting thing that happened was that there really wasn't any candy given out. I haven't been trick-or-treating in quite some time, so I may have missed the memo about that. I did give some money though to a giant inflatable penis that walked through our dorm on Friday night.

The O.C.: I never realized how much I missed television until I got together with my hall mates to watch the season premier of the hit show *The O.C.* The fourth floor lounge was packed with students all gathered around the television mounted high in the corner of the room, anxious to return to the lives of Seth, Marissa, Ryan, and Summer, the four stars of the show. The thing that made the experience so memorable was the absolute passion and reverence that was given to the show. During the show, the lounge was extremely silent and all those that trespassed on that silence were immediately dealt with, either with a loud *shuhh* or some curse word or another, which usually ended the comment very quickly. As soon as the commercials began the room exploded with talking and laughter and expressions of surprise at what had just developed.

Math 111: Unfortunately, I did not do well in Math 112 (2nd semester Calculus) and had to drop down in the sequence to Math 111 (1st semester Calc). Surprisingly, even though the semester was almost over, I was still able to drop down into the course. The grades from the other class did not follow me as well, I was fresh as a new-born baby. The only potential problem was that since I had missed the majority of the class, all that remained to have my grade based on was a prelim and a final. That was fine by me. I moved into a class with a real professor instead of just a T.A. and worked hard to catch up to the class.

# PETER GRECZNER

## CLASS OF 2009

Scrapbook entries, 2005. My First College Class. I didn't know what to expect. My previous notions about college classes were that they are provocative and engaging between the professors and the students. I felt that the material to be discussed was going to be at a much higher level than anything I had ever witnessed in a classroom. I feared that the other students would be out of my league intellectually speaking, yet I cherished that I was going to be in an environment no longer surrounded with a majority of morons. With all these thoughts penetrating my head I woke up early, ate my PowerBar and headed off to my first class. I looked at all the beautiful scenery that surrounded my walk and it just felt right. I was still nervous, but the campus feel reassured me. I arrived for my Nanotechnology class in B17 Kimball Hall about 15 minutes early. To my surprise there was already about 50 of the 150 students situated. I found my seat, got a pencil, opened up my blue notebook, and patiently in my demeanor, yet anxiously in my thoughts, waited for the professor and 10:10 A.M. to arrive. The professor, Professor Gianellis, walked into his room with a smile on his face, as to reassure us; it didn't work for me, I was still nervous. Shortly after, the syllabus was passed out, and the professor went over it. I noticed something familiar with what was happening. This familiarity was that this was no different than high school. Everything was laid out in the syllabus and I knew what to expect for everything. The only thing different was that this was going to be a lot harder than high school classes. Once the syllabus was finished, we actually started learning the background and some interesting facts about nanotechnology. I thought the professor seemed pretty cool; he even agreed to let us out 10 minutes early because when he was in college he never liked it when the professor would actually try teaching on the first day. Before I knew it, the class was over. It was nothing special. It seemed like all of my worries and anxieties failed to present themselves in those 40 minutes of class, because it turned out class was exactly like what I was used to and the obvious exception would be the difficulty. Maybe the only difference was that there was no engaging dialogue, but what can you really expect in the first class of an extremely introductory level course of nanotechnology? The best thing that I took from that first class was that college was going to be ok and that I would be able to handle it because there isn't going to be anything that I haven't seen before.

~~~

Basketball at Helen Newman. A few weeks into the school year, my hall sponsored a party at Helen Newman. A party was an over exaggerating term for what occurred. In the gym they had a drunk goggle free throw contest, a football throwing contest, and pick-up games of basketball. On the outskirts of the gym they had a raffle, prizes, and a karaoke machine.

I convinced my friends to go there to check it out with me. When we got there, they were not enthused by the activities, and shortly left. However, I decided to stay and play some basketball. That would turn out to be the best decision I made that night.

I shot around for a while, and after some time passed there were enough other guys there to get a game on. I was really excited, because basketball is my favorite sport and I am extremely competitive when I play. I don't really remember who was on my team, except that both teams were very even. I wasn't the best player, but I wasn't the worst, I was in the middle. Naturally, my team didn't expect much out of me. Why "naturally," because I am of modest height, overweight and I wear glasses. If I were looking at myself I wouldn't expect much athleticism. However, I was soon able to prove them wrong.

Despite how I look I am actually very good at basketball, especially shooting, and I have an unexpected quickness. I was able to get open a few times, but they didn't pass it to me. Finally, when I was open once again, I got the ball behind the three-point line, and without hesitation, shot, and drained it. My team was a little shocked, but also excited that I made the basket. I got open three or four more times and was able to make the basket yet again. The game was nearing the end and the score was tied, but I was so into the game I didn't know this; not knowing probably helped me out, otherwise I would have been nervous. I got open once more, we were playing win by 2 points, received the pass, shot the ball, and drained one from behind the three-point line for 3 points. We won and my team was impressed. We would play one more game, and although I did well in it, and I had the other team saying to their players, "You need to guard him," I didn't hit the game winning shot.

I must note that earlier in the day I played two pick-up games at the outdoor courts behind RPU and in one of those games I had the game winning three-pointer. Also, the night before in a pick-up game, I had a game winning three-pointer. This gave me three game winning three-pointers, out of the last 5 games I had played. I de-
~~~

cided to refer to myself as "Mr. Clutch" the rest of the night.

Going to Mall. As of the week of September 18th I had been at Cornell for a whole month. I was really enjoying myself and everything was going well. However, during this month I had never stepped off campus (not including Collegetown). That weekend I decided to take the bus over to the mall to buy some drinks, paper towels, and birthday presents for my brother.



I wasn't expecting anything special at the mall. The only thing I expected was for it to be smaller than my mall back home. However, I had such a weird feeling stepping off the bus and into the mall. It felt almost like freedom. Being in the new environment was exhilarating. I was so used to the same sights and sounds of the Cornell campus for a month that I seemed to forget what real life was like. Walking through the mall I no longer saw students with backpacks; I saw adults young and old and families with children walking around. It was as if I entered a whole new environment.

The main feeling I had was relief. It was such a relief to be off campus and in a place that had a non-educational reality to it. I enjoyed seeing the many types of people. I enjoyed looking at the shops. It was a pleasure to see a food store beyond that of Appel and RPU.

Hockey Tickets. You can not go to Cornell and not know about Cornell Hockey. Coming into Cornell I was very excited about getting season tickets for Hockey. However, I failed to realize how excited everyone else is, and how limited the number of season tickets were. To obtain tickets you would have to line up in some location and wait to receive a number for the camp-out date. To find out where to line up you would have to listen to a radio station for 5 days and on a random day at a random time between 9:30 P.M. and 11:00 P.M., the location would be announced. I listened every night until they announced it. I stuttered a little in my approach because I wanted to see if anyone else would come; big mistake. I ended up getting to Lynah rink about 2000 students back. However I didn't know how the line worked and thought I was at worst 800 students back. This misperception resulted because the line wrapped inside the building as well as outside; I had thought that it only wrapped outside.

I waited in line for approximately an hour. During that hour there was much pushing and shoving, cutting in line, and a girl fainted. Everyone in the crowd was pissed when after an hour they told us that there were no more tickets left. Since no one had knowledge of the inside line the crowd got quite rowdy because we couldn't understand how the tickets could be filled. I was one of the 50 or so people that refused to leave. I don't know if I was shocked, angry, or disappointed. I was shocked because I didn't realize how so many people could get to the rink in less than 10 minutes. I was angry that I checked to see if anyone else wanted to come with me and potentially caused my missing of the tickets. I was disappointed in how I was too dumb to realize that hockey tickets were a big thing and I should have been more prepared.

A good thing that came out of it, although some might say not so good, is that I got to be part of the "Lynah Stampede." I don't know how long that name will live on, or this story would live on, but if it does, maybe some day when my kids or grandkids ask if I was part of the Lynah Stampede, I will be able to tell them about it. I didn't get Hockey Tickets that night, but I was able to procure a story that could live with me forever.



First Chemistry Prelim. The first prelim that I ever had at Cornell was a chemistry prelim. I studied my ass off for this test. I studied my ass off for two reasons, one, I had heard that Cornell prelims were a force to be reckoned with and two, I wanted to do well and prove to myself that I belonged at Cornell. The day of the test came and I was extremely nervous, but I had studied hard, and felt like I knew the material pretty well. After the test I didn't feel too good about it. I was able to answer all of the questions, so that was a good sign.

A week later we got the tests back. From the talk of the other students I felt like I had at least gotten the mean. If I got the mean, that would mean I got a B, and for Cornell a B is a decent grade to earn. After the lecture I went downstairs, fought my way through the crowd, and got my test from the TA. If you want to understand how nervous I was, I didn't even look at my test until I was outside and on my walk back to the dorm. I opened it up and saw 82, and I gave myself a high-five right on my thigh in excitement. An 82 meant that I scored 1 standard deviation above the mean, and that is good enough for a grade around an A– or A, however they curve it. I couldn't believe it, all my hard work had paid off, and not just with a B, with an A. I got the same exhilaration with the game winning three-pointers as I did with this grade.

Math Prelim #2. I had done rather well on my first math prelim. My grade earned me a B+. It wasn't as well as I had hoped for, but that was only because I made a careless mistake which cost me 10 points, and an A. For this prelim I studied very hard, and knew the material very well. I was able to do the examples and understand the concepts.

As I walked to the prelim with Dave, I was nervous, but also excited because I felt like I knew the material. When we got the test, I was able to do the first problem fine. Then I looked at #2, and said let me see #3, and so on until #7. I was taken aback by the difficulty of the questions. I was getting really nervous, and all my hopes were gone. Eventually I calmed myself down. I looked at numbers 5, 6, and 7 and was able to do them well. Then I went to number 3, worth 20 points, the big question, and was able to do it well. There were only 2 questions left and I had done fine so far on the other 5. I looked at number 2, and knew where the question was coming from. It was a question from an obscure homework problem which was only one example out of the entire book. I thought it was totally unfair, and did my best,.which wasn't much at all. Finally there was #4. I knew exactly how to do number 4; I had done many examples of its type. It was a LaGrange Multiplier problem. There was one problem, the coordinate on the test to be used was (0,–5). For some reason, my stupid brain interpreted it as (–5,0). I worked and worked through the problem, but I just couldn't figure it out. I tried over and over again. I wasted so much time on that seemingly simple problem. I had done the hard problems, but I couldn't get this problem worth 18 points.



Later on when I realized that I had mixed up the coordinate system, I was devastated. That was the reason why all of my math was wrong and nothing was making sense. I had done so well on the rest of the test, but bombed one of the more expensive (18 points) problems. When I got my prelim back I ended up getting a B. Had I not mixed up the coordinate system I would have gotten an A. This was so frustrating. I even said to my friends, "I am glad I don't drink, because if I did, I would be getting so drunk right now." I hope I never feel this type of pain and disappointment ever again in my Cornell career, because it killed me. I even felt like getting tested for dyslexia. My friends told me that it was fine, since I knew how to do it, and it was just a stupid mistake. Sure, that makes sense, but making sense doesn't get me into grad school or give me a high GPA, an A is what does that, not a B.

... I hope when I look back on this, I can say that that is the last time I ever made a mistake like that ...

Making the Scrapbook. ... I don't know when I will ever come to the archives to see my scrapbook in later years, but I do know that I will come. I hope that when I come I am still able to relive these memories, but most likely they will be vague images due to the time that has passed. My greatest wonder is what I will think of myself then. All the time while I was making the scrapbook I had that thought in the back of my mind. I hope my future self enjoys what I put together for him. I also hope that my future self has lived up to my expectations, but I'll never know that.

... I also wonder if anyone else besides me (and Mrs. Kammen, my teacher) will ever open the scrapbook to read it. I would like to think that one day my kids will read it if they ever come to Cornell, but I don't know if they would want to. If you do read my scrap book and have managed to get this far, what did you think? It's not like many other typical scrapbooks, at least in my opinion. Most scrapbooks are a little bit of writing with a bit of pictures and items. I decided to write enough so that you would feel and witness things as I witnessed them, and had the items there to help. It was also meant to be interactive.

The final word count for this entire book turned out to be 14,511 words. That is quite a lot and I don't think I have ever written that much before on one assignment. However, those are 14,511 words that I enjoyed writing. The making of this scrapbook was very pleasurable and I am lucky that I was forced into making it; otherwise, I would have little to nothing to remind me of my first semester. Lastly, I feel like this semester was nothing like I had anticipated in every aspect; however, I feel that my semester has exceeded in every aspect, and I can only hope that the rest of my time at Cornell will be as pleasurable.

# SOURCES

Most of the letters, diaries, and other writings excerpted in this book are in the Rare and Manuscript Collections (RMC). Scrapbooks created for History 126 are on deposit at RMC.


Ang, Angelina: On-line web log.

Appell, Stephen E.: Courtesy of Stephen Appell.

Ashong, Niiamah: Scrapbook.

Banks, Reilly: The letters appeared for sale on eBay and are now at RMC.

Bean, David Richard: *David: A Collection of the Letters, Journals, and Artwork of David Richard Bean* (Wichita, 1972).

Bennett, Elizabeth: Scrapbook.

Boulton, Jessie Mary: RMC 37/5/2289.

Brick, Alvan, Jr.: Courtesy of Alvan Brick.

Bullard, Helen: RMC 6501 Box 2/16 journal Nov. 22, 1917.

Carpenter, Evie: RMC 37/5/2880.

Chasalov, Elizabeth: Scrapbook.

Cornell Gay Liberation Office Notebook: RMC 37/6/1589.

Curtin, Maeva: Scrapbook.

Darneider, Molly: Scrapbook.

Davis, John Y.: RMC 37/5/m.188.

Detmold, John Hunter: RMC 37/5/2354.

Fessenden, Mary: RMC 37/5/2547 Box 1.

Finch, J. S.: RMC 37/5/2041.

French, Charles M.: RMC 37/5/1099.

Ghent, Ann Meigs: RMC 37-5-3303.

Goldin, Anita Ades: Courtesy of Mrs. Anita A. Goldin.

Goldsmith, Howie: Scrapbook.

Greczner, Peter: Scrapbook.

Gulvin, Harold E.: RMC 37-5-2197.

Hamber, Janet: RMC 37/5/2907.

Hayes, Webb: RMC 37/5/m427; the original comes from the Colonel Webb C. Hayes Collection, Rutherford B. Hayes Presidential Center, Fremont, Ohio.

"Jill": The original letters have been deposited in RMC; box number withheld at the writer's request

Kiplinger, Knight: Courtesy of Knight Kiplinger.

Klingele, Karen: Scrapbook.

Kogan, David S.: *The Diary of David S. Kogan*, edited by Meyer Levin (Beachhurst Press, New York, 1955).

Kowalski, Geoff: Courtesy of Geoff and Christine Kowalski.

Kraus, George A.: RMC 37/5/2507.
LaVallee, Donna Fulkerson: Courtesy of Donna LaVallee.
Lee, W. Forrest: RMC 37/5/2316.
Lloyd, David: Scrapbook.
Lyon, Katherine: RMC 37/5/1414.
Manzo, Justin: Scrapbook.
Mathur, Abhiskek: Scrapbook.
Moffatt, John Little: RMC 37/5/1460.
Neiderbach, Margaux: Scrapbook.
Nelson, Gertrude and Ruth: RMC 37/5/717.
Newman, Floyd: RMC 37/5/1619 Box 2 Folder 1.
Nieh, Nick: Scrapbook.
Putnam, Kathleen Pierce: RMC 37/5/3471
Taft, Royal: RMC 37/5/61.
Thomas, M. Carey: The M. C. Thomas Manuscripts are in the Marian Coffin Canady Library, Bryn Mawr College; they are addressed to Dear Father & Mother. Those interested in reading additional letters from Thomas written while she was at Cornell should see *The Making of a Feminist,* edited by Marjorie Housepian Dobkin (Kent State University, 1979).
Todd, Walter L.: RMC 3167.
Warner, Elizabeth Severinghaus: RMC 6552
Wessels, Arthur K.: RMC 37/5/2921.
Young, Adelaide Taber: RMC 37/5/820.
Zeller, Adelheid: RMC 37/5/930.

# INDEX

This index is a selective topical guide to themes found in the students' writings, including places, organizations, and attitudes; noteworthy Cornell professors and administrators and nationally known off-campus figures and events are also included.

Eric Tobis, class of 2008